From Jim 1979

20ct4

To Bud

The Bettor's Guide to
Harness Racing

The Bettor's Guide to
Harness Racing

by Ronald Roblin, Ph.D.

CITADEL PRESS   Secaucus, N.J.

First edition
Copyright © 1979 by Ronald Roblin
All rights reserved
Published by Citadel Press
A division of Lyle Stuart Inc.
120 Enterprise Ave., Secaucus, N.J. 07094
In Canada: George J. McLeod Limited
Don Mills, Ontario
Manufactured in the United States of America

Library of Congress Cataloging in Publication Data

Roblin, Ronald.
The bettor's guide to harness racing.

   1. Horse race betting. 2. Harness racing.
I. Title.
SF333.5.R63   798'.46   78-23195
ISBN 0-8065-0645-8

CONTENTS

Acknowledgments

The following persons and publishers offered their kind assistance in the preparation of this book. Marie Marra, president of Marra Program and Past Performance Form; Martin G. Holleran, house counsel of the New Jersey Sports and Exposition Authority for the Meadowlands; the Colonial Press, publisher of the Pompano Park program; Sara Short, publicity director of the United States Trotting Association; Ed Bonze, editor of *Star Weekly,* who gave permission to reprint sections of my article "Taking Account of the Driver in Harness Racing"; and Max Robinson, public-relations director at Batavia Downs.

My father, Alex L. Roblin, assisted by collecting and organizing materials from Pompano Park programs; my wife, Esther, gave me help and encouragement throughout its writing; and my mother-in-law, Martha Tinjanoff, was a constant source of fresh ideas.

Finally, I owe a debt of gratitude to my department secretary, Marilyn Coyne, who gave unstintingly of her time in typing the early drafts and, later, the final version of the book.

Preface

This guide is intended for persons who enjoy harness racing but have little background or experience in handicapping trotting races. The professional handicapper, able to handicap races with demonstrated success, will not find this book of much value. By *demonstrated success* I mean a "track record" in which winnings outweigh losses, by a large margin. Unfortunately, there aren't many such persons around, and they make up a very small percentage of the people who bet on harness races.

Two other groups will have little use for a book on handicapping. The first is made up of those who believe that the outcome of every race is fixed. The less said about these folks the better! The second group is composed of people who believe that the outcome of a race is just a matter of chance. The first group will have to rely on doubtful tips from "inside" sources who can tell them beforehand what the results will be, assuming that such "information" is available to them. (The touts found around race tracks are seldom reliable, incidentally.) The second group should bet the date of their birthday or the date of the month or some equally irrational method for getting occasional winners.

Still another group of people—those who go to the track a few times a year for the fun of it—will get their money's worth from the entertainment value of a night out, assuming it doesn't turn out to be too expensive. There's certainly nothing wrong in going to the races, expecting to lose, and writing off one's losses to an enjoyable evening spent with friends.

But this guide is meant for the bettor who really wants to win, or at least to minimize his losses. Anyone who enjoys wagering regularly on the trotters and who believes that his chances of winning will be improved by intelligent handicapping should be able to profit from

the approach taken in this book. In particular, a novice in the art and science of handicapping will find this book useful, and so should someone who wagers regularly on the trotters with little success, if he's willing to put up with someone else's point of view.

But readers must be patient and cautious in using this manual to best advantage. This means laying off many races that are difficult or perhaps impossible to handicap effectively. It also means using the ideas outlined in the chapters to follow to increase their percentage of winners in races that are playable and should be wagered on.

I have had more than twenty years' experience handicapping and betting on trotting races. I have had my ups and downs but have wound up ahead because I stuck to handicapping races for myself and bet my own choices instead of listening to tips or following the tote board. This, of course, requires making up one's mind for oneself instead of following every suggestion or tip from people who probably know less than you do. As a rule, bad tips are free and good tips are favors, which the giver expects you to return. In fact, most good "tips" are kept as quiet as possible. Why give something for nothing?

There is no solution to the problem of winning at the races except to do your own handicapping and bet selectively—certainly not on every race—on the horse that is the clear choice after the race has been carefully handicapped. Keep in mind that the racetrack is no place for tender hearts and sentiment. You can win only by taking a tough-minded attitude toward every race you bet. The handicapping procedures outlined in this book have been gained by first-hand experience in the school of hard knocks during many evenings in which I have attended and bet on trotting races. My aim in this book is not merely to instruct the beginner in how to read a program, but to help him improve his chances in selecting a high percentage of winners at the trots.

In successive chapters I give the reader some basic information about harness racing, show him how to read a program, and then discuss the art of handicapping from the standpoint of such fundamentals as the level of competition in a particular race; a horse's speed, consistency, and current form; the importance of the driver and of post position; and some features of racing strategy as they apply to specific races ("how the race will be run"). These are the most important considerations in handicapping trotting races.

Throughout this book I use illustrations of races run during the 1977 summer and fall seasons at Batavia Downs. I teach handicapping methods not merely by precept, but also and mostly by example. This should make the important points far more clear than a book with very few examples and much advice.

The best advice that can be given the beginner is not to bet every race, but to select with care the races he will bet. Before laying down a $2 or a $20 wager, the bettor should take some pains to justify his choice to himself. He should be able to make clear the reasons why he placed a certain bet on a certain animal.

But the subject of betting will be discussed in a later chapter. I am more reluctant to advise my readers on how to bet than I am to furnish them with the principles of a system that should produce a high percentage of horses that win, place, or show.

1

Basic Information on Harness Racing

Claiming and Conditioned Races

The two most prevalent types of races in harness racing are claiming races and conditioned races. In a claiming race, any horse in the race can be claimed for a specified amount of money. This means that an owner who enters his horse in a claimer must risk losing his horse to someone willing to pay the specified amount.

As a rule, very young horses are seldom entered in claiming races unless the claiming price is high. A two-, three-, or four-year-old horse has most of its racing life ahead of it, and an an owner would be foolish to risk losing such a horse in a claiming race if he thought it showed potential for real improvement. When I started attending harness races, claiming prices began at $1,000. Nowadays, claiming prices at the larger tracks start at $2,000 and continue on up the scale to races in which a horse can be claimed for $30,000 or more.

In this book, my illustrations are taken exclusively from claimers, and my point system is designed for play on claimers. Over the years, I have found that the animals in higher-priced claiming races tend to run more consistently than those in most conditioned races.

A conditioned race is a race open only to horses that meet certain conditions specified by the racing secretary responsible for making up the race card. For example, conditioned races may be for nonwinners of a race this meet; for nonwinners of $225 per start in 1978 or last ten starts; for winners of at least two races and $3,000 in 1978–79; etc. In specifying the conditions in this way, the race secretary tries to match contestants as evenly as possible. Otherwise, races would be too one-sided, favoring older, faster, and more experienced animals.

When handicapping a conditioned race, it is important that you read the conditions carefully and determine how each horse in that race fits the conditions. All too often, however, it is difficult to determine the potential of the horses in certain conditioned races,

especially when they are composed of maidens (horses that have never won a race) or of young horses that are inexperienced and therefore tend to be erratic.

One more point about claiming races: A claiming allowance race is one in which certain horses, such as mares, are allowed an additional amount upon the claiming price. For example, a claiming allowance race for mares and four-year-olds may be priced at $4,000. A horse that is both a mare and a four-year-old may be allowed 40 percent more for a total price of $5,600. In this way mares and younger horses will have an advantage in allowing races. Often a mare will do better against cheaper company than if she had to run in a $5,000 claimer, and this is a point worth noting in handicapping.

Front-runners, Quitters, and Closers

As a rule, a horse has a specific style of racing. Fundamentally, there are three different ways in which horses are raced, and a horse is usually trained to run in just one of these ways. A front-runner is a horse at its best when it is leading the pack. Front-runners are trained to get off fast at the beginning of a race and to take the lead as quickly as possible. For a front-runner to be successful, it must have a quick opening burst to seize the lead and enough in reserve late in the race to fight off challengers in the stretch.

If a front-runner is parked outside for the first quarter or more of a race, at least on ½-mile track, or has to fly in the first quarter to take the lead, it often will not have enough in reserve to hold up in the stretch. A driver who can "move" his horse will take a front runner into the lead, slow down the pace, and hope that the animal will hold up in the last quarter.

A quitter is a horse that will go all out in the first half or more of a race but will invariably fade in the stretch. Quitting is not a style of racing so much as a liability in a horse that might otherwise be a successful front-runner. Whereas a driver will take a front-runner to the front of the pack and then slow the pace so that the horse has enough in reserve in the final quarter, a quitter will go all out for two or three quarters and then fade out of sight.

The mark of the quitter, as opposed to the front-runner, is that the quitter will cut the first half of the race in a much faster time than the second half. For example, in a race run in 2:04 (2 minutes and 4 seconds), both a front-runner and a quitter may capture the lead in :30, but the quitter may go to the half in 1:01 and the three-quarter

mark in 1:32, winding up five lengths behind the winner in 2:05. (One second is equivalent to five lengths.) This means that the quitter raced each quarter in the following times: :30, :31, :31, and :33. In contrast, the front-runner slows down the pace after taking the lead, goes to the half in 1:02 (hypothetically), holds the lead through the third quarter in 1:33, and holds up with a :31 final quarter.

A closer is a horse that sits back and waits until sometime in the last quarter before making its move, frequently not moving until the stretch. As we will see, a closer is at a decided advantage when the pace of the race through the first three quarters is especially fast, for then the "stretch horse" will be able to make up ground in a slow last quarter. A stretch horse is at a disadvantage when a front-runner takes the lead and slows down the pace, because then the last quarter is apt to be run in a fast time. When this happens the horses racing up front have the best shot at winning the race.

In addition to front-runners and closers, there are horses a driver will move at the half or even at the first quarter. A driver who moves his horse at the quarter mark does not want to race on the outside for the remainder of the race. Unless his horse is in peak shape, he can't afford to tire the animal by running it on the outside for the last three quarters. The driver who moves at the quarter therefore hopes to get to the rail by the half, slow down the pace, and rally in the stretch.

More commonly, a driver will move his horse at the half. If he's well back, this is a good stretegy, for otherwise his horse will be too far back by the fourth quarter to rally and win, especially if the last quarter is run in a fast time.

But how much ground does it cost a horse to run a quarter or more on the outside? Probably about 1 second (five lengths) per ½-mile by comparison with horses on the rail. And this is a great deal when we consider that the majority of harness races are won or lost by a length or less. For this reason, post position is very important in harness racing. A horse that begins the race at or near the front has a big initial advantage.

We should also stress that many horses are maneuverable or can run just as well in the front as by moving at the half or closing quickly in the stretch. Such horses are at a decided advantage in many races because they can either go for the lead immediately or wait until later in the race, depending upon the race situation. In a race dominated by quitters and front-runners, no sane driver would use up a maneuverable horse in the first quarter over a battle for the lead. Instead, he will

sit back during the fast pace, moving at just the opportune moment—when the horses in front are beginning to run themselves out. Likewise, a maneuverable horse can run in front effectively, particularly in a race made up of closers. A maneuverable horse is therefore in the best position to win, everything else being equal in a race. But everything else is *seldom* equal in a race!

Drivers, Trainers, Owners

Next to the horse, the most important factor in a race is the driver. A knowledge of the drivers at a raceway is indispensable for anyone who expects to win at the races. Many raceways, such as Batavia Downs, are dominated by no more than ten to fifteen drivers who win with astonishing regularity. Almost 50 percent of all the races in a season are won by the members of this clique. As a result, the difference between successful and unsuccessful drivers at a raceway is a hard fact of life that you must consider in every race you handicap.

Driver A, who has raced here for the past ten years, wins between 15 and 20 percent of his races over a season. Driver B, another regular, has been a consistent loser over approximately the same number of years. Driver C, just in from another raceway, seems to have his stable in peak condition and is winning more than one race in three and finishing in the money (finishing first, second, or third) in more than half of his races. Driver D, also a recent face at the Downs, seems to be taking the horses in his stable out for fresh air in race after race.

One of the points in this book is that you should keep tabs of the leading drivers at the track you frequent. You will find that of the sixty races run each week, a high percentage are won by a select group of drivers who probably average two to three winners a week.

Some drivers train the horses they drive, and if these drivers win consistently, they must be watched closely and played often. Other drivers specialize in catch driving. When a driver catch drives for a particular stable on a steady basis, it is essential to keep track of whether he is winning regularly. Other drivers, who catch drive for different trainers and stables, are less apt to be consistent in their winning and losing.

Because of the importance of the driver to the outcome of a race, you should be aware at all times which drivers are winners and whether they are winning in streaks. (Much more will be said on this

subject in chapter 3.) One rule central to my approach to racing is: Bet only strong drivers, that is, drivers who win a high percentage of their races, and bet them when they are on winning streaks.

Because of the high degree of specialization nowadays, many horsemen specialize only in training. Others drive as well as train the horses in their stable, although it is not unusual for a capable driver who has a large stable to hire a number of assistant trainers. It is useful to know whether a particular trainer has a high winning percentage, for trainers, like drivers, have winning streaks when their stable is in top shape.

Obviously, a good trainer will keep his stable in peak condition as long as possible, and his horses will perform according to their optimum capacity. When a first-rate catch driver is joined to a winning trainer, the combination is deadly. Obviously, it is often worth giving his horse consideration in a race, unless unfavorable conditions compensate for these advantages.

Last and least is the owner, usually a poor sucker who bets money on his pride and joy whether or not it can perform. Owners call themselves horsemen, but unless they train or drive the animals they own, they are no more horsemen than you or I. Anyone who can afford to claim or otherwise buy a horse and hire a trainer and/or driver is in a position to become an owner. It costs about $5,000 a year and up to maintain a horse, including stabling, training and veterinarian costs, entrance fees for races, etc. As a result, fewer than 10 percent of owners make money after their horses' winnings have been deducted from maintenance costs. Of course, the owner who wagers on his horse when it wins is in an excellent position to realize profits from his venture into racing. But as we all know, not all owners are successful in wagering on their pride and joy. Most are not.

The Race Track

In handicapping, the size of the race track and the placement of the finish line are important.* Most tracks in America are ½-mile ovals, around which the horses run twice, for a total of 1 mile. On the ½-mile track, turns are crucial, because a horse parked on the outside invariably loses ground on the sharp turns. A horse going for the lead

---

*The handicapping procedures in this book are designed primarily for play on ½- and ⅝-mile tracks.

at the beginning of the race, after starting from an outside post position, is often parked two, three, or even four horses from the rail at the first turn. This can take so much starch out of a horse that it fails to hold on in the stretch. It is also worth mentioning that some horses simply have trouble negotiating the sharp turns on a ½-mile track.

At the opposite extreme is the 1-mile track, in which there are no sharp turns for the horses to negotiate. On a 1-mile track, a horse does not pay nearly as great a price for having to trot on the outside. On ⅝- and ¾-mile tracks there is usually a long straightaway at the beginning of the race, so that horses going for the lead are not parked wide on the first turn. These tracks give front-runners a definite advantage over closers. On the average, ⅝- and ¾-mile tracks are 1 to 2 seconds faster than ½-mile tracks, and a 1-mile track is about 4 seconds faster. This means that a 1-mile race run in 2:10 on a ½-mile track will go in about 2:06 on a mile track and 2:08 to 2:09 on a ⅝- or ¾-mile track.

The condition of the track is another important element in handicapping. A fast track differs from one that is good, sloppy, slow, heavy, or muddy.

Good means that a light rain has just begun to fall or the track is drying off after a light rain.

Sloppy—because of a moderate rain, the footing is more difficult than with a good track. There may be puddles on the track.

Slow—the rain has so saturated the track that the footing is even more insecure than on a sloppy track.

Muddy is self-explanatory.

Heavy—the track is mud through and through.

Although there is no hard-and-fast rule for determining how much slower a race will go on an off track, it is probably safe to assume that a good track is only slightly slower than a fast track, that a sloppy or slow track is 1 to 2 seconds slower than a fast track, and that a muddy to heavy track will cause a race to run about 2 to 3 seconds slower. It is important to note that some horses do better on an off track than on a fast track.

Although a track classified good is not apt to make much of a difference in any race, sore or slightly lame horses might benefit from the soft footing.

In addition, some horses are "mudders" and do especially well on off tracks. The only way to determine whether a horse is a mudder is to go back through its last several months or more of races and check

out its performance on off tracks. If a horse does much better in the mud, it will be a good bet under such conditions. However, the work involved takes more time than most handicappers are willing to spend. As a result, it is probably better not to wager at all on a race run in the mud. Off tracks are notorious for spawning more than the usual share of long shots. For these reasons, unless you know that the horse you wish to bet is a mudder or will most likely perform as well in the mud as on a fast track, it is better to lay off the race.

A word now about further differences among ½-mile, ⅝-mile, and 1-mile tracks and the way in which differences in track size dictate important differences in driving strategy.

½-mile tracks. On a ½-mile track, the race begins in front of the grandstand and continues around the clubhouse turn into the backstretch to the quarter. From the quarter mark, the race proceeds around the far turn to the stretch and past the grandstand for the first time. This is the halfway point. The field then circumnavigates the oval again, to the finish.

It's important to note that the turns on a ½-mile track are sharp and that a horse on the outside almost inevitably loses ground on the turns. Not only that, but the hairpin turns take a good deal more out of a horse than the wider turns on ⅝- and 1-mile tracks. Races on the ½-milers tend to be closer than on larger tracks, and favorites are upset a greater percentage of the time.

The best racing strategy on a ½-mile track is for a horse to get to the front at the outset and to avoid being boxed in the rest of the way. Horses having the outside post positions are at a greater disadvantage on ½-mile tracks because their drivers are faced with the problem of either going for the lead at the start and being parked outside for a quarter or more, or sitting back until there is clearance, at which time the driver can encounter traffic problems. Again, if a driver goes for the lead right off and is hung up on the first turn in a fast quarter, the result is usually a lost race. But this can happen just as frequently if the horse has to go three or four wide on the far turn after getting stuck behind horses already outside in the backstretch. By then it's often too late to catch the leaders. For these reasons, post positions 1 to 4 offer a great advantage to the driver on the ½-milers, although a skillful driver from an outside post position will offset the advantages of a weak driver with an inside post.

⅝-*mile tracks.* On the ⅝-milers, the race begins in the backstretch, three-eighths of the track length before the finish line. This means that horses pass in front of the grandstand on their way to the three-eighths mark and then go around the track once completely. As a result of the larger size of the track, horses take three turns instead of four. Races tend not to be as close as in the ½-milers, and there is not as much wear and tear on the horse.

Another difference is that front-runners have a better chance of winning on the ½-milers because of the shorter stretch, whereas horses with the ability to close strongly enjoy an advantage on the longer stretch in ⅝-milers. A horse that moves from a ½-miler to a ⅝-mile track should be watched for a race or two to see whether it has sufficient stamina to hold up in the stretch, especially if the horse is a front-runner. It may also take a while for a horse racing on ½-mile strips to adjust to the requirements of the ½-milers, particularly if the horse gets off slowly.

1-mile tracks. The 1-milers are said to be the best tests of a horse's racing ability, because so little is left to chance and luck. Horses circle the track only once, minimizing the effect of the turns on a horse's performance. Sheer speed therefore counts for more on a 1-mile track. Most of the important stake races for younger horses are held on 1-mile tracks. However, the number of 1-mile tracks is comparatively small, and because of the greater expense involved in building them, it is unlikely that many more will be constructed.

Major Harness Raceways in the United States and Canada

½-mile Tracks (*major ½-milers)
Balmoral Park (Crete, Illinois)
Batavia Downs (Batavia, New York)
Buffalo Raceway (Hamburg, New York)
Freehold Raceway (Freehold, New Jersey)
*Maywood Park (Maywood, Illinois)
Monticello Raceway (Monticello, New York)
Northfield Park (Northfield, Ohio)
Northville Downs (Northville, Michigan)
Richelieu Park (Montreal, Quebec)
Rockingham Park (Rockingham, New Hampshire)
*Roosevelt Raceway (Westbury, New York)
Rosecroft Raceway (Oxon Hill, Maryland)
Saratoga Harness (Saratoga, New York)
*Yonkers Raceway (Yonkers, New York)

⅝-mile Tracks (*major ⅝-milers)
  Atlantic City Raceway (Atlantic City, New Jersey)
*Blue Bonnets Raceway (Montreal, Quebec)
*Brandywine Raceway (Wilmington, Delaware)
*Greenhold Raceway (Toronto, Ontario)
*Hazel Park (Hazel Park, Michigan)
  Laurel Raceway (Laurel, Maryland)
*Liberty Bell Park (Philadelphia, Pennsylvania)
  Los Alamitos Harness (Los Alamitos, California)
  Mohawk Raceway (Campbellville, Ontario)
  New England Harness Raceway (Foxboro, Massachusetts)
  Pompano Park (Pompano Beach, Florida)
  Scioto Downs (Columbus, Ohio)
*Sportsman's Park (Cicero, Illinois)
  The Meadows (Meadow Lands, Pennsylvania)
  Windsor Raceway (Windsor, Ontario)

1-mile Tracks (*major 1-milers)
  Bay Meadows (San Mateo, California)
  Fairmount Park (Collinsville, Illinois)
  Golden Bear Raceway (Sacramento, California)
*Hawthorne (Cicero, Illinois)
*Hollywood Park (Inglewood, California)
*The Meadowlands (East Rutherford, New Jersey)
*Washington Park (Chicago, Illinois)
*Wolverine Raceway (Livonia, Michigan)

Public Handicappers

Each evening when there is racing, the sports pages of your newspaper list the horses entered in every race on the evening's card. In most metropolitan areas with race tracks, the newspapers hire so-called experts who predict the order of finish in the nine or ten contests on the card.

For several good reasons, the public selector should not be taken seriously. First, the newspaper handicapper does not usually distinguish between those races which are playable and those which are not. As a result, an "open" contest—that is, a race in which there are several strong contenders—is not distinguished from a race in which a single horse stands out. One of the most important things we need to know is when to bet and when to lay off; yet the public selector does not give us this vital information—except for the one "best bet" he singles out for the evening.

Statistics show that even if wagering is confined to the "best bet" race, the results will be much the same as if we bet the public selector's choices in every race, because the "best bet" is usually a

heavy favorite that will net a small return on our wager—*if* it wins. And it's impossible to wind up ahead betting *every* race. So in either case we will end up the same if we follow the selector—in the poor house.

Moreover, the public selector may be devoting only a small part of his time to handicapping harness races. He may also be the selector for Thoroughbred racing, as well as a reporter of other sports events.

Obviously, the choices of public selectors should be taken with many grains of salt. If you devote your attention strictly to harness racing and confine your betting to no more than two or three races on the card, you are apt to get a much higher percentage of winners than the newspaper or any other public selector can give you.

In addition to newspaper selectors, a track hires a handicapper to assign odds to each horse on an evening's card. The track handicapper's rating is known as the day's morning line and is included in the official program. Since the program is printed a day or more in advance, the morning line cannot take account of certain driver changes, late scratches, and so on. The track's handicapper does not determine the actual odds but merely states his opinion of what the probable odds will be. There is a specific method by which such odds are calculated, but they are not the same as those which will be employed in this book.

On an average, the track handicapper selects from two to four winners an evening, almost always at short odds. As a result, anyone who wagers exclusively on the track handicapper's selections, whether to win, place, or show, will go broke. If anything, the odds the track handicapper assigns can be misleading because they do not always tally with the actual odds established by public wagering.

You would do best to ignore the morning-line odds altogether when you handicap a race.

Hanky-panky at the Races?

In the preface I dismissed the individual who is convinced that every race is fixed. Now I want to add a word about shady practices that are believed to go on at the races. But first, I must state my conviction that very few races are fixed, if by a fixed race we mean one in which all the drivers conspire to predetermine the outcome. Is it likely that the eight drivers in tonight's fifth race sit down over tea and crumpets beforehand to decide who will win? Not very likely, when we reflect that the state supervises the goings-on at a raceway

with an eagle eye, and a driver risks permanent suspension for throwing a race.

A second point: At Buffalo Raceway and Batavia Downs, stables from Canada, Ohio, and Pennsylvania move in and out during the season. As a general rule, raceways are hospitable to new stables and try to make space available to them. In this way the influx of new drivers helps to ensure that hanky-panky does not go on, although it is both legal and profitable for a stable to wager on its choice. (For more on this subject, see chapter 3.)

A third point: Trainers and drivers depend for their livelihood upon a percentage of the earnings of the horses they train and drive. For example, in a race with a purse of $2,000, the winner ordinarily receives $1,000, the place horse $500, and so on. A driver has good reason to make every effort to win, because he earns 10 percent of the horse's earnings. The trainer, if he's not driving, may also receive a share of the purse money.

It would therefore seem to be in the driver's interest to win as many races as he can. After all, most of his income depends upon it. The premier drivers at a raceway have an established reputation, not only among their fellow drivers, with whom they compete for income, but also among the best trainers at the raceway. For this reason alone, I believe that most drivers are trying most of the time, although I concede that if a driver is told by an owner *not* to try in a particular race, he may follow orders. This practice, incidentally, is referred to as "stiffing" a horse, and it happens much less often than persons who lose at the races are willing to believe.

What sorts of shady practices, then, do go on at a harness raceway? It is not unusual for a driver with a horse from an outside post position simply to take the horse for a ride, unless it's the class of the field. This should not be frowned upon too much, since trotting on the outside can take a great deal out of a horse while not appreciably increasing its chances of finishing in the money. Racing on the outside, especially on a ½-mile track, is both tiring and, for cheaper horses, a sure way to finish well back. For this reason, be wary of betting horses from the outside post positions, particularly if the program shows that they did nothing from these posts in their previous starts.

This rule applies even more to animals that have been idle for a month or more. Standardbreds need to race regularly to keep in shape, and an animal coming off a lengthy layoff is seldom sharp.

More often than not, if a horse has been idle for a long period it will be taken out for a freshener, and not to win. Moreover, it is not uncommon for an animal to be trained lightly for a certain period and then to be trained very hard in preparation for a specific race.

There is nothing illegal about a horse's running poorly for a number of races and then "popping" after it has been trained intensively for a week. The only drawback for us poor bettors is that we probably have no way of learning whether the horse is up in its *next* start.

Incidentally, this is a nice way for a stable to make a bundle—the odds usually go up week after week because of a horse's poor showing. In the interest of fairness, we must add that in such situations a driver need not be stiffing a horse in race after race. Until the horse has been trained to peak condition, it's simply not ready and can't win. No driver, no matter how capable, will win with an out-of-shape horse.

A final note: In harness racing, just over one race in three is won by the favorite, the most heavily bet horse in the race. And about 60 percent of odds-on favorites (horses that go off at less than even money) win in harness racing. Of the remaining two-thirds of all races, a large majority are won by horses that go off at odds of less than 5 to 1. As the odds continue to rise, a decreasing percentage of horses enter the winning circle. Very few long shots can be *handicapped* as the best horse in the race. Playing long shots as a way of life is a sure way to go broke on the trotters.

As a rule, Standardbreds run more closely according to form than Thoroughbreds, and sharp discrepancies in a Standardbred's level of performance from race to race can result in a stable's being obliged to move from the premises.

At the Track

Most racing fans do not take full advantage of the information it is possible to get at the track. A catalogue of Joe Q. Punter's actions at the race track might show him trying to handicap each race from the program in the brief interval before the start of the race, searching about for tips from people "in the know" or relying on tip sheets, and watching the tote board for possible clues to the outcome of the race.

Contrast this haphazard approach with that of the serious handicapper who zeroes in on what is important. He has obtained the

program and studied it carefully well before the first race. He has decided which races are playable and which horses in those races are good bets before he arrives at the track. He pays no heed to prerace gossip; he ignores tips and refuses to panic once his choices have been made. And he watches each race not merely to root for his own choice, but to find out which horses will run well and which will not, as well as to confirm (or disconfirm) his ideas about the way the race will be run.

The main difference, then, between the casual horseplayer and the serious horseplayer is that the serious horseplayer is able to learn many things by watching the race and the prerace warmups carefully.

The Warmups. The Standardbred, being a sturdy animal, usually takes 2 or 3 miles of warmups before its race, usually at intervals of an hour or two. In addition, a horse "scores" just prior to the start of the race, usually working the mile about 10 to 20 seconds slower than in the actual race. This is the time for a handicapper to check out the condition of the horse he intends to wager on. The horse should move freely and easily, showing no signs of pain or distress. A horse that is lame, hurting, or strained by overwork will often reflect this by its inability to stay flat or by favoring a leg or foot. Similarly, an unruly horse, especially a puller, will be difficult for a driver to restrain during the warmups. (This is not the same as his keeping a tight hold on a horse that wants to run.)

So if an animal is unruly or appears uncomfortable, ailing, or tired, it is best to save your money. These are not certain indications that a horse is sore, ailing, or unstrung, but they are more cause than not for the player to keep his money in his pocket.

On the other hand, there are occasions on which you may wish to bet a horse solely on the basis of its impressive workouts—especially if it has shown something in its last start.

By and large, however, the warmups should be used to *disqualify* a horse from further consideration.

The race. First, it is important to find a good seat in the grandstand, directly above the finish line, if possible. Binoculars are useful in following the action closely during the race. In addition, I recommend that you watch the replay on closed-circuit television. If you bet the race, you undoubtedly kept your eyes riveted on your choice

throughout. The replay offers an opportunity to follow the progress of the remaining horses, particularly those which finished in the money—along with your own selection!

Here are some things to look for and to keep in mind when you watch a race: any horses parked outside for a good part or all of the race; any that are boxed in (trapped against the rail by horses on the outside) from the half through the stretch; and any that get stuck in the backstretch on the outside behind other animals and must go three wide at the head of the stretch, necessarily losing ground.

You will want to include all this information in a "handicapper's notebook" (see chapter 4). You will then have on file a record of which animals in the race were lucky (for example, got through on the rail in the stretch), and which were unlucky (hung three wide on the first turn, boxed all the way from the half, got out at same time as horses in front). Knowing these things helps the handicapper to account for the effects of racing luck, to take what's on the program with a grain of salt, and to foresee so-called upsets next time out. Many or most of them cannot be learned by reading the program alone. They are the principal advantage, if put to good use, that the experienced racegoer has over the stay-at-homes.

2
The Business of Betting

How to Determine the Payoff on a Wager

To determine what a horse will pay if you bet on it to win and it does win, let's look at the chart below:

MUTUELS FOR EACH $2.00 BET

ODDS	PAYS	ODDS	PAYS	ODDS	PAYS	ODDS	PAYS	ODDS	PAYS	ODDS	PAYS
2 - 5	2.80	1	4.00	8 - 5	5.20	3	8.00	5	12.00	9	20.00
1 - 2	3.00	6 - 5	4.40	9 - 5	5.60	7 - 2	9.00	6	14.00	10	22.00
3 - 5	3.20	7 - 5	4.80	2	6.00	4	10.00	7	16.00	15	32.00
4 - 5	3.60	3 - 2	5.00	5 - 2	7.00	9 - 2	11.00	8	18.00	20	42.00

A horse that goes off at odds of 1 to 5 will pay $1 for each $5 bet on it. This means that a $5 bet will return $6 to the bettor, including the $5 he wagered and his $1 in winnings. To determine what a $2 bet will pay on a horse at the odds of 1 to 5, simply multiply each figure by 4, and you will get 4 to 20, the sum of which is 24. A $2.00 bet, then, will net a return of $2.40, including the $2.00 wager.

A horse that wins at odds of 8 to 5 will return a net of $13 on a $5 straight-win bet, with $8 in profits. Again, to determine the payoff of an 8-to-5 shot on a $2 win bet, multiply each number by 4 and you will get 32 to 20. Add these, and you get 52, or a $5.20 return on a $2.00 bet.

A horse which wins at odds of 2 to 1 will pay $15 on a $5 win bet, including $10 in winnings. Once you get in the habit of making these calculations, they will come naturally to you.

Win, Place, and Show Wagering

In New York State, about 20 percent of the total amount bet on all the horses in a given race to win is deducted for taxes, etc. The remaining 80 percent is returned to the winning bettors. For example, if $10,000 is the total amount bet in the win pool in a race, $8,100 will be returned to the winning bettors.

Suppose that $1,000 has been bet to win on the horse that does win. Then each dollar bet on this horse to win will return to the winning bettor $7.10 in profits. This means that the horse will go off at odds of just over 7 to 1. Of the $8,100 returned to winning bettors, $1,000 was bet by them originally on the horse and the remaining $7,100 comes out of the pockets of the losers.

Again, if $2,000 of the total win pool has been bet on the winning horse, each dollar will yield a profit of approximately $4, so that the odds on the horse to win will now be about 4 to 1. Now suppose that $5,000 of the original $10,000 wagered has been bet on the winning horse. Then each winning dollar bet will net a return of only $.60. In this instance the $5,000 bet on the horse will bring a return of only $3,000 and the odds will accordingly be just over 3 to 5.

Place and show betting are more complicated in their returns, because the odds shown on the tote board correspond only very roughly to expected payoffs for place and show wagers. Payoffs for a place wager are always divided between backers of each of the horses that finish first and second. This requires that the total amount of the return on successful place wagers be cut in half. If $4,000 of a $10,000 total place pool is wagered on the two horses that win and place, the return will be approximately $4 on a $2 wager. First, deduct about $2,000 from the total for the tax cut. Then divide the remaining $8,000 equally between the winners since the same amount of money was wagered on each of the two horses which won and placed. As a result, for each $2 wager the place bettor will net a return of $4, including $2 in winnings.

Similar considerations hold for show betting. On the average, place bets pay close to $4.00 (less on favorites), so that you must expect to collect more than 50 percent of your bets in order to finish ahead, betting straight place. The average show price is about $2.80, so that you must cash at least three-fourths of the show tickets you buy in order to win betting straight show. During a brief period (including more than thirty nights of racing) I kept a record of show betting on favorites. I found that if a punter wagered $20 to show on the favorite in every race on the card, he would realize an average *profit* of just under $20 an evening over this period. However, exceptions were races in which two or more horses go off as co-favorites, usually at odds of close to 2 to 1 each. In such cases, one co-favorite often finishes in the money and the other out.

At this juncture an attentive reader will wonder why he should continue reading this book. For if my claims about show betting hold up, he can go to the races each evening and come home with small but predictable profits. My answer is that the better the handicapper you are, the more profits you will realize at the races whether you bet win, place, show, exactas, trifectas, etc. In many races you will find that the favorite is unplayable either because the horse has too little form to be worth a bet or because the favorite is simply not the best bet in the race. You will discover that if you lay off certain types of races, especially maiden races and conditioned trots with young and inexperienced horses, your profits will be considerably higher. In a race of formless or near formless animals, it's almost impossible to handicap effectively, and the favorite in an "open" race is often an arbitrary selection.

If low-percentage profit taking is acceptable to you (after all, it is money won), I suggest that you accumulate past programs, look at the results charts, and check the possibility of profit-taking by betting exclusively to show on favorites. However, you can do even better *if* you are a good handicapper by betting the horse you think is best in the race to show whether or not it's the favorite. Generally, your chances of winning will be much improved on evenings in which the majority of races are made up of higher-class animals with better form.

It's sometimes argued that if you are a good handicapper, you will select more horses to win than to place or show, and that your profits will be still higher if you stick to straight win play. I can't agree completely. If you're a good handicapper, you may still find that you bet as many horses to place and show as to win. Selecting winners in at least one-third of the races you play is probably the minimum you need to make a profit by straight win betting, and this is not easy. But a good handicapper can probably select horses in such a way that more than 70 percent of his choices finish in the money. And he can bet many more races with confidence than if he restricts himself to straight win betting.

Some experts on money management at the races recommend that you begin with an exact amount, such as $200, and bet exactly 5 percent of your total on each wager. So if you lose your first two $10 bets, you will be left with $180, and you will then bet $9 on each of your choices. Should you lose two more bets in a row, your bankroll

will be reduced to $160, and you will bet $8 per race. If you then make a comeback you can wager 5 percent of your total kitty.

However, I would recommend that the show bettor follow a 10 percent instead of a 5 percent rule for the following reasons: your chances of losing a show wager are about two times less than your chances of losing a straight win bet, so you can bet with more confidence and therefore more funds to show. Second, your profits are so much lower when you bet to show that you must bet at least twice as much to make up the difference. A $20 show bet makes very good sense if you are a capable handicapper and happy to go home with a $20 to $40 profit on an average evening.

Exactas, Trifectas, and the Daily Double

It is most tempting to bet exactas, trifectas, and other kinds of exotic wagering. There is one and only one condition under which I would advise your betting an exacta. That is when two horses in the same race seem equally strong to you, and you are at a loss whether to bet one or the other. This assumes that only those two horses are attractive bets. Under any other conditions, it is advisable to avoid exacta wagering.

I recommend that you avoid trifectas completely. Selecting horses in a 1-2-3 order is like searching for a needle in a haystack. If you are serious about winning consistently, exacta and trifecta wagering must be dispensed with.

Betting daily doubles, however, makes sense under one and only one condition—when each race in the daily double is worth wagering on in its own right. Of course, this involves parlay wagering, which is the same thing as betting your winnings on the first race entirely upon a horse in the second to win. The major advantage to betting the daily double, as opposed to parlay wagering on the first two races, is that the daily double ordinarily pays at least 20 percent more than a parlay wager on the first two races. Perhaps this is because there is more speculation on long shots in the daily double than in other races. In any case, the daily double is seldom worth betting because there are seldom two playable consecutive races, particularly when the caliber of horses that race in the double is considered.

There are four reasonable approaches to take toward betting on a race. These are: (1) straight win betting on one horse: (2) straight win

betting on two or even three horses; (3) straight place wagering; and (4) straight show wagering. Let's consider each of these.

The major advantage of straight win wagering is the size of the return on each bet, which is considerably higher than the return on place and show bets. Moreover, the percentage of breakage deducted from place and show winnings is proportionately greater than from profits earned on straight win bets. A horse that wins at odds of 2 to 1 will return a profit of $4 on a $2 win wager. A horse that wins or places at these odds will return a $1 to $2 profit on most place bets, and a $2 show bet on a horse that finishes in the money will seldom reward the bettor with much more than a $1 in winnings.

The disadvantage of straight win betting is the obvious difficulty of selecting the one horse that will win the race. Betting consistently on favorites to win will not enable you to realize a profit in the long run. Favorites win, on an average, slightly more than one-third of all harness races. But if you confine your play to favorites, you must be able to cash at least one-third of your tickets at average odds of 2 to 1 in order to break even. However, the average odds on a favorite to win have been calculated to be about 7 to 5 (1.40 to 1). Moreover, a substantial number of favorites go off as odds-on choices and the great majority at odds of less than 2 to 1. As a result, most of the money you will make at the track betting to win will be realized on overlays, or horses that go off at somewhat higher odds than a good handicapper would assign them.

A capable handicapper may give a horse a fifty-fifty chance of winning its race and discover to his surprise that the horse is 5 to 2. In that case he will hasten to the window to put down a wager on the animal. If, however, this same horse goes off as odds-on favorite at 3 to 5, he will pass the race altogether rather than risk his money on an underlay. The straight win wager on a true overlay, a horse that is an excellent bet at odds of 2 to 1 or more, is what will yield a consistent margin of profit at the races. Straight win wagering on favorites alone, even if you are selective, is likely to lead to bankruptcy. By contrast, straight win betting on overlays is one path (and probably the best) to financial success at the races. (For more on overlays, see chapter 5.)

Some writers on racing advocate betting on more than one horse in a single race when, after careful handicapping, two or three equally

strong contenders emerge. This advice makes good sense under special circumstances, when the two (or more) horses you believe have equal chances go off at reasonably high odds. But if one horse goes off at even money and the other at 2 to 1, it will make little sense to bet both horses. For suppose that you wager $10 on each of these horses. Then if the even-money shot wins, you break even; if the 2-to-1 shot wins, your overall profit is only $10; but if both horses lose, you are out $20.

Is it worth risking $20 to win a maximum of $10? I doubt it. But if one horse goes off at 2 to 1 and the other at 5 to 1, it may be worthwhile betting on both horses. This means that your net profit will be $10 if the 2-to-1 shot wins and $40 if the 5-to-1 shot wins. Still, it would seem even more reasonable to bet your entire $20 on the animal with favorable odds of 5 to 1 if you think it has a fifty-fifty chance to win.

So the only circumstance under which betting two or more horses in a race makes sense is when there is no basis for a choice among the contenders and each goes off at odds that will ensure a handy profit on each play. Otherwise, I recommend betting the horse with the best odds or simply passing the race.

Straight place betting has the advantage that you will most likely cash tickets about twice as often as when you bet straight win. To realize a profit from straight win betting, you must cash at least one-third of the tickets you buy, at average odds of 2 to 1 or higher. As place prices average between $3.50 and $4.00, you must cash at least two-thirds of your wagers to finish ahead by straight place betting. Place betting makes sense only for someone who finds that a substantially higher percentage of the horses he bets finish second rather than first.

Show betting will be profitable if you are able to cash at least 70 to 80 percent of your tickets, and not just on favorites. You need this high a percentage of winning tickets because the average show ticket pays no more than $2.60 to $2.80. However, if you are willing to bet large sums on horses to show, you may find that you can realize a fair margin of profit by selecting the races you bet carefully and wagering only on solid choices.

I do not recommend show betting unless you intend to wager a substantial amount on each race you play. Otherwise, your profits

will be nugatory. For a person who is unable to handicap and who can't resist wagering on every race on the card, wagering on the favorite to show is probably the safest way to minimize losses. For a capable handicapper, show betting is at best an unappetizing venture. Why bet to show if you're good enough to handicap a high percentage of winners (or horses to place) on selected races?

The "Hidden Factor" in Wagering

According to certain writers on racing, another factor besides handicapping must be taken into account if you are to win at the races. This "hidden factor" is the probability that a horse is ready, willing, and able to win tonight's race, not because it looks good on the program but because those "in the know" are betting it heavily.

Who or what is the "stable"? Most likely the horse's owner, trainer, and driver and any other interested parties who feel confident enough of their horse to risk hard-earned greenbacks on its chances. The size of the barn's wager can run from a few hundred to many thousands of dollars, depending upon their estimate of their horse's condition, the competition and other elements such as post position, driver, etc.

It is not unusual for an animal to turn in several mediocre races and shortly thereafter to reach peak form. Reaching peak condition can be due to the horse's quickly finding itself or, more likely, its rounding into shape through intensive training over several days or weeks. When this happens, the barn is apt to bet its choice, particularly when the level of competition and other factors in the race make a large wager right.

Here is a typical example. You have handicapped the second race on the card, a $3,000 claiming pace. Your choice is Alphonse Pick, a thirteen-year-old horse who has run consistently well in his last several starts. The odds on your choice are good—you expect Alphonse Pick to go off at odds of 2 to 1 or less, but instead he is 7 to 2 on the tote board.

Suddenly, looking at the board just before you go to place your bet, you notice that Gaston Direct, which should be 6 to 1 in this race, has been bet down to 8 to 5. How, you ask yourself, can an animal that shows almost nothing on the program go off at 8 to 5 tonight?

The odds on Gaston Direct are too low—should it win, it will complete a Daily Double of just $25, less than one would win betting

a two-horse parlay on the first and second races. Moreover, it's most unlikely that the public would back this animal to anything like 8 to 5 on a busy Friday evening. Only one conclusion seems possible, and in this instance it is personally confirmed by a friend of the owner. The barn has trained the horse to a T for more than a week, and the animal is ready.

With an inside post position and a strong driver, our 8-to-5 shot wins going away! Naturally Gaston Direct was bet heavily by the owner and his associates.

Moral: Get on the bandwagon whenever the tote board shows that a stable is emptying its coffers on its pride and joy.

The advice to get on the bandwagon in such cases often sounds more promising than it turns out in reality. A number of complications often make this advice difficult or impossible to act on.

First, you can't always tell whether a horse is bet heavily because the stable is going with it tonight or because the animal is naturally attracting the public's money. Only when a horse is obviously *over-bet* in a race, considering its likely chances from the program, do we have any business believing that stable money makes the difference.

Second, the stable's bet may be made at the last minute so that it registers on the tote board too late for us to make any use of it. The very last time the betting-pool total is flashed on the board is just after the race has started.

Third, the barn's wager may be pumped through the machines so slowly that the odds on its choice never fall sharply enough for us to notice any marked changes on the board. Or the wager, placed in a heavily bet race, may be so modest relative to the entire pool that it fails to make a real dent on the tote board. In most races, a $1,000 bet will lower the odds on a horse only marginally.

Fourth, more than one barn may be emptying its piggy bank in a particular race! It is not unusual to see two or even three horses bet far more heavily than one might expect.

Fifth, a stable can overestimate its entry's chances. On more than one occasion I have seen a heavily bet horse just miss after its odds had dropped at the last minute. In fact, I used to think that the best rule was to bet the "smart money" horse to *place*. It is not unusual for a stable's choice to get boxed in or parked out for the entire race and finish well back. By and large, these smart-money animals don't do much better than your everyday run-of-the-mill favorites. And if you confine your wagering to claiming races, you have even less to

worry about. Most of these "heavies" run in conditioned races because the barn doesn't want to risk losing a prize animal in a claimer.

What do you do, then, when you hit a race in which you like a horse other than the stable's choice? Three alternatives are open to you: (1) stick to your original choice; (2) change your selection to the barn's choice; or (3) lay off the race altogether.

Here are the pros and cons. If you stick to your original choice and win, you will have the obvious satisfaction of beating the "smart money's" choice, but if you lose on your horse, you will curse yourself for not getting on the bandwagon. If you bet the stable and win, you will get the satisfaction of being with the smart money. "If you can't beat them, join them." But if you change your choice and lose, you will be utterly miserable for having "switched hats." If you lay off the race, you will at least not find yourself hung up trying to decide what to do at the last minute. I recommend sticking with your original choice unless you feel very strongly that you're on the wrong track (no pun intended) after noticing the change on the tote board and looking again at the program.

But if you get confused, *always* lay off betting a race. Getting confused and losing money at the races are bedfellows.

New York State's OTB

Off-track-betting offices are in business throughout New York State. Anyone interested in wagering on harness races has ample opportunity to do so without making a trip to the raceway or finding a bookmaker. The advantages of OTB are obvious—offices throughout the state in which one can place a bet with a minimum of bother.

The disadvantages are not so obvious. These have to do with the additional 5 percent charge OTB deducts from a winning ticket *after* take and breakage have been deducted. This means that in addition to the 20 cents out of each dollar the state and raceway tax the winning bettor, OTB levies an additional 5 percent surcharge for the privilege of placing your bet at one of their offices.

How does this work out in relation to the actual prices paid out by OTB as opposed to the track? Suppose you wager $2 to win on an even-money shot, that is, a horse that pays $4 at the track. OTB will deduct 5 percent of $4.00, the winning price, with the result that your return is $3.80. Actually, 10 percent has been lopped off your winnings of $2.00, which are now $1.80 instead of $2.00.

The situation is even worse for the show bettor, because OTB takes

a minimum of 20 cents off each ticket up to $4.00. So a show price of $2.80 is good for only $2.60 at OTB, a 25 percent reduction in one's profits. The moral is clear—if you bet favorites or bet consistently to place or show, OTB is not for you unless you wager very small sums. For the bettor who plays long shots, daily doubles, and trifectas, there is little or no penalty for using OTB. Someone who gets a $50.00 daily double needn't fret about the $2.50 takeout. But for the more serious player who wagers substantial sums on favorites, the track is the place to be. Also, as we have seen, an astute observer can learn something, from being at the track, that the program may not reveal.

3
Reading the Program and the Charts

Handicapping: Reading the Program Intelligently

Handicapping is 100 percent a question of being able to read a program intelligently and select the best bet in a race. In this chapter we will cover the basics of reading a program. First, keep in mind that nearly every race is either a claiming or a conditioned race and either a pace or a trot.

Paces are as a rule easier to handicap than trots. Moreover, claiming races are usually easier to handicap than conditioned races, because there is usually a single claiming price in a claiming race. Even here, though, horses may race for different claiming prices in a race because a mare or a younger horse may be allowed an additional 20 to 50 percent in claiming price. Therefore, don't be deceived if a horse in a $3,000 claiming pace has a $3,600 claiming price. The $600 difference is an additional 20 percent because the horse is a mare or a four-year-old.

Examples from Actual Races

We will consider claiming paces because past experience shows that these are the easiest harness races to handicap. Let's begin with a $3,500 claiming pace in which there is a field of eight horses. Look at the record for the number-1 horse in the race, Single Johnnie. On the far left is indicated the horse's post position, which is 1. Under the post position are the letters *MS,* which indicate that the horse is driven with a modified sulky. Under *MS* is the horse's claiming price, $3,500.

Turning now to information about the horse, we find above the horse's name in parentheses that Single Johnnie's best previous winning time was 2:08 4/5 on a ½-mile track when the horse was four years old. After the dash are recorded the horse's lifetime earnings up

(6) PACE CLAIMING

EXACTA Wagering This Race

1 Mile — Purse $1500

Claiming Price $3500
Mares allowed 20%.

ASK FOR HORSE BY PROGRAM NUMBER

Saddle Cloth
BLUE

---

1 SINGLE JOHNNIE
MS 3500

(4, 2.08¼ (½) — $3603)

DRIVER—FRED GRIFFIN—White, Red and Blue

blk. g. 8, by Johnnie G—Rosy Dolly
Thomas Agosti, Tonawanda, N.Y.

Trainer: T. Agosti (Griffin Stable)

1977   14   5   7   1 $ 4818
2.07¾ B.R.   Last Raced in 1975

6-28⁷⁷	Btva	ms	1500	ft	3500	clm						(FGriffi)	
6- 7⁷⁷	B.R.	ms	1600	ft	3500	clm						(FGriffi)	
5-21⁷⁷	B.R.	ms	1600	ft	3500	clm						(FGriffi)	
5- 4⁷⁷	B.R.	ms	1600	sy	4000	clm						(FGriffi)	
4-26⁷⁷	B.R.	ms	1500	ft	3500	clm CD						(FGriffi)	
4-19⁷⁷	B.R.	ms	1500	ft	3500	clm						(FGriffi)	
4- 8⁷⁷	B.R.	ms	1300	gd	3500	clm						(FGriffi)	

---

2 FRISCO BENNIE
MS 3500

(6, 2.08¾ Q (½) — $8067)

DRIVER—MARC BOURGON (P)—Blue, Gold and White

b. g. 7, by Maynard Hanover—April C
Marc Bourgon, Montreal, Que., Can.

Trainer: M. Bourgon (Bourgon Stable)

2.07¾ B.R.
2.08¾ Btva Q

---

3 TWILA
MS 4200

(4, 2.06¾ (¼) — $21432)

DRIVER—CARMEN CAPPOTELLI—Gray, Red and Gold

b. m. 7, by Fort Knox—Twinkle Patch
Carmen & Archie Cappotelli, Caledonia, N.Y.

Trainer: C. Cappotelli

1977   11   1   0   2 $ 1400
2.09 Btva
2.08 Btva

---

4 NORA'S LAST BOY (N)
MS

(8, 2.02½ (¼) — $57152)

DRIVER—JAN FILER—Brown and Gold

b. g. 10, by Glendale Direct—Nora Hal
Carl Labate, Rochester, N.Y.

Trainer: C. Welty (Labate Stable)

1977   6   0   0   1 $ 192
2.05½ Btva

5 3500

(4, 2.04 (⅝)) — $28454
JOHN SILVER
DRIVER—GEORGE GOVEIA—Brown and Sand
b. g. 9, by Philip Frost—Dalyce Blue
Juniors III, Buffalo, N.Y.   Trainer: C. Monti

6-23⁷⁷	B.R.	cs	1600	ft	3500 clm	1	.31¹	1.03¹	1.35²	2.06³	2	2.07²	6.60	(GGoveia)	EbenJones,LarryLinn,JohnSilver			1977 10 0 0 2 $ 737
6-14⁷⁷	B.R.	cs	1600	ft	4000 clm	1	.31¹	1.03¹	1.37	2.07⁴	2	2.08²	12.50	(GGoveia)	DaringDrexel,ButlerKnight,AQEquador			1976 20 0 4 1 $ 2669
6- 1⁷⁷	B.R.	cs	1700	ft	4000 clm	1	.33	1.05³	1.37	2.08	4	2.10	16.20	(GGoveia)	SargeGunner,LarryTiz,ScotlandAgnes			75
5- 4⁷⁷	B.R.	cs	1600	sy	4000 clm	1	.32³	1.06⁴	1.40²	2.11³	1x	2.10	4.30	(JSchroe)	BuckeyeKnight,SingleJohnnie,BonVic			75
4-27⁷⁷	B.R.	ms	1600	ft	4000 clm	1	.31	1.03¹	1.36¹	2.07²	5	2.17³	3.60	(JSchroe)	SargeGunner,VeraclyN,JohnSilver			66
4-16⁷⁷	B.R.	ms	1400	ft	4000 clm	1	.31	1.03¹	1.36¹	2.07³	4	2.08³	13.60	(JSchroe)	MyBrothersHorse,JsJane,DealersDream			55
4- 5⁷⁷	B.R.	ms	1400	gd	4000 clm CD	1	.32²	1.37²	2.09³	2		2.13	14.70	(GGibson)	BeverlysJune,GraysPat,SlippersBoy			36

6 3500

(10, 2.02⅞ (⅝)) — $70032
DREAMER LOBELL
DRIVER—PHILIPPE LAFRAMBOISE—Blue and White
b. h. 13, by Airliner—Gay Dream
P. Laframboise & E. Ingenito, Masson, Que. Can. & Olean, N.Y.   Trainer: R. Horton (Laframboise Stable)

6-23⁷⁷	B.R.	ms	1600	ft	3500 clm	1	.31	1.03¹	1.34	2.06	5	2.07²	1.90	(PLaframb)	CptainCrunch,DreamerLbell,BuddyVelbob			1977 9 2 1 0 $ 1150
6-15⁷⁷	B.R.	ms	1500	ft	3000 clm	1	.32	1.04²	1.36³	2.08	4	1.80*	(PLaframb)	DreamerLobell,LisaGa,KeystoneDBrien			1976 9 0 1 5 $ 316
6- 3⁷⁷	B.R.	ms		gd	Qua	1	.32	1.03¹	1.37	2.08	3	2.094	NB	(PLaframb)	Squall,RacingGene,JinniesFicka			77
11-24⁷⁶	RldC⅝		600	ft	nw200La6CD	1	.30⁴	1.01¹	1.32	2.05⁴	5	2.10	3.95	(RODwyer)	AdiosEarl,MapleHillMmaid,ParisNctrn			57
11-17⁷⁶	RldC⅝		600	ft	nw200La6CD	1	.31²	1.34	1.35⁴	2.06²	6	2.10	2.35	(RODwyer)	ByeridgeGene,CapePinePowl,DrlrmLobell			
11-10⁷⁶	RldC⅝		650	gd	nw200La6CD	1	.32	1.04¹	1.35⁴	2.08²	3	2.101	13.90	(JLancas)	ButtwoodPrince,AdiosEarl,RebPammy			63
11- 5⁷⁶	B.R.	ms	650	ft	nw220La6CD	1	.31¹	1.03¹	1.36¹	2.08³	9	2.11²	13.30	(RChartr)	KevnDvrtrck,DavidABrk,MapleHillMmd			78

7 4000 MS

(4, 2.05⅜ (½)) — $18189
WESTERN'S MYRTLE
DRIVER—DAN SARAMA—White, Orange and Red
ro. m. 6, by Everett Chief—Zulu Hal
Mardan Stable, Corfu, N.Y.   Trainer: M. Sarama

6-23⁷⁷	B.R.	ms	1700	ft	4800 clm	1	.31²	1.04³	1.36	2.06⁴	6	6⁴¹	2.70	(DSarama)	PearlieChita,IndianRuler,PeanutB			1977 13 4 2 1 $ 4425
5-28⁷⁷	B.R.	ms	2150	ft	7200 clm	1	.31³	1.04³	1.36	2.08	7	7	8.20	(DSarama)	BurleyGuy,RacingGene,ColeHillJohn			1976 9 0 2 6 $ 2107
5-21⁷⁷	B.R.	ms	2150	ft	7200 clm	1	.31³	1.04¹	1.33³	2.05⁴	6	x86⁴	3.95	(DSarama)	Squall,RacingGene,WesternsMyrtle			75
5-14⁷⁷	B.R.	ms	2150	ft	7200 clm	1	.30	1.01³	1.33	2.05⁴	5	6³	5.30	(DSarama)	BernitaHanover,WaitABit,Quickem			58
5- 7⁷⁷	B.R.	ms	2050	ft	7800 clm	1	.32	1.04¹	1.35²	2.06¹	6	6¹²	2.50*	(DSarama)	BernitaHanover,WaitABit,Quickem			62
4-30⁷⁷	B.R.	ms	2050	ft	7200 clm	1	.31¹	1.04	1.37²	2.08	7	6⁷	13.90	(DSarama)	MerryJohnA,TredonScott,BeverlysJune			54
4-20⁷⁷	B.R.	ms	2000	ft	7200 clm hcp	1	.30³	1.34	2.06⁴	5	5²⁴		1.40*	(DSarama)	WstrnsMyrtle,BethOregon,MrshmllowFluff			63
									1ns		5	5¹⁴²	4.90	(DSarama)	WesternsMyrtle,Sophrunia,KissyVon			78

8 3500 MS

(6, 2.03⅜ (½)) — $50385
STANLEY PICK
DRIVER—BOB ALTIZER—Gold, Green and White
ch. h. 11, by Easy Adios—Rockette Wick
You & Me Stables, Inc., Batavia, N.Y.   Trainer: Jo. Altizer (Altizer Stable)

6-24⁷⁷	B.R.	ms	1400	ft	c-2500 clm	1	.31¹	1.02⁴	1.34⁴	2.08¹	4	5	7.40	(DWelch)	SpanglerFrost,BrackenField,MaryAWil			79
6-13⁷⁷	B.R.	ms	1400	ft	2500 clm	1	.32²	1.05³	1.38	2.10	7	7¹³	7.90	(DWelch)	StanleyPick,HappyAcres,Susie,MrGlenby			72
6- 7⁷⁷	B.R.	ms		gd	Qua	1	.31¹	1.03	1.35²	2.06¹	6	5⁴⁴	NB	(DWelch)	StarettaCharm,WallysSue,EddieForbes			53
6- 3⁷⁷	B.R.	ms		gd	Qua	1	.31¹	1.04	1.38²	2.12	4	3³¹	NB	(DWelch)	GlendalePisa,DannysDilema,TripleJ			57
5-14⁷⁷	B.R.	ms	1400	ft	Qua	1	.31²	1.03¹	1.35⁴	2.09²	5	5¹¹²	NB	(DWelch)	CounselQuick,CCTempo,StanleyPick			85
5-24⁷⁷	B.R.	ms		gd	2500 clm	1	.31²	1.03¹	1.35⁴	2.09²	6	6³²	4.90	(DWelch)	MikeKabbe,StanleyPick,JeboroExpress			85
1-24⁷⁷	B.R.	ms	900	gd	2500 clm CD	1	.32³	1.07	1.40²	2.12⁴	5	2nk	3.90	(KBall)	RobbyCarLith,GameGreek,VicsTar			25

to the present year, $3,603. Below the horse's name is the name of the driver, Fred Griffin, and his colors, white, red, and blue.

Directly to the right is further information about the horse. It is a black gelding, eight years old, sired by Johnnie G out of Rosy Dolly. Below this information is the name of the horse's owner. Moving further to the right we find that the horse's owner, Thomas Agosti, is also its trainer and that Single Johnnie is part of the driver's (Fred Griffin's) stable.

More important is the horse's record for the present year (1977). He has raced fourteen times, with five wins, seven places, and one show, and his total winnings this year have been $4,818. His fastest winning time was 2:07 2/5, as shown to the left of 1977.

Now let us look at the information directly below the driver's name and colors. In this space we find the record of the horse's last seven races, the most recent of which was June 28, 1977, at Batavia Downs. Single Johnnie's previous six races were at Buffalo Raceway. (For abbreviations of the major American harness tracks and comparative times for these tracks, look elsewhere in your program.) After the names of the tracks we see that the horse raced on every occasion with a modified sulky. The purse of his last race was $1,500 and of the previous three races on June 7, May 21, and May 4, it was $1,600.

After the amount of the purse is stated the condition of the track, which was fast on June 28, June 7, and May 21, sloppy on May 4, fast on April 26 and April 19, and good on April 8. Keep in mind that if a track is good to sloppy, races are usually run one to two seconds slower than on a fast track.

After the condition of the track is stated the amount of the claiming race, which was $3,500, except for the race on May 4, which was a $4,000 claimer.

To the right we are given the distance of Single Johnnie's races, which in every case was 1 mile, the usual length of trotting races. Then we are given the time at which each quarter of the race was run. In the race on June 28, the first quarter was run in 30 4/5 seconds. The first half of this race went in 1:03, which means that the second quarter was run in just over 32 seconds. The three-quarter mark of the race was at 1:34, from which it follows that the third quarter was run in 31 seconds. The race was won in 2:05, so the final quarter also went in 31 seconds.

Following the times at which each quarter of the race was run, we are given the horse's post position and then its position at each quarter. Single Johnnie's post position in his June 28 race was 5, and his position during the race was fourth at the first quarter, fourth at the half, fifth on the outside at the three-quarter mark, fifth at the head of the stretch, 4½ lengths behind the leader, and fifth at the finish, 12½ lengths behind the winner. This account of the horse's position at each quarter of the race can be shown as follows:

Post Position	¼	½	¾	Head of Stretch	Finish
5	4	4	5	5	5

The small *O* next to five at the three-quarter mark means that Single Johnnie was running on the outside for at least one quarter of the last half of the race. This means that the driver took the horse to the outside at the half and attempted to catch the horses in front of him—in this instance unsuccessfully. Single Johnnie finished fifth, 12½ lengths behind the winner, and his time for the race was 2:07 2/5. Since the race was won in 2:05 and Single Johnnie was 12½ lengths behind the winner, you can see that a length is run in about 1/5 second.

Next we are given the betting odds on Single Johnnie in this race, which were 6.30 to 1, then the name of the driver (F. Griffin), and then the horses that finished first, second, and third in the race. At the end of this line is 77, the temperature on the evening of June 28. Asterisks after the odds of the races on June 7, May 21, and May 4 show that Single Johnnie was the favorite in these races.

Let us consider a second example, in this case of a horse that runs, not in claiming, but in conditioned races. Nicotine, a four-year-old chestnut gelding, has started four races in 1977 and won three. In his last start at Batavia Downs on July 14, 1977, he finished first by a neck in a $2,500 conditioned race. Specifically, this race was open to nonwinners of three races lifetime.

In his race on July 7, 1977, Nicotine finished fifth, 8¼ lengths behind the winner, in another $2,500 conditioned race. The race of July 7 was open to nonwinners of $2,500 lifetime.

In the race on June 23, 1977, Nicotine was raced with a conventional sulky, and he won a $1,900 conditioned race open to nonwinners of two races lifetime.

(None — $000)

NICOTINE

DRIVER—RONALD FITZGERALD—Red and White

ch. g. 4, by Atomic Pick—Fairy House
Vincent C. Caserta, Kenmore, N.Y.

Trainer: R. Fitzgerald
2.05¾ Btva

1977   4   3   0   0 $ 3125
First Start

7-14⁷⁷	Btva	2500	ft	nw3RLtCD	1	.31²	1.03²	1.34	2.05²	1	2	2	2⁰	2²	1nk	2.05²	1.20*	(RFitzge)	Nicotine,WiscoyPatsy,AddiesDuke	80
7- 7⁷⁷	Btva	2500	sy	nw2500LtCD	1	.31	1.03³	1.35	2.05	6	7	8	8	8⁸³	5⁸⁴	2.06³	2.70	(RFitzge)	EddoThorpe,OBriensPrincess,AdieuRose	67
6-23⁷⁷	B.R.	cs 1900	ft	nw2RLtCD	1	.30³	1.02³	1.34³	2.05²	3	1⁰	1	1	1¹⁴	1¹⁴	2.05²	1.40*	(RFitzge)	Nicotine,AvonFairline,FullConnection	75
6-15⁷⁷	B.R.	cs 1600	ft	Mdn CD	1	.30³	1.02²	1.35²	2.08	7	2⁰	2	1½	1½	1³⁴	2.08	1.70*	(RFitzge)	Nicotine,OlympicRob,SharpDeputy	77
6- 3⁷⁷	B.R.	cs	gd	Qua	1	.31⁴	1.05²	1.38¹	2.10²	5	3	3	3²	3²	2ns	2.10²	NB	(RFitzge)	BigValue,Nicotine,KeystoneDebut	
5-10⁷⁷	ScD⅝	‡	ft	Qua	1	.31¹	1.02⁴	1.33⁴	2.03⁴	1	2	3	3x	x34½	5dis	2.10⁴	NB	(JPolloc)	HMC,BattleKnight,KeyHill	57

(4, 2.05¾ (½) — $5636)

DUTCH HOLLOW KAT(N)

DRIVER—PETER ARRIGENNA (P)—Red, White and Blue

b. g. 5, by Kat Byrd—Ellie B
William Stoltman & William A. Brogan, Avon, N.Y.

7-26⁷⁷	Btva	ms	2700	ft	nw2500LtCD	1	.31²	1.04²	1.34⁴	2.06	7	2	1²	1²⁴	2.06	2.50* (PArrige)	DutchHollowKat,SpurGauman,LadyVanessa 68
7-21⁷⁷	Btva	ms	2700	ft	nw2500LtCD	1	.30⁴	1.05	1.36²	2.07²	5	6	4⁰	4²¹	2ns	4.30 (TLanphe)	WiscoyPatsy,DtchHollowKat,FlmeGauman 78
7-14⁷⁷	Btva	ms	2500	ft	nw3RLtCD	1	.31²	1.03²	1.34	2.05²	8	8	8⁷²	4⁴¹	2.06¹	25.00 (TLanphe)	Nicotine,WiscoyPatsy,AddiesDuke 80
7- 7⁷⁷	Btva	ms	2500	sy	nw2500LtCD	1	.31	1.03³	1.35	2.05	6	6	3⁰	4⁷	2.06²	8.30 (FHaslip)	EddoThorpe,OBriensPrincess,AdieuRose 67
7- 1⁷⁷	Btva	ms	2400	ft	nw3RLtCD	1	.30⁴	1.02¹	1.33	2.04⁴	5	6	2⁰	3²³	2.06⁴	4.10 (TLanphe)	JsseGlnnbrooke,OBrnsPrncss,DtchHllwKt 77
6-21⁷⁷	B.R.	ms	2050	ft	76-7nw4000CD	1	.29¹	1.00	1.33¹	2.05¹	2	2	1	1²	2.05³	13.10 (TLanphe)	StrettaChrm,DtchHllowKat,SenatrDuglas 70
6-16⁷⁷	B.R.	cs	2350	ft	76-7nw5000CD	1	.30²	1.03²	1.34²	2.05⁴	6	5	4⁰	8³³	2.06³	41.10 (DWelch)	AvonAngelo,Silicon,ClayAttack 80

Trainer: P. Arrigenna

	2.06 Btva	;, 1977	9	1	2	1	$ 3342
	2.05½ Btva	1976	20	3	5	8	$ 5527

Nicotine's preceding start, on June 15, was a $1,600 conditioned race open to maidens, or horses that have never won a race. Although Nicotine was parked on the outside for more than ½ mile in this race, he won easily by 3¾ lengths.

The races on June 3 at Buffalo Raceway and at Scioto Downs on May 10 are merely qualifying races and do not count as part of a horse's record. A qualifying race is to determine whether a horse can run a sufficiently fast time to run in regular races, with a purse. Therefore, a qualifying race should not be taken very seriously. The driver is often not pushing the horse beyond the point of running the time necessary to qualify. We should note, however, that Nicotine broke stride after the three-quarter mark in his qualifying race on May 10 and that he was distanced, or left so many lengths behind the winner that the lengths are not stated.

Dutch Hollow Kat, a five-year-old bay gelding, has won once, placed twice, and showed once in nine starts in 1977. Notice that in this race the horse's trainer is driving. Its last start was a $2,700 conditioned race for nonwinners of $2,500 lifetime.

In its start July 21, Dutch Hollow Kat finished second by a nose in a race whose conditions were the same as those on July 26. In the race on July 14, open to nonwinners of three races lifetme, Dutch Hollow Kat finished fourth, as he did in the race on July 7, open to nonwinners of $2,500 lifetime.

In the race on June 21, open to nonwinners of $4,000 in 1976–77, Dutch Hollow Kat finished second, losing 4½ lengths in the stretch. In the race on June 16, Dutch Hollow Kat ran with a conventional sulky, finishing last. Notice that this horse has been driven by four different drivers in the last seven races and was a favorite only in his last start.

How to Read and Utilize the Results Charts.

It is also useful to be able to interpret the racing charts for previous evenings, which are printed at the back of the program and show how races unfolded. By reconstructing the race, we can often learn a number of important things about the horses in it. For example, we can discover whether a horse had an easy or a difficult race, and we can get some idea of its racing ability, beyond what we could get from just looking at the program. What we will get in the results charts is what every horse in the race did at the quarter, the half, the three-quarter point, the stretch, and the wire.

As an example, let's consider a race we have already analyzed in this chapter ·

SECOND RACE — 1 Mile							$3500 Claiming Pace		$1800
Stanley Pick ms	3	3	3	3	2hd	1½	B. Altizer	2.50
Bright Promise ms	2	2	2	2	3¹	2½	J. Wetzel	9.60
Lucky Lang	5	5	5	4	4¹½	3½	M. DeMenno	34.70
Eben Jones ms	6	1	1	1	1¹	4⁴½	T. Swift	3.30
Moon Mission ms	8	7	6	5⁰	5¹	5nk	G. Sarama	10.60
Top Mission ms	7	6	7	6	6⁴½	6⁵	P. Laframboise	35.90
I'll Never Tell ms	4	4	4	7	7⁵	7⁸³	P. Cecchini	5.10
Gold Prize	x1x	8	8	8	8	be8	J. Goodenow	*2.20

$2 MUTUEL PRICES	3. Stanley Pick	7.00	4.40	4.00
Official Program Nos.	2. Bright Promise		8.00	5.60
	5. Lucky Lang			12.40

Time — .32   1.04⅗   1.36⅖   2.07⅗

The chart shows that Stanley Pick, driven by B. Altizer, was third at each quarter and second at the head of the stretch. (If we look down the chart to see which horse was leading at the stretch, we see that Eben Jones led Stanley Pick by a full length, indicated by the small figure 1.) Stanley Pick won this race by ½ length.

Bright Promise, driven by J. Wetzel, was second through the first three quarters, just a head back of Stanley Pick at the head of the stretch, and finished ½ length behind Stanley Pick and ½ length ahead of Lucky Lang. The chart also shows that Eben Jones, the number-6 horse, took the lead and held it at least until the head of the stretch but tired in the stretch, finishing 1½ lengths behind Stanley Pick.

At the bottom we are given the fractional times of each quarter of the race. After getting the lead in a :32 quarter, Eben Jones slowed down the pace, going to the half in 1:04 3/5 and three-quarter mark in 1:36 2/5 but finishing the race in about 2:08. The race was won in 2:07 3/5 by Stanley Pick.

It is worth noting that the favorite, Gold Prize, broke stride just before and just after the race began and then broke equipment in the stretch. Gold Prize was the favorite at odds of 2.20 to 1, Stanley Pick the second choice at 2.50 to 1, and Eben Jones the public's third choice at odds of 3.30 to 1. The mutuel prices are stated directly below the chart of the race.

For practice, let us take a second example of a more complicated claiming pace.

THIRD RACE — 1 Mile							$4000 Claiming Pace		$2100
c Chester Devil ms	8	8	7	2º²	2¹¼	1nk	T. Turcotte, Jr.		5.00
Terr Adios ms	1	5	6	8	4¹	2¾	C. Cappotelli		5.00
c Captain Crunch ms	4	6	5	10º²	1²	3¾	D. Ackley		2.40
Benton Blue ms	5	7	8	3	3²	4⁶	D. McNeight		8.20
Game Guy Pick ms	2	3	4	7	5²	5¹	R. Bompczyk		39.80
Flag In Front	3	2º	3	4	8	6³	F. Haslip		*2.00
Game Effort ms	7	4º	2º	6º	7¾	7¹¼	J. Holmes		28.90
Gingham ms	6	10²	1	4	6½	8	M. Bouvrette		10.20

$2 MUTUEL PRICES		
Official Program Nos.	8. Chester Devil	12.00 5.20 3.00
	1. Terr Adios	6.20 3.80
	4. Captain Crunch	2.80

Time — .30⅘   1.02⅖   1.34⅘   2.06⅔

EXACTA — 8 AND 1 $67.00

Chester Devil claimed by P. D. Anderson, No. Tonawanda, N.Y. (Tr. N. Bauch)
Captain Crunch claimed by Andrew Strano, Mumford, N.Y. (Tr. G. Rapone, Jr.)

It is easier to reconstruct the course of this race if we begin with each horse by post position from 1 to 8.

Number 1, Terr Adios, the horse that placed in this race, fell back to fifth place at the quarter, which was run in :30 4/5, and was sixth at the half and eighth at the three-quarter mark. Terr Adios made its move in the last quarter. At the head of the stretch this horse was 5¼ lengths behind the leader, Captain Crunch, and it finished just a neck behind the winner, Chester Devil. In other words, Terr Adios made up more than 5 lengths, probably far on the outside, over the last quarter.

Number 2, Game Guy Pick, also gave ground through the first three quarters, running in seventh position at the three-quarter mark. Game Guy Pick was 6¼ lengths behind the leader at the head of the stretch and finished 7½ lengths behind the winner.

Number 3, Flag in Front, ran second in a :30 4/5 first quarter and faded steadily after that. This horse was out of the race by the head of the stretch and finished 8½ lengths back. Note that he was the favorite at odds of 2 to 1.

Number 4, Captain Crunch, fell back to sixth position at the quarter mark, moving before the half. At the half, Captain Crunch was fifth and went three wide to gain the lead at the three-quarter mark. At the head of the stretch, Captain Crunch was first, two lengths ahead of Chester Devil, but faded in the stretch, finishing 1½ lengths behind Chester Devil.

Number 5, Benton Blue, also fell back and was eighth at the half,

rallying at the half to run third at the three-quarter mark and third at the head of the stretch, 3¼ lengths behind Captain Crunch. Benton Blue finished fourth, 1½ lengths behind the winner.

Number 6, Gingham, going for the lead, was parked three wide in the first quarter when Flag in Front cut in front of Gingham, also going to the front. After getting the lead, Gingham held on until the half and was finished before the three-quarter mark.

Number 7, Game Effort, also was in a fight for the lead and was parked out for the mile, tiring in the third quarter and finishing seventh.

Number 8, Chester Devil, the winner, moved at the half going three wide around Game Effort. Chester Devil was 2 lengths behind Captain Crunch at the three-quarter mark and won the race by a neck over Terr Adios. Finally, note that Chester Devil and Captain Crunch were claimed after this race, as indicated by the *c* to the left of their names.

Here is a third example of a results chart, which you may wish to work out for yourself.

FIFTH RACE — 1 Mile				Conditioned Pace				$3400
Royal Hunch	3	1^0	2	3	$3^{1¼}$	1^1	A. Waddell	17.90
Sunrise Best ms	4	2^0	1	1	1^1	2^{ns}	D. Vance	2.40
L G Blaze ms	2	3	3	2^0	$2^{1¼}$	3^1	G. Aiken	*1.90
Pistol Almahurst ms	1	4	4	5	4^{hd}	4^{nk}	M. Bouvrette	6.20
Clay Attack ms	5	5	5	7	6^{nk}	$5^{3¾}$	D. Rothfuss	18.20
Prairie Song ms	7	7	6	4^0	5^1	$6^{9½}$	A. Bordner	4.60
Wild Kit ms	6	6	7	6	7^{ix}	7	F. Haslip	5.40

$2 MUTUEL PRICES	3. Royal Hunch	37.80	8.60	3.60
Official Program Nos.	4. Sunrise Best		4.00	2.60
	2. L G Blaze			2.80

Time — .32⅖   1.03⅖   1.35   2.05⅖
EXACTA — 3 AND 4 $107.80

Make sure that you answer the following questions:

1. Which horse or horses went to the front?

2. Was the first quarter fast or slow relative to the rest of the race? What were the times of each quarter?

3. Which horse or horses moved at the half?

4. Which horse or horses moved up in the stretch? How much ground, if any, did they make up?

5. In what time was the final quarter run? Was this fast relative to the first three quarters?

Other Information in the Program

Besides the races on the program and the results charts, it is important that you acquaint yourself with three other items on the program.

First, a list of the ten leading drivers in the meet is usually provided on the back cover of the program. A complicated formula, based upon a driver's percentage of in-the-money finishes, is used to determine which drivers are "leading." It is essential to know who the leading drivers happen to be, but you should also be aware of their relative percentages of win, place, and show finishes. Driver A may win more than 20 percent of his races but finish in the money less than 40 percent of the time, whereas Driver B may win only 10 percent of his races, yet finish in the money almost 50 percent of the time. There is no reliable correlation between a driver's percentage of wins and the driver's number of win, place, and show finishes. Second, in using the Universal Driver Rating (UDR) to our best advantage, we must keep in mind that the ten leading drivers must have a minimum number of starts (eighty-five in our example, below). However, a number of very successful drivers with fewer starts are not included in the list. Consequently, you will find it useful to keep tabs on several drivers who, although very successful, drive comparatively infrequently, probably because they have smaller stables.

Further, unless it is quite early in the season, the UDR does not inform us whether a driver has been on a winning or losing streak during the last two or three weeks. However, anyone who follows the leading drivers at a raceway will be interested in their comparatively recent drives. For this reason, the UDR, however helpful, is not the last word on the leading drivers.

TEN LEADING DRIVERS   (with 85 or more starts)
Through Monday, October 3, 1977

GASTON GUINDON	111	27	20	11	.374	BOB ALTIZER	122	27	15	13	.32
GERALD SARAMA	271	57	51	41	.366	DAVE VANCE	251	34	49	52	.31
TOM ARTANDI	85	16	20	8	.350	TED TURCOTTE, JR.	97	19	13	10	.30
TOM SWIFT	106	23	18	11	.346	ED MCNEIGHT, JR.	87	13	15	13	.29
JIM RANKIN	102	20	18	12	.333	PHILIPPE LAFRAMBOISE	147	27	16	22	.29

A second item of interest on the program is the breakdown of wins during a racing season by post position alone. Ordinarily, there are eight horses in a harness race, and on ½-mile raceways, the closer a horse is to the rail at the start, the better are its chances winning or

finishing in the money. Here is a sample from the October 3, 1977, program at Batavia Downs.

			WINS BY POST POSITION				
1	2	3	4	5	6	7	8
153	146	134	132	105	91	66	42

In chapter 3 we will discuss post position more fully in relation to handicapping. Please note that the percentage of wins by post position on ⅝-, ¾-, and 1-mile raceways is not apt to be as large for the inside (1 to 4) post positions as on ½-mile raceways.

A third item of information you can utilize is the list of comparative speed ratings for different raceways. You will find ½-, ⅝-, ¾-, and 1-mile raceways listed in this chart. As a rule of thumb, a ⅝-mile track will be an average of 1 to 2 seconds faster than a ½-mile track, and ¾- and 1-mile tracks are about 4 seconds faster than ½-mile tracks.

A word of warning: It is much less safe to compare times at various raceways, even using this chart carefully, than to compare times at the same track.

I will argue later that time is not as important in handicapping as class, consistency, and current form. So if a horse has just moved in from another raceway, it is doubly unsafe to estimate its chances in a race by considering the times of its latest races. As a rule, it is almost always a mistake to predict a horse's performance by averaging the times of its most recent starts to within a second or two and expecting it to perform accordingly in its next start.

TRACK ABBREVIATIONS AND COMPARATIVE SPEED RATINGS

Track	Abbrev.	Time
Atlantic City 5/8	A.C. 5/8	2.03 2/5
Aurora	Aur	2.07
Balmoral Park	BmlP	2.06
Batavia	Bva	2.05 1/5
Bay Meadows (1)	B.M. (1)	2.04
Blue Bonnets 5/8	B.B. 5/8	2.03 1/5
Brandywine 5/8	Brd5/8	2.02 3/5
Buffalo	B.R.	2.05 1/5
Cahokia Downs 3/4	Cka3/4	2.04 1/5
Cal-Expo (1)	Sacr(1)	2.03 2/5
Centennial	Cen(1)	
Connaught Park	Conn	2.06 1/5
Delaware	Dela	2.04 3/5
Detroit (1) (Wolverine)	Det(1)	2.01 2/5
Dover Downs 5/8	D.D. 5/8	2.04 2/5
DuQuoin (1)	DuQ(1)	2.01 3/5
Flamboro Downs	FlmD	2.05
Foxboro 5/8	Fox5/8	2.03 2/5
Freehold	Fnld	2.04 3/5
Frontenac Downs	F.D.5/8	2.04 1/5
Garden City 5/8	GdnC5/8	2.04 3/5
Georgetown Raceway	Grgtn	2.05 2/5
Goshen	Gosh	2.05
Greenwood Raceway 5/8	GrR5/8	2.04
Green Mountain 13/16	GM13/14	2.04 3/5

Track	Abbrev.	Time
Hanover	Hnvr	2.05 4/5
Harrington	Harr	2.05 2/5
Hawthorne (1)	Haw(1)	2.03 4/5
Hazel Park 5/8	H.P. 5/8	2.04
Hinsdale	Hin	2.06 1/5
Hollywood Park (1)	Hol(1)	2.01 4/5
Indianapolis (1)	Ind(1)	2.01 4/5
Kawartha Downs 5/8	K.D. 5/8	2.04
Kingston	Kngst	2.06
Latonia (1)	Lat(1)	2.03
Laurel 5/8	Lau5/8	2.03 1/5
Lebanon	Leb	2.06 2/5
Lexington (1)	Lex(1)	2.01 2/5
Liberty Bell 5/8	L.B. 5/8	2.02 3/5
London	Lon	2.05 4/5
Los Alamitos 5/8	L.A. 5/8	2.03 4/5
Louisville Downs	LouD	2.05 2/5
Maywood	May	2.04
Meadowlands (1)	M(1)	
Midwest Harness	Mid	2.05 2/5
Mohawk Raceway 5/8	Moh5/8	2.04 1/5
Monticello	M.R.	2.05 1/5
Northfield	Nfld	2.04 3/5

Track	Abbrev.	Time
Northville	Nor	2.05
Ocean Downs	O.D.	2.04 3/5
Orangeville	Ornvl	2.06 1/5
Pocono Downs 5/8	PcD5/8	2.03 1/5
Pompano Park 5/8	P.Pk5/8	2.03 1/5
Quad City Downs5/8	QCD5/8	
Raceway Park 5/8	R.P.5/8	2.03 2/5
Richelieu Park	Rich	2.03 2/5
Rideau Carlton 5/8	RidC5/8	2.04 1/5
Rockingham	Rock	2.04 1/5
Roosevelt	R.R.	2.03 2/5
Rosecroft	RcR	2.04 1/5
Saratoga	Stga	2.03 2/5
Scioto Downs 5/8	ScD5/8	2.02 3/5
Sportsman's Park 5/8	Spk5/8	2.03 4/5
Springfield (1)	Spr(1)	2.01 3/5
Syracuse (1)	Sycs(1)	
The Meadows 5/8	Mea5/8	2.03 1/5
Three Rivers	T.R.	2.05 1/5
Vernon Downs 3/4	V.D.3/4	2.01 4/5
Washington Park (1)	Was(1)	2.03 1/5
Wheeling Downs	W.D.	2.05 3/5
Windsor Raceway 5/8	WR5/8	2.03 1/5
Yonkers	Y.R.	2.04

General Factors in Handicapping

The Three C's: Class, Consistency, and Current Form

Class

In handicapping trotting races we must first consider each horse's ability to compete successfully on a very specific level of competition. A horse's class is determined by the level of competition on which it can compete successfully. It is therefore essential to know what class of horses are running in a race.

This is easy to determine for claiming races, for here, horses are graded along a price scale beginning with $2,000 claimers and continuing up to $30,000 and higher claimers. It is easy to pinpoint the class of horses in such races because a $5,000 claiming race is one in which every horse can be claimed for that price (with certain possible qualifications). Moreover, the purse for $5,000 claimers may be $2,000, of which the winner gets $1,000, the place horse $500, etc. In this way a horse's earnings over a season become a fairly reliable guide to its class, unless the animal has been moving steadily up in company.

It is important to keep in mind that a horse can go up or down in class. After each race, an animal is either getting sharper, closer to peak condition, or losing its edge from previous races. Whether it is doing one or the other will ordinarily explain why it is being moved up or down in class. A successful competitor will be moved up in class until it reaches its proper level. In each race thereafter the animal will perform more or less well *in that class*, depending upon its condition as it nears its next race. A horse that has been competing in $3,000 claimers will, everything else being equal, have a better chance of taking a $2,500 claimer than an animal moving up in class from $2,000 claimers.

But seldom is everything else equal. The horse stepping down in

49

class has most likely performed poorly in higher-priced races, and this is undoubtedly why it is being put down in class. On the other hand, a horse successful in a lower class race may be put up in class. There is no hard-and-fast rule whether one should bet a horse in such cases, although my experience with *claiming races* tends to show that a horse moving up in class is more apt to be a good bet than one moving down. This is the case only because the public tends to *overbet* a horse going down in class and to *underestimate* a horse's chances if it has been successful against cheaper competition.

In any case, class is always an important consideration in handicapping a race.

Consistency

After class, consistency is an important consideration in handicapping. A consistent animal is one that turns in a representative performance from race to race. By contrast, an inconsistent animal is erratic and therefore unpredictable from week to week. A trotter of the "break or win" variety may run exceptionally well one week and jump all over the track the next. A cheap pacer may forget its lameness in one race, winning easily, and refuse to move in its next start. What we seek for betting purposes are consistent animals that are competitive in their class.

One test of consistency is the time a horse runs from race to race, but this criterion must be used with great care. A consistent horse may run a 2:06 mile one week and a 2:08 mile the next. Where then is the consistency? There may be a number of possible explanations. First, the 2:08 race may have had a 1:06 half because the lead horse slowed down the pace over the first half enough to cause the race to be run more slowly than would be expected. Second, the track condition in the second race may be good or sloppy, helping to account for the slow time. Third, if our horse is parked on the outside for ½ mile or more in the second race, his time will be slower. Fourth, the animal may simply not be as sharp in his second race for one of many reasons such as illness, lack of training, etc. Obviously, week to week changes in a horse's performance are often more apparent than real.

If a horse's times are not the best test of its consistency, can we find a more suitable test? I believe that a horse's actual record of in-the-money finishes is the best test. Consider the following two cases:

Buttons Diamond	16	1	1	4	$2,048
Doc's Duke	27	9	4	8	$8,702

Between these two horses, the choice is clear. Buttons Diamond has won only once in sixteen starts, whereas Doc's Duke has nine wins in twenty-seven starts. In addition, Doc's Duke has been in the money more than 75 percent of the time, whereas Buttons Diamond has paid off less than 40 percent of the time.

However, considerations of consistency must be tempered by those of class and current form. A horse that has won consistently against cheaper animals but is going up in class cannot be accorded the same chances as previously. Early in the year, it is not uncommon for promising-looking colts or fillies to win race after race against inferior competition. After several races, however, the youngster may not be able to meet the test of more severe competition. Easy wins in maiden races, etc., are not designed to challenge our horse's potential. So if a horse's record is consistently good against cheaper animals we must temper our enthusiasm when it moves up in class. The horse is no longer as good as its record.

A third consideration, current form, is even more important. Whatever a horse's record may be, if it has gone sour in its last few starts, the horse shouldn't be bet. This happens frequently with horses that perform well early in the year but tire after a number of good races.

Standardbreds are probably the most consistent, or "formful," animals in any sort of racing. Unless there is a definite explanation for marked differences in performance levels from week to week, you should assume that an animal will perform on a par with its last two or three races. Variations in the quality of performance over an animal's last few races should show either that it's becoming sharper or that it has already peaked and is losing its edge.

However, if a horse has been pressed very hard in the last quarter of a tough race, it's not unusual for the animal to be raced lightly for a while. When you see a horse being whipped home from the three-quarter pole in a close decision, think twice about betting it the next time out.

To summarize, the assumption of consistency is fundamental to any handicapping scheme, for it is unreasonable to guess that a horse's performance will take a quantum jump. In harness racing 35 percent of all races are won by favorites. The factor of consistency,

along with class and current form, will usually be instrumental in establishing an animal as the favorite in a race.

Current Form

The most important element of all in handicapping is a horse's current form in its appropriate class. The best clue to what a horse can do in a given race, unless it is being moved up in class, is how successfully it competed in its last few starts. This is a far more important consideration than the times the horse ran in those races. Generally speaking, a horse's finishing in the money in its last start is more important than the time in which its races were run. To see this clearly, examine the times of Happy Acres Susie's last seven races.

Notice the difference in times over the past several races. Happy Acres Susie's last three races were $3,000 claimers (Because the horse is a mare, her claiming price was an additional 20 percent, or $3600). In her last race, the time was 2:08, but in the two previous races the times were 2:10 and 2:09. This suggests that $3,000 claimers are ordinarily run in about 2:08 to 2:10, which is about right. But also notice that the race on May 20, 1977, which was a $2,000 claimer, was run in the very fast time of 2:05 2/5. Compare this with the times of the $2,000 claimers on April 29 and April 25, which went in 2:11 and 2:12. The extraordinary difference shows why time is often unreliable in predicting a race's outcome.

The reasons for this are many. First, such conditions as hot or cold weather result in a race's being run faster or slower. Again, a race run on a fast track will be run faster than one on a good, sloppy, slow, or muddy track.

Second, it is not uncommon for a driver to get the lead and then slow down the pace. This is good driving strategy because by slowing down the field the driver will be able to save his horse for the stretch. If he cuts the first quarter or half too quickly, he may use his horse up too early. When this happens, horses farther back are able to make up ground, because the third and fourth quarters are apt to be much slower. This happens often in races where there are two or more front-runners vying for the lead.

As a rule, a race with a very fast first half will be run in a faster time than one in which the first half is slow. This should be taken into account in handicapping races, for it shows that time *per se* is not as crucial as many people think. So be wary of emphasizing a horse's times at the expense of where it finished in its last few outings.

(3. 2.06⅗) (½) — $15698)

HAPPY ACRES SUSIE(NY)
DRIVER—BOB ALTIZER—Gold, Green and White

b. m. 6, by Zorro Hanover—Bonny Hilda
You & Me Stables, Inc., Batavia, N.Y.

Trainer Jo Altizer (Altizer Stable)
2.05⅗ B.R.   1977 11 3 3 1 $ 3030
2.07⅗ B.R.   1976 34 3 3 2 $ 5463

6-20'' B.R. ms 1500 ft 3600 clm 1 31 1 04¹ 1 36⁴ 2 08 6 6 6 5 4½ 2¹ dh2 08¹ 3 40 (BAltize) TarSahbra,(NossiBe,HappyAcresSusie) 74
6-13'' B.R. ms 1400 ft 3000 clm 1 32² 1 05³ 1 38 2 10 7 5 4 2º 2¹ 2 10¹ 1 20* (BAltize) StanleyPick,HappyAcresSusie,MrGlenby 72
6- 1'' B.R. ms 1500 ft 3600 clm 1 32 1 03⁴ 1 36⁴ 2 08⁴ 5 3 3 3½ 2 09 1 10* (BAltize) TerrAdios,HappyAcresSusie,Bombay 67
5-20'' B.R. ms 1300 ft 2400 clm 1 31 1 03¹ 1 34¹ 2 05² 6 2 2 2½ 1¼ 2 05² 2 10 (BAltize) HppyAcresSusie,LivelyGne,JrnesADandee 80
5-10'' B.R. ms 1400 ft 3000 clm CD 1 31⁴ 1 03 1 35⁴ 2 07¹ 7 8 8 6⁴ 5³ 2 07⁴ 4 50 (BAltize) MightyKen,RobbyCarLith,AdiosTheGirl 56
4-29'' B.R. ms 1200 ft 2400 clm 1 33⁴ 1 06³ 1 38³ 2 11 5 5 8 6 1² 2 11 1 10* (BAltize) HappyAcresSusie,RElementLeft,ElmaHy 45
4-25'' B.R. ms 1200 gd 2400 clm 1 32⁴ 1 06³ 1 40 2 12 3 1 1 2º 1½ 1½ 2 12 1 20* (BAltize) HappyAcresSusie,MissLadyByByrd,PlaidTme 48

(7) PACE

CONDITIONED
1 Mile — Purse $5500

Winners over $5000 in 1976-77 or lower money winners of a race in last 4 starts.

ASK FOR HORSE BY PROGRAM NUMBER

Saddle Cloth RED

---

1 ▶ (3, 2.02½ (⅝) — $20669)
TERRY HERBERT
DRIVER—JACK DARLING—Red and White
b. h. 4, by Replica Herbert—Tami Herbert
Jack Darling, Exeter, Ont., Can.
Trainer: J. Darling

8-12⁷⁷	Btva	ms 2600	ft	76-7nw250ps	1	.30	1.02	1.32	2.03	2	2⁰	1¹	1¹	14¹	2.03²	1.00* (JDarlin)

---

2 ◆ (3, 2.02⅗ (⅝) — $75722)
SILICON (W)
DRIVER—JIM RANKIN—Red, Blue and White
b. h. 5, by Meadow Paige—Icon
H.J.Stewart, S.Proctor,J. & A.Rankin, St.Catharines, Ont., Can.
Trainer: T. Dunlap (Rankin Stable)

---

3 ◆ (6, 1.58⅗ (1) — $32321)
BREV HANOVER
DRIVER—CHRIS CHRISTOFOROU—Blue, White and Gold
br. g. 7, by Stars Pride—Brief Romance
Alan Parker, St. Catharines, Ont., Can.
Trainer: C. Christoforou

---

4 ◆ (5, 2.01⅘ (⅛) — $137059)
HOGAN ‡
DRIVER—GERALD AIKEN—Red, White and Blue
br. g. 10, by Excel Knight—Penny Worthy
John C. Fletcher, Melbourne, Ont., Can.
Trainer: G. Aiken

5. (2, 2.08¾) (½) — $4489
EDDO THORPE(W)
DRIVER—ANTHONY MacRAE—Maroon, Gold and Gold

blk. c. 3, by Thorpe Hanover—Vive La Myrt
Irma M. MacRae, Casselberry, Fla.

7- s¹⁷⁷	Btva	ms‡5500	ft	wo5000hcp	1	.30³	1.01³	1.31¹	2.01¹	4	4	4	x5x4⁴	d2.02	9.70 (GAiken)
7- 2⁷⁷	Btva	ms‡6000	ft	Inv. hcp	1	.29⁴	1.00¹	1.31¹	2.01¹	5	x6	6dis	6dis	15.90 (GAiken)
6-25⁷⁷	B.R.	ms‡5500	sl	Inv. hcp	1	.31¹	1.01²	1.31¹	2.01²	4	4	3¹⁵	1¹⁵	13.60 (GAiken)

Trainer: A. MacRae

	1977	14	6	3	1	$15943	77
2.02 Btva	1976	18	2	1	2	$ 4889	65
2.08¾ Btva							

PennState,FarmSkipper,RealQuick(PI 6)
SeedlingHerbert,PatrickWill,PennState
Hogan,BaronToo,LimelightTime

6. (4, 2.04¾) (½) — 11255
MAY O'NEIGHS
DRIVER—KEN BALL—Brown and Gold¹

b. m. 5, by Rebel Leader—Reliable Duchess
Fred G. McLean, Silver Creek, N.Y.

Trainer: F. W. Mays

	1977	29	6	5	4	$16837	77
2.01% Btva	1976	35	8	6	5	$10435	77
2.04% Btva							

MayONeighs,FrostFire,HawthorneRoad
HawthorneRoad,FrostFire,Sangria
HawthorneRoad,RuthsMary,BaronWhiz
PrincessDeeDee,Hogan,BrevHanover
AvonAngelo,EddoThorpe,WildKit
BretsAmour,MayONeighs,MissBonnVicar
LovelyGene,MayONeighs,MissBonnVicar
MayONeighs,Woodhillben,SparkyChris

7. (3, 2.12¾) (½) — $850
HAWTHORNE ROAD
DRIVER—JOSE DELGADO—Gold, Black and White

b. m. 4, by Kat Byrd—Rockville Brook
John J. Wallace, (Lessee), Dunkirk, N.Y.

Trainer: J. Delgado

	1977	18	7	0	2	$ 9982	77
2.00% V.D. ¾	1976	5	1	0	1	$ 850	60
2.12% B.R.							

MayONeighs,FrostFire,HawthorneRoad
HawthorneRoad,FrostFire,Sangria
HawthorneRoad,Mary,BaronWhiz
MissBonnVicar,MayONeighs,Salnan
RaceTimeKlean,PnnState,Shipoke(PI 6)
HawthorneRoad,Salnan,KathyBright
TeensJudy,PassWithCare,RvelileTme

8. (5, 2.03¾) (½) — $34585
MISS BONN VICAR
DRIVER—JOE HODGINS—Maroon and White

b. m. 6, by Vicar Hanover—Bonnie Gene Scott
Fair Fields Enterprises, Inc., Hamburg, N.Y.

Trainer: J. Hodgins

	1977	25	8	1	2	$ 13323	77
2.02 Btva	1976	35	9	3	3	$ 17630	80
2.03% B.R.							

MissBonnVicar,LovelyGene,FrostFire
MissBonnVicar,MayONeighs,Salnan
LovelyGene,MayONeighs,MissBonnVicar
BretsAmour,WillaAlmahurst,LovelyGene
MissBonnVicar,Tarvon,ClayAttack
BreezyNite,DoubleJinn,PistolAlmahurst
MissBonnVicar,StNick,BernitaHanover

Why an analysis of times is not necessarily an effective way of getting winners can be seen from the 7th race at Batavia Downs on September 2, 1977. Notice that the time of the August 13 race won by Hogan was 2:04 3/5. This was a $5,500 conditioned pace with the same conditions as the present race. On that same evening, August 13, a $4,600 conditioned pace for mares included May O'Neighs and Hawthorne Road, who are in the present field. The time of this lower-class pace was 2:01 1/5.

Anyone who tried to handicap this race solely on the basis of time, irrespective of class, would be completely misled. Although the $4,600 pace was run in an exceptionally fast first half of 1:00 2/5, the first half of the higher-priced pace went in 1:02 3/5, a difference of more than 2 seconds. When this is taken into account, a careful handicapper will realize that the $5,500 pace was run in a slow time because a front-runner captured the lead and slowed down the pace. In the $4,600 race, Hawthorne Road moved at the quarter mark, causing the first half to be run very fast. Anyone who interpreted this as evidence of the superiority of May O'Neighs and Hawthorne Road over the rest of the field in tonight's race would be mistaken—neither finished in the money.

We can learn a second lesson from this race about the ways in which final times can be misleading. This is illustrated by Terry Herbert and Eddo Thorpe, two horses moving up in class after victories against inferior competition. Notice that Terry Herbert won his last two starts with apparent ease in times of 2:03 2/5 (August 12) and 2:02 4/5 (August 10). This is no less true of Eddo Thorpe's last three starts, which he won in times of 2:02 (August 11), 2:03 (August 4), and 2:04 (July 27).

Because neither horse was really pushed in these races, their times cannot be taken as a reliable index of what each really can do. In point of fact, Terry Herbert won this race and Eddo Thorpe was second after being parked out in a blazing first quarter. Obviously, previous times were no help in handicapping this race!

Taking Account of the Driver

In the first chapter we referred to the hard facts of life at a raceway for the average driver. Of the one hundred or more licensed chauffeurs at a raceway, only a handful are successful week after week, season after season. I surveyed the records of September 17 to October 11, 1977, of the leading drivers at Batavia Downs. During this

twenty-day racing period, exactly two hundred races were run at the Downs. Here is a breakdown of the number of races won by the twelve leading drivers.

1.	G. Sarama	11
2.	T. Turcotte	10
3.	F. Haslip	10
4.	J. Wetzel	9
5.	T. Artandi	9
6.	G. Guindon	8
7.	P. La Frambois	7
8.	C. Hie	7
9.	Y. Demers	7
10.	T. Swift	7
11.	D. Vance	6
12.	A. MacRae	6
	Total	97

This means that almost half of the races were won by twelve of the more than one hundred drivers active at the raceway. Is the message clear? Keep a close tab on the successful drivers at the raceway and confine your bets as much as possible to them. How to take maximum advantage of their "hot" and "cold" streaks is explained in this section.

What makes a driver topnotch? The driver who knows how to rate his horse well can make a real difference to the outcome of a race. The point at which the driver makes his move in the race is crucial, and a good driver will move at just the right moment. He will take the lead if it opens up but won't wear his horse out fighting for it. When he takes the lead, he will usually know just how much to take out of another driver's horse coming up on the outside, in order to overtake him in the stretch. Moreover, a capable, experienced driver does not permit himself to get boxed in, but he is adept at boxing in a horse that is a real threat to him in a race. Last but not least, he gets maximum performance out of the horse he's driving. Obviously, the quality of a driver is often crucial to the outcome of a race.

We can see the difference a capable driver can make to the outcome of a race, if we look at a few instances where a horse's performance was improved with an improvement in the caliber of the driver. One of the best drivers at Batavia Downs is Gerald Sarama, who has won the dash championship there for the past several years. It is not unusual for Sarama to catch drive a horse to victory for the

first time after it has previously been a consistent loser. Here are two well-chosen but not uncharacteristic cases of Sarama's magical effect on a horse's performance:

But however skillful a driver may be, he is not worth betting if his percentage of in-the-money finishes is quite low. A driver who rarely wins a race and who has a low percentage of in-the-money finishes relative to his total number of drives is by our definition a poor driver. It doesn't matter how well he handles a horse—if he doesn't win, place, or show in at least 40 percent of his drives, he's not worth betting.

A good driver wins at least 15 percent of his races during a season, usually more, and his percentage of place and show finishes is usually also high (above 40 percent). A driver who wins more than 20 percent of his starts is formidable indeed, and you should think twice before betting against him—at least when the horse he's driving is a definite contender in the race.

How do you know whether a particular driver is good? Only by following the results from day to day and keeping tabs on how several of the better-known drivers are doing. At any track there are a number of drivers with reputations for getting good results. These are the drivers—perhaps ten to twenty overall—that you should follow regularly to find out whether they are finishing consistently in the money. Usually, you can find the winning percentages of the top drivers in the program, but this will not tell you if the driver is on a winning or losing streak during the last two weeks or so. It's not uncommon for a driver to win in streaks, and when this happens you will be well advised to bet him often, but only if he's driving a horse that has a good chance in a specific race.

Let's call a driver who has finished in the money in his last five starts (excluding catch or one-shot drives) "hot" and the streak of his in-the-money finishes a "hot streak." The reason many drivers win in streaks seems to be that they get their stable in top shape—when they train the horses they drive—at pretty much the same time. When this happens, they bring horses in to win, place, or show in clusters rather than off and on.

How can you tell whether a driver is hot? Simply keep a record of his finishes from day to day. Specifically, pick out about ten or fifteen drivers who have been in the money frequently and see if they are hot. If they are, bet them frequently. But be sure through handicapping that the horse has a good chance in any race in which you bet

3
7 MB

(6. 2.08½) (½) — $13710)
CHARLIE DOUBLE E
DRIVER—GERALD SARAMA—Orange and Red

b. g. 7, by Hal Sampson—Pattie Fingo
Carole J. Duffy & Marguerite A. Murphy, Rochester, N.Y.

Trainer: N. Bauch

| | | | | 2.07½ Btva sy | 1977 | 31 | 1 | 4 | 5 | $ 4145 |
| | | | | 2.08½ M.R. | 1976 | 28 | 4 | 5 | 4 | $ 5142 |

9-26⁷⁷ Btva ms 1600 sy 3500 clm 1.30² 1.03² 1.35 2.07¹ 8 8 5 3 1 2.07¹ 5.80 (GSarama) ChrlieDoubleE,BrightPrmise,DaveyShal
9-13⁷⁷ Btva ms 1600 ms 3500 clm 1.31² 1.05³ 1.38¹ 2.09³ 5 5 5 5 5 2.07¹ 6.90 (TEichas) VeracityN,DaveyShal,BrightPromise
9- 2⁷⁷ Btva ms 1800 ft 4000 clm 1.32² 1.04⁴ 1.35² 2.06⁴ 7 5 30 4³¹ 5²¹ 2.10 9.40 (TEichas) RowdyGTime,NedaSal,Spohn
8-23⁷⁷ Btva ms 2100 ft 4000 clm 1.31¹ 1.05 1.35⁴ 2.07⁴ 8 8 7 7⁶² 4³⁴ 2.08³ 12.60 (TEichas) VeracityN,NedaSal,Gingham
8-15⁷⁷ Btva ms 2100 ft 4000 clm 1.31³ 1.04⁴ 1.35⁴ 2.07¹ 6⁰ 7 7⁶ 5⁵ 2.08¹ 8.50 (TEichas) WinnieSong,EasternQueen,LisasLucky
8- 5⁷⁷ Btva ms 2000 ft 4000 clm 1.30¹ 1.01⁴ 1.34¹ 2.07 5 5⁰ x6x 86 5²⁴ 2.07² 2.10 (TEichas) BeckysAdora,TerrAdios,CaptainCrunch
7-26⁷⁷ Btva ms 1900 ft 3500 clm 1.31 1.03² 1.35¹ 2.07⁴ 6 6 5 5⁴ 3¹ 2.08 5.90 (TEichas) MarysPenn,GoldPrize,CharlieDoubleE

3
2 MS
5000

(8. 2.05½) (½) — $31442)
HONOR KENNEDY (W)
DRIVER—GERALD SARAMA—Orange and Red

br. h. 9, by Honor Dares—Glendale Crescent
Perry Wilson & Anthony Orsini, Springville, N.Y.

Trainer: P. Wilson

| | | | | 2.05½ Btva | 1977 | 20 | 5 | 4 | 1 | $ 7701 |
| | | | | 2.05½ Btva | 1976 | 45 | 6 | 9 | 9 | $10135 |

10-14⁷⁷ Btva ms 1800 ft 5000 clm 1.31⁴ 1.04³ 1.36⁴ 2.09 2 3 3 2 1¹¹ 2.09 1.80* (GSarama) HonorKennedy,EasternQueen,Spohn
10- 4⁷⁷ Btva ms 2100 ft 5000 clm 1.30³ 1.03² 1.36² 2.08⁴ 2 5 6 4ix¹ 46³ 2.10¹ 3.10 (JHodgin) AdiosWilla,IanHill,EasternQueen
9-22⁷⁷ Btva ms 2100 ft 5000 clm 1.30⁴ 1.02³ 1.34¹ 2.03³ 6 7 8 7⁴² 67⁴ 2.07 9.70 (JHodgin) FaysThunder,Downpour,EasternQueen
9-15⁷⁷ Btva ms 2100 ft 5000 clm 1.31² 1.04 1.34² 2.06 4 4 40 6⁶ 43¹ 2.06³ 6.40 (JHodgin) GigiLamour,EasternQueen,GoodLuck
9- 5⁷⁷ Btva ms 2100 ft 5000 clm 1.31 1.02⁴ 1.34¹ 2.06 4 7 7 3²¹ 4²² 2.06² 8.80 (JHodgin) TopSkipper,AdiosWilla,SuccessGrant
8-31⁷⁷ Btva ms 2100 ft 5000 clm 1.30³ 1.04² 1.35² 2.07 6 6 4 2 1³ 2.07 5.40 (GSarama) HonorKennedy,ShadyHillDaisy,BredByrd
8-20⁷⁷ Btva ms 2400 ft 5000 clm 1.31³ 1.03¹ 1.34³ 2.06³ 3 4 4 5⁰ 1¹ 2.06³ 1.10* (GSarama) HonorKennedy,SlippersBoy,SteadyMoran

this driver. Be wary also of betting hot drivers who are catch driving a horse for the first time. This is not a reliable index of whether a driver is hot.

Here is a fairly simple procedure for determining whether a driver is indeed on a hot streak. First, put the driver's name on an index card with the names of the horses he regularly drives beneath his name. For example:

Driver: *La Framboise, P.*
Stable (arranged alphabetically):

Black Vic	Lemon Tar
Dreamer Lobell	Leta's Lad
G. P. Obeyond	Lincoln's Valor
Hosi Guy	Star G.
L'Ami Bambi	Thunder Imp

Second, list the dates consecutively on which he is driving and after the date write the results in this way:

Won the race	1
Finished second	2
Showed	3
Out of the money	0

Here is how five consecutive days of this driver's record during a hot streak will look:

6/20/77	:	1 (Star G).
6/22/77	:	2 (Hosi Guy).
6/23/77	:	2 (Dreamer Lobell); 1 (Leta's Lad); 1 (L'Ami Bambi).

To simplify matters, you can assign letters to the horses' names and write in the letter instead of the horse's name after his performance on a specific date:

a. Black Vic	f. Lemon Tar
b. Dreamer Lobell	g. Leta's Lad
c. G.P. Obeyond	h. Lincoln's Valor
d. Hosi Guy	i. Star G.
e. L'Ami Bambi	j. Thunder Imp

Now, the dates will look like this:

6/20/77	1 i [Star G. won]
6/22/77	2 d [Hosi Guy placed]
6/23/77	2 b − 1 g − 1 e
6/25/77	3 j − 2 a − 1 f − 0 c
6/27/77	1 g

Actually, we caught this driver in the midst of a hot streak that began before the week of June 20. So if we had got on the bandwagon even earlier by betting this driver to win or place through the week of June 20, we would have ended the week in good shape financially. And this would be true if we bet this driver consistently, even though some of his horses went off as solid favorites.

Here is another example:

Bourgon, W. (with G. and M. Bourgon)

a. Curiosity A.	e. Nev Hanover
b. Frisco Bennie	f. Notable Baron
c. Great Notion	g. Sangria
d. Miss Move	h. Spangler Frost

6/20/77	1 e
6/21/77	1 a − 1 c
6/24/77	1 h
6/27/77	2 d
6/28/77	2 b − 0 e

In this case, we caught the driver at the tail end of a win streak begun some time earlier. (In one race, on June 21, the winner was Great Notion at odds of 25 to 1.)

I will mention still another example of a driver on a hot streak. The difference between this example and the two previous ones is that this driver, after a long winless stretch, won a race on each of the last three cards.

(The driver, Fred Haslip, then proceeded to win two races the following evening and three more on the next evening's card, for a total of eight wins in five evenings of racing. Compare this hot streak with the previous two weeks in which Haslip won a total of one race in thirty-five starts.)

The chart showing the beginning of this hot streak follows:

7/22/77	1 c
7/23/77	1 e
7/25/77	1 f

If you do try to catch a hot driver, two warnings are in order. First, stop betting a driver who *was* hot but has failed to win or place in his last three starts. He's no longer hot! Second, confine your bets to drivers who either train the horses they drive or drive certain horses on a regular basis. In other words, avoid betting on drivers who are last-minute substitutions for a horse's regular driver. A catch drive is a risky bet. As a rule, one should also avoid betting on a driver who is taking out a new horse in his stable for the first time, although a hot driver will often finish in the money here, too.

We have talked about hot drivers, but there are also drivers who have cold streaks, who go a certain length of time finishing only occasionally in the money. This happens to good drivers too, but a cold streak is a hard fact of life for the large majority of drivers. When a driver is on a cold streak, never bet him. Wait until he shows signs of life before starting to bet him again. This is especially true of drivers on cold streaks whose horses are favorites or usually go off at relatively low odds, because the return on your wager will be modest in any case. Why increase the odds against your winning even more by betting on a driver when he's not doing much of anything?

Here is an example of a good driver on a cold streak:

Altizer, R.

a. Acropolis	f. Happy Acres Susie
b. Admiral Mark	g. Holly's Champ
c. Arlas E. Junkin	h. J.J. Byrd
d. Dealer's Dream	i. Keystone Gallant
e. Doc's Duke	j. Merry John A.

6/20	2 f − 2 e − 0 b
6/21	0 g
6/22	0 d
6/23	0 h − 0 c
6/24	0 a − 0 i
6/28	0 b
6/29	0 c
7/1	1 e − 0 j
7/4	2 a

Perhaps it's worth mentioning that in most of Altizer's races from June 21 through July 1 his horses usually went off at short odds or as the favorite. Obviously, the bettor who was able to "lay off" Altizer during this period had an advantage. This cold streak on the part of a

very successful driver is really not unusual. It happens to several good drivers during a racing season.

A useful method for determining whether a driver is on a hot streak is to keep a record of his day by day performance together with other leading drivers at the track. You may be surprised by the extent to which drivers win in streaks—excluding catch drives, of course. The following chart is an example of a record of recent driver performances.

Driver's Name	8/8/77	8/9/77	8/10/77	8/11/77
*Artandi, P.	1	1–1	2	3
Bourgon, W.	1–0	—	3	—

*Driver on hot streak

This is a convenient means by which you can record a driver's performance from day to day with a minimum of bother. All you need do is indicate by number (1 = win, 2 = place, 3 = show, 0 = out of the money) what a driver has done on each day he raced, and you will discover whether he is winning with any consistency. You will be surprised at the length of many drivers' hot or cold streaks and will find that it's not unusual for a driver who is hot to finish in the money 80 or 90 percent of the time on a streak covering twenty or thirty races. Even more commonly a "cold" driver will go for a month or more without finishing in the money more than a few times.

How can you best put this information to your advantage? When a driver is hot, bet him to finish in the money *every time* until he finishes out two or at most three straight times. Sometimes this can be a paradise for show bettors, because a hot driver will manage to finish in the money race after race even if he doesn't win repeatedly. Likewise, cold streaks (three or more races out of the money) often have a way of extending themselves to your monetary advantage. Moreover, you can utilize this rule effectively to find overlays in races you would otherwise pass.

We can summarize the results of this discussion as follows:

1. Avoid betting provisional drivers and drivers who seldom win.

2. Bet only experienced drivers with consistent winning records over the long haul.

3. Bet drivers on hot streaks.

4. Don't bet drivers on cold streaks.

Sample Chart of Drivers' Performances for Seven Days

	9/5	9/6	9/7	9/8	9/9	9/10	9/12
*Altizer, R. 4-14 [indicates four wins in last fourteen starts]	2	2-1	0	0-1	0		0-1-1-2
*Artandi, P. 5-22	1			2	2 0-0	2-1-0	
Bourgon, W.	0		0-2	—	0-3	0	2
Christoforu, C. 4-25	2-2		2	2-0	0	2-0-0 0	
Darling, J. 3-11	0					1-1-0	
*Demers, Y. 3-6		1-3	0	1	1	3	0
*Guindon, G. 7-22	1			0	1	0 0-0	2-0
Haslip, F. 10-40			0-0-0 0-1-0	0-0-0 0-0-2	3 1-3-0	1-0-0 3-0	0-0-0
*Harner, L. 2-4						0-1	1
*LaFramboise, P. 8-21			0	1-0	0-0-0		0-1
MacRae, A. 0-14	0-0	3			0-0-1		0
Manges, L. 1-5				0-2	1	0	0
McNeight, E. 5-13	3-0		3-2				
Rankin, J. 7-25			2	0-3-0	0-2	3-3-3	
*Sarama, G. 7-13	0-0-0 2-3	3	0 0-0-1		0-1-2	2-1-0 3-0-1	0-0-1-2
Swift, T. 1-9	0		1-0-1	0			
*Waddell, A. 4-15	1	2-1-2	0	3-3-1		2	

*Indicates driver on a hot streak preceding week of September 5.

The Importance of Post Position

The importance of post position cannot be underestimated in handicapping harness races. Over a period of several months I kept a record of winning post positions at Buffalo Raceway and Batavia Downs. The results show that the odds favor the bettor who confines his wagers to horses starting from the advantageous post positions 1 to 4, usually referred to as the inside positions.

A rundown of the winning post positions for this period follows:

Post Position	Winning Percentage
1	18%
2	17
3	15
4	14
5	12
6	10
7	8
8	6

Slightly over one-half of all trotting races during this period were won from the first three post positions. Almost two-thirds of all races were won from positions 1 to 4. Three-fourths of the races were won from post positions 1 to 5.

The moral of this story, which I believe is characteristic of ½-mile tracks, is obvious: Confine your bets as much as possible to horses with good post positions. Moreover, it is often wiser, if you must bet a horse with a poor post position, to bet it to place or show because of the high odds against its winning from "holes" 5 to 8.

There are exceptions to nearly every rule, however, and the exception to this one is a race in which a horse with a poor post position outclasses the field. In this case one should either bet the horse or lay off the race. The only circumstances conducive to betting a horse from post positions 6 to 8 are those in which the superiority of the horse, the caliber of the driver, and the driver's racing strategy ("how the race will be run") make the wager a worthwhile risk.

The reasons why horses win less frequently from poor post positions are clear. If a driver goes for the lead from the 6, 7, or 8 holes, he is apt to be parked on the outside by a horse that has already taken the lead from an inside post position. There are often horses going for the lead ahead cf him, which means that our horse could be stuck on the outside for the first quarter or more of the race. Furthermore, a driver who has an outside position and who sits back most of the race

must go around the entire field ahead of him if he's to win. This is no easy thing to do, considering that the ground to be made up is not just the lengths of the horses in front of him but includes their sulkies as well.

If he moves at the half, horses in front of him may start their move on the outside, and he will have to go three wide to get around them. This move often takes too much out of a horse for it to win the race, especially if the first half is run in a comparatively slow time, for then the last half figures to be run much faster. But if the driver waits until the stretch to go all out, the horse may simply have too far to go to win.

For all these reasons, it is not uncommon for a driver to take a horse for a ride from the 7 or 8 positions, especially if nothing opens up during the race. This is not necessarily unethical, for there is no sense in taking too much out of a horse in order to finish second or third instead of third or fourth, providing the driver is ready to take advantage of any openings during the race.

In the chapter on scoring a race according to a point scheme, we will assign points on the basis of post position in addition to those for caliber of horse and driver and for how a race figures to be run.

In summary, confine your bets to post positions 1 to 4 as much as you can. Bet on horses from post positions 5 through 8 only when the superiority of the horse, the caliber of the driver, and the conditions of the race combine to make the bet a favorable exception to this rule.

Racing Strategy: How the Race Will Be Run

Another important element that should be taken into account in handicapping trotting races is "how the race will be run" or in other words how, given the information in the program, we can expect the race to unfold. Because it is quite common for a driver to use the same strategy again and again in racing a specific horse, it is often possible to predict successfully how a race will unfold. This is a most valuable asset for the serious handicapper.

There are three common ways a driver can elect to race a horse. First, he may race the horse in front. This means that he will try to get the lead as soon as he can and keep it the entire race. In a race in which there is only one front-runner, the horse's chances are usually quite good because the animal will not be worn out fighting for the lead against other front-runners.

Here is a classical example of a front-runner (on facing page):

INDIAN RULER

(4, 2.03¾) (½) — $50905)
DRIVER—TOM SWIFT—Blue, Black and White

b. g. 11, by Good Time—Indian Idol
Mamipa Stable & Mary Marotta, Lockport, N.Y.

Trainer: F. Marotta

	1977	21	10	3	3	$ 8625
2.06¾ B.R.	1976	35	9	9	2	$ 8507
2.07¾ Btva						

6-23⁷⁷	B.R.	ms	1700	ft	4000	clm	1	.31²	1.04³	1.36	2.06⁴	7	1	1	1	2¹ᐟ⁴	2.07¹	3.40	(TSwift)	PearlieChita,IndianRuler,PeanutB	75
6-16⁷⁷	B.R.	ms	1700	ft	4000	clm	1	.31¹	1.03	1.35	2.06⁴	3	1	1	1	1hd	2.06⁴	2.10*	(TSwift)	IndianRuler,RBPride,ScottMeadow	80
6- 6⁷⁷	B.R.	ms	1700	ft	4000	clm	1	.30⁴	1.03³	1.35²	2.07²	4	1	1	1	1¹ᐟ⁴	2.07²	1.80*	(TSwift)	IndianRuler,CaptainCrunch,JeffW	57
5-30⁷⁷	B.R.	ms	1700	ft	4000	clm	1	.30²	1.04²	1.36³	2.07⁴	3	1	1⁰²	1	1¹ᐟ²	2.08¹	3.20	(TSwift)	DellLynch,GigiLamour,IndianRuler	75
5-20⁷⁷	B.R.	ms	1700	ft	4000	clm	1	.31¹	1.05²	1.36³	2.07²	1	1	1	1	1¹ᐟ²	2.07²	1.60*	(TSwift)	IndianRuler,SlippersBoy,TThree	80
5-13⁷⁷	B.R.	ms	1500	ft	3000	clm	1	.30¹	1.03⁴	1.36¹	2.07¹	5	1	1	1	1¹ᐟ⁴	2.07¹	3.00	(TSwift)	IndianRuler,ThirdSon,KeystoneOBrien	56
5- 4⁷⁷	B.R.	ms	1400	sy	3000	clm CD	1	.31	1.04¹	1.37¹	2.10	7	1⁰	2	1	1nk	2.10	3.10	(TSwift)	IndinRuler,VictoriaString,SusnRowGil	56

Notice in particular the races on May 20 and May 30. On May 20, the driver took the lead in :31 3/5 and went to the half in a relatively slow 1:05 2/5, giving the horse breathing space for the last half, which went in 1:02. On May 30, on the other hand, the driver had to fight for the lead, going three wide to get it in :30 2/5, a very fast time for the first quarter for a 2:07 horse. And although the driver slowed things down, going to the half in 1:04 2/5, the horse did not have enough left to win. Ditto for the horse's last race on June 23. A very fast first quarter often takes so much out of a front-runner that it has nothing left for the stretch.

For the record, on page 69 is an example of a front-runner that ran out of gas in almost every race.

Notice that this horse quits in the stretch regardless of whether it gets the lead in a very fast time, as in the races on May 27, June 3, or June 9, or whether it gets the lead more easily, as in the races on June 20 and June 28. Generally speaking, one should lay off betting horses that "die" in the stretch, even if they are going down in class. A horse that runs out of steam in the stretch race after race is almost always a bad bet.

In contrast to front-runners, a "closer" will be saved for the final quarter, the driver making his move sometime between the three-quarter mark and the stretch. On page 70 is an example of a horse that has rallied in the last quarter in its last five races. On June 24, Peerless Lobell was fifth at the three-quarter mark, was second at the head of the stretch, ½ length behind the leader, and won going away with a burst of speed in the stretch. In his two previous races, however, Peerless Lobell was unable to make up enough ground in the last quarter to win.

A third way of driving a horse is to move at the halfway mark. This strategy makes good sense if the horse does not get off well at the start and in addition does not have enough closing speed to make up several lengths in the stretch. In a race that goes in a fast first half, there is a real advantage to moving at the half, because the time of the third and last quarters are apt to be comparatively slow. For this reason, a horse can gain a lot of ground in the third quarter and be in a good position to catch the horse or horses in front of it in the stretch. A good example of a driver who moves at the half is illustrated in the last two races of this horse:

On June 25, the first half went in the fast time of 1:01 1/5, and the

(None in U.S.A. — $2360)

SUPER DEAL N
DRIVER—ANTHONY STROLLO—White, Black and Red

b. g. 7, by Garrison Hanover—Russian Time
Mark & Tanis Lewis, Northeast, Pa.

Trainer: A. Strollo
2.07¾ B.R.Q

							1977	12	0	1	1	$	954
None in U.S.A.							1976	20	4	1	1	$	2360

Date	Track		Dist	Cond									Time	Odds	Driver	Order of finish	Rec
6-28⁷⁷	Btva	ms	1600 ft	76-7nw175ps	1	.32⁴	1.05³	1.37	2.08	3	1¹	4²³	2.08³	3.90	(AStroll)	MartyG,WeeChance,RedArgotKid	77
6-20⁷⁷	B.R.	ms	1850 ft	76-7nw3500CD1	.32²	1.04³	1.35⁴	2.06³	2	1	1	5²¹	2.07	3.70	(AStroll)	QueeniePaige,WildKit,MannartDamsel	74
6- 9⁷⁷	B.R.	ms	1700 ft	76-7nw3000CD1	.31	1.03	1.34¹	2.06	4	1	1	2²	2.06	1.50	(AStroll)	MightyYankee,SuperDealN,AdiosRowdy	64
6- 3⁷⁷	B.R.	ms	1850 ft	76-7nw3500CD1	.30³	1.02⁴	1.33⁴	2.04	3	1⁰²	1	3¹⁴	2.05	8.30	(AStroll)	Squall,SunriseBest,StrollAwayN	60
5-27⁷⁷	B.R.	ms	1850 ft	76-7nw3500CD1	.30¹	1.02⁴	1.34²	2.06¹	6	1	2	65¹	2.06³	7.30	(AStroll)	BermudaSmoke,FrostFire,SuperDealN	78
5-20⁷⁷	B.R.	ms	1850 ft	76-7nw3500CD1	.30⁴	1.03¹	1.34⁴	2.07³	2	1	1	1⁴	2.07³	NB	(AStroll)	SprDealN,DtchHllowKat,PrquimnsIndian	81
3-24⁷⁷	Penrith	ft	Qua	1	.30⁴	1.03	1.34	2.07	1	2	3²	1¹			(LHarple)	ComeAgain,Runkeno,PrinceOforna	

Raced apx. 1⅞ miles in 3.18⁴, finished 6th.

PEERLESS LOBELL
(b. 2.05½) (½) — $15964)
DRIVER—TOM SWIFT—Blue, Black and White

b. m. 8, by Stephan Smith—Penny Arden
Joseph Buscaglia & F. P. Sirianni, Kenmore & Tonawanda, N.Y.

Trainer: T. Swift
2.06½ B.R.
2.05¾ Btva

| | 1977 | 18 | 3 | 2 | 4 | $ | 5225 |
| 1976 | 33 | 4 | 4 | 3 | $ | 7912 |

6-24⁷⁷ B.R.	ms 2150 ft 6000 clm	1	.30⁴	1.04	1.36¹	2.06⁴	3	4	4	5	2½	1¹³	2.06⁴	2.00	(TSwift)	PeerlessLobell,SteadyMoran,EljayJoe	79
6-18⁷⁷ B.R.	ms 2150 ft 6000 clm	1	.33	1.04⁴	1.36¹	2.07¹	6	2	2	2¹	2¹	2.07¹	2.20*(TSwift)	NotableBaron,PrlessLobell,FreightBaron	78
6-17⁷⁷ B.R.	ms 2150 ft 6000 clm	1	.31¹	1.03	1.34³	2.05⁴	4	5	6	4³³	22½	2.06¹	1.70*(TSwift)	BurleyGuy,PeerlessLobll,RusselTorrnce	68
6- 2⁷⁷ B.R.	ms 1900 sy 5000 clm	1	.30²	1.02²	1.36²	2.08²	2	3	2	1²	1³²	2.08²	1.90*(TSwift)	PeerlessLobll,RussellTorrnce,MarysHeel	49
5-24⁷⁷ B.R.	ms 1900 ft 5000 clm	1	.30³	1.03³	1.36²	2.06³	6	6	6	6⁷⁴	3²³	2.07¹	6.20 (TSwift)	RowmarsAngel,YankeeJean,PeerlssLobell	80
5-14⁷⁷ B.R.	ms 1900 ft 5000 clm	1	.31	1.03	1.34⁴	2.05²	2	3	4	3²½	5⁴⁴	2.06¹	2.10*(TSwift)	GurnSpringsScott,MarysHeel,Squall	62
5- 7⁷⁷ B.R.	cs 1800 ft 5000 clm	1	.30⁴	1.01³	1.34⁴	2.07³	8	8	8	7⁴³	5²³	2.08¹	18.30 (BAItize)	KittysHope,MissMargaretEd,NotableBaron	54

(4, 1.50¾ TT (1) — $39718)
SUPER WHIZ(N)
DRIVER—LARRY MANGES—Red and White

ro. h. 5, by Rebel Leader—Misty Tona
Morris D. Miller & Betty A. Miller, Cassadaga, N.Y.

Trainer: L. Manges
2.06¾ B.R. gd
2.03 Btva

		1977	14	2	3	2	$ 7942
		1976	38	7	8	7	$24167

6-23⁷⁷ B.R. ms 4000 sl nw100000CD 1 .30² 1.01¹ 1.32¹ 2.03² 4 5 4 2o² 2¹ 23 2.03³ 4.40 (LManges) LemonTar,SuperWhiz,LyronHanover 70

6-18⁷⁷ B.R. ms 3700 ft 76-7nw8500CD 1 .29⁴ 1.00² 1.31¹ 2.02¹ 6 6 6 3o² 3⁷ 2.03³ 3.90 (LManges) LimelightTime,AvonSweetsng,SuprWhiz 78

6- 4⁷⁷ B.R. ms 4500 ft 76-7wo5000 1 .30³ 1.01² 1.31⁴ 2.01² 6 4 4 4³¹ 5⁵³ 2.02³ 21.00 (LManges) Shipoke,ArmbroRambler,LimelightTime 68

5-28⁷⁷ B.R. ms 6500 ft wo inv. hcp 1 .30⁴ 1.01¹ 1.32¹ 2.03³ 1 4 6 6³ 8³² 2.04¹ 13.80 (LManges) FarmSkipper,Hogan,RealQuick 58

4-30⁷⁷ B.R. ms 4200 ft 76-7wo5000 1 .32³ 1.03¹ 1.34³ 2.04² 4 4 4 2¹ 3² 2.04⁴ 11.70 (LManges) RaceTimeKillean,SuperClint,SuperWhiz 63

4-23⁷⁷ B.R. ms 4200 sy 76-7wo5000 1 .32¹ 1.05² 1.37 2.08 5 5 5 2o² 2¹ 2.08¹ 5.10 (LManges) RaceTimeKillean,SuperWhiz,HardyKing 44

4-16⁷⁷ B.R. ms 4000 ft 76-7w5000hcp 1 .30² 1.01² 1.32³ 2.04¹ 2 4 3 2o 3¹ 5³¹ 2.04⁴ 18.50 (LManges) Shipoke,(HardyKing,ArmbroRambler) 55

driver made his move three wide over the third quarter. The horse, however, did not have enough left to win the race.

Not every horse is run in the same way each race. In our next example the horse is rated differently from race to race. In Terry Herbert's last outing, the driver waited until the last quarter before making his move. But in the qualifying race on June 10, he simply took the lead and held it throughout. In the race of December 19, Darling went for the lead right off and then moved again at the half. In his three previous starts he moved at the half, finishing strongly in the races on December 4 and December 11.

A horse like Terry Herbert can be called *maneuverable,* because such a horse is confined to no one style of racing. Obviously, a driver with a maneuverable animal has a great advantage over one whose horse can race in only one way. A good driver will exploit this advantage as fully as possible.

We can summarize the results of our discussion of how the race will be run with the following advice: Bet a front-runner that can be expected to get the lead easily and not to have to give it up. But make sure the horse you bet has shown staying power in previous races.

Bet a closer when there are several front-runners in the same race. The front-runners will probably fight it out for the lead, and this will result in a fast first half or even three quarters. This will provide the driver who sits back with the opportunity to use his horse in the final quarter to overhaul the leaders. The same point applies to drivers who move their horses at the half, especially if they are not likely to get stuck behind other horses. Everything else being equal, bet a maneuverable horse when the conditions of the race favor it.

Do's and Don't's of Betting

As a summary of our previous discussions of handicapping and betting, here are some rules that, if applied intelligently, should help increase your chances of winning. None of these is meant to be without exception. There are exceptions to every rule, and the wise bettor and handicapper will treat these do's and don't's as useful guides to success.

Let's start with the don't's, because there are so many more of them.

Don't bet horses starting from outside post positions.

(3, 2.02¾) (¾) — $20669

TERRY HERBERT
DRIVER—JACK DARLING—Red and White

b. h. 4, by Replica Herbert—Tami Herbert
Jack Darling, Exeter, Ont., Can.

Trainer: J. Darling

										2.06¾ Lon Q			1977	1	0	0	1	$ 276
										2.02¾ GdnC ¾			1976	34	7	4	6	$20669

6-18⁷⁷ Lon 2300 ft wo2000La6CD 1 .31 1.03¹ 1.34 2.04⁴ 3 4 4 5 3⁴ 3²¹ 2.04⁴ 6.25 (JDarlin) WilcorStephen,GameWilliam,TerryHrbrt

6-10⁷⁷ Lon 5000 ft Qua 1 .32² 1.04³ 1.36 2.06² 3 1⁰ 1 1 1² 2.06² NB (JDarlin) TerryHerbert,AprilWood,SkipElla

12-19⁷⁶ W.R.⅝ 5000 ft 3yr Opn 1 .30² 1.02¹ 1.32³ 2.03 6 3⁰ 2 2⁰ 6⁴³ 2.70 (JDarlin) RumWave,RobertsRidge,RebelGrattan

12-11⁷⁶ Lon 2400 gd Pref 1 .32 1.05⁴ 1.37¹ 2.07³ 6 6 4 4⁰ 1½ 1.25* (JDarlin) TerryHerbert,PamelaWave,WinningClass

12- 4⁷⁶ Lon 2600 gd Pref 1 .31⁴ 1.05⁴ 1.37² 2.07⁴ 7 6 5 3¹ 2nd 2.07⁴ 5.80 (JDarlin) MrFulla,TerryHerbert,PamelaWave

11-28⁷⁶ W.R.⅝ 6500 ft 3yr Opn 1 .30³ 1.02³ 1.33² 2.04¹ 1 4 4 4½ 3²³ 2.04⁴ 7.75 (JDarlin) FortuneBookie,JRDecker,TerryHerbert

11-20⁷⁶ Lon 2700 gd Pref' 1 .31⁴ 1.04³ 1.35³ 2.06 6 5 6 2⁰ 3⁴½ 2.06⁴ 3.70 (JDarlin) WBArnie,PamelaWave,TerryHerbert

Don't bet horses starting for the first time after a layoff of three weeks or more.

Don't bet horses that haven't raced well in at least one of their last three starts.

Don't bet horses that have a history of breaking stride.

Don't bet maidens (horses that have never won a race) or horses with little racing experience.

Don't bet horses that are inconsistent—off again, on again from race to race.

Don't bet horses that lose ground in the stretch race after race (quitters).

Don't bet horses that keep going down in class but aren't able to win in lower-class races.

Don't bet every race on the card. Three or four races are the most that are usually playable on an average evening.

Don't bet a horse just because it's the favorite.

Don't bet a horse because it's a long shot or because the odds are attractive, when you don't really like its chances.

Don't bet trifectas unless you enjoy searching for needles in haystacks.

Ditto for most daily doubles and exactas.

Don't "reach" for good prices if you get behind and need a winner to make up your losses.

Don't bet $20 on a horse that "looks great" when your regular bet is $5 a race. Horses that look great have a way of not winning on the day you play them.

Don't bet on a tip unless your source has proved his reliability many times in the past.

Don't bet drivers that finish in the money once every leap year.

Don't bet a driver on a cold streak.

Don't bet provisional drivers.

A list of Betting do's

Bet horses from inside post positions (1 to 4).

Bet horses that perform consistently from race to race.

Bet higher-class claiming paces.

Bet drivers with winning percentages.

Bet drivers on hot streaks.

Bet horses favored by the probable pacing of the race.

Bet on overlays whenever you can find them.

Bet straight win, place, or show.

Bet the same amount on each race you choose to wager, and no more than 5 percent of your entire bankroll on any one race.

Examples of Races to Test Your Handicapping Skills.

We have completed our discussion of the major factors required for successful handicapping. In the next chapter I will provide you with a point system that is effective in handicapping claiming races, particularly paces, according to these guidelines. Before I outline this system, it would be a good exercise for you to handicap a number of claiming races using the criteria discussed in this chapter.

In order of importance, these are:

1. Current form
2. Class
3. Consistency
4. How the race will be run
5. Caliber of driver
6. Post position

I suggest that before you begin handicapping you prepare to spend at least ten minutes or more on each race. When you sit down to handicap, make sure that you can give 100 percent of your attention to studying the program. If you are distracted by business concerns, personal problems, etc., your chances of success will be greatly diminished.

Next, select four or five claiming paces on the program and devote your attention to them. It probably will not be worthwhile attempting to handicap every race on the card. An hour or two spent on claiming races should provide you with the two or three races you will find worth wagering on that evening.

Having settled on a specific race, your first task is to eliminate every entry that doesn't deserve serious consideration. Generally, two or more horses can be eliminated from contention almost immediately. You will be able to eliminate noncontenders for a number of possible reasons—because they show no current form, are inconsistent, are up too high in class, etc. Any animal that lacks good current form should be dismissed. In addition, you must consider whether a horse can overcome a weak driver or an outside post position. Finally, you may have to eliminate a horse from further

6 PACE

CLAIMING
EXACTA Wagering This Race

1 Mile — Purse $3100

Claiming Price $10000
Mares allowed 20%.

Saddle Cloth
BLUE

ASK FOR HORSE BY PROGRAM NUMBER

---

1 12000 MS

(4, 2.05½ (½)) — $7895)

ERINDALE ROBIN
DRIVER—DAN SARAMA—White, Orange and Red

b. m. 5, by Matador—Constance Adio
Mary Ann Sarama, Corfu, N.Y.

Trainer: M. Sarama

		1977	29	8	5	4	$12233
2.05½ Btva sy		1976	23	5	3	1	$ 5633
2.05½ GdnC ⅝							

8-20⁷⁷	Btva	ms	3700	ft	15000 clm hcp 1	.30¹	1.03²	1.33⁴ 2.04⁴	7	10	1	1	1ʰᵈ	2.05²	10.40	(DSarama)	DonRamon,IconAdios,Squall	65
8-13⁷⁷	Btva	ms	15000 clm	.31	1.32² 2.03³ 6x	6²¾	5⁴¼	2.05²	7.00	(DSarama)	StNick,PeblokhanⅬ,AmiBamby	77
8- 6⁷⁷	Btva	ms	5000 ft	21000 clm hcp 1	.28⁴	1.31² 2.02¹	2	1⁰	7⁵¼	5⁴¼	2.03²	2.80	(DSarama)	MrJoeKool,MajesticCreed,SunnyShell	76
7-30⁷⁷	Btva	ms	5000 ft	18000 clm hcp 1	.30	1.03 1.34 2.05	2	2ⁿˢ	2ⁿˢ	4.90	(DSarama)	LennTar,JillyJohnJohn,SunnyShell(PI 6)	77
7-22⁷⁷	Btva	ms	4000 ft	C-12000 clm	.30¹	1.03² 1.34¹ 2.05²	2	2²¼	2²¼	d2.05	4.90	(DJarlin)	MuddyDave,ErindaleRobin,ColeHillJohn	74
7-15⁷⁷	Btva	ms	4000 sy	12000 clm hcp 1	.30¹	1.03¹ 1.34¹ 2.05²	4	2⁰	1⁷²	2ⁿᵈ	2.05³	2.70	(JDarlin)	ErindaleRobin,ConestogaCash,WiscoyBird	80
7- 7⁷⁷	Btva	ms	3100 sy	10800 clm	.30¹	1.03¹ 1.34² 2.06¹	2	4	4	2ⁿˢ	2.06¹	1.50*	(JDarlin)	GinnyClay,ErindaleRobin,ArmbroProfit	67

---

2 12000 MS

(6, 2.05 (½)) — $45078)

GINNY CLAY NY
DRIVER—KEITH HAASE—Gold and White

b. m. 7, by Clay—Virginia Kay
Osten Dion, Schomberg, Ont., Can.

Trainer: O. Dion

| 2.06½ Btva sy | | 1977 | 30 | 5 | 3 | 5 | $13407 |
| 2.05 B.R. | | 1976 | 26 | 7 | 6 | 4 | $12672 |

8-26⁷⁷	Btva	ms	3100	ft	12000 clm	.30	1.01⁴ 1.32³ 2.04³	7	1¹	1¹	7⁵³	2.05⁴	3.20	(KHaase)	RlhomWarren,BnkDeposit,IconAdios(PI 6)	'76
8-19⁷⁷	Btva	ms	3400	ft	12000 clm	.31	1.33⁴ 2.04⁴	6	4⁰	5⁴¼	2.04¹	24.10	(KHaase)	MuddyDave,GinnyClay,ThunderImp	60
8-19⁷⁷	Btva	ms	3700	ft	12000 clm	.31	1.33⁴ 2.04⁴	5	75	7⁵	2.06	5.50	(KHaase)	FrankTSmith,ThunderImp,MuddyDave	71
8-12⁷⁷	Btva	ms	2600	ft	12000 clm	.30¹	1.33⁴ 2.05	4	4⁰	4⁰	2.04¹	9.70	(KHaase)	StNick,BeautyBoy,ArmbroProfit	76
8- 6⁷⁷	Btva	ms	4300	ft	15000 clm	.31¹	1.02³ 1.33 2.03⁴	4	4¹	4⁷²¼	2.20¹	4.90	(KHaase)	ThunderImp,GinnyClay,GreenviewAnn	73
7-29⁷⁷	Btva	ms	4000	sy	12000 clm hcp 1	.33	1.36⁴ 2.08	7	5²¼	5²¼	2.08¹	17.10	(BSlade)	MuddyDave,ErindaleRobin,ColeHillJohn	74
7-22⁷⁷	Btva	ms	4000	ft	12000 clm hcp 1	.33¹	1.34¹ 2.05²	7	2¹	2¹	2.05¹	2.20*	(KHaase)	MuddyDave,GinnyClay,ColeHillJohn	—
7-15⁷⁷	Btva	ms	4000	sy	12000 clm hcp 1	.30¹	1.03¹ 1.34² 2.05³	5	6²¾	5³¼	2.06¹	1.50*	(BSlade)	ErindaleRobin,ConestogaCash,WiscoyBird(PI 6)	80

---

3 10000 MS

(3, 2.04½ (½)) — $38041)

ICON ADIOS
DRIVER—LARRY MANGES—Red and White

br. g. 6, by Adios Boy—Icon
F. W. & Fred Stewart, St. Catharines, Ont., Can.

Trainer: T. Dunlap (Rankin Stable)

| 2.05 Btva | | 1977 | 12 | 0 | 3 | 5 | $ 4040 |
| | | 1976 | 46 | 7 | 9 | 5 | $14101 |

8-26⁷⁷	Btva	ms	3100	ft	10000 clm	.30	1.01⁴ 1.32³ 2.04³	2⁰	2ⁿᵏ	2ⁿᵏ	2.04⁴	2.40	(JMcNeJr)	RlhomWarren,BankDeposit,IconAdios	76
8-20⁷⁷	Btva	ms	3700	ft	11000 clm hcp 1	.30¹	1.33 2.04⁴	6	4	4	4	2.05¹	9.80	(JRankin)	DonRamon,IconAdios,Squall	65
8-12⁷⁷	Btva	ms	2600	ft	10000 clm	.30¹	1.33⁴ 2.05	4	4	40	2.05²	8.20	(JRankin)	StNick,BeautyBoy,ArmbroProfit	76
8- 2⁷⁷	Btva	ms	2600	ft	10000 clm	.32¹	1.04 1.34 2.05²	3	3	3	2.05²	9.70	(JRankin)	TerryHerbert,WiscoyPatsy,IconAdios	71
7-27⁷⁷	Btva	ms	2600	sy	76-7w225ps	.30²	1.32¹ 1.34² 2.04¹	1	1¹	1ʰᵈ	2.04¹	1.30*	(JRankin)	AvonSongByrd,AllwinKnick,IconAdios	76
7-27⁷⁷	Btva	ms	2800	sy	76-7w225ps	.30²	1.02¹ 1.33² 2.03⁴	4	4	5³	2.04³	2.30	(JRankin)	AChoiceGuy,IconAdios,SaraABByrd	74
7-21⁷⁷	Btva	ms	2600	sy	76-7w225ps	.30²	1.03 1.33² 2.04⁴	3	5⁴¼	5⁴¼	2.05³	15.20	(JRankin)	HilltopAndrs,RoyalHnch,Jsse6Innbrooke	78
7-16⁷⁷	Btva	ms	2800	sy	76-7w250ps	.30²	1.34 2.05⁴	4	2⁶	2⁶	2.06¹	NB	(RHillJr)	TriangleBoy,IconAdios,EasternGold	

---

4 10000 MS

(7, 2.06⅓ (⅓)) — $18639)

BANK DEPOSIT NY
DRIVER—ED McNEIGHT, JR.—Orange, Black and White

b. g. 8, by Razzle Dazzle—Catch Me
A. R. Clauss, Boston, N.Y.

Trainer: A. Clauss

| 2.06½ B.R. | | 1977 | 38 | 3 | 11 | 4 | $11697 |
| 2.06⅓ Btva | | 1976 | 46 | 5 | 13 | 4 | $11949 |

8-26⁷⁷	Btva	ms	3100	ft	10000 clm	1	.30	1.01⁴ 1.32³ 2.04³	5	3²	2³¼	2.05¹	6.40	(EMcNeJr)	RelhomWarren,BankDeposit,IconAdios	76
8-19⁷⁷	Btva	ms	3400	ft	10000 clm	1	.31	1.33² 2.04⁴	7	6	5⁴	2.05³	8.20	(EMcNeJr)	MuddyDave,GinnyClay,ThunderImp	60
8-15⁷⁷	Btva	ms	3100	ft	9000 clm	1	.30¹	1.02 1.34 2.05¹	3	6	6³¼	2.05¹	4.50	(EMcNeJr)	BddyFrndale,BankDeposit,OldeSoftShoe	71

5 • 10000

(8, 2.04½) — $56584

THUNDER IMP

DRIVER—PHILIPPE LAFRAMBOISE—Blue and White

br. g. 11, t γ by Dale Spring (F)—Imperial Jewel
Edward Ingenito & Philippe Laframboise, Olean, N.Y. & Quebec, Can.

Trainer: R. Horton (Laframboise Stable)

8- 3⁷⁷	Btva	ms	3100	ft	8000	clm	1	.29² 1.01² 1.32⁴ 2.05	1	3	4	2⁰	4.2½	2.05²	4.50	(PLafram)	MissMaryDl,WaitABit,LincolnsValor		
8-28⁷	Btva	ms	3100	ft	8000	clm	1	.31 1.03 1.34³ 2.05³	2	2	2	2²	3²	2.06	15.20	(AClauss)	MerryJohnA,KeystoneWhiz,BankDeposit		
7-22⁷	Btva	ms	3100	ft	8000	clm	1	.30³ 1.02² 1.33 2.04⁴	8	8	8	8⁶³	8⁷½	2.06¹	11.10	(AClauss)	GreenviewAnn,BurleyGuy,MerryJohnA		

1977: 21 6 2 3 $13432
1976: 37 7 8 3 $13773
2.03¾ B.R.
2.04½ Btva

---

6 • 12000

(4, 2.05) (½) — $18275

RUTH BAKER

DRIVER—PETER RADNO—Red and White

ch. m. 5, by Sky Hanover—Patsy Lynn
A. Cooper & R. Preszler & P.J.R. Stables, Laurel, Ont. Can.

Trainer: P. Radno

8-24⁷	Btva	ms	3100	ft	10000	clm	1	.30² 1.01¹ 1.32⁴ 2.04¹	1	2	3	5	8⁷³	2.05	8.40	(PRadno)	RedFlyer,MarConCash,Rightful
8-13⁷⁷	Btva	ms	5500	ft	76-7wo5000	1	.30 1.02³ 1.34 2.04³	7	1	1⁰	1²	6²½	2.05	45.60	(PRadno)	Hogan,Silicon,PrincessDeeDee	
8-	Btva	ms	3400	gd	10800	clm	1	.30³ 1.02² 1.34² 2.05¹	4	5	5	3²	3³	2.05¹	6.40	(PRadno)	RuthBaker,ColeHillJohn,ClassicAffairN
8-	Btva	ms	2000	ft	76-7nw175ps	1	.30¹ 1.01⁴ 1.33¹ 2.04¹	5	6	5	6²½	6⁷¾	2.04²	7.90	(PRadno)	NobleMoran,RuthBaker,LadyIntruder
7-26⁷⁷	Btva	ms	2300	ft	76-7nw200ps	1	.31² 1.03 1.33 2.04³	6	6	4	6½	6¹⁰⁴	2.05²	6.30	(PRadno)	StNick,BeautysBoy,ArmbroProfit
7-	Btva	ms	4000	sy	10000	clm	hcp 1	.33 1.05¹ 1.36⁴ 2.08	4	3	3	4	4³	2.08	2.30	(PLafram)	ThunderImp,GinnyClay,GreenviewAnn
5- 7⁷⁷	GrR%	ms	2500	ft	10000	clm	hcp 1	.30² 1.02 1.34 2.05¹	2	4	4	2⁴	2⁴	2.05¹	37.35	(PRadno)	MuddyDave,ErindaleRobin,ColeHillJohn
6-26⁷³	Moh%	ms	2200	ft	8000	clm	1	.30 1.02¹ 1.32³ 2.03¹	9	6	6⁰	7⁷	3¹ d-dh2.05⁴	1.50*	54.10	(PRadno)	FrontierFrd,BuddyFrndale,StellaYnkee

1977: 20 3 3 1 $ 5166
1976: 7 2 2 5 $11727
2.04½ Btva gd
2.05 Fhid

---

7 • 10000

(6, 2.03¾) (½) — $28293)

RELHOM WARREN

DRIVER—BRUCE TUBIN (P)—Blue, White and Red

b. g. 7, by Senga Duke—Catherine Anne
Ronald Smith, Endicott, N.Y.

Trainer: N. Fluet (Tubin Stable)

8-26⁷⁷	Btva	ms	3100	ft	10000	clm	1	.30 1.01⁴ 1.32³ 2.04³	5	7	8	8	7⁵¾	2.04³	81.30	(BTubin)	RelhomWarren,BankDeposit,IconAdios
8-19⁷⁷	Btva	ms	3400	ft	10000	clm	1	.31 1.02³ 1.34 2.04⁴	4	7	7	6	8³½	2.05¹	21.30	(BTubin)	MuddyDave,GinnyClay,ThunderImp
8-13⁷⁷	Btva	ms	2900	sy	c-8000	clm	1	.31² 1.02³ 1.33¹ 2.04³	7	7	5⁴	5⁴	3.3	2.05¹	29.50	(TArtand)	ClassicAffairN,LncInsValor,RelhomWarn
8- 9⁷⁷	Btva	ms		ft	Qua	1	.31⁴ 1.04³ 1.36¹ 2.08²	4	2⁰	2¹	1³	1³	2.08²	NB	(TArtand)	RelhomWarren,GlindalePisa,FoFo
8- 2⁷⁷	Btva	ms		ft	Qua	1	.31 1.03² 1.35⁴ 2.07¹	6	4	4x	x6dh	6¹⁰⁴	2.08	NB	(JGerrar)	Mr.SperWhiz,WndmillAngel,MyBrthrsHorse
5- 7⁷⁷	GrR%	ms	2500	ft	10000	clm	hcp 1	.30² 1.02² 1.34 2.05³	4	6	6³⁴	6³⁴	2.06²	11.50	(TArtand)	LyndenBrian,RuthBker,NavalPrinceN	
5- 1⁷⁷	Moh%	ms	2900	ft	10000	clm	1	.29¹ 1.01¹ 1.32³ 2.02⁴	3	9	8	7¹³	7⁹	2.04³	6.20	(PRadno)	CrwnHanoverA,GinbysThorpe,LatsINewsGB

1977: 22 4 2 2 $ 6538
1976: 17 1 1 $19480
2.04½ Btva
2.03¾ W.R. %

---

8 • 12000

(5, 2.05¾) (¾) — $14582)

FROSTY SHIRBERT

DRIVER—TOM ARTAND—White and Brown

b. m. 6, by Philip Frost—Gay Reel
R. C., Brian, Glenn & Wm. Hamilton, Caledonia, Ont. Can.

Trainer: W. Robinson

8-24⁷⁷	FlmD	ms	1800	ft	c-9600	clm	1	.29¹ 1.01¹ 1.32¹ 2.04³	5	7	7	1²	1²	2.04³	3.75	(MLHerue)	FrostyShirbert,DreamySusan,Dr.Dale
8-18⁷⁷	FlmD	ms	2000	ft	12000	clm	1	.30 1.02³ 1.34 2.05	8	7	7	7⁶	8³½	2.06	11.60	(MLHerue)	CountDan,JustBGun,StoneSkipper
8-11⁷⁷	FlmD	ms	2000	ft	12000	clm	1	.30¹ 1.03 1.34³ 2.05	8	7	7	10	3³³	2.05¹	3.95	(MLHerue)	HurricaneChrle,Kymala,FrostyShrbrt
8- 4⁷⁷	FlmD	ms	2000	ft	12000	clm	1	.30³ 1.03 1.33² 2.03²	4	4	10	4⁵½	4⁵½	2.04³	3.25	(MLHerue)	ForwardBay,JstADrger,FrstyShirbrt(Pl 3)
7-28⁷⁷	FlmD	ms	2000	ft	12000	clm	1	.31² 1.03⁴ 1.36¹ 2.04³	2	5	5	3³½	3²½	2.05⁴	4.25	(MLHerue)	JstADodger,FrstyShrbrt,JustBGun(Pl 2)
7-21⁷⁷	FlmD	ms	2000	ft	12000	clm	1	.29¹ 1.01¹ 1.32³ 2.04²	7	6	5¹³	5²	2.04⁴	9.20	(MLHerue)	JstADodger,SevenFifteen,EasternWi	
7-14⁷⁷	FlmD	ms	2000	ft	12000	clm	1	.30¹ 1.03 1.34 2.05¹	6	6	7	7³²	7³³	2.06	3.15	(MLHerue)	CountDan,FrstyShirbrt,WickedMir

1977: 25 5 4 5 $ 6268
1976: 47 6 6 10 $12422
2.05½ FlmD

consideration because the likely pacing of the race is not conducive to its chances of winning.

Let's assume that you have eliminated at least two horses as apparent contenders in the first stage of your selection process. Now you are left with the remaining entries. At this point you must weigh each of the six factors in relation to the horses you consider *bona fide* contenders. At this stage, however, there are no hard-and-fast rules available for you to determine which horse is the best bet.

For example, the current form of horses A and B is virtually identical, but A's post position is better, and B has a better driver. What will you do? At this stage you are dependent solely on subjective judgment in utilizing each of the six factors to estimate the contender's chances.

The following three races are taken from the October 19, 1977, program at Batavia Raceway. Read my discussion and analysis of the second race on the program before going on to handicap the next two races yourself. Also keep in mind that these races were handicapped "fresh" and reflect my own doubts and hesitations over their outcome.

We will score every horse in the race first and eliminate noncontenders afterward.

Batavia Downs   2nd Race   October 19, 1977

Eliminate the following horses:

2 Lord Overseer

Although Lord Overseer finished fourth in his last start, no more than 1½ lengths back, he was never in contention and never moved off the rail. His preceding two starts are even worse. Unplayable because of poor recent form.

3 Flyaway Pro

With three straight seventh-place finishes, this horse must be eliminated on grounds of poor current form.

4 Hill Billy Pat

Hill Billy Pat has not rounded into shape yet after thirteen starts. This horse has only two second-place finishes and has been out of the money in his last seven trips.

Claiming Price $3000 to $4500
Mares allowed 20%. Post position drawn to price.
SECOND HALF OF DAILY DOUBLE

**Saddle Cloth
GRAY**

1
3000
MS

(2, 2.19 (½) — $1539)
MR EVANS(N)
DRIVER—MICHEL BOUVRETTE—Gray, Red and Black

9-28⁷⁷	Btva	ms	1800	sl	4000 clm hcp	1	.33¹	1.08¹	1.41²	2.14¹	8	8	6⁵¹	6²	2.14³	14.90	(JHodgin)	PridesFashion,Rayette,HastyEarl
9-19⁷⁷	Btva	ms	1700	sy	76-7nw17ps	1	.32¹	1.04³	1.38¹	2.12	1	2	2⁰²	6⁴²ex	2.12	6.90	(MBouvre)	PridesFashion,Lovelty,GrampasBoy
9-9⁷⁷	Btva	ms			Qua h-dr	1	.31¹	1.04²	1.37²	2.09³	1	4	2⁰	12¹	2.09³	NB	(RMillet)	MrEvans,LuckyPlay,SongBonus
9-7⁷⁷	Btva	ms	1300	ft	76-7nw150ps	1	.31¹	1.05²	1.37¹	2.01¹	3	4	4⁹	4⁰²	02.12	1.90*	(YDemers)	AmrcnScne,AmzinMily,FshinMndy(PI 6)
8-22⁷⁷	Btva	ms	1600	ft	3000 clm hcp	1	.32¹	1.06¹	1.39¹	2.11³	8	7	2nd	2nk	2.11³	16.10	(JHodgin)	CaprKey,MrEvans,SpaceLeader
8-17⁷⁷	Btva	ms			Qua	1	.31⁴	1.04¹	1.36²	2.09³	4	3	*3³	3⁵	2.09⁴	NB	(MBouvre)	MoonlightProphet,KerryBarmin,MrEvans
8-1⁷⁷	Btva	ms	1600	ft	3000 clm hcp	1	.31⁴	1.05⁴	1.38²	2.10⁴	7	6	4x	5⁵⁴	2.11⁴	5.50	(TSwift)	PridesFashion,PerkyMike,MrEvans

Trainer: J. R. Millette

| | 1977 | 25 | 2 | 5 | 3 | $ 3162 |
| 2.07% V.D. ¾ | 1976 | 5 | 0 | 0 | 1 | $ 184 |

b. g. 5, by Rain Water—Kelly Fisherman
J. Real Millette, Mascouche, Que., Can.

2
3000
MS

(11, 2.07 (½) — $4212)
LORD OVERSEER
DRIVER—PHILIPPE LAFRAMBOISE—Blue and White

9-28⁷⁷	Btva	ms	1800	sl	3000 clm hcp	1	.33¹	1.08¹	1.41²	2.14¹	2	4	5	7	6⁵¹	62	2.14²	2.80	(PLafram)	PridesFashion,Rayette,HastyEarl
9-14⁷⁷	Btva	ms	1800	ft	3500 clm hcp	1	.31⁴	1.05⁴	1.39	2.11	4	5	6x⁵	6¹⁰⁴	2.13	3.20	(MGrieJr)	HastyEarl,EliPick,Polsyn
8-25⁷⁷	Hin		600	ft	nw1200CD	1	.31²	1.04	1.36²	2.09	4	5	50	7¹¹¹	2.11	6.20	(MGrieJr)	TillyTally,MrSharpness,SpeedyRelease
8-17⁷⁷	Hin		600	gd	nw1200CD	1	.31³	1.04³	1.37	2.09¹	1	2	2³	2¹	02.10*	2.10*	(MGrieJr)	TillyTally,LordOverseer,CraneHillBrnda
8-1⁷⁷	Hin		600	ft	nw1200CD	1	.32¹	1.04¹	1.38²	2.10⁴	6	7	7⁴¹	3¹³	2.11¹	5.20	(MGrieJr)	DealersCheck,POsBoy,LordOverseer
8-1⁷⁷	Hin		600	ft	nw1100CD	1	.32¹	1.04⁴	1.36²	2.07³	7	7	7⁶¹	7¹¹¹	2.09⁴	25.20	(MGrieJr)	TranquilLinda,DealrsCheck,MrShrpness
7-27⁷⁷	Hin				Qua	1	.32³	1.07¹	1.38²	2.10	3	4	4x	*3³	2.13	NB	(MGrieJr)	TillyTally,CraneHillBrnda,DayProspect

Trainer: M. Grieco, Jr.

| | 2.08% Hin | 1977 | 20 | 3 | 2 | 1 | $ 1873 |
| | 2.07 Hin | 1976 | 22 | 5 | 4 | 3 | $ 2288 |

b. g. 12, by Overseer—Dares Always
Mike Grieco, Jr. & Henry Florence, Depew & Niagara Falls, N.Y.

3
3000
MS

(4, 2.10% Q — $4622)
FLYAWAY PRO
DRIVER—ED McNEIGHT, SR.—Orange, Black and White

9-28⁷⁷	Btva	ms	3000	ft	3000 clm hcp	1	.33¹	1.08¹	1.41²	2.14¹	2	4	5	76	74	2.15	27.20	(EMcNeSr)	PridesFashion,Rayette,HastyEarl
9-14⁷⁷	Btva	ms	1800	ft	3000 clm hcp	1	.31⁴	1.05⁴	1.39	2.11	2	10	6x	7¹⁸⁴	2.14³	13.90	(EMcNeSr)	HastyEarl,EliPick,Polsyn
9-5⁷⁷	Btva	ms	1400	ft	3000 clm hcp	1	.31³	1.05	1.37⁴	2.10³	1	6x	5²	7⁵	2.13³	27.60	(EMcNeSr)	PridesFashion,SomeMatter,Worry
8-15⁷⁷	Btva	ms	2500	ft	2500 clm hcp	1	.31³	1.04¹	1.36²	2.09¹	6	6	2²	2³¹	2.10¹	12.00	(EMcNeSr)	DollieLane,CaprKey,FlyawayPro
8-1⁷⁷	Btva	ms	1600	ft	3000 clm hcp	1	.31⁴	1.05⁴	1.38²	2.10⁴	5	7	7⁸	6⁹³	2.12¹	12.00	(EMcNeSr)	PridesFashion,PerkyMike,MrEvans
7-2⁷⁷	Btva	ms	1700	ft	3000 clm hcp	1	.32⁴	1.06¹	1.38²	2.10⁴	6	8	6⁹³	6¹²⁴	2.13¹	25.20	(EMcNeSr)	TrimDemon,PerkyMike,MrEvans
6-22⁷⁷	B.R.		1550	ft	3000 clm hcp	1	.32¹	1.04⁴	1.36²	2.07³	1	6	5	4	5⁴³	2.13¹	12.00	(EMcNeSr)	TrimDemon,JollyoC,ProFuse
6-17⁷⁷																		

Trainer: E. McNeight, Sr.

| | 2.10% B.R. | 1977 | 10 | 1 | 1 | 2 | $ 1556 |
| | | 1976 | | | | 0 | $ 100 |

b. g. 7, by Worthy Pro—Chockoyotte Gold
Edward G. McNeight, Orchard Park, N.Y.

4
3000
MS

(4, 2.07% (½) — $26074)
HILL BILLY PAT
DRIVER—WILLARD JENSEN—Gray and Blue

10-11⁷⁷	Btva			ft	Qua tp	1	.31¹	1.04¹	1.36³	2.09²	3	4	4²⁴	4¹³	2.09⁴	NB	(WJensen)	SangerSam,RegalOak,CedarwoodKit
10-5⁷⁷	Btva		2000	ft	3500 clm hcp	1	.32¹	1.05³	1.38³	2.11¹	4	5	7²³	52	2.12¹	16.90	(WJensen)	Polsyn,SpaceLeader,NewHanover
9-21⁷⁷	Btva		1800	gd	3500 clm hcp	1	.31⁴	1.04²	1.37	2.10³	6	6	7⁵	8⁵²	2.11³	23.00	(WJensen)	NationalAnthem,EliPick,SpaceLeader
9-14⁷⁷	Btva		1800	ft	3500 clm hcp	1	.31⁴	1.05⁴	1.39	2.11	7	8	8	5⁴¹	2.11⁴	14.10	(WJensen)	HastyEarl,EliPick,Polsyn

Trainer: W. Jensen

| | 2.10 B.R. | 1977 | 13 | 0 | 2 | 0 | $ 1362 |
| | | 1976 | 34 | 3 | 4 | 3 | $ 3756 |

b. g. 8, by Hickory Hill—Patsy Dean
Charles E. & Clara Ann Knell, Williamsville, N.Y.

3

3500

8-31⁷⁷	Btva		2200	ft	3500 clm hcp	1	.31⁴ 1.04¹ 1.36⁴ 2.10	2 2 2 3²	4¹³	2.10² 11.30 (WJensen) Polsyn,EliPick,Rayette
8-21⁷⁷	Sycs(1)		800	ft	77nw2500	1	.30⁴ 1.04¹ 1.31 2.04	5 2 2 4dis	4dis	2.04 42.90 (WJensen) JoanCollins,GoodInvestmnt,Rbertas,Jaspr
8-14⁷⁷	Sycs(1)		800	sy	77nw2500	1	.31³ 1.03 1.35³ 2.09	5 4 5be 5 5¹⁷₄	5dis	2.14 18.80 (WJensen) Corona,RosarioB,LJB

(5, 2.08% Q (%) — $8674)

DOLLIE LANE

DRIVER—ANTHONY STROLLO—White, Black and Red

b. m. 8, by Mr Bloom—Lola Lane

Billy Kaye & Lynne Strollo, Northeast, Pa., & Batavia, N.Y.

Trainer: A. Strollo

2.09% Btva

2.09 RIdC %

	1977	1976	
	26	32	
	6	4	
	4	0	
	2	6	$
			5484
			3642

RosieD,RedWhiz,DinoBoy — 80
DarlinHussy,JackFlood,MistyMessenger — 71
DollieLane,RosieD,DarinHussy — 68

5

MS

4200

10- 4⁷⁷	Btva	ms	2500	ft	6000 clm	1	.31³ 1.04¹ 1.36⁴ 2.10	2 2 2 3²	4¹³	2.10² 17.70 (AStroll) SpaceLeder,NewHnvr,(DlleLne,KrkwoodVic) — 66
10- 4⁷⁷	Btva	ms	2700	gd	7800 clm	1	.31³ 1.04¹ 1.31 2.08²	5 5 5⁰ 7³⁴	7³³	2.104 5.70 (AStroll) DollieLane,RosieD,BlackRockCandy — 63
9-28⁷⁷	Btva	ms	2300	my	5400 clm	1	.32 1.03 1.36¹ 2.09²	2 2 2¹ 8⁵⁴	8⁵⁴	2.093 1.40* (AStroll) Coldspot,RosieD,BlackRockCandy — 67
9- 7⁷⁷	Btva	ms	2200	ft	4200 clm	1	.31⁴ 1.04² 1.37 2.09¹	2 2 1³	1³	1.70* (AStroll) DollieLane,CapriKey,FlyawayPro — 71
8-23⁷⁷	Btva	ms	2300	ft	4200 clm	1	.31² 1.03¹ 1.35¹ 2.08	3 3 3³⁴	3³⁴	2.09 2.10* (AStroll) Athlone,Yankee,DollieLane,RedWhiz — 74
8-15⁷⁷	Btva	ms	1600	ft	3000 clm	1	.31 1.04 1.35² 2.09¹	3 3 3 4⁶	13¹	

(7, 2.10 Q (%) — $14118)

SPACE LEADER

DRIVER—ANGUS MacDONALD (P)—Red and White

br. g. 10, by Squadron Leader—Twinkle Hal

John & Angus MacDonald, Lancaster, N.Y.

Trainer: A. MacDonald

2.09 Btva

6

3500

10-11⁷⁷	Btva			ft	Qua tp h-dr	1	.31¹ 1.04¹ 1.36 2.09²	6 6 6 5⁵⁴	5⁵⁴	2.094 NB (BHolmes) SangerSam,RegalOak,Cedarwood Kit — 60
10- 4⁷⁷	Btva		3500	clm	3500 clm hcp	1	.32¹ 1.05¹ 1.38³ 2.11¹	6 6 4⁰ 2³	2³	2.10* (AMacDon) Polsyn,SpaceLeader,NewHanover — 60
10- 5⁷⁷	Btva		2000	ft	Qua h-dr	1	.33 1.03² 1.38² 2.11	3 4 4 1¹²	1¹²	NB (WBourgo) SpaceLeader,NewHnvr,(DlleLne,KrkwoodVic) — 52
9-28⁷⁷	Btva		1800	ft	3500 clm	1	.31⁴ 1.04² 1.37 2.09³	4 4 2⁰ 1¹	1³	NB (WBourgo) SpaceLeader,BombsBooBoo,ProFuse — 58
9-21⁷⁷	Btva		2200	ft	3500 clm	1	.31² 1.03² 1.37 2.09	6 7 6⁵ 3³⁴	3³⁴	2.09¹ NB (BHornbe) NationalAnthem,EliPick,SpaceLeader — 52
9- 7⁷⁷	Btva		2200	ft	Qua	1	.31² 1.03² 1.37¹ 2.09¹	2 2 2⁰ 1¹⁴	1¹⁴	2.09 NB (AMacDon) SpaceLeder,NewHnvr,(DlleLne,KrkwoodVic) — 63
8-26⁷⁷	Btva			ft	Qua	1	.31¹ 1.03¹ 1.34 2.09¹	1 1 1³ 1³	2¹	2.09 NB (AMacDon) FrancisMood,MarConBewtched,SikaLilwier — 75
8-22⁷⁷	Btva		1600	ft	2900 clm hcp	1	.32² 1.06¹ 1.39² 2.11³	6 6 5⁰ 4²	3¹	2.11³ NB (AMacDon) CapriKey,MrEvans,SpaceLeader — 67

(6, 2.06% Q (%) — $19402)

NEV HANOVER

DRIVER—PERRY WILSON (P)—Green, Tan and White

br. g. 8, by Caleb—Netina Hanover

Perry Wilson & Anthony Orsini, Springville, N.Y.

Trainer: P. Wilson

2.08% B.R.

2.06% B.R.

	1977	1976	
	18	23	
	1	5	
	4	5	
	2	6	$
			3607
			1946

Polsyn,SpaceLeader,NevHanover — 60
NationalAnthem,EliPick,SpaceLeader — 52
SpaceLeder,NevHnvr,(DlleLne,KrkwoodVic) — 63
CapriKey,MrEvans,SpaceLeader — 67
BlackRockCandy,Rayette,RosieD — 70
SpaceLeder,NevHnvr,(DlleLne,KrkwoodVic) — 63
Rayette,NevHanover,CapriKey — 72
SwordHanover,BlackRockCandy,HastyEarl — 84

7

3600

10- 5⁷⁷	Btva		2000	ft	c-3000 clm hcp	1	.32¹ 1.05¹ 1.38³ 2.11¹	8 8 8 8⁹²	3³	2.124 4.90 (VAquino) MarConBewitched,Coldspot,Rayette — 58
9-20⁷⁷	Btva		2300	gd	6000 clm	1	.37⁴ 2.09³	2 1 1 1	2x¹	2.08¹ 2.60 (DSnyder) Edgewood,Grania,SwiftDecision,VonTaylor — 52
9- 7⁷⁷	Mea⅝		2600	ft	7000 clm hcp	1	.30¹ 1.03 1.34³ 2.05⁴	2 1 1 5⁴	6¹¹³	2.081 5.30 (WPocza) GalaGold,Edgewood,Grania,TeeVeeNfty — 77
8-26⁷⁷	Mea⅝		2600	ft	7000 clm hcp	1	.29¹ 1.03 1.31² 2.02¹	1 1 3 6¹⁸	6¹⁸²	2.06 .80* (LRapone) DarnPro,AutumnLady,Plunker — 65
8-21⁷⁷	Mea⅝		1600	ft	c-5000 clm	1	.30¹ 1.03¹ 1.32 2.06²	5 1 4⁸ 1¹⁴	1¹⁴	2.062 NB (LRapone) Haste,DarnPro,WorthyTrot —
8-10⁷⁷	Nild		3000	gd	CD	1	.30¹ 1.03¹ 1.34² 2.06	6 5 3² 2⁵	2⁵	2.07 5.10 (LRapone) StClairEric,GalaGold,Edgewood,Grania —
8- 4⁷⁷	Mea⅝		2200	ft	6000 clm	1	.30 1.03¹ 1.31² 2.02	3 3 3⁰ 4⁶	4⁶²	2.03¹ 2.00 (LRapone) StClairEric,GalaGold,Edgewood,Grania — 78
7-28⁷⁷	Mea⅝		2200	ft	7000 clm	1	.31² 1.02 1.33 2.04⁴	4 10 1⁰ 1²	5⁸	2.062 5.40 (GPurcel) StClairEric,TeeVeeNfty,GalaGold — 72

(4, 2.06% Q (%) — $5909)

DARN PRO

DRIVER—VINCE AQUINO—Blue and Gold

br. g. 6, by Worthy Pro—S S Mitzi

Richard Snyder, Meadow Lands, Pa.

Trainer: V. Aquino

2.04 Mea %

2.09% Mea %

7 Nev Hanover

Besides moving up in class after being claimed on October 5, Nev Hanover has a weak driver and an outside post position. Need I say more?

8 Darn Pro

After being claimed on August 21 for $5,000, this horse has been moved steadily down in class. Since being catch driven on August 26 and September 7, Darn Pro now has a capable regular driver and trainer. However, Darn Pro has been idle for almost a month and has the extreme outside post position; we must pass him by.

The seeming contenders are:

1 Mr Evans

Mr Evans ran a good qualifying race on September 9 and has excuses for finishing back in his last two starts. On September 19 an equipment break may have been a factor in the horse's finishing fifth, and the outside post position excuses the sixth-place finish on September 28. Still, Mr Evans is far from being a strong contender in this race.

5 Dollie Lane

Dollie Lane is stepping down in class after having competed unsuccessfully in $5,000 and $6,000 claiming trots. However, Dollie Lane's previous starts, showing two victories, a place, and a show, make her the favorite in this race. On September 13, Dollie Lane licked tougher competition than her opposition in this race.

6 Space Leader

Space Leader is a remarkably consistent horse, finishing in the money in twenty-five out of thirty starts. However, Space Leader has acquired the nasty habit of finishing third in almost half his starts. From the six hole, with a provisional driver, Space Leader cannot be given a very good chance to win this race.

Analysis. Dollie Lane should go for the lead at the beginning of the race and will probably have no difficulty getting to the rail. There is no good reason to believe that any of the other horses in this race will be able to overtake Dollie Lane in the stretch. Dollie Lane is the play.

Results.

SECOND RACE — 1 Mile								$3000 - 4500 Claiming Hcp. Trot		$1700
Dollie Lane ms	5	1	1	1	1^6	1^7	A. Strollo		*1.10
Mr. Evans ms	1	6	6	4	4^1	$2\frac{1}{2}$	M. Bouvrette		5.20
Space Leader	6	8	8	6	$5\frac{3}{4}$	$3\frac{1}{2}$	A. MacDonald		5.40
Hill Billy Pat	4	7	7	5	6^3	$4\frac{1}{2}$	W. Jensen		10.50
Lord Overseer ms	2	4	3	2°	2nk	5^5	P. Laframboise		8.40
Flyaway Pro ms	3	2	2	3	$3\frac{1}{2}$	$6^{1}\frac{1}{2}$	E. McNeight, Jr.		37.90
Nev Hanover	7	3°	$x5^o$	7°	7^4	be7^8	P. Wilson		19.50
Darn Pro	8	5^{o2}	4^{o2}	8°	8	8	V. Aquino		5.10
$2 MUTUEL PRICES		5. Dollie Lane						4.20	3.20	2.60
Official Program Nos.		1. Mr. Evans							5.20	3.20
		6. Space Leader								2.80

Time — .31⅖   1.04⅖   1.37   2.10
DAILY DOUBLE — 4 AND 5 $58.20

Batavia Downs   4th Race   October 19, 1977

The following horses must be eliminated from contention:

1 Scotch Rice

We can eliminate this horse right off. No current form after several months of idleness.

4 Peachtree Parader

This horse has shown nothing in his last four starts and must be eliminated for this reason alone.

5 Victoria Sterling

Victoria Sterling has finished in the money in two of her last three starts but did not move on the outside to make up ground in either race. From the number-5 hole, Victoria Sterling can't be considered a threat here.

7 Mini Grattan

With very poor recent form, an outside post position, and one win in twenty-six starts, Mini Grattan can safely be consigned to the wastebasket.

8 Reveille Dan

With an unimpressive showing in his last two starts and the extreme outside post position, Reveille Dan must be eliminated from contention.

We are left with three apparent contenders:

2 Eben Jones

After winning seven races in a row earlier in the year, Eben Jones has been gradually returning to peak form. In his last three regular starts Eben Jones has run very well against a stiff level of competition. His last race on October 3 can be excused because of the outside post position and comparatively fast second half. A definite contender.

3 Mister Salty

The change to the modified sulky may account for Mister Salty's success in his last start. It is not unusual for this change to result in several seconds' improvement in a horse's time over the mile. On this basis alone, Mister Salty is a formidable contender. However, the change from an outstanding to a provisional driver is not in Mister Salty's favor. If Mister Salty has to struggle to gain the lead, Eben Jones will probably win this race.

6 G. V. Grattan

G. V. Grattan is going down in class but has not raced well in his last several starts. Even the race on August 29 is by no means exceptional, since the competition was weak. Nonetheless, he must be considered a contender in this race on the basis of class alone.

Analysis. Between the two horses, Mister Salty is the faster, although Eben Jones has a slight edge in post position and a far more experienced driver. An exacta wager on these two horses seems called for.

Results.

FOURTH RACE — 1 Mile							$3000 Claiming Pace			$1400
d Mister Salty ms	3	2	2	1	1²	1²	A. GuilianiP8		2.10
GV Grattan ms	6ix	6	6	5⁰	3½	2²	D. SaramaP1		3.10
Eben Jones ms	2ix	5	5	4	2¹	3¹½	T. SwiftP2		*1.70
Scotch Rice ms	1ix	3	4	3	5¹¼	4²½	F. BondP3		25.40
Mini Grattan ms	7ix	7	7	6	6⁶	5⁶½	P. SorgeP4		58.70
Peachtree Parader ms	4	1	1	2	4x² be6²½	F. MahiquesP5		6.50
Victoria Sterling ms	5ix	4	3⁰	7	7⁸	7¹³	E. McNeightJrP6		13.00
Reveille Dan ms	8ix	8	8	8	8	8	C. MancinelliP7		70.10

$2 MUTUEL PRICES	6. GV Grattan	8.20	4.20	3.20
Official Program Nos.	2. Eben Jones		3.40	2.60
	1. Scotch Rice			4.60

Time — .32   1.04¾   1.37⅖   2.09⅖

EXACTA — 6 AND 2 $23.60

Mister Salty finished 1st, placed 8th for interference at the first turn.

④ PACE CLAIMING

1 Mile — Purse $1400

EXACTA Wagering This Race

Claiming Price $3000
Mares allowed 20%, 4 year olds allowed 30%.

ASK FOR HORSE BY PROGRAM NUMBER

Saddle Cloth
TANGERINE

10

1
MS
3000

(7, 2.06½) (¾) — $17856)

SCOTCH RICE
DRIVER—FRANCS BOND—Blue, Black and White

br. g. 8, by Scotch Mercury—Meadow Betz
Vincent A. Puglisi, Buffalo, N.Y.

Trainer: V. Puglisi

10- 37¾	Btva	ms	1400	gd	3000	clm	1	.31	1.04¹	1.37	2.09¹
9- 17¾	Btva	ms	1400	gd	3000	clm	1	.31²	1.04	1.36¹	2.09⁴
4- 57	B.R.	ms		gd	Qua	h-dr	1	.32¹	1.04¹	1.41¹	2.11
4- 17	B.R.	ms		gd	Qua	h-dr	1	.32⁴	1.06¹	1.40³	2.14¹
2- 17¾	B.R.			ft	Qua		1	.32⁴	1.06¹	1.43³	2.18
1- 25¾	B.R.			sy	Qua		1	.34³	1.08⁴	1.43²	2.24
1- 21¾	B.R.			gd	Qua		1	.31³	1.05	1.39¹	2.15³

2.06½ B.R.

1977 · 1 · 0 · 0 · 0 · $ 000
1976 · 37 · 8 · 5 · 6 · $ 8744

7-2

2
MS
3000

(9, 2.03) (¾) — $67512)

EBEN JONES(N)
DRIVER—TOM SWIFT(N)—Blue, Black and White

ch. g. 13, by Adios Day—Handy Flirt
Emmett & Marilyn Koch, Lockport, N.Y.

Trainer: T. Swift

2.06½ Btva

1977 · 27 · 12 · 4 · 1 · $10628
1976 · 35 · 7 · 7 · 3 · $ 7714

5-2

3
MS
3900

(3, 2.07¾) (1) — $2957)

MISTER SALTY
DRIVER—ALEX GIULIANI (P)—Gray, Red and Black

ch. h. 4, by Calcaneus—Amoretta
Alex Giuliani, Batavia, N.Y.

Trainer: A. Giuliani

2.07¾ FlmD
2.07½ Lat (1)

1977 · 27 · 2 · 5 · 7 · $ 3357
1976 · 27 · 1 · 1 · 3 · $ 2600

8

4

(4, 2.03¾) (¾) — $35780)

PEACHTREE PARADER
DRIVER—FRANK MAHIQUES—Red, Gray and White

ch. g. 11, by Sparkle Way—Persuade
Frank Mahiques, Buffalo, N.Y.

Trainer: F. Mahiques

2.04¾ Hin
2.11¾ Leb Q

1977 · 29 · 4 · 6 · 3 · $ 2948
1976 · 7 · 0 · 1 · 0 · $ 313

VICTORIA STERLING
(5, 2.12¾ (½) — $2862)
DRIVER—ED McNEIGHT, JR.—Orange, Black and White

b. m. 6, by Noble Victory—Strange Music
Richard L. Hall, Frank R. May & Joan A. May, Eden & Angola, N. Y.

Trainer: J. Glair

Date	Trk		Dist		Cond						Time	Odds	Driver	First Three Finishers
8- 6⁷⁷	Hin	900 ft	3000 clm hcp	1	.30	1.01	1.33	2.05²	5 2⁰ 2 2 2³	2.05⁴	1.50*	(Chorner)	JboroExprss,PeachtreeParader,GramasBoy
7-30⁷⁷	Hin	900 ft	3000 clm hcp	1	.30³	1.02	1.33⁴	2.04²	2 2 2 2² 2³⁴	2.06¹	1.00*	(Chorner)	Jstalong,PeachtreeParader,SparHillMax
7-23⁷⁷	Hin	900 ft	3500 clm hcp	1	.31⁴	1.04²	1.36	2.08²	5 3⁰ 1 1 1½	2.08⁴	.80*	(Chorner)	OJSwiftlee,RckMapleDverli,PeachtreePrader

2.12¾ B.R. gd

	1977	24	0	3	5	$ 2347
	1976	27	1	2	2	$ 1751

G. V. GRATTAN
(5, 2.11 (½) — $4368)
DRIVER—DAN SARAMA—White, Orange and Red

b. m. 6, by Maynard Hanover—Sara A Grattan
Mary Ann Sarama, Corfu, N.Y.

Trainer: M. Sarama

Date	Trk		Dist		Cond						Time	Odds	Driver	First Three Finishers
10- 3⁷⁷	Btva	1400 my	3600 clm	1	.31	1.04⁴	1.37	2.09			4.90	(DSarama)	BlueAdios,ThirdSon,GlendalePisa
9- 1⁷⁷	Btva	1400 ft	3600 clm	1	.30²	1.03¹	1.34³	2.07¹			15.40	(DSarama)	SaratogaBarbara,IndianRuler,StrmyPro
8-18⁷⁷	Btva	1400 ft	3600 clm	1	.31²	1.05²	1.36	2.07³			1.80*	(DSarama)	DaringDrexel,Dsiradios,SaratogaBarbra
8-13⁷⁷	Btva	1700 ft	Qua	1	.31	1.04	1.35²	2.08⁴			1.70*	(DSarama)	GlanaradsBoy,GVGrattan,StormyPro
8- 5⁷⁷	Btva	1600 ft	3600 clm	1	.31	1.02³	1.34¹	2.07¹			7.60	(DSarama)	Peetong,RowdyGTime,BarbVolo
7-25⁷⁷	Btva	1600 ft	3600 clm	1	.30¹	1.01²	1.32⁴	2.06²			3.70	(DSarama)	BrackenField,ScottMeadow,MarysPenn

2.11 Btva

	1977	33	5	2	6	$ 7088
	1976	28	3	6	6	$ 4368

MINI GRATTAN
(5, 2.07½ (½) — $12617)
DRIVER—PHIL SORGE—Sand and Brown

b. m. 9, by Grattan Creed—Gay Coleen
Joseph M. Siracuse, Rochester, N.Y.

Trainer: P. Sorge

Date	Trk		Dist		Cond						Time	Odds	Driver	First Three Finishers
10- 4⁷⁷	Btva	1600	4200 clm	1	.31²	1.04¹	1.37	2.09			4.90	(PSorge)	BretVan,LadyColdFront,GoodAccount
9-21⁷⁷	Btva	1600 gd	4200 clm	1	.31	1.03³	1.35²	2.07²			22.20	(PSorge)	Dreamer,Lobel,Bluejayjanet,Nozzle
9- 8⁷⁷	Btva	1600 ft	4200 clm	1	.30³	1.03⁴	1.34⁴	2.07			50.10	(PSorge)	Bluejayjanet,LadyAmbro,FaysThunder
8-29⁷⁷	Btva	1600 ft	4200 clm	1	.31⁴	1.05³	1.35⁴	2.08			29.10	(PSorge)	MiracleBeau,KeystoneGallant,Nozzle
8-17⁷⁷	Btva	2100 ft	3600 clm	1	.32	1.03⁴	1.36	2.07⁴			14.00	(PSorge)	SratogaBarbara,HezaMoney,ButtnsDiamond
8- 8⁷⁷	Btva	2000 gd	4800 clm	1	.31³	1.04¹	1.36⁴	2.09²			48.30	(PSorge)	BrghtPrmise,DleonRbel,ChrminCountess
7-30⁷⁷	Btva	2300 ft	6000 clm	1	.30¹	1.01²	1.32²	2.05⁴			21.00	(PSorge)	AdmiralMark,DRsRhythm,ChrminCountss

2.08⅘ B.R.
2.12½ Btva my Q

	1977	26	1	3	2	$ 2608
	1976	35	0	4	1	$ 2410

REVEILLE DAN
(3, 2.11¾ (½) — $1265)
DRIVER—CARL MANCINELLI—Green, Gray and Black

br. g. 4, by Jeremiah Hanover—Nite Folly
Carl Mancinelli & Joseph DeAntonis, Buffalo, N.Y.

Trainer: D. Kausner

Date	Trk		Dist		Cond						Time	Odds	Driver	First Three Finishers
9-30⁷⁷	Btva	1400 my	3900 clm	1	.30³	1.02	1.35	2.10²			17.70	(CMancin)	AvnCarefree,EmpireAdios,SaintClairBuck
9- 9⁷⁷	Btva	1400 ft	3900 clm	1	.32	1.05¹	1.37²	2.09⁴			9.30	(CMancin)	EmpireAdios,GenseeCheryl,SctIndAgnes
8-29⁷⁷	Btva	1400 ft	4450 clm	1	.30⁴	1.03¹	1.34³	2.08⁴			22.50	(CMancin)	DringDrexel,RevelleDan,SratogaBarbra
8-18⁷⁷	Btva	1050 ft	3750 clm	1	.31¹	1.05	1.37²	2.07³			2.70	(CMancin)	RevelleDan,PttysBlckBird,Darneedle
8-15⁷⁷	Sycs(1) ms	900 ft	3750 clm	1	.32	1.03⁴	1.36	2.07⁴			4.90	(DKausne)	Desiradios,RevelleDan,MistyWhiz
8-13⁷⁷	Sycs(1) ms	900 gd	3750 clm	1	.30²	1.01²	1.34	2.06			7.30	(DKausne)	Tilthmmer,PttysBlackBird,DougEGrttn
8- 9⁷⁷	PcD⅝ ms		Qua dr	1	.32¹	1.03⁴	1.35²	2.07⁴			NB	(MPatst)	RevelleDan,KokoSpinner,MickeyCarol

2.07⅘ Sycs (1)
2.11½ Btva

	1977	26	1	2	4	$ 2364
	1976	9	1	1	3	$ 1265

(8) PACE CLAIMING

1 Mile — Purse $2000
EXACTA Wagering This Race

Claiming Price $6000
Mares allowed 20%, 4 year olds allowed 30%

Saddle Cloth YELLOW

ASK FOR HORSE BY PROGRAM NUMBER

---

1 — MS 7200 — 12 — 7-2

MABEL BYRD
(5. 2.06) — $12872)
DRIVER—LARRY MANGES—Red and White
b. m. 6, by Parker Byrd—Roxburgh Ruth
Nancy A. Gregor, Arcade, N.Y.

Trainer: B. Maniace (Gregor Stable)

2.06 Ornvl

	1977	32	0	4	7	$8109
	1976	42	3	13	10	$8533

---

2 — MS 6000 — 8

OLDE SOFT SHOE
(4. 2.06½ (½) — $5806)
DRIVER—JOE SARAGO—Brown and Orange
b. g. 5, by Kings Choice—Miss Volstadt
Joseph Sarago, Cheektowaga, N.Y.

Trainer: J. Sarago

2.07% Btva
2.06½ K.D. %

	1977	36	5	10	6	$10120
	1976	36	5	5	7	$5272

---

3 — MS 7200

MISS MARY DI
(6. 2.06½ (½) — $16203)
DRIVER—FRED HASLIP—Blue, White and Gold
b. m. 7, by Painter—Fuzzy Direct Guy
Mr. & Mrs. Donald Stevens, Hilton, N.Y.

Trainer: D. Stevens

2.05 Btva
2.06½ Btva

	1977	21	2	2	3	$5575
	1976	34	8	3	6	$8257

---

4 — 3

RITZY GIRL
(6. 2.04 (½) — $22109)
DRIVER—GASTON GUINDON—Brown and Gold
br. m. 7, by Ritzy Don—Dougs Girl
Jamison Acres, Elma, N.Y.

Trainer: G. Guindon

2.05 Btva gd
2.04 Btva

	1977	30	4	5	3	$9292
	1976	46	4	7	9	$12253

15

7200

8-27⁷⁷ Btva ms 2300 ft 7200 clm 1 .30² 1.02¹ 2.05³ 3 1 1 1½ 1³ 2.05³ 3.30 (GGuindo) RitzyGirl,Quickem,BeverlysJune
8-17⁷⁷ Btva ms 2500 ft 7200 clm 1 .31² 1.03 1.33² 2.07 7 6 7 5⁶ 6⁴ 2.07 9.10 (GGuindo) RaiseHobb,FreightBaron,MightyYankee
8-11⁷⁷ Btva ms 2600 ft 7200 clm 1 .30³ 1.04 1.34² 2.05⁴ 6 6 7 7 5⁴ 2.06³ 5.10 (GGuindo) EljayJoe,RaiseHobb,KennyYankee

5

6000

(5, 2.00⅗ (½) — $97987)

BROWN SONG

DRIVER—PHILIPPE LAFRAMBOISE—Blue and White

b. h. 10, by Brown Star—Melody Time
R. & J. Horton & P. Laframboise, Corfu, N.Y. & Masson, Que., Can.

Trainer: R. Horton (Laframboise Stable)

	1977				1976				

2.02⅘ Fox %

10-11⁷⁷ Btva ms 2300 ft 6000 clm 1 .31³ 1.05¹ 1.37 8 8 8 88½ 77½ 2.112 35.70 (PLafram) Crisp,IronPrince,EljayJoe
9-21⁷⁷ Btva ms 2500 gd 7000 clm 1 .33¹ 1.06 1.38 2.11 2 2ns NB (RHorton) JnnlferAdios,BrownSng,KatrinkaWann
6-18⁷⁷ Hin gd Opn 1 .30⁴ 1.04³ 1.36 2.07⁴ 3 3 2¼ 5⁷ 2.09¹ 14.10 (AGuidel) HarryW,MagicMirrorMan,KatrinkaWann
6- 5⁷⁷ Rock ms 2900 ft 7000 clm hcp 1 .30 1.01¹ 1.32² 2.03 5 7 9 8¹⁰ 2.053 34.00 (AGuidel) Glenbrae,KingVicar,SpecialRockette
5-25⁷⁷ Rock 2900 ft 7000 clm hcp 1 .30¹ 1.01² 1.32¹ 2.04² 1 1 2 6⁴ 2.051 13.90 (AGuidel) LrdBernie,KimmysDreamHigh,PrefectushHanovr
5-18⁷⁷ Rock 2800 gd 7000 clm hcp 1 .31² 1.03¹ 1.35⁴ 2.03³ 7 4 5 4½ 2.092 14.80 (AGuidel) StdyBlckBoy,KimmysDreamHigh,EmbssyIrsh
5-11⁷⁷ Rock 2400 ft 7000 clm hcp 1 .30¹ 1.01³ 1.32⁴ 2.04³ 7 7 7 6⁴½ 2.06³ 78.80 (AGuidel) HarryW,SteadyBlackBoy,BestBye

10

(6, 2.03⅘ (½) — $84371)

LUCKEY BOB DAY

DRIVER—GORD BAXTER—White, Green and Gold

gr. h. 8, by Minick Byrd—Rose Richelieu
Julian Bertozzi, Hamilton, Ont., Can.

Trainer: G. Baxter

6

6000

2.04 FlmD M.R.

10-11⁷⁷ Btva ms 2300 sy 6000 clm 1 .31³ 1.05 1.37 8 8 8 6⁵½ 65½ 4.80 (GBaxter) Crisp,IronPrince,EljayJoe
10- 3⁷⁷ Btva ms 2500 sy 7000 clm 1 .31¹ 1.02⁴ 1.35¹ 2.08² 8 7 7 40 44½ 11.80 (GBaxter) Parkwood,ScotchChaser,GoldenJuelka
9-24⁷⁷ Btva ms 2100 sy 5000 clm 1 .31 1.03² 1.34¹ 2.07 2 1 1 1² 53½ 9.20 (GBaxter) LuckeyBobDay,GoldnJuelka,MountainHavn
8-29⁷⁷ Btva GrR⅜ 2000 ft 6000 clm 1 .30⁴ 1.02⁴ 1.34¹ 2.04³ 3 2 3 7¼ 65½ 11.90 (GBaxter) CompanyMan,GranpaHnry,SaundersBoyGB
7-28⁷⁷ Btva FlmD 1400 ft 6000 clm 1 .31 1.01² 1.33² 2.05⁴ 2 3 4 2¼ 4½ 4.85 (GBaxter) BaronReal,StrfireNncy,JustSociety
6-30⁷⁷ Btva FlmD 1600 gd 7000 clm 1 .30² 1.04¹ 1.35² 2.09³ 7 4 5 5⁴ 76½ 7.75 (GBaxter) ValiantAlmhrst,MrExpo,EdgewoodKry
6- 2⁷⁷ Btva ms 2000 ft 9000 clm 1 .29³ 1.01³ 1.32² 2.04¹ 3 6 8 8¹² 45 5.90 (GBaxter) WickedMir,JeffOmaha,DonniPatch

7

5-2

(4, 2.01⅘ (⅞) — $34222)

CRISP

DRIVER—TED TURCOTTE, JR.—Yellow and Red

ch. g. 6, by Airliner—Overwhelm
Mannpa Stables, Lockport, N.Y.

Trainer: F. Marotta

	1977				1976				

2.07⅗ Btva gd

10-11⁷⁷ Btva ms 2300 sy 6000 clm 1 .31³ 1.05³ 1.37 3 4 4 2⁰ 1³ 2.10 3.20 (TTurcJr) Crisp,IronPrince,EljayJoe
10- 3⁷⁷ Btva ms 1900 gd 77nw200psCD 1 .31 1.03² 1.34¹ 2.07¹ 2 1 1 1² 1½ 2.07¹ 2.90 (TTurcJr) Crisp,ArihanoverR,GemDuval
9-24⁷⁷ Btva ms 2100 sy 5000 clm 1 .31⁴ 1.04 1.36¹ 2.08⁴ 2 1 1 1² 1¼ 2.084 1.50* (TTurcJr) Crisp,Medastar,BrackenField
9-15⁷⁷ Btva ms 1300 ft 76-7nw150ps 1 .31 1.03¹ 1.36 2.07³ 5 5 5 1nk 1¼ 2.073 3.40 (TTurcJr) Crisp,ShinnyShot,LondoHanover
9- 7⁷⁷ Btva ms 1700 ft 76-7nw175ps 1 .30³ 1.02³ 1.35² 2.06 5 10 20 43½ 1¼ 2.06 68.10 (TTurcJr) PerfectJackie,MaryMeadow,BitOfAdios
8-30⁷⁷ Btva ms 1700 ft 76-7nw175ps 1 .31³ 1.04² 1.35² 2.08 4 8 20 75³ 62½ 2.07 6.80 (TTurcJr) ReallyRoyal,EVC,HydleBird
8-19⁷⁷ Btva ms 1900 ft 76-7nw175ps 1 .31⁴ 1.04¹ 1.36² 2.08² 4 7 8 8⁸ 69¼ 2.10¹ 12.90 (TTurcJr) EVC,RadiantLady,CindyLands

6

6000

(4, 2.06⅘ (½) — $7817)

DEL LYNCH(W)

DRIVER—GERALD SARAMA—Orange and Red

b. h. 5, by Lynch Hanover—Del His Sis
James Fallon & Mae Culligan, Rochester, N.Y.

Trainer: J. Fallon

	1977				1976				

2.06⅗ Btva

10- 8⁷⁷ Btva ms 2300 sl 6000 clm 1 .32² 1.06 1.38³ 2.11³ 2 3 4 4² 62½ 2.30¹ (FHaslip) Kenwooddim,OldeSoftShoe,ProTestor
9-30⁷⁷ Btva ms 2300 my 6000 clm 1 .33 1.06¹ 1.39¹ 2.10³ 1 1 1² 1½ 1.70¹ (FHaslip) DelLynch,MugWump,RoyalU
9-21⁷⁷ Btva ms 2300 gd 6000 clm 1 .30¹ 1.03 1.34² 2.05³ 2 2⁰ 22 14 1.30¹ (FHaslip) Quickem,DelLynch,EljayJoe
9-10⁷⁷ Btva ms 2100 ft 5000 clm 1 .31¹ 1.04 1.34⁴ 2.06 1 1½ 1½ 8.90 (FHaslip) DelLynch,Peetong,Torque
8- 3⁷⁷ Btva ms 2100 ft 5000 clm 1 .30¹ 1.02¹ 1.34² 2.06² 7 7 8⁴½ 14.50 (FHaslip) EqualKash,ScottMeadow,BrackenField
8-30⁷⁷ Btva ms 1700 gd 5000 clm 1 .30⁴ 1.03⁴ 1.36 2.08 3 4 4 23 NB (GSarama) SonnyDirect,DelLynch,GrandPro
7-16⁷⁷ Btva ms 2400 ft 5000 clm 1 .35² 2.06² 8 6 74½ 3.20 (GSarama) RusselTorrence,TrueProject,BradleysGay

Note: You can't win them all. Mr. Salty won, all right, but not fair and square. After being interfered with at the start, Eben Jones finished behind G. V. Grattan, who was declared the winner.

Batavia Downs   8th Race   October 19, 1977

Let's begin by eliminating the apparent noncontenders.

1 Mabel Byrd

Although Mabel Byrd is going down in class, she has raced poorly in her last three starts and has not won a race in 1977. Lack of current form and consistency rule Mabel Byrd out as a contender.

3 Miss Mary Di

Miss Mary Di has shown next to nothing in her last four races and can be disqualified on grounds of poor recent form.

5 Brown Song

This horse shows nothing at all on the program. The qualifying race on September 21 was run in a slow time and is not in the horse's favor.

6 Luckey Bob Day

This horse ran a good race on September 24 but has not shown much in his last two starts. Outside post position is also a hindrance.

8 Del Lynch

After being idle for more than a month, this horse ran impressively in three straight races. In his last race Del Lynch was boxed in over the last half. However, even making allowances for this race, Del Lynch does not figure to be a contender here because of his outside post position and the caliber of his opposition.

The contenders stack up as follows:

2 Olde Soft Shoe

This horse was claimed for $6,000 two months ago and has been unsuccessful racing in $7,000 and $8,000 claimers. However, Olde Soft Shoe is now in a class in which he can compete successfully, as is evidenced by the race on October 8. Definitely a contender.

4 Ritzy Girl

After three straight wins in this class, Ritzy Girl has been unimpressive in her last two starts. Her last race on October 8 can be

excused in part because of a poor post position and Ritzy Girl's being trapped behind Olde Soft Shoe over the last half.

7 Crisp

How can we argue with a horse that has won his last four starts, all easily? With a good driver, Crisp is handicapped only by his post position. He may run into trouble going for the lead or moving at the half, whichever course the driver decides on.

Analysis. Ritzy Girl is a maneuverable horse, and her driver can either take her to the front right away or wait until the half before making a move. Ditto for Crisp and Del Lynch. Olde Soft Shoe will probably go at the half. If Crisp is able to gain the lead easily, he will be tough. However, since Crisp has an outside post position and the remaining contenders are evenly matched, it is a good idea to pass this race.

Results.

EIGHTH RACE — 1 Mile							$6000 Claiming Pace			$2000
Olde Soft Shoe ms	2	4	4	2o	2¹⁴	1ns	J. Sarago			5.80
Crisp ms	7	1o	1	1	1nk	2¹½	T. Turcotte, Jr.			2.40
c Ritzy Girl	4	2o	2	3	3¹⁴	3hd	G. Guindon			*1.60
Del Lynch ms	8	8	7	6o	5³	4nk	G. Sarama			6.90
Mabel Byrd ms	1	3	3	5	6³	5¹½	L. Manges			17.20
Miss Mary Di ms	3	5	5	4o	4hd	6½	F. Haslip			5.50
Brown Song ms	5	6	6	7	8	7¹⁴	P. Laframboise			45.00
Luckey Bob Day ms	6	7	8	8	7½	8	G. Baxter			20.00
$2 MUTUEL PRICES		2. Olde Soft Shoe						13.60	6.80	2.80
Official Program Nos.		7. Crisp							6.00	3.80
		4. Ritzy Girl								2.80

Time — .31   1.03³⁵   1.35⅓   2.07
EXACTA — 2 AND 7 $71.60
Ritzy Girl claimed by Loubred Stable, Louisville, Ky. (Tr. W. Witten)

6 PACE CLAIMING

1 Mile — Purse $2200

EXACTA Wagering This Race

Claiming Price $7000
Mares allowed 20%, 4 year old geldings allowed 30%, 4 year old mares allowed 50%.

ASK FOR HORSE BY PROGRAM NUMBER

Saddle Cloth
BLUE

1
MS
10500

SHADY HILL DAISY
(3, 2.14¼ (½) — $638)
DRIVER—LARRY WITTCOP (P)—Red and Gold
br. m. 4, by Tarport Robbie—Daisy Lochinver
Gerald Gilbert Lockport, N.Y.

										Trainer: G. Gilbert			
										2.05½ Btva	1977	27 7 4 4 $ 8740
										2.14¼ Btva sl	1976	7 1 0 0 638
10-15⁷⁷	Btva	ms	2200	ft	10500 clm	1.31¹	1.03²	1.35¹	2.08	2	5²	5²³	2.08³	5.70	(LWittco)	Prkwood,JustASpiner,GoldenJuelka(Pl 4)	60
10- 8⁷⁷	Btva	ms	2300	sl	9000 clm	1.32	1.06³	1.39⁴	2.12²	6	6³⁴	6³⁴	2.13	3.90	(TSwift)	Sphrunia,MyBrothersHorse,ScotchChaser	50
10- 1⁷⁷	Btva	ms	2500	sy	9000 clm	1.31³	1.04²	1.42¹	2.08³	7	7⁴	5¹	2.084	4.70	(Teichas)	TerrAdios,JimmieCollins,MEPoplar	53
9-22⁷⁷	Btva	ms	2100	ft	7500 clm	1.31¹	1.03¹	1.344	2.07¹	7	2²	5¹	2.07¹	6.70	(Teichas)	ShdyHillDaisy,JffersnSloPke,RwdyGTime	52
9-10⁷⁷	Btva	ms	2300	ft	9000 clm	1.31¹	1.04¹	1.35	2.06	3	3³	1⁴	2.06	5.80	(Teichas)	StarMon,ShadyHillDaisy,MugWump	62
8-31⁷⁷	Btva	ms	2100	ft	7500 clm	1.30¹	1.04²	1.35²	2.07	5	2¹	2²	2.07¹	1.70	(Teichas)	HonorKennedy,ShadyHillDaisy,BredByrd	80
8-18⁷⁷	Btva	ms	2400	ft	7500 clm	1.30⁴	1.03	1.35²	2.064	5	6	7⁸³	46	.70	(Teichas)	SuperLaird,TerrAdios,SuccessGrant	65

2
MS
7000

COMBAT SPUD
(6, 2.06¹ (½) — $3254)
DRIVER—AL MARIACHER—White, Gold and Red
ch. g. 7, by Combat Time—Our Elizabeth
Kathleen Mariacher, Buffalo, N.Y.

										Trainer: A. Mariacher			
										2.06⅗ Btva Q	1977	10 1 0 0 669
										2.06⅕ Btva sl	1976	17 5 1 2 1501
10-14⁷⁷	Btva	ms	1600	ft	77nw200pscD	1.31	1.02³	1.35³	2.08	2	2¹	4³¹	2.083	2.60*	(AMariac)	KathyBright,FlyStraight,AriHanoverR	40
10- 3⁷⁷	Btva	ms	2900	gd	9000 clm	1.30²	1.02⁴	1.34¹	2.06¹	4	4³¹	6³³	2.07	17.50	(AMariac)	HoneyGun,ThunderImp,StNick	51
9-26⁷⁷	Btva	ms	2300	sy	77nw225gCSD	1.30³	1.02⁴	1.33²	2.05¹	8	5¹	6⁴¹	2.07	38.40	(AMariac)	PagesAdios,LegsGinnBrooke,MannrtDamsl	60
9-16⁷⁷	Btva	ms	1700	ft	76-7nw175ps	1.31¹	1.05²	1.38	2.09¹	7	8	6³¹	2.10	12.20	(AMariac)	StansPride,Perquimansindian,RadiantLady	63
9- 5⁷a	Btva	ms	1700	gd	76-7nw175ps	1.30⁴	1.03	1.34²	2.05⁴	1	3	4⁴³	2.06	3.20	(AMariac)	SiriusRuss,CombatSpud,ScotchMeadow	72
8-30⁷⁷	Btva	ms	1800	ft	5000 clm	1.31²	1.02¹	1.34²	2.06¹	2	1¹	1⁵	2.06¹	5.80	(AMariac)	CombatSpud,OoTarGratn,BanrsPrince	75
8-26⁷⁷	Btva	ms	2400	ft	Qua	1.31¹	1.03²	1.35²	2.07	4	6	7⁶³	4⁴¹	NB	(AMariac)	CaptainRed,JRBlaze,GreyBelleGerry	75

3
MS
8400

LITTLE HOT SHOT(w)
(3, 2.03¾ (½) — $19588)
DRIVER—DON CROSSETT(w)—Tan and Brown
b. m. 6, by Pioneer Pick—Meadow Fanny
Donald & Nellie Crossett, Holcomb, N.Y.

										Trainer: D. Crossett			
										2.02⅔ V.D. ¾	1977	32 8 1 4 6850
										2.04⅗ Stga	1976	26 4 4 2 6305
10-12⁷⁷	V.D. ¾	ms	8400	clm hcp	1.29²	1.02²	2.05¹	2	2	8¹¹	2.07²	10.20	(DCrosse)	MyMyBrooklyn,DoubleRoan,Prime	45
10- 5⁷⁷	V.D. ¾	ms	1900	ft	7000 clm hcp	1.28⁴	1.02¹	1.32¹	2.03⁴	4	2	2²¹	2.034	3.90	(TSwift)	LittleHotShot,MissBettingTime,Custmry	55
9-28⁷⁷	V.D. ¾	ms	1900	ft	7000 clm hcp	1.29¹	1.03	1.33²	2.06²	5	1	5³	2.07	4.40	(TSwift)	MissBettingTime,Customary,SndownPrince	55
9-20⁷⁷	V.D. ¾	ms	1800	ft	7000 clm hcp	1.29¹	1.02¹	1.32²	2.05³	6	1¹	1³	2.05³	3.00	(BKomell)	LittleHotShot,RaceyBel,SamBengazi	50
9-13⁷⁷	V.D. ¾	my	5000	clm	1.30²	1.04	1.36⁴	2.09¹	2	2	4¹¹	2.09²	3.40	(BKomell)	TimeForFrills,SomeNerve,FigaroDixyDo	60
9- 6⁷⁷	V.D. ¾	ms	1800	ft	5000 clm	1.28³	1.01¹	1.314	2.02³	2	1¹	1³	2.02³	3.50	(BKomell)	LittleHotShot,TimeForFrills,BentonBoss	60
8-30⁷⁷	V.D. ¾	ms	5000	clm	1.29¹	1.01¹	1.314	2.05³	4	5	7⁴	2.032	8.70	(BKomell)	HartTJ,TwentyTwo,BentonBoss	70

4
MS
8400

KEYSTONE WHIZ
(5, 2.02¼ (½) — $158855)
DRIVER—TOM SWIFT—Blue, Black and White
b. h. 11, by Lehigh Hanover—Winged Foot
Tom Swift & Beverly Ann Caprio, Akron, N.Y.

										Trainer: T. Swift			
										2.05 Btva	1977	35 5 11 8 14508
										2.05⅓ Btva	1976	43 8 9 6 15839
10-13⁷⁷	Btva	ms	2500	ft	7000 clm	1.30²	1.01⁴	1.33²	2.06¹	4	4⁵³	4⁴¹	2.06¹	3.80	(TSwift)	Baratony,IconAdios,MarkMinbar	40
10- 6⁷⁷	Btva	ms	2500	ft	7000 clm	1.30	1.01⁴	1.33	2.06	5	2¹	2²¹	2.06¹	10.30	(TSwift)	MarkMinbar,Merry,JohnA,Baratony	53
9-29⁷⁷	Btva	ms	2500	ft	7000 clm	1.31⁴	1.03¹	1.342	2.054	5	5³	66¹	2.064	16.10	(TSwift)	NotableBaron,MarkMinbar,MarysHeel	55
9-20⁷⁷	Btva	ms	2500	gd	7000 clm	1.29	1.314	1.32²	2.05³	3	5	4²¹	2.054	1.40*	(TSwift)	NotableBaron,MarkMinbar,AvonFairline	58

5-2 · 7000 · LADY WILLOWAY

DRIVER—YVON DEMERS—White, Black and Red

(3, 2.11¾ (½) — $1353)

b. m. 4, by Meadow Gene—Bills Flame
Guy Joanis, Montebello, Que., Can.

Trainer: Y. Demers

9- 7⁷⁷	Btva	2500	ft	7000 clm	1	.30² 1.01⁴ 1.33⁴ 2.05	1	3	3	2	1²	2.40	(TSwift)	KeystoneWhiz,AvonFairline,MarysHeel	63
8-26⁷⁷	Btva	2500	ft	7000 clm	1	.32 1.03 1.34 2.04	2	3	3	3½	3½	2.05¹	(TSwift)	MarkMinbar,NotableBaron,KeystoneWhiz	76
8-20⁷⁷	Btva	2700	ft	7000 clm	1	.29⁴ 1.00⁴ 1.33² 2.05¹	4	5	5	4½	4²½	1.60*	(TSwift)	MarkMinbar,KeystoneWhiz,ScotchChaser	65

2.03¾ Rich · 2.11¾ Emira

---

8 · 10500 · NOTABLE BARON

DRIVER—MARC BOURGON—Blue, Gold and White

(5, 2.05¾ (½) — $17791)

b. g. 6, by Baron Hanover—Lady Beth
Wilfrid J. Bourgon, Montreal, Que., Can.

Trainer: M. Bourgon (Bourgon Stable)

10-13⁷⁷	Btva	2500	ft	7000 clm	1	.30 1.01⁴ 1.33² 2.06¹	7	8	7⁸	7⁸½	6⁶¹	4.20	(MBourgo)	Baratony,IconAdios,MarkMinbar	40
9-26⁷⁷	Btva	2500	sy	13500 clm	1	.30 1.01⁴ 1.33 2.06	5	6	6	7	4²³	4.90	(MBourgo)	MarkMinbar,MerryJohnA,Baratony	55
9-20⁷⁷	Btva	2700	sl	9600 clm	1	.31¹ 1.03¹ 1.34³ 2.05³	2	2	2¹	1¹	1¹	4.20	(MBourgo)	NotableBaron,MarkMinbar,MarysHeel	58
9-13⁷⁷	Btva	1900	ft	7000 clm	1	.29 .59⁴ 1.32² 2.05²	2	2	2	1	1²	1.60*	(WBourgo)	NotableBaron,AvonFairline	66
9-5a⁷⁷	Btva	2700	gd	8000 clm	2	.30⁴ 1.02⁴ 1.34 2.05	3	4	4	6³½	6⁴½	4.80	(YDemers)	LAmiBamby,LadyWilloway,ConchoByrd	73
8-26⁷⁷	Btva	2500	ft	13500 clm	1	.32 1.03 1.34 2.04	6	6	7	4	2¹	4.70	(MBourgo)	MarkMinbar,NotableBaron,KeystoneWhiz	72
8-16⁷⁷	Btva	2700	sy	7000 clm	1	.30 1.02 1.32² 2.03¹	8	7	7⁰	3	3²	17.70	(MBourgo)	JustASpinner,SirAladoh,NotableBaron	75

2.03¾ Btva · 2.05¾ B.R.

---

15 · 7000 · GRAY EDNA

DRIVER—BRUCE TUBIN (P)—Blue, White and Red

(4, 2.08½ (½) — $7478)

ro. m. 5, by Glendale Indian—Ednas Lady
Ronald Smith, Endicott, N.Y.

Trainer: N. Fluet (Tubin Stable)

10-14⁷⁷	Btva	1600	ft	77nw200psCD	1	.31 1.02³ 1.35² 2.08	5	5	5	6⁶½	7¹⁰⁴	12.50	(BTubin)	KathyBright,FlyStraight,AriHanoverR	40
10- 6⁷⁷	Btva	8400	ft	77nw200ps	3	.30 1.01⁴ 1.33² 2.06	2	4	4	4²³	6²²	17.00	(BTubin)	MarkMinbar,MerryJohnA,Baratony	53
9-28⁷⁷	Btva	9600	sy	76-7nw200ps	7	.30² 1.03 1.34³ 2.05²	4	7⁰	8⁶½	7⁴	7⁰	34.10	(BTubin)	DuzHerbert,WiscoyByrd,LadyWilloway	58
9-22⁷⁷	Btva	1900	ft	76-7nw200ps	4	.30² 1.03 1.34² 2.07	5	7	7	6¹⁴	6¹¹	6.40	(BTubin)	OJWiscoy,AdieuRose,NobleMoran	52
9-10⁷⁷	Btva	1900	ft	76-7nw200ps	1	.30² 1.03¹ 1.34² 2.05²	20	3	3	8¹	7⁹³	3.30	(BTubin)	JfftersonPlayboy,BulletBill,NobleMoran	62
9- 5⁷⁷	Btva	1900	ft	76-7nw200ps	1	.30¹ 1.01⁴ 1.34 2.04⁴	4	6¹	16	6⁶²	2¹⁴	9.50	(NFluet)	IrtonPrince,StansPride,OldeSoftShoe	73
8-29⁷⁷	ms	2700	sy	7000 clm	1	.30¹ 1.03 1.34 2.05²	5	6	4⁰	2¹⅓	2¹⅓	8.00	(BTubin)	PaulJ,GrayEdna,Romero	75

2.05¾ Btva · 2.08½ Btva

---

5 · 9100 · BARATONY

DRIVER—FRED BRANSTON—Green and White

(3, 2.07¾ (½) — $4765)

br. g. 4, by Lochinver Tony—Queenie Blossom
Raymond Chebott & Beverley Gallant, London, Ont., Can.

Trainer: F. Branston

10-13⁷⁷	Btva	2500	ft	9100 clm	1	.30² 1.01⁴ 1.33² 2.06¹	5	3⁰	3¹¼	1ns	2.50	(FBranst)	Baratony,IconAdios,MarkMinbar	40
9-26⁷⁷	Btva	2500	ft	9100 clm	1	.30 1.01⁴ 1.33 2.06	6	4⁰	4	3¹⅓	3¹⅓	1.60*	(FBranst)	MarkMinbar,MerryJohnA,Baratony	53
9-26⁷⁷	Btva	2900	sy	11700 clm	1	.30 1.03² 1.34³ 2.05²	4	2⁰	2⁰	8⁷	8⁵²	17.90	(FBranst)	ThunderImp,BeautysBoy,HoneyGun	60
9-14⁷⁷	Btva	1900	ft	9100 clm	1	.30 1.02¹ 1.32⁴ 2.04¹	4	5	5	4²¼	2.20	(FBranst)	Baratony,MountainHaven,GoldenJuelka	62
9- 2⁷⁷	Btva	1900	ft	9100 clm	1	.30 1.01 1.32⁴ 2.04⁴	3	3³¼	3²¼	4.00	(FBranst)	DelmerWynwood,AdiosFlyboy,Baratony	75
8-26⁷⁷	Btva	2500	ft	9100 clm	1	.32 1.03 1.33 2.04	8	8	8⁰	5⁵	17.00	(FBranst)	MarkMinbar,NotableBaron,KeystoneWhiz	76
8-20⁷⁷	Btva	2700	ft	9100 clm	1	.29⁴ 1.00⁴ 1.33² 2.05¹	8	8	8	6⁸²	30.50	(FBranst)	MarkMinbar,KeystoneWhiz,ScotchChaser	65

2.04½ Btva · 2.07¾ Sudly

	1977	1976				
	36	14	9	9	5	$ 16145
	25	7	2	4	$ 11133
	32	4	2	6	$ 5999
	22	4	2	3	$ 6790

Analysis. Little Hot Shot will no doubt go to the front and will park out all challengers in a fast first quarter. To be successful here, Baratony may have to fall in second or third behind the leader. Keystone Whiz and Lady Willoway may be sent at the half, although it is likely that Keystone Whiz will be saved for the stretch. Lady Willoway is the class of this race and the best choice to win.

Results.

SIXTH RACE — 1 Mile								$7000 Claiming Pace	$2200
Lady Willoway ms	5	6	5	2^{02}	2^2	$1\frac{3}{2}$		Y. Demers	*1.40
Keystone Whiz	4	2	3	1	1hd	$2^{1}\frac{1}{2}$		T. Swift	2.20
Little Hot Shot ms	3	3	4	3^0	3^1	3hd		D. Crossett	8.20
Combat Spud ms	2	x5	7	6	5^6	4^1		A. Mariacher	19.40
Baratony ms	8	8	6	5^0	$4\frac{1}{2}$	5^2		F. Branston	6.00
Shady Hill Daisy ms	1	4	x8	8	6^3	6^3		L. Wittcop	26.60
Gray Edna ms	7	7	2^0	7^0	$7\frac{1}{2}$	$7^5\frac{1}{2}$		B. Tubin	30.50
Notable Baron ms	6	1^0	1	4	8	8		M. Bourgon	6.60
$2 MUTUEL PRICES		5. Lady Willoway					4.80	3.20	2.40
Official Program Nos.		4. Keystone Whiz						3.40	2.60
		3. Little Hot Shot							3.00

Time — .30⅘   1.03⅗   1.35⅖   2.07⅕
EXACTA — 5 AND 4 $13.20

The Handicapper's Notebook

We have already emphasized the value of saving the results charts of previous evenings' programs. For the serious handicapper, this is but one valuable means for predicting the results of future races. A committed handicapper will also retain programs as a basis for comparing the competition in specific races from week to week. These are particularly useful to someone who views a race rationally and wishes to make notes about it. Suppose that watching the first race on the card, you notice the following occurrences: Horse A was boxed in during the entire last half of the race; horse B was parked three wide in the stretch; horse C was parked out for almost the entire mile and was forced to go three wide in the backstretch to circle the pack.

Why might these notes be valuable to the handicapper? Isn't this information included in the results chart of the race and in future programs? The answer is, unfortunately, no. Most raceway programs do not show that horse A was boxed in, that B was forced to go three wide at the head of the stretch, or that C was on the outside for almost the entire mile—and not just the last half. The wise handicapper will

therefore note these happenings and attach them in written form to the appropriate page in his program. This will enable him to give more weight to the performances of these horses than the program permits. He will not be able to write off A as a horse without a stretch kick but will consider the horse a genuine contender in its next start. Similarly, he will recognize that B and especially C have excuses for not winning and that C in particular may be an excellent bet next time out.

In addition to notes about specific races, the notebook will contain a "book" on a number of horses worth watching. It will show, for example, that a particular horse races well in the slop, and the book may even contain a file on "mudders." Additionally, a handicapper's notebook will group together the horses in a number of important stables and will show whether the horses in a particular stable are improving as a lot, whether only one or two are in peak condition at a time, or whether none are yet in peak form. In this way, tabs can be kept on the leading trainers and trainer-drivers to see whether they are on winning or losing streaks.

Last but not least, the notebook will contain a rather delicate bit of information. This is the handicapper's "track record," his play-by-play account of the profits and losses he undergoes from day to day. Most of us are all too willing to exaggerate our triumphs and minimize our setbacks. An accurate record of credits and debits is required in the interests of honesty and enables the handicapper to take a hard-boiled, realistic look at how he is doing. Too many setbacks will indicate that a fresh appraisal of either handicapping procedures or betting patterns, or both, is essential.

This means that the notebook will contain a strict statement of every bet made and the precise amount won or lost right up to the present. It will also include a report of the amounts spent on nightly jaunts to the raceway, on programs, etc. By keeping this record, one can learn quickly enough whether betting on races should be a vocation, a hobby, or even a cause for visitation to a psychiatrist. It might even, if it shows success, convince an angry spouse that all the time we have been devoting to those damned horses is really going to pay off in dollars and cents. Well, maybe!

5
A Point System for Handicapping Harness Races

How to Handicap a Race by Assigning Points to Each Horse

This system is designed for play on claiming races, especially paces. It has proved its success over many years of wagering on harness races at Buffalo Raceway and Batavia Downs. My experience shows that the system is far less successful when used to handicap conditioned races. Moreover, it will not work well for *cheap* claiming races in which the animals show little or no consistency. It should be applied to claiming races in the range of $3,000 and up.

The system does not pretend to be more than a helpful *guide* to successful handicapping. At the very least it is a successful tool for eliminating noncontenders. It may not do the job of separating two or three genuine contenders in some races. In other words, it does not always guarantee to produce the *one* best bet in a race.

Handicapping is still an art and depends in no small measure on a sense of what's going on in a race. A smart handicapper will pass on many races simply because no one or even two horses are the play. When this happens, the point system should score an almost equal number of points for each of the contenders. And unless you can find a bona fide overlay in the race, you should pass.

The Six Major Criteria
The point system takes six basic factors into account:

1. Current form
2. Consistency
3. Class
4. Driver
5. Post position
6. Racing strategy

Current Form

Current form is probably the most important consideration in handicapping a race. Assign two points for each win and one point for each place *up to four points* in the horse's last three starts. This means that a horse that won two of its last three starts will receive the maximum four points; a horse that placed twice in its last three starts will receive only two points.

But suppose a horse has been idle for a month since its last start? In that case, don't bet the animal at all, for it has no *current* form. Current form, to be current, can't take us back more than a month or so.

For a number of reasons, it's necessary to go back at least three starts and sometimes more in assigning points for current form. The first reason has to do with a horse's starting from outside post positions in some or all of its recent trips. Often a driver will not push a horse if it is too far back at the beginning of a race unless an opportunity offers itself—and frequently, not even then. If the program shows that a horse started from an outside post position (especially 7 or 8) and *ran out of form,* finishing well back in contrast to other recent starts, discount that particular race. Go back still another race and count that instead.

A second exception to our three-race rule deals with races in which a horse goes for the lead and is parked outside for most or all of the mile. This usually takes so much out of the animal that it has nothing left for the stretch. Again, such races should not be counted as a fair test of a horse's current form.

Last, a horse boxed for the mile or the last part of it cannot be considered as turning in a representative performance. This, too, should be discounted when you assign points for current form.

Consistency

The test of consistency, as we have seen, is crucial in handicapping. An on-and-off horse is seldom, if ever, worth betting. We wish to confine our wagering to horses that demonstrate consistency over the season. The best test of consistency is the overall record of a horse's finishes during the year. A steed that winds up either first or second in more than half of its races is a very consistent animal indeed. One that wins or places in less than 20 percent of its races is an inconsistent animal, for our purposes. Here is a scheme for awarding points according to a horse's overall record for the year:

4 points—win or place 50 percent of all starts
3 points—win or place 40 to 50 percent of all starts
2 points—win or place 30 to 40 percent of all starts
1 point—win or place 20 to 30 percent of all starts
0 points—win or place less than 20 percent of all starts

Class

We propose to treat class differently than current form and consistency. If a horse is going down in class, I would add two points to its total for each identifiable class the horse is being dropped. For example, if a horse is being dropped from a $5,000 to a $4,000 claimer, add two points to its total. But if it is being dropped from a $5,000 to a $3,000 claimer, add four points. By the same token, subtract two points for each step a horse is being moved *up* in class. So a horse being moved from a $3,000 to a $4,000 claimer will have two points deducted from its total score.

Driver

Up to three points can be awarded for the caliber of driver in a race. A driver who is in the money in more than 50 percent of his races or who wins more than 20 percent of his races should be assigned three points. A driver on a hot streak or one who has been in the money in his last five starts should also be assigned three points. A driver who wins about 15 percent of his races and is in the money about 40 percent of the time should be awarded two points. Drivers who are less successful but who finish in the money up to 40 percent of the time get one point. Finally, drivers on cold streaks, provisional drivers, and drivers who are generally unsuccessful receive no points.

To summarize:

On hot streaks—3 points
In the money 50 percent of the time—3 points
In the money 40 percent of the time—2 points
In the money up to 40 percent of the time—1 point
On cold streaks—0 points
Provisional drivers and losers—0 points

Post Position

Post position is the easiest factor in a race to handicap. Assign points as follows:

1 or 2—3 points

3 or 4—2 points
5 or 6—1 point
7 or 8—0 points

Racing Strategy

How a race will be run is another crucial factor in handicapping, but it is often difficult to assign points in this category simply because we have no clear idea how a race will go. However, in races in which the strategy is fairly clear and favors a specific horse, award the animal 1 to 3 points.

For example, a front-runner that can be expected to get the lead easily from the 4 hole and to hold it without difficulty should be assigned three points. A stretch horse in a race chock full of front-runners would also receive a three-point bonus. But a strong closer sitting behind one or two other stretch horses would probably get no points.

You can also *deduct* points for a horse's being in a very unfavorable position in a race. For example, a front-runner leaving from the 5 hole, with another front-runner inside him in the 3 or 4 hole, is at a decided disadvantage. Points should be deducted for such a horse.

You must use subjective judgment in awarding points in this category, since no cut and dried formula seems applicable to quantifying how a race will be run.

Recent Change to Modified Sulky

The modified sulky has come into prominence at harness tracks only during the last year or two. Since then, a large number of horses which formerly raced with the conventional sulky have been converted to it, although not every track permits its use.

For many horses, the change to a modified sulky adds precious seconds to their performance. It can therefore become an important factor in the outcome of a race, particularly if a horse is just changing to it.

Example: During the past few months, a number of horses have been claimed out of races at tracks that do not permit the modified sulky and moved to tracks that do. In virtually every instance the horse's performance improved dramatically. Here are two examples:

However, not all horses increase their speed with the adoption of the modified sulky. Some perform exactly as before, and a few can-

(6, 2.03¾) (½) — $31246)

MARK MINBAR

DRIVER—CARMAN HIE—Blue and Gold

blk. g. 7, by Thorpe Hanover—Harrys Carol
Michael Kuzub, Burlington, Ont., Can.

Trainer: C. Hie

	1977	26	5	4	2	$ 7160
2.04¾ Btva	1976	35	6	4	9	$16443
2.03¾ B.R.						

8-26⁷⁷	Btva	ms	2500	clm	1	.32	1.03³	1.34	2.04⁴	1	2	2	2¹	2.044	1.70* (CHie)	MarkMinbar,NotableBaron,KeystoneWhiz
8-20⁷⁷	Btva	ms	2700	clm	1	.29⁴	1.00⁴	1.33²	2.05¹	2	2	2	1¹	2.05¹	2.00 (CHie)	MarkMinbar,KeystoneWhiz,ScotchChaser
8- 4⁷⁷	GrR%		2000	ft	1	.30¹	1.01³	1.32¹	2.04	6	1	1	1¹	2.041	4.35 (CHie)	GaysBequest,MarkMinbar,MaggiesFlight
8- 1⁷⁷	GrR%		2200	ft	1	.31	1.02¹	1.32²	2.03²	9	5	5	4	2.043	6.60 (CHie)	DanLoblI,BelyeArnknight,CrowdPleasr
7- 6⁷⁷	GrR%		Qua		1	.31²	1.01³	1.32²	2.04⁴	4	1	3	4⁵₄	NB	(CHie)	KeystoneSwatara,ArmrHill,ByeByeIrish
7-20⁷⁷	GrR%		1800	ft	1	.30¹	1.01	1.31²	2.03	5	3	3	4⁵₄	4.90 (CHie)	HJFashion,NativeHill,MarkMinbar
7-14⁷⁷	GrR%		1800	clm	1	.30³	1.01³	1.32¹	2.05	x7	9	9	2¹₂	21.20 (CHie)	BermacNorma,MarkMinbr,BelyeArnknight

---

(5, 2.03¾) (½) — $22189)

PERFECT JACKIE

DRIVER—GERALD SARAMA—Orange and Red

b. m. 6, by Perfect Wave—Jacqueline Chief
Howard Dinning, Windsor, Ont., Can.

Trainer: H. Dinning

	1977	29	1	3	4	$ 3388
2.06 Btva	1976	48	2	5	8	$ 8750
2.03¾ Btva						

8-30⁷⁷	Btva	ms	1700	ft	76-7nw175ps	1.33²	2.06	2	4	4⁰	4²₂	1nk	2.06	3.90 (GSarama)	PrfectJckie,Prquimans,Indian,ClaudsTwn	76
8- 9⁷⁷	FlmD		1100	ft	c-4800	1.33²	1.34⁴	2.06³	7	1	1	2²₄	2.07¹	1.40* (JMuttar)	KnotreKatie,PerfectJckie,HastyDandy
8- 2⁷⁷	FlmD		1200	ft	c-4800	1.33¹	2.07²	3	6	2⁰	3¹₄	2.07³	4.55 (JMuttar)	RoyalLeeN,Mr.Expo,PerfectJackie
7-27⁷⁷	FlmD		1200	ft	6000	1.30⁴	1.03	1.35³	2.07²	4	4	2⁰	3¹	2.08¹	2.60 (JMuttar)	TaybroTarka,KngMacMillan,KBEllen
7-21⁷⁷	FlmD		1200	ft	6000	1.30¹	1.03¹	1.34³	2.07	4	9	20	5³₂	2.08¹	2.60 (JMuttar)	TaybroTarka,KngMacMillan,KBEllen
7-21⁷⁷	FlmD		1200	ft	6000	1.30¹	1.02³	1.35	2.08	x3	9	8	7⁹₄	2.094	2.10* (JMuttar)	TrportBloom,SokysColt,PrkwoodByeBye
7-12⁷⁷	FlmD		1100	ft	c-4800	1.30¹	1.01¹	1.33²	2.06⁴	4	4	2	2⁹	2.90* (RKenned)	ManassasJoe,PrfectJckie,MidWay
7- 5⁷⁷	FlmD		900	ft	3600	1.30¹	1.02¹	1.33²	2.04⁴	6	2	1	2¹	2.05	5.25 (RKenned)	LstAttorneyJhn,PerfctJackie,RindyBeeAdios	69

not adapt to the new sulky at all. However, when a horse shows visible improvement after being changed to the modified sulky, add two points to its total. If a horse is changing to a modified sulky for the first time, you may wish to bet the animal providing that it figures as a contender by ordinary handicapping.

I suggest that you assign points first for consistency and current form, taking class into account, and then assign points for driver and post position. Last, analyze the race in terms of the way you think it will be run and assign points accordingly.

A horse should have a minimum of eight points before you play it. Moreover, a horse should have two points under current form and two points under two of the following three headings to be playable: consistency, driver, and post position. A favorite, to be playable, should have a minimum of two points in all four respects.

In addition, the horse you favor should be at least two points better than any other horse in the race. This is not a hard-and-fast rule, but you will ordinarily want to play horses that have proven success as well as an advantage in their race (driver, post position). This will translate into a high point total.

Often, but not always, such horses will be favorites in their races. The public often passes up a good bet to back another horse, particularly when its apparent times are better than the horse that figures by our system. In fact, you will probably discover that the horse with the most points in a race will be a favorite about 50 percent of the time. As a result, you will get a respectable share of overlays using the point system.

Your first response might be that this system leaves you with almost no races to bet. But that is untrue. On the average, you will find at least three or four races on an evening's card in which a horse scores a minimum of eight points and is at least two points higher than any other horse in the race. Moreover, the point system yields an exceptionally high percentage of horses that finish in the money. I suggest that you employ it to handicap a number of claiming paces during a week or two and analyze the results in terms of straight win, place, and show betting. You may conclude that the system is more effective for place or show betting than for straight win wagering.

Close Decisions
What happens when there is a difference of at most a point or two

between contenders in a race? Suppose that two or even three horses are separated by no more than a point or two. Should the race be thrown out as unplayable or can a test be proposed for breaking the deadlock?

Close decisions are inevitable in a system of the kind we have elaborated, because we have used only a few handicapping criteria, together with an uncomplicated procedure for assigning points. In addition, racing secretaries take great pains to match horses as closely as possible. On ½-mile tracks it is not unusual for a race to be decided by 1/5 second or less.

Three tests, which can be used to compare the current form of contenders, follow. In each case the test offers the means of assigning bonus points by which close decisions can be resolved. These tests—stretch gain, early speed, and roughing it on the outside—should be applied to recent starts in which the contenders have finished first or second. In so doing, it will be possible to determine how vigorously the contenders competed in the races used to assign point totals.

Stretch Gain

The first test for comparing the form displayed by different animals in recent starts is the amount of ground each gained in the stretch in their races. Assume that the performance lines for horses A and B are from races of the same class with hypothetically identical fractional times of :31, 1:04, 1:35, and 2:06.

	PP	¼	½	¾	str.		fin.
A	1	2	2	2	$2^{1/2}$		2^2
B	2	4	5	7	7^6	2^2	

Which horse ran a better race? A's performance leaves much to be desired. Leaving from the rail, A was able to tuck in behind the leader, having the advantage of a windscreen until the three-quarter mark. From this point to the finish A was in excellent position to take the lead and win but instead faded badly in the stretch, finishing two lengths behind the winner.

B, on the other hand, was shuffled back to seventh place, six lengths behind the leader at the head of the stretch, yet was able to pick up four lengths through the stretch.

A had no excuse for quitting in the stretch after having a "perfect trip" from the start—plenty of racing room, no interference, etc. A

was merely sucked along by the leader to a deceptively fast time (2:06 2/5) and a second-place finish.

B, on the other hand, after being boxed for most of the last half, showed a strong kick in the stretch. For this reason alone, we must consider B a far better wagering prospect next time out. As a rule of thumb, a stretch gain of three lengths or more should be assigned a bonus point when the races of contenders are being compared.

Roughing It

A still more important consideration is a horse's ability to rough it on the outside for a quarter of a mile or more, yet finish first or second. A horse that can pace on the outside must be fit, for roughing it requires an animal to add several lengths to the distance it has to run each quarter. A horse is to receive one bonus point for *each* quarter mile it is parked out. Keeping the same fractional and final times as in the previous example, consider the following variation:

	PP	¼	½	¾	str.	fin.
A	1	2	2	2	1^1	1^{ns}
B	4	5	7	5^0	3^2	1^2

Again, B's race is far superior to A's. A was barely able to hang on in the stretch after having everything its own way. B, losing ground until the half, pulled out and roughed it over the last ½ mile, destroying the field with its stretch kick.

B deserves two bonus points here—one for roughing it over the last half and one for stretch gain. Clearly, if A and B are contenders in tonight's race, B is the stronger of the two, at least on the basis of a comparison of their recent winning efforts.

Early Speed

A final element that can be used to separate contenders is the ability to show early speed without faltering in the stretch. Compare the following three races:

	PP	¼	½	¾	str.	fin.
A	3	2	2	2	1	1^{hd}
B	6	1^0	1	1	1^1	1^2
C	5	2^0	2	2	2^1	1^1

Notice that while A made a good move to get within striking position in the first quarter, it showed no stretch kick after taking the lead before the stretch. Contrast the efforts of B and C. Both were parked in the first quarter and either extended their lead in the stretch, as did B, or came on in the stretch for a convincing victory, as in C's case. B and C can therefore be awarded an extra point for combining early speed with an ability to hold up in the stretch.

In any race, then, in which there are closely matched contenders, examine the races in which they earned points for current form by finishing first or second. Then add bonus points for any races in which a horse gained at least three lengths in the stretch, roughed it for one quarter or more (one bonus point for *each* quarter on the outside), or showed early speed while gaining or maintaining ground in the stretch. The number of additional bonus points a contender earns will make it the best bet.

Application of the Point System to Actual Races

On page 104 are three examples of claiming paces run in August 1977 at Batavia Downs. Each is handicapped according to the requirements of the point system. In each case, I deferred an analysis of "pacing" in the race until after points were assigned under the remaining headings. A consideration of pacing in each race supported my conclusion about the most probable winner.

PACE CLAIMING

1 Mile — Purse $2600

EXACTA Wagering This Race

Claiming Price $6000
Mares allowed 20%, 4 year olds allowed 30%.

ASK FOR HORSE BY PROGRAM NUMBER

Saddle Cloth
YELLOW

---

1 — 7200

YANKEE JEAN (4, 2.13½) (½) — $3216)
DRIVER—ED BEADLE—Red, Gold and Black

b. m. 5, by Yankee Hanover—Chiquita Adios
Edward Beadle & Richard Flemming, Holley & Brockport, N.Y.

Trainer: R. Flemming

7-23⁷⁷ Btva	ms	2600	ft	7200 clm	1	.32	1.05²	1.36³	2.08²	1	4	4	4½³	2.08⁴	6.40 (EBeadle) Cuba,THAlmighty,TiogaCardigan
7-12⁷⁷ Btva	ms	1900	ft	c-6000 clm	1	.31	1.04⁴	1.36	2.07	8	8	8⁶	5³⁴	2.07³	7.30 (TLanphe) GlendalePisa,IanHill,RowmarsAngel
7- 6⁷⁷ Btva	ms	2200	gd	7200 clm	1	.31	1.01³	1.33	2.04⁴	4	3	4	4⁴	2.05³	7.30 (TLanphe) VickyBojo,WaitABit,YankeeJean
6-29⁷⁷ Btva	ms	1800	ft	6000 clm	1	.31	1.04	1.36¹	2.08²	6	7	4²⁴	3³⁴	2.09²	5.60 (TLanphe) YankeeJean,NedaSal,Scooter Jones
6-20⁷⁷ Btva	ms	1800	ft	6000 clm	1	.31¹	1.03	1.36²	2.06²	7	6	4²⁴	1½	2.06²	4.60 (TLanphe) YankeeJean,NedaSal,Scooter Jones
6-13⁷⁷ B.R.	ms	1900	ft	6000 clm	1	.31³	1.05	1.35	2.06⁴	4	6	6⁴⁴	3²⁴	2.06⁴	2.20 (TLanphe) StarG,AdiosPeterCooper,YankeeJean
6- 7⁷⁷ B.R.	ms	1900	ft	6000 clm	1	.31³	1.06	1.35⁴	2.06⁴	5	5	5½³	3hd	2.06⁴	3.40 (TLanphe) NotableBaron,BuckeyeKnight,YankeeJean
6- 7⁷⁷ B.R.	ms	1900	ft	nw2RLtCD	1	.31²	1.03	1.35⁴	2.07¹	5	4	6³	1½	2.07¹	4.00 (TLanphe) YankeeJean,FullConnection,AdieuRose

	1977	23	2	4	4	$ 5371
2.07½ B.R.	1976	19	2	2	4	$ 3166
2.13½ Btva						

---

2 — 7200

MARY'S HEEL (3, 2.02½) (¼) — $12204)
DRIVER—ED McNEIGHT, JR.—Orange, Black and White

b. m. 6, by Tar Mite—Marys Mite
Geraldine & Ervin Johnson, E. Pembroke, N.Y.

Trainer: E. McNeight, Jr.

7-26⁷⁷ Btva	ms	2600	ft	7200 clm	1	.30³	1.03¹	1.34²	2.05	6	7	5³⁴	3²	2.06	5.00 (EMcNeJr) GrayEdna,IanHill,MarysHeel
7-16⁷⁷ Btva	ms	2400	ft	6000 clm	1	.32	1.03	1.34¹	2.05³	2	4	3²	1²⁴	2.05³	6.90 (EMcNeJr) MarysHeel,SargeGunner,PearlieChita
7- 9⁷⁷ Btva	ms	1900	ft	6000 clm	1	.30³	1.01⁴	1.33	2.04⁴	8	8	4⁴	2¹	2.06⁴	7.30 (EMcNeJr) MyBrothersHorse,AdiosWilla,MarysHeel
6-29⁷⁷ Btva	ms	1800	ft	6000 clm	1	.31	1.04	1.36¹	2.08²	1	1	1¹	5³⁴	2.09³	5.50 (EMcNeJr) YankeeJean,NedaSal,Scooter Jones
6-22⁷⁷ Btva	ms	1600	ft	c-4000 clm	1	.30²	1.04¹	1.35⁴	2.06⁴	4	20²	1³	8⁵³	2.09³	2.10 (BSchroe) YankeeJean,NedaSal,Scooter Jones(Pl 7)
6- 7⁷⁷ B.R.	ms	1100	ft	3000 clm	1	.29	1.01	1.33²	2.06¹	3	3	3³	3⁷⁴	2.07⁷	7.80 (BSchroe) PeerlessLobil,RusselTorrence,MarysHeel
5-24⁷⁷ B.R.			ft	0ua		.31¹	1.03¹	1.34²	2.05⁴	4	1	1²	3³	2.06²	NB (EMcNeJr) StarettaCharm,MarysHeel,LordAlbion
5-24⁷⁷ B.R.			ft	0ua		.31²	1.03¹	1.34²	2.06²	2	2	1¼	1½	2.06³	NB (EMcNeJr) MarysHeel,MarysHeel,AChoiceGuy

	1977	20	4	5	4	$ 6510
2.05½ Btva	1976	35	5	6	6	$ 7947
2.04½ B.R.						

---

3 — 6000

SAM C (7, 2.04½) (¼) — $6372)
DRIVER—ANTHONY MacRAE—Maroon, Gold and White

b. g. 8, by Tasselman—Hope Grattan
Philip Passarell, Holley, N.Y.

Trainer: P. Passarell

7-23⁷⁷ Btva	ms	2600	ft	6000 clm	1	.32	1.05²	1.36²	2.08²	6x	6x	6dis	6dis		16.60 (AMacRae) Cuba,THAlmighty,TiogaCardigan
7-15⁷⁷ Btva	ms	2600	sy	6000 clm	1	.32	1.36²	2.07³×6x	8	8	8dis	8dis		17.20 (AMacRae) BverlysJne,MyBrthersHrse,PeerlessLbil
7- 9⁷⁷ Btva	ms	1900	ft	6000 clm	1	.30³	1.01⁴	1.33	2.04⁴	2	1	1²	1²¹	2.06	1.40* (JWetzel) MyBrothersHorse,AdiosWilla,SamC
6-30⁷⁷ Btva	ms	1600	ft	c-4000 clm	1	.30	1.04¹	1.33²	2.06¹	1	1	1³	1¹	2.06¹	2.10 (BSchroe) SamC,JeffersonVictory,GlendalePisa
6-22⁷⁷ B.R.	ms	1500	ft	3000 clm	1	.31	1.04¹	1.35⁴	2.06⁴	3⁰	3	2²	2²¹	2.07	7.80 (BSchroe) SamC,Becket,GlendalePisa
6- 3⁷⁷ V.D.¾	ms	1300	ft	3000 clm	1	.29	1.03²	1.34³	2.06¹	3	3	4⁰	1¹	2.06¹	3.40 (JConlJr) GayAbe,CameronAro,Calhoun
5-26⁷⁷ V.D.¾	ms	1300	ft	4000 clm	1	.30¹	1.03¹	1.34³	2.06²	2	2	3¹	5²	2.06³	7.30 (BCottre) HalGamaun,Fanfare,CordiallyYours

	1977	12	2	1	2	$ 3488
2.06½ Btva	1976	23	3	4	5	$ 4275
2.04½ V.D.¾						

---

4 — $13948

BUTLER KNIGHT (5, 2.06½) (½) — $13948)
DRIVER—JOHN CONLON, JR.—Gold and Green

b. h. 7, by Adios Butler—Pammy Hanover
John W. Conlon, Jr., Batavia, N.Y.

Trainer: J. Conlon, Jr.

7-23⁷⁷ Btva	ms	2400	ft	5000 clm	1	.30⁴	1.04²	1.36	2.07²	1	1	1ns	1ns	2.07²	12.90 (JWilkes) ButlerKnight,TrueProject,IndianRuler
7-15⁷⁷ Btva	ms	2100	sy	4000 clm	1	.30²	1.03²	1.34²	2.06³	3	2	2³⁴	2²³	2.07¹	2.40 (JConlJr) IndianRuler,ButlerKnight,JohnSilver
7- 8⁷⁷ Btva	ms	1900	ft	6000 clm	1	.31	1.03	1.35	2.07¹	8	1⁰²	1³	1²⁴	2.07¹	33.30 (JConlJr) IndianRuler,ButlerKnight,MssMargaretEd
7- 8⁷⁷ Btva	ms	1700	ft	4000 clm	1	.31¹	1.03	1.35	2.07¹	8	1⁰	2²	2nk	2.08¹	2.30* (JConlJr) ButlerKnight,MarysPenn,LivelyGene

	1977	16	2	3	1	$ 3488
2.07½ Btva	1976	26	4	2	5	$ 2986
2.10 B.R.						

5 · MS 6000

CUBA (P)
DRIVER—

(8, 2.04½ (½) — $10863)

br. g. 10, by Aksarben (F)—Shepherds Pride
C. Crissman, Jr. & A. Mastandrea, Lakeview, N.Y.

Trainer: Jo. Altizer (Altizer Stable)

											2.04½ B.R. %	2.07½ W.R. %	1977	25	4 1 1	$ 5420	75
													1976	23	1 1 4	$ 2982	72
6-14⁷⁷ B.R.	cs	1600	ft	3500 clm	1	.31³	1.05	1.37	2.07⁴	5	5	5	5³	2.08	15.00 (JConLdr)	DaringDrexel,ButterKnight,AOEquador	75
5-31⁷⁷ B.R.	cs		ft	Qua	1	.32³	1.05	1.37	2.09⁴	3	2	1	19²	2.09⁴	NB (JConLdr)	ButterKnight,Shamokin,InTime	79
5-26⁷⁷ B.R.	cs	1600	ft	3500 clm	1	.31²	1.03²	1.35	2.08³	7	10x2	6³	6³	2.09¹	23.80 (JConLdr)	JJByrd,KnightsMarion,FilmFlamGirl	72

6 · MS 7200

McINTOSH MAGIC
DRIVER—JIM ACKLEY—Green and White

(4, 2.03½ (½) — $22581)

ch. m. 5, by Freight Special—Susan O
James C. Ackley & Dr. Elmo Corsette, Springville, N.Y.

Trainer: C. Whitmer

											2.03½ Btva	2.07½ Btva	1977	6	1 0 0	$ 1336	74
													1976	28	3 4 6	$ 6334	79
7-23⁷⁷ Btva	ms	2600	ft	7200 clm	1	.32	1.05²	1.36³	2.08²	4	1	1	1¹	2.08²	1.00* (BAltize)	Cuba,THAlmighty,TiogaCardigan	74
7-15⁷⁷ Btva	ms	2600	sy	7200 clm	1	.31²	1.05	1.36²	2.07³	7	6³	6⁵	6⁷²	2.08³	19.60 (DAckley)	Facile,Stonecutter,HarryW	77
7-9⁷⁷ Btva	ms	2200	ft	7200 clm	1	.30⁴	1.01	1.32²	2.04⁴	5	3	4	4 10³	2.05²	5.10 (CCrislr)	SaucyMix,HarryW,Facile	77
7-1⁷⁷ Btva	ms	1800	ft	6000 clm	1	.30²	1.01³	1.33²	2.04²	5	4	4³	4²⁴	2.05³	8.10 (CCrislr)	Facile,Lightinginjoe,Cuba	77
6-24⁷⁷ B.R.	ms	2150	ft	7200 clm	1	.30⁴	1.04	1.36¹	2.06⁴	7	6	6⁵	6³⁶	2.07⁴	9.50 (CCrislr)	McIntoshMagic,PearlieChita,RoyalShdw	79
6-18⁷⁷ B.R.	ms	1900	ft	7200 clm	1	.31	1.04²	1.34	2.05¹	8	7	8³	8⁷²	2.05⁴	29.20 (CCrislr)	PeerlessLobell,SteadyMoran,Eljayjoe	79
5-14⁷⁷ B.R.	ms	2150	ft	7200 clm	1	.30²	1.04¹	1.36¹	2.07¹	8	8	8⁷	8⁹⁴	2.08¹	31.00 (CCrislr)	NotableBaron,PriessLobell,FreightBaron	78
5-14⁷⁷ B.R.	ms	1600	ft	3500 clm	1	.31²	1.03²	1.32³	2.04²	7	5	4	1³	2.04²	NB (CCrislr)	GlendalePisa,McIntoshMagic,FrostCollins	85

7 · MS 7800

IAN HILL
DRIVER—FRED HASLIP—Blue, White and Gold

(3, 2.06⅘ (½) — $5236)

b. g. 4, by Hi Hill—Impeccable
Edward Wittenberg, West Seneca, N.Y.

Trainer: E. Wittenberg

											2.06⅘ Btva	2.05⅘ Btva	1977	24	2 4 6	$ 5131	68
													1976	31	4 2 4	$ 4086	68
7-26⁷⁷ Btva	ms	2600	ft	7800 clm	1	.30³	1.02³	1.34³	2.05³	8	8	8⁷	7⁵²	2.07¹	6.10 (FHaslip)	GrayEdna,IanHill,MarysSheel	68
7-19⁷⁷ Btva	ms	2400	ft	6500 clm	1	.31³	1.05	1.36²	2.07³	4	3	4⁴	3¹¹	1.40* (FHaslip)	SctchChsr.BckyKnght,WlleyedWillie(Pl,5)	79
7-12⁷⁷ Btva	ms	1900	ft	6500 clm	1	.31	1.04¹	1.36	2.07	4	4	4 10³	3³²	2.40 (FHaslip)	GlendalePisa,IanHill,Rowman'sAngel	84
7-4⁷⁷ Btva	ms	2200	ft	6500 clm	1	.30¹	1.01³	1.33¹	2.04³	4	5	6²	6⁷²	11.90 (FHaslip)	Torque,StardustMiracle,IanHill	81
6-24⁷⁷ B.R.	ms	1900	ft	6500 clm	1	.30³	1.03⁴	1.35	2.06³	2	4	3³	3³³	2.40* (DMcNeig)	DelLynch,SlippersBoy,IanHill	79
6-18⁷⁷ B.R.	ms	1900	ft	6500 clm	1	.31³	1.03	1.35⁴	2.07⁴	5	3	2x1	2x¹	4.00 (FHaslip)	MyBrothersHorse,HonorKennedy,GraysPat	78
6-16⁷⁷ B.R.	ms	6250	ft		1	.31³	1.03	1.35²	2.06⁴	1	1	1²	1³	2.06⁴	6.90 (FHaslip)	IanHill,Acropolis,GraysPat	68

8 · MS 6000

QUICKEM
DRIVER—AL MARIACHER—White, Gold and Red

(5, 2.06⅗ (½) — $14981)

b. g. 6, by Quick Pick—Easily
Harry Mariacher, Greenville, Pa.

Trainer: A. Mariacher

											2.05⅘ Btva	2.05⅘ Btva	1977	29	3 2 8	$ 6258	74
													1976	40	5 3 7	$ 7025	80
7-27⁷⁷ Btva	ms	2800	ft	7000 clm	1	.31⁴	1.04³	1.35³	2.06²	8	8	7	5³	2.07¹	36.80 (AMariac)	WaitABit,EljayJoe,MissMaryDi	74
7-20⁷⁷ Btva	ms	2200	ft	6000 clm	1	.31¹	1.04⁴	1.34⁴	2.05⁴	8	2	2¹	1²¹	4.80 (AMariac)	Quickem,RaiseHobb,CoTarGrattan	88
7-12⁷⁷ Btva	ms	2200	ft	6000 clm	1	.30²	1.03	1.33	2.05	7	3	3²	3²¹	5.00 (AMariac)	ProTestor,FamousJulie,Quickem	84
7-6⁷⁷ Btva	ms	2100	gd	6000 clm	1	.30¹	1.01¹	1.33¹	2.04⁴	3	4	4³	4⁵²	2.30* (AMariac)	VickyBojo,WaitABit,YankeeJean	63
6-28⁷⁷ B.R.	ms	2250	ft	7000 clm	1	.30¹	1.02	1.33¹	2.06²	7	4	4¹	4¹¹	13.40 (AMariac)	MightyOtto,BeverlysJune,StarG	77
6-22⁷⁷ B.R.	ms		gd	7000 clm	1	.31¹	1.03	1.35²	2.05⁴	3	3	4³	4³³	8.30 (AMariac)	BurleyGuy,HosiGuy,KeystoneWhiz	72
6-16⁷⁷ B.R.	ms	2550	ft	8000 clm	1	.30³	1.02¹	1.32⁴	2.04	6	6	6³	8⁶³	34.00 (AMariac)	ConestogaCash,RacingGene,LAmbBamby	80

Batavia Downs 8th Race August 3, 1977

1 Yankee Jean			**5 Cuba**	
Current form	0		Current form	2
Consistency	1		Consistency	1
Class	0		Class	0
Driver	0		Driver	2
Post position	3		Post position	1
Total	4		Total	6

2 Mary's Heel			**6 McIntosh Magic**		
Current form	2		Current form	2	(discount 7/15
Consistency	3		Consistency	0	race)
Class	0		Class	0	
Driver	0		Driver	1	
Post position	3		Post position	1	
Total	10		Total	4	

3 Sam C			**7 Ian Hill**	
Current form	0		Current form	2
Consistency	1		Consistency	1
Class	0		Class	0
Driver	2		Driver	2
Post position	2		Post position	0
Total	5		Total	5

4 Butler Knight			**8 Quickem**	
Current form	4		Current form	2
Consistency	2		Consistency	0
Class	−2		Class	2
Driver	1		Driver	1
Post position	2		Post position	0
Total	7		Total	5

Analysis. Mary's Heel has an advantage in this race because the only other contenders on paper, Butler Knight and Cuba, are both front-runners. It's likely that the first quarter of this race will be run in a fast time and that Mary's Heel will be in an ideal position to move at the half or later and win going away.

Results. Mary's Heel won easily at odds of 2 to 1. Cuba, the even-

money favorite, was parked in a fast first quarter and wound up third, fading in the stretch. Mary's Heel, moving at the half, finished almost 2 lengths ahead of Butler Knight, the place horse.

Batavia Downs   8th race   October 8, 1977

Let's begin by eliminating the noncontenders in this race.

1 Burley Guy

Raced poorly in its last three starts against this level of competition, finishing no better than fourth. Not a factor in this race.

2 Happy Brooke

After being idle for more than a month, Happy Brooke resumed racing on September 20. Unimpressive in his last two starts, probably because of lameness, he is unplayable.

3 Mabel Byrd.

Can be eliminated because of poor recent form as well as inconsistency.

7 C F Guy

Can be eliminated because of poor recent form as well as outside post position.

The contenders are:

4 Terr Adios		**6 Mary's Heel**	
Current form	2	Current form	0
Consistency	3	Consistency	3
Class	0	Class	0
Driver	2	Driver	2
Post position	2	Post position	1
Total	9	Total	6

5 Golden Juelka			**8 Parkwood**	
Current form	3	(omit 10/1 race)	Current form	2
Consistency	3		Consistency	4
Class	0		Class	0
Driver	2		Driver	3
Post position	1		Post position	0
Total	9		Total	9

Claiming Price $7000
Mares allowed 20%.

ASK FOR HORSE BY PROGRAM NUMBER

---

1 — 7000

(2, 2.02¾) TT (1) — $57912)
BURLEY GUY ‡
DRIVER—KEITH HAASE—Gold and White
b. h. 7, by Bret Hanover—Rilda Guy
Osten Roy Dion, Schomberg, Ont., Can.

Trainer: O. Dion
2.05¾ Btva   1977   20   5   1   1 $ 7624
2.02¾ Btva   1976   33   8   7   3 $15230

10- 1⁷⁷	Btva	‡2500	sy	7000 clm	1	.31¹¹	1.02⁴	1.35¹	2.08²	6	2	2⁰	7⁷³	2.10⁴	5.80	(KHaase)	Parkwood,ScotchChaser,GoldenJuelka
9-24⁷⁷	Btva	‡2500	sy	7000 clm	1	.34²	1.08	2.11¹		6	5	4³	4³½	2.05¹	5.10	(KHaase)	LuckeyBobDay,GoldnJuelka,MountainHavn
9-14⁷⁷	Btva	‡2500	ft	7000 clm	1	.30²	1.02¹	1.33²	2.04¹	5	4	4⁴	4⁵	2.05¹	3.10	(KHaase)	Baratony,MountainHaven,GoldenJuelka
9- 3⁷⁷	Btva	‡2300	ft	6000 clm	1	.31²	1.02¹	1.34¹	2.07	6	8	8⁵	3¹½	2.07	6.90	(KHaase)	BrleyGuy,BeverlysJune,Sophrunia(P1 1)
8-27⁷⁷	Btva	‡2300	ft	6000 clm	1	.29²	1.01¹	1.33	2.03	6	5	5⁵	2ns	2.03¹	5.00	(KHaase)	IrtonPrince,ScotchChaser,Sophrunia
8-22⁷⁷	Btva	‡2500	ft	6000 clm	1	.30²	1.02⁴	1.34	2.05⁴	2	3	3²	4⁶½	2.05³	1.80*	(KHaase)	MarysHeel,PetronBetsy,FamousJulie
8-13⁷⁷	Btva	‡2900	sy	8000 clm	1	.30⁴	1.02²	1.33³	2.04³	6	2⁰x8	8dis	8dis		7.70	(KHaase)	ClssicAffairN,LncInsValor,RelhomWarrn

---

2 — 7000

(4, 2.04¾) (½) — $4055)
HAPPY BROOKE
DRIVER—PERRY SMITH—Maroon, Gold and White
b. g. 5, by Adioway—Dolly M Brooke
Anthony Asher, Rocky River, Ohio

Trainer: P. Smith
2.07⅗ Spk ⅝   1977   17   2   1   2 $6724
2.04¾ Nfld   1976   15   2   2   2 $2605

9-28⁷⁷	Btva	2700	gd	8000 clm	1	.31¹	1.03	1.36²	2.08¹	5	2	2⁰	8⁵²	2.09¹	2.40*	(PSmith)	ConchoByrd,GreenviewAnn,CalKnight
9-17⁷⁷	Btva	2700	ft	9000 clm	1	.29¹	1.00¹	1.32¹	2.04³	2	3	3¹	4¹²	2.06	4.70	(PSmith)	DuzHerbert,Wiscoy,Byrd,LadyWilloway
9-20⁷⁷	Btva	2900	gd	9000 clm	1	.30³	1.02	1.34³	2.07	1	1	1³¹	1¹⁴	2.06⁴	NB	(PSmith)	HappyBrooke,Armonk,AlmightyDollar
9- 9⁷⁷	Btva		ms	Qua	1	.30¹	1.02⁴	1.33	2.03⁴	4	4	4¹	4³¹	2.04³	46.10	(PSmith)	ShortySmith,JoeyLimbo,MightyDream
8-11⁷⁷	Btva	4700	ft	10000 clm	1	.30³	1.02⁴	1.33³	2.03⁴	7	2	2²	2²	2.04	20.80	(PSmith)	IdlewhilesMike,Jefferies,JustlyGenius
8- 4⁷⁷	Spk⅝	5800	sy	12000 clm	1	.30⁴	1.03¹	1.34²	2.06³	7	8	9⁹	9⁹³	2.08³	31.90	(PSmith)	TheGrmbler,Tensor,IdlewhlesMike
7-26⁷⁷	Spk⅝	5700	ft	12000 clm	1	.29²	1.01²	1.32²	2.03	3	5	4⁴	4⁴²	2.04	31.90	(PSmith)	TheGrmbler,Tensor,IdlewhlesMike
7-15⁷⁷	Spk⅝	5000	ft	11000 clm	1	.31¹	1.01⁴	1.33	2.02³	4	6⁰	2⁰x8	5⁵½	2.04	5.30	(PSmith)	AbbeCrry,DesotoDuke,PrettyPatrick

---

3 — 8400

(5, 2.06) (½) — $12872)
MABEL BYRD
DRIVER—LARRY MANGES—Red and White
b. m. 6, by Parker Byrd—Roxburgh Ruth
Nancy A. Gregor, Arcade, N.Y.

Trainer: B. Maniace (Gregor Stable)
2.07¾ Btva B.R.   1977   31   2   2   4 $8109
2.06 Ormvl   1976   42   3   13   10 $8533

9-29⁷⁷	Btva	2500	ft	8400 clm	1	.31⁴	1.03¹	1.34³	2.05³	3	3	4³²	4⁴³	2.06²	52.00	(LManges)	NotableBaron,MarkMinbar,MarysHeel
9-17⁷⁷	Btva	2700	ft	9600 clm	1	.29¹	1.00¹	1.32¹	2.04³	1	1	7¹¹²	6¹⁰⁴	2.06³	43.90	(BManiac)	HoneyGun,WaitABit,AdiosRowdy
8-24⁷⁷	Btva	2100	ft	76-7nw200ps	1	.30³	1.02	1.33	2.03⁴	3	7	7¹¹³	7⁷³	2.06	34.40	(LManges)	WilLorGem,OJWiscoy,NobleMoran
8-16⁷⁷	Btva	2400	sy	76-7nw225ps	1	.31²	1.02³	1.36²	2.07²	2	4	4⁴	4²⁴	2.08¹	4.60	(AMacRae)	PhntomAlmahrst,ArniesEllen,FissiesBby
8- 8⁷⁷	Btva	3400	gd	10800 clm	1	.30¹	1.02¹	1.33	2.03³	7	6	6⁵	6³³	2.05⁴	39.90	(BManiac)	RuthBaker,ColeHillJohn,ClassicAffairN
7-29⁷⁷	Btva	4000	sy	12000 clm hcp	1	.33	1.03¹	1.34²	2.08	5	7	7⁷	6⁷²	2.08²	25.90	(LManges)	ThunderImp,GreenviewAnn
7-22⁷⁷	Btva	3100	ft	9600 clm	1	.30³	1.02¹	1.33	2.04⁴	1	3	3⁶	6⁴³	2.05³	3.30	(LManges)	GreenviewAnn,BurleyGuy,MerryJohnA

---

4 —

(5, 2.07½) (½) — $4013)
TERR ADIOS
DRIVER—CARMEN CAPPOTELLI—Gray, Red and Gold
ch. g. 5, by Adios Boy—Terry N
John J. Saeva, Scottsville, N.Y.

Trainer: C. Cappotelli
2.06 Btva   1977   16   4   3   2 $6129
2.07½ B.R.   1976   20   1   2   1 $ 1583

10- 1⁷⁷	Btva	ms	2500	ft	7000 clm	1	.31³	1.04³	1.35⁴	2.08³	3	4	4³	4³²	2.08³	13.30	(CCappot)	TerrAdios,JimmieCollins,MFPoplar
9-24⁷⁷	Btva	ms	2500	sy	7000 clm	1	.34²	1.08	1.40	2.11²	7	7	2⁰	7⁷³	2.12⁴	16.90	(CCappot)	LuckeyBobDay,GoldnJuelka,MountainHavn
9-14⁷⁷	Btva	ms	2500	ft	7000 clm	1	.30²	1.02¹	1.33²	2.04¹	6	2	5⁶	5⁶⁴	2.05²	15.00	(CCappot)	Baratony,MountainHaven,GoldenJuelka
9- 5⁷⁷	Btva	ms	2100	ft	5000 clm	1	.31³	1.04¹	1.35²	2.06	3	2	1²	1²	2.06	3.30	(CCappot)	TerrAdios,EasternQueen,WinnieSong

5 MS **7000**

(3, 2.01¼ TT (1) — $10331)

GOLDEN JUELKA
DRIVER—JACK DARLING—Red and White

b. m. 5, by Golden Money Maker—Juelka
Jack Darling, Exeter, Ont., Can.

Trainer: J. Darling

	1977	34	4	12	4	$ 9422	75
2.04½ FlmD	1976	30	3	1	1	$ 3471	65
2.08⅓ Btva							71

PearlieChita,SuccessGrant,TerrAdios
SuperLaird,TerrAdios,SuccessGrant
ChesterDevil,TerrAdios,CaptainCrunch

6 MS **8400**

(3, 2.02¾ (1) — $12204)

MARY'S HEEL
DRIVER—ED McNEIGHT, JR.—Orange, Black and White

b. m. 6, by Tar Mite—Marys Mite
Geraldine & Ervin Johnson, E. Pembroke, N.Y.

Trainer: E. McNeight, Jr.

	1977	28	6	6	7	$10903	55
2.04½ Btva	1976	35	5	6	6	$ 7947	70
2.04¾ B.R.							63

NotableBaron,MarkMinbar,MarysHeel
HoneyGun,WaitABit,AdiosRowdy
KeystoneWhiz,AvonFairline,MarysHeel
GoldenJuelka,MissMaryDl,MarysHeel
MarysHeel,PetronBetsy,FamousJulie
IronPrince,FreightBaron,MightyYankee
OldeSoftShoe,MarysHeel,BradleysGay

7 MS **7000**

(6, 2.03¾ (¾) — $42114)

C F GUY
DRIVER—NORMAND FLUET—Gold, Black and White

ch. g. 8, by Greatheart Pick—Piper Day
Robert Moser & Rene Robert, Buffalo, N.Y. & Trois Rivieres, Que., Can.

Trainer: N. Fluet (Tubin Stable)

	1977	31	2	4	5	$ 7715	53
2.05% N.E. %	1976	42	5	6	3	$ 8955	52
2.05⅓ Fox %							68

TerrAdios,JimmieCollins,MEPoplar
Squall,ArmbroProfit,LincolnsValor
LincolnsValor,MerryJohnA,Parkwood
CFGuy,MyBrothersHorse,SharpiesBeta
SirAladon,CFGuy,RacingGene
CFGuy,FreightBaron,TrueProject
Quicken,RaiseHobb,CoTarGrattan

8 MS **7000**

(6, 2.03½ (¾) — $25128)

PARKWOOD
DRIVER—YVON DEMERS—White, Black and Red

b. h. 7, by Shadow Wave—Gay Bett
Guy Joanis, Montebello, Que., Can.

Trainer: Y. Demers

	1977	13	4	3	4	$ 6882	53
2.04% B.B. %	1976	14	3	2	2	$ 5194	52
2.03⅓ B.B. %							68

Parkwood,ScotchChaser,GoldenJuelka
Squall,ArmbroProfit,GoldenJuelka
LincolnsValor,MerryJohnA,Parkwood
Parkwood,JustaplainLady,DuanesJane
ArmbroMcKee,Prkwood,BaronMichael
Parkwood,Nereva,ArmbroMckee
Parkwood,TrueCreed,WaverlysGem

Analysis. A difficult race to handicap for a number of reasons. First, the apparent contenders, with the exception of Terr Adios, have outside post positions. Second, three of the contenders tally nine points. Third, this race was run on a slow track (2 to 3 seconds slow), and it is difficult to rate the comparative strengths of contenders under these circumstances. Finally, no clear pattern emerges when we ask how we can expect the race to be run. Will Parkwood go to the front? Will Mary's Heel move at the half? Will Terr Adios and Golden Juelka move at the half or later? No discernible pattern seems to emerge. As a result, this race is unplayable.

Results.

EIGHTH RACE — 1 Mile							$7000 Claiming Pace		$2500
Parkwood ms	8	4	5	5	$5^1\frac{1}{2}$	$1\frac{1}{2}$	Y. Demers		5.80
Marys Heel ms	6	7	6	4^{02}	$3\frac{3}{4}$	$2^2\frac{1}{2}$	E. McNeight, Jr.		5.70
Terr Adios ms	4	6	7	6	$6^1\frac{1}{4}$	3ns	C. Cappotelli		5/00
Golden Juelka ms	5	1^0	1	1	1hd	4^1	J. Darling		*2.60
Burley Guy ‡	1	2	2	3	4^1	$5\frac{1}{2}$	K. Haase		4.90
Happy Brooke ms	2	3	3	2	$2^1\frac{1}{4}$	6dh	P. Smith		3.40
C F Guy ms	7	8	8	8	7nk	$6dh^2\frac{1}{2}$ N. Fluet			49.80
Mabel Byrd ms	3	5	4	7^0	8	8	L. Manges		15.80

$2 MUTUEL PRICES	8. Parkwood		13.60	5.00	3.20
Official Program Nos.	6. Marys Heel			4.80	3.80
	4. Terr Adios				3.40

Time — .31⅗   1.04⅘   1.37½   2.10¼
EXACTA — 8 AND 6 $116.80

Batavia Downs   10th race   October 8, 1977

Again, we begin by eliminating the noncontenders.

1 J J's Newsweek
No recent form. Unplayable.

5 Olde Soft Shoe
Again, poor recent form eliminates this horse, even though it is stepping down in class.

8 Famous Julie
Eliminate because of poor recent form and outside post position.

2 Del Lynch		**6 Ritzy Girl**	
Current form	3	Current form	4
Consistency	4	Consistency	2
Class	0	Class	0
Driver	2	Driver	2
Post position	3	Post position	1
Total	12	Total	9

3 Torpids Aytch

Current form	4
Consistency	2
Class	−2
Driver	2
Post position	2
Total	8

7 Kenwood Jim

Current form	1
Consistency	2
Class	0
Driver	3
Post position	0
Total	6

4 Pro Testor

Current form	1
Consistency	2
Class	0
Driver	2
Post position	2
Total	7

Analysis. Three horses seemed evenly matched in this race according to the point system—Del Lynch, Ritzy Girl, and Torpids Aytch—with Pro Testor and Kenwood Jim also having a shot. Moreover, it is difficult to determine how this race will be run, since the contenders do not seem to follow a consistent pattern. Del Lynch, Torpids Aytch, Pro Testor, and Ritzy Girl are all maneuverable horses. For this reason, and because the race is being run on a slow track, we elect to pass.

Results.

TENTH RACE — 1 Mile							$6000 Claiming Pace			$2300
Kenwood Jim ms	7	1	1	1	2¹�¼	1ns	Y. Demers			11.70
Olde Soft Shoe ms	5	3	3	2⁰	1hd	2¾	J. Sarago			14.10
Pro Testor ms	4	6	6	6	7⁸	3¹	T. Dufford			2.60
Famous Julie ms	8	8	8	7	6nk	4hd	L. Manges			25.60
Ritzy Girl	6	7	7	5⁰	5¹	5¾	G. Guindon			3.30
Del Lynch ms	2	3	3	4	4½	6¹¼	F. Haslip			*2.30
Torpids Aytch ms	3	5	5	3⁰	3¾	7⁸½	A. MacRae			5.10
JJ's Newsweek ms	1	4	4	8	8	8	A. Strollo			18.90
$2 MUTUEL PRICES		7. Kenwood Jim						24.20	6.80	4.40
Official Program Nos.		5. Olde Soft Shoe							10.20	4.80
		4. Pro Testor								4.20

Time — .32⅗   1.06   1.38⅖   2.11⅗

TRIFECTA — 7 — 5 — 4 $1,342.00

Pro Testor claimed by James Helfeldt, Buffalo, N.Y. (Tr. J. Helfeldt)

–Recorded from photo chart film)

TRACK: SLOW
WEATHER: CLOUDY, WINDY, COOL, (50°)

(10) PACE CLAIMING
$2 TRIFECTA Wagering This Race
1 Mile — Purse $2300

Claiming Price $6000
Mares allowed 20%, 4 year olds allowed 30%.

Saddle Cloth PURPLE

ASK FOR HORSE BY PROGRAM NUMBER

---

1 — JJ'S NEWSWEEK
(3, 2.01) (¾) — $392283
DRIVER—ANTHONY STROLLO—White, Black and Red
blk. h. 8, by Overtrick—Precise Time
Billy Kaye, Northeast, Pa.

Trainer: A. Strollo
2.03¾ B.B. %
2.05⅗ RidC %

9-30⁷⁷	Btva	ms	2300	my	6000 clm	1	.33	1.06¹	1.39¹	2.11²	15.00	(AStroll)	DelLynch,MugWump,RoyalJ
9-19⁷⁷	Btva	ms	2300	sy	6000 clm	1	.32¹	1.05¹	1.36²	2.10	8.50	(AStroll)	RitzyGirl,RaiseHobb,FamousJulie
9-7⁷⁷	Btva	ms	2500	ft	7000 clm	1	.30²	1.01⁴	1.33⁴	2.06³	68.30	(AStroll)	KeystoneWhiz,AvonFairine,MarysHeel
9-1⁷⁷	Btva	ms	2500	ft	7000 clm	1	.31	1.03	1.34²	2.07³	17.80	(AStroll)	GoldenJuelka,MissMaryDl,MarysHeel
8-14⁷⁷	RidC%		1000		5500 clm hcp	1	.30¹	1.03¹	1.33⁴	2.05¹	11.25	(YPlouff)	ChoreBoyPat,OverDares,JJsNwswk
8-7⁷⁷	RidC%		950		5500 clm hcp	1	.29¹	1.03³	1.32⁴	2.05¹	5.40	(YPlouff)	ChoreBoyPat,TopGun,Estwoodjuno
7-29⁷⁷	RidC%		950	sl	5000 clm hcp	1	.31¹	1.04	1.35⁴	2.09³	8.10	(JPlouff)	OverDares,JJsNewsweek,FashionScott

---

2 — DEL LYNCH (N)
(4, 2.06⅗) (½) — $7817
DRIVER—FRED HASLIP—Blue, Gold and White
b. h. 5, by Lynch Hanover—Del His Sis
James Fallon & Mae Culligan, Rochester, N.Y.

Trainer: J. Fallon
2.06⅗ Btva

9-30⁷⁷	Btva	ms	2300	my	6000 clm	1	.33	1.06¹	1.39¹	2.11²	1.70*	(FHaslip)	DelLynch,MugWump,RoyalJ
9-21⁷⁷	Btva	ms	2300	gd	6000 clm	1	.30²	1.03	1.34³	2.06	1.30*	(FHaslip)	Quicken,DelLynch,EljayJoe
9-10⁷⁷	Btva	ms	2100	ft	5000 clm	1	.31¹	1.03	1.34⁴	2.06	8.90	(FHaslip)	DelLynch,Peetong,Torque
9-3⁷⁷	Btva	ms	2100	ft	5000 clm	1	.30¹	1.02¹	1.34¹	2.07¹	14.50	(FHaslip)	EqualKash,ScottMeadow,BrackenField
8-30⁷⁷	Btva			gd	Qua	1	.30⁴	1.03¹	1.36²	2.06²	NB	(GSarama)	SonnyDirect,DelLynch,GrandPro
7-16⁷⁷	Btva	ms	2400	ft	5000 clm	1	.30¹	1.04¹	1.35²	2.06²	3.20	(GSarama)	RusselTorrence,TrueProject,BradleysGay
7-9⁷⁷	Btva	ms	1900	ft	5000 clm	1	.31¹	1.03	1.34²	2.06	1.50*	(GSarama)	DelLynch,RusselTorrence,SargeGunner

---

3 — TORPIDS AYTCH
(3, 2.03¼) (¼) — $26076)
DRIVER—ANTHONY MacRAE—Maroon, Gold and White
b. h. 6, by Torpid—Miss Buckeye
Mario & Josephine Schiano, Rochester, N.Y.

Trainer: J. Mulcahy
2.05⅗ P.Pk %
2.03⅘ V.D. ¾

9-27⁷⁷	Btva	ms	2100	ft	5000 clm	1	.30¹	1.04¹	1.34²	2.06²	3.90	(DVance)	TorpidsAytch,SuccessGrant,KittysHope
9-17⁷⁷	Btva	ms	2100	ft	5000 clm	1	.29¹	1.02	1.34²	2.06²	5.70	(DVance)	SuccessGrant,TorpidsAytch,BigFrosty
9-9⁷⁷	Btva	ms	1800	ft	4000 clm	1	.30³	1.04²	1.36¹	2.07⁴	2.40*	(FHaslip)	TorpidsAytch,LarryLinn,LuckyLang
8-30⁷⁷	V.D.¾		1500	ft	4000 clm	1	.30¹	1.01⁴	1.32¹	2.07³	10.60	(RMcNult)	CordiallyYours,SandTony,Lewiston
8-23⁷⁷	V.D.¾		1800	ft	5000 clm	1	.28³	1.01⁴	1.31²	2.03	52.20	(RMcNult)	TimeForFrills,Viveza,HartJ
8-16⁷⁷	V.D.¾		1800	ft	5000 clm	1	.28²	1.01³	1.31²	2.04²	21.40	(RMcNult)	Carefully,BabyBoots,Viveza
8-9⁷⁷	V.D.¾		1800	ft	5000 clm	1	.28¹	.59⁴	1.31²	2.01¹	14.70	(TDufford)	GoonbilsPride,LindsaysDouble,Dr.Beebe

---

4 — PRO TESTOR
(3, 2.06⅜) (¾) — $3536)
DRIVER—TOM DUFFORD—White, Red and Green
br. g. 4, by Pro Test—Miss Amy Jean
Thomas L. Dufford, Roanoke Rapids, N.C.

Trainer: T. Dufford
2.05 Btva
2.06¾ Mea %

10-1⁷⁷	Btva	ms	2500	sy	9100 clm	1	.31³	1.04²	1.35	2.08³	1.80*	(TDufford)	TerriAdios,JimmieCollins,MEPoplar
9-23⁷⁷	Btva	ms	2300	ft	7800 clm	1	.30²	1.02	1.34²	2.06³	4.90	(TDufford)	ColeHillJohn,ProTestor,ScotchChaser
9-14⁷⁷	Btva		2500	ft	9100 clm	1	.30²	1.02¹	1.33²	2.05³	1.40*	(TDufford)	Baratony,MountainHaven,GoldenJuelka
9-5⁷ᵃ	Btva		2300	gd	7800 clm	1	.31¹	1.02³	1.33	2.05	7.30	(TDufford)	RitzyGirl,ProTestor,TrueProject

---

	1977				1976			
	21	1	5	$ 4580	31	2	2	$ 4753
				57				66
								63
								80

(Right-margin summary statistics, per horse)

Trainer A. Strollo — 1977: 21 1 5 $4580 / 1976: 31 2 2 $4753
Trainer J. Fallon — 1977: 25 8 2 $9060 / 1976: 28 3 5 $4737
Trainer J. Mulcahy — 1977: 17 4 2 $4033 / 1976: 20 3 3 $3767
Trainer T. Dufford — 1977: 18 2 3 $4281 / 1976: 15 3 2 $3536

5 • 7800

(4, 2.06½) (½) — $5806)

OLDE SOFT SHOE

DRIVER—JOE SARAGO—Brown and Orange

b. g. 5, by Kings Choice—Miss Volstadt
Joseph Sarago, Cheektowaga, N.Y.

Trainer: J. Sarago

8-25⁷⁷	Btva		1900	ft	76-7nw175ps	1	.31²	1.03⁴	1.36²	2.07²	2	2	1	1hd	1hd	2.07²	(TDuffor)	ProTestor,KingMacMillan,Goodluck	65
8-17⁷⁷	Btva		2500	ft	7800 clm	1	.29¹	1.02	1.33²	2.04²	3	3	3	3½	2¹	2.04³	(TDuffor)	IronPrince,ProTestor,ButerAbbot	67
8- 9⁷⁷	Btva		2600	ft	7800 clm	1	.32³	1.04	1.35³	2.07¹	1	6	7	7	6½	.90*	(TDuffor)	OldeSoftShoe,MarysHeel,BradleysGay	72

2.07½ Btva 1977 35 6 5 6 $ 9545
2.06% K.D. % 1976 36 5 5 7 $ 5272

6 • 7200

(6, 2.04) (½) — $22109)

RITZY GIRL

DRIVER—GASTON GUINDON—Brown and Gold

br. m. 7, by Ritzy Don—Dougs Girl
Jamison Acres, Elma, N.Y.

Trainer: G. Guindon

9-29⁷⁷	Btva		2500	ft	8400 clm	1	.31¹	1.03¹	1.34³	2.05³	4	4	3⁰	4²³	6⁶	3.10	(GGuindo)	NotableBaron,MarkMinbar,MarysHeel	55
9-19⁷⁷	Btva		2300	sy	7200 clm	1	.32⁴	1.05¹	1.36⁴	2.09³	8	8	7	75ª	8⁹	8.40	(GGuindo)	RitzyGirl,RaiseHobb,FamousJulie	66
9- 7⁷⁷	Btva		2300	gd	7200 clm	1	.31¹	1.02	1.33⁴	2.05	3	3	2	32⁴	78³	1.00*	(GGuindo)	RitzyGirl,ProTestor,TrueProject	72
8-27⁷⁷	Btva		2300	ft	7000 clm	1	.30²	1.02¹	1.34¹	2.05³	3	2	1½	1⅓	8¹¹	3.30	(GGuindo)	RitzyGirl,Quickem,BeverlysJune	82
8-20⁷⁷	Btva		2700	ft	7000 clm	1	.29¹	1.00⁴	1.33²	2.05¹	6	6	7	56	89	9.10	(GGuindo)	RaiseHobb,FreightBaron,MightyYankee	67
8-13⁷⁷	Btva		2500	ft	7200 clm	1	.30²	1.02²	1.33²	2.06¹	7	6	7	6⁴½	5⁴½	5.10	(GGuindo)	EllayJoe,RaiseHobb,KennyYankee	77
8- 7⁷⁷	Btva		2800	ft	8400 clm	1	.30¹	1.02¹	1.34²	2.06²	4	2	2	2³	3½	9.80	(GGuindo)	SirAladdin,CFGuy,RacingGene	79

2.04 Btva 1976

7 • 6000

(4, 2.03½) (½) — $7830)

KENWOOD JIM

DRIVER—YVON DEMERS—White, Black and Red

b. g. 5, by Adoras Dream—Ginny Byrd
Robert Maynard, Ottawa, Ont. Can.

Trainer: Y. Demers

9-27⁷⁷	Btva		2300	ft	6000 clm	1	.30	1.03¹	1.34²	2.06²	5	5	5	57	8¹²½	16.50	(YDemers)	BriarLeaDwight,Kenwoodjim,RaiseHobb	60
9-14⁷⁷	Btva		2500	ft	7000 clm	1	.30²	1.02¹	1.33²	2.04¹	3	3	3	32¹	32	15.00	(YDemers)	Baratony,MountainHaven,GoldenJuelka	62
8-26⁷⁷	Btva		2300	ft	7000 clm	1	.31	1.03	1.34	2.04⁴	4	5	5	76³	76²	45.50	(YDemers)	MarkMinbar,NotableBaron,KeystoneWhiz	76
8-20⁷⁷	Btva		2700	ft	7000 clm	1	.29¹	1.00⁴	1.33²	2.05¹	6	6	7⁸³	89	89	13.90	(YDemers)	MarkMinbar,KeystoneWhiz,ScotchChaser	77
8-13⁷⁷	Btva		2900	ft	8000 clm	1	.30⁴	1.02²	1.33²	2.05³	6	4	4	56	55	13.00	(YDemers)	ClassicAffairN,LncInsValor,RelhomWarrn	77
8- 8⁷⁷	Btva		3400	gd	9000 clm	1	.30³	1.01²	1.34	2.04²	8	4	3	43	55½	11.00	(YDemers)	RuthBaker,ColeHillJohn,ClassicAffairN	70
8- 4⁷⁷	RidC⅝	ms	1400	ft	8500 clm	1	.31	1.02⁴	1.33¹	2.04¹	5	5	2⁰¹	54½	2²	2.25	(YDemers)	SilentSlade,KnwdJim,MightyCasey	

2.03% Det (1) 1977 25 2 7 2 $ 7621
2.03% H.P. % 1976 33 4 1 6 $ 5306

Trainer: D. Manges

8 • 7200

(7, 2.04) (¾) — $40641)

FAMOUS JULIE

DRIVER—LARRY MANGES—Red and White

ch. m. 8, by Julep Time—Bonnie Gene Scott
Dorothy Manges, Harrington, Dela.

9-29⁷⁷	Btva		2100	ft	77nw200psCD	1	.30¹	1.01³	1.33²	2.05¹	3	5	5	81²¹	8¹²½	10.30	(LManges)	SuperDealN,HonstHbbyHrse,QueeniePaige	55
9-19⁷⁷	Btva		2300	ft	7200 clm	1	.32⁴	1.05¹	1.36⁴	2.10	2	3	3	3²	3²	9.80	(LManges)	RitzyGirl,RaiseHobb,FamousJulie	66
9-10⁷⁷	Btva		2300	ft	7200 clm	1	.31¹	1.04¹	1.35	2.07¹	2	2	2	63	76¹	8.80	(LManges)	StarMon,ShadyHillDaisy,MugWump	62
9- 1⁷⁷	Btva		2500	ft	8400 clm	1	.31	1.03	1.34²	2.07⁴	2	3	2	2¹	76²	7.00	(LManges)	GoldenJuelka,MissMaryDl,MarysHeel	80
8-22⁷⁷	Btva		2300	ft	7200 clm	1	.30²	1.02⁴	1.34	2.06³	4	5	5	34	3.4	17.00	(LManges)	MarysHeel,PetronBetsy,FamousJulie	67
8-11⁷⁷	Btva		2300	ft	7200 clm	1	.30²	1.02¹	1.34	2.06³	5	5	5	43³	55½	6.80	(LManges)	StphnDemon,DlmrWynwood,MountainHavn	77
8- 4⁷⁷	ms	2400	ft	76-7nw200ps	1	.30⁴	1.03²	1.35²	2.07¹	3	20	3	2²	2²	3.70	(LManges)	GoodLittleArb,FamousJulie,MountainHvn	82

2.04% B.R. 1977 18 1 3 2 $ 3131
2.04 Btva 1976 40 9 2 8 $ 12627

PACE CLAIMING
EXACTA Wagering This Race
1 Mile — Purse $1700

Saddle Cloth
TANGERINE

ASK FOR HORSE BY PROGRAM NUMBER

Claiming Price $3000
Mares allowed 20%, 3 year olds allowed 50%.

---

1 3000

(6. 2.07) (½) — $10422
LIVELY GENE ‡
DRIVER—ANTHONY MacRAE—Maroon, Gold and White

b h 8, by Gene Abbe—Lively Time
Philip Passarell, Holley, N.Y.

Trainer: P. Passarell
1977 12 2 3 2 $ 3217
1976 18 2 1 0 $ 2059

8-12⁷⁷	Btva	‡1700 ft	3000 clm	1	32¹	1	03⁴	1	35	2	07¹	2	2²	76	2.08²	4.60	(AMacRae)	LarryLinn,BabyArizona,MightyKen	71
8- 2⁷⁷	Btva	‡1900 ft	3500 clm	1	31³	1	04²	1	35.²	06³	1	3⁰	8⁵	2.07³	29.80	(AMacRae)	Edstime,GurnSprings,Scott,GoldPrize	76
7-22⁷⁷	Btva	‡2000 ft	4000 clm	1	30⁴	1	34¹	1	34¹	2	05²	3	64¹	2.07¹	5.00	(AMacRae)	ChesterDevil,Audt,MichaelsEdct	74
7-15⁷⁷	Btva	‡2100 ft	4000 clm	1	31⁴	1	05	1	37	2	09¹	3	6¹⁸¹	2.09¹	50°	(AMacRae)	BrackenField,ChesterDevil,LivelyGene	80
7- 1⁷⁷	Btva	‡1500 sy	3500 clm	1	31³	1	03²	1	35³	2	08⁴	2	1¹³	2.08⁴	2.10°	(AMacRae)	LivelyGene,MarysPenn,Governorette	67
6-30⁷⁷	Btva	‡1400 ft	3500 clm	1	30³	1	03	1	35¹	2	08¹	6	1¹²	2.08²	4.70°	(AMacRae)	ButlerKnight,MarysPenn,LivelyGene	79
6-20⁷⁷	B R	cs‡1700 ft	4000 clm	1	30⁴	1	03³	1	35²	2	06²	6	4³	2.07²	5.90	(AMacRae)	ScooterJones,GoldPrize,SmithHy	74

---

2 3600

(6. 2.05¾ (½) — $18665
GENESEE CHERYL (N)
DRIVER—BRUCE DINEEN—Grey, Red and Green

b m 9, by John A Hanover—Grand Girl
Bruce J. Dineen, Ellicottville, N.Y.

Trainer: B. Dineen
1977 23 3 4 1 $ 4221
1976 23 4 4 1 $ 1906

8-15⁷⁷	Btva	ms 1900	4200 clm	1	32³	1	04³	1	36	2	07⁴	3	3⁰	77	2.09³	20.70	(BDineen)	QuebecFleurie,CCTempo,LadyGoldFront	71
8- 3⁷⁷	Btva	ms 1600	3600 clm	1	32¹	1	03²	1	36³	2	08⁴	4	5	68²	2.08⁴	3.70	(BDineen)	AmyJo,GeneseeCheryl,BabyArizona	75
7-25⁷⁷	Btva	ms 1600	3600 clm	1	31¹	1	36	1	36	2	08¹	4	4	2¹½	2.08¹	4.30	(BDineen)	GeneseeCheryl,SuccessGrnt,VictriaString	72
7-18⁷⁷	Btva	ms 1700	3600 clm	1	31¹	1	04²	1	36	2	07¹	7	7	7¹¹²	2.09¹	33.60	(BDineen)	DRSRhythm,Salimar,ThrdSon	90
7- 6⁷⁷	Btva	ms 1400	3600 clm	1	31³	1	06³	1	39¹	2	10¹	4	5	5⁴²	2.10⁴	12.20	(BDineen)	MichaelsEdct,MightyMcKiyo,ThrdSon	63
7- 6⁷⁷	Btva	ms 1900	7500 clm	1	31	1	06¹	1	38	2	08	2	2	1¹½	2.08	NB	(BDineen)	RitzyGirl,SpeedyStrut,GeneseeCheryl	70
6-28⁷⁷	B.R.	ms	Qua	1	32	1	04³	1	37	2	08⁴	2	2⁰	3³¹	2.09⁴	NB	(BDineen)	GeneseeCheryl,GreatSullivan,EmilyC	78
		ms	Qua tp	1	31⁴	1	05²	1	38¹	2	10¹	6	6	1³⁴	2.10¹			

---

3 4500

(None — $000)
HEZA MONEY
DRIVER—LARRY MANGES—Red and White

b c 3, by Tar Mite—Sucker's Money
Muriel & Hiram Harrington, East Aurora, N.Y.

Trainer: L. Manges
1977 20 2 4 3 $ 4270
First Start

8-10⁷⁷	Btva	ms 1600	4500 clm	1	32	1	03⁴	1	36	2	07⁴	3	5	2¹	2.08²	4.70	(LManges)	SratogaBarbara,HezaMoney,ButtnsDiamond	78
8- 2⁷⁷	Btva	ms 1600	4500 clm	1	31²	1	03²	1	35⁴	2	07⁴	6	5	2³⁴	2.08⁴	4.20	(LManges)	TopMission,Impossible,HezaMoney	74
7-19⁷⁷	Btva	ms 2100	6000 clm	1	32²	1	04²	1	35²	2	07¹	5	3⁰	3⁵	2.09²	16.10	(LManges)	GVGrattan,CaptainCrunch,BentonBuddy	79
7- 6⁷⁷	Btva	gd 6000	6000 clm	1	33²	1	05¹	1	38¹	2	09²	8	8	7¹¹²	2.12	5.30	(LManges)	ScottMeadow,ChesterDevil,BentonBlue	62
6-29⁷⁷	Btva	ms 1800	7500 clm	1	33²	1	06¹	1	36¹	2	08²	4	4	7⁵²	2.09¹	4.70	(LManges)	YankeeJean,NedaSal,ScooterJones(PI 4)	62
6-18⁷⁷	B R.	ms 1900	7500 clm	1	31³	1	03	1	35¹	2	08²	1x6⁰	7	8dis		24.60	(LManges)	MyBrothersHorse,HonorKennedy,GraysPat	78
6-11⁷⁷	B.R.	ms	7500 clm	1	30⁴	1	03¹	1	35²	2	06⁴	5	x8	8dis	2.07⁴	24.50	(LManges)	IanHill,Acropolis,GraysPat	68

---

4 4500

(6. 2.05¾ (½) — $23789)
COPPER T LITE
DRIVER—TERRY EICHAS—Red, Gold and Black

b. g. 8, by Henry T Adios—Copper Flower
Edward Thomas, Rochester, N.Y.

Trainer: N. Bauch
1977 25 1 3 5 $ 3288
1976 19 4 1 2 $ 4224

8-12⁷⁷	Btva	ms 1700	3000 clm	1	30²	1	02¹	1	34	2	07	7	2	2	2.07²	4.40	(TEichas)	MissMove,JJByrd,CopperTLite	71
8- 4⁷⁷	Btva	ms 1800	3500 clm	1	31³	1	05²	1	35²	07.²	2	3	4⁵³	2.09	4.40	(TEichas)	BentonBlue,LittleEtta,WorthyRoger	82
7-29⁷⁷	Btva	sy 3000	3500 clm	1	31¹	1	03⁴	1	36²	2	09⁴	5	6	5⁸	2.10¹	4.40	(TEichas)	DocsDuke,KeystoneGallant,CopperTLite	73
7-20⁷⁷	Btva	ms 1600	3000 clm	1	31	1	04¹	1	34⁴	2	07⁴	7	7	4¹⁴	2.08	10.30	(TEichas)	RogerFarr,TactileBay,TarAlmahurst	88

5

BARBS TUFFY (7, 2.08) — $74373
DRIVER—DON HOLMES—Light Blue and White

blk. m. 10, by Timely Topic—Barbara Grattan K
Gordon Gent, Milton, Ont., Can.

																	Driver	
8-13??	Btva	ms	1400	ft	3000 clm	1	.31¹	1.03¹	1.35⁴	2.07⁴	7	1o	1	2²	3⁷	2.09¹	3.30	(GGent)	BudDDuke,Keystone,Joel,FantasticIrish
8- 1??	FimD	ms	900	ft	3000 clm	1	.29⁴	1.03⁴	1.36³	2.08⁴	3	3	6	85	35³	2.09⁴	7.75	(GGent)	LastAttorney,John,DoctorC,BarbsTuffy
8- 6??	FimD	ms	900	ft	3000 clm	1	.30³	1.02	1.33	2.04³	1	5	5	3³⁴	4⁴¹	2.05⁴	—	(BAltzr)	BarbsTuffy,SociaJet,DimplesDeb
7-28??	Ornvi	ms	650	ft	c-2500 clm	1	.32	1.03	1.36	2.03³	1	6	6	2²	1nk	2.03³	3.95	(AMorris)	BarbsTuffy,SociaJet,DimplesDeb
7-21??	Ornvi	ms	650	ft	2500 clm	1	.31²	1.04²	1.36	2.10³	5	5	4	4²¹	4²¹	2.11	1.55	(AMorris)	ParkerMaid,DimplesDeb,DaggerLobell
7- 9??	Ornvi	ms	650	ft	2500 clm	1	.31²	1.06	1.38	2.10³	3	3	1	3¹	12⁴	2.11	—	(AMorris)	BarbsTuffy,HaroldsPrncss,KnightGloom
7- 6??	Ornvi	ms	650	ft	3600 clm	1	.31	1.04	1.36	2.09	2	2	2	2²	2nd	2.09	3.10	(AMorris)	BarbsTuffy,HaroldsPrncss,GoodOldFlo
7-14??	Ornvi	ms	650	ft	2500 clm	1	.31	1.03	1.36	2.08⁴	2	2	3	2¹	2nd	2.08⁴	2.20	(AMorris)	PinedaleTris,BarbsTuffy,GoodOldFlo
7-12??	Ornvi	ms	650	ft	2500 clm	1	.30³	1.03¹	1.37³	2.05²	4	2	2	3¹	3⁴¹	2.08²	2.20	(AMorris)	LancersDust,DimplesDeb,BarbsTuffy

Trainer: D. Holmes

	1977	33	6	9	11	$ 4443
2.08% Ornvi	1976	52	11	9	6	5569
2.10% Ornvi						70
						77
						64

6

GLENDA MAHONE (7, 2.05½) — $17339)
DRIVER—BOB ALTIZER—Gold, Green and White

b. m. 9, by Glendale Direct—Winnie Mahone
You & Me Stables, Inc., Batavia, N.Y.

8- 5??	Btva	ms	1600	ft	3600 clm	1	.32	1.05	1.38²	2.09²	2	1	1	2¹	35³	2.10³	3.10	(JeAltz)	PennysBenny,ColdStreak,GlendaMahone
7-26??	Btva	ms	1400	ft	3000 clm	1	.32	1.04¹	1.36³	2.09⁴	2	3	6	6⁴	4⁴¹	5.70	(BAltzr)	DevereauxRader,DillerVolo,SponDilly
7-19??	Btva	ms		ft	3000 clm	1	.31³	1.03	1.35	2.07¹	6	4	4	4¹¹	4¹¹	2.09³	—	(AMorris)	Acropolis,DalePro,AdiosPeterCooper
7- 9??	Btva	ms		ft	Qua h-dr	1	.31¹	1.04	1.36	2.07²	7	3	4	4	DNF	NB	(JeAltz)	Excalibur,CindyLands,MrshmllowFluff
7- 6??	Btva	ms	1400	ft	Qua h-dr	1	.33	1.04	1.36¹	2.09	4	50	6	7	7dis	—	(JeAltz)	HilltopBenny,WhiteFace,GoJhnnyGo
6-24??	B.R.	ms	650	ft	3600 clm	1	.31	1.06¹	1.39	2.10	ck			3²¹	DNF	3.10	(GSarama)	MichaelsEdict,MightyMcKiyo,ThirdSon
6-17??	B.R.	ms	650	ft	2500 clm	1	.31	1.03¹	1.36	2.09	2	3	2	2²	65³	2.10¹	3.10	(AGiulia)	Twila,Sallimar,LastWii
6-16??	B.R.	ms	650	ft	3500 clm	1	.30¹	1.02¹	1.35³	2.08³	5	2	2	3¹	4¹³	2.08²	12.80	(AGiulia)	DaveysShai,CharminCountess,FlimFlamGirl

Trainer: Jo. Altizer (Altizer Stable)

	1977	19	5	1	2	$ 4218
2.05½ Btva	1976	30	6	4	5	6996
						79
						68
						84
						72
						63
						78
						80

7

POPLAR TUXEDO (5, 2.05½) — $16450)
DRIVER—TED TURCOTTE, JR.—Yellow and Red

b. g. 6, by Tuxedo Hanover—Poplar Annabel
David G. Gerstner, Rochester, N.Y.

8-10??	Btva	ms	1600	ft	3000 clm	1	.31¹	1.03¹	1.35³	2.08²	4	2o	5	5²³	74¹	2.09¹	1.70*	(TTurJr)	KeystoneGallant,AvonCarefree,Nozzle
8- 1??	Btva	ms	2000	ft	4000 clm	1	.30	1.01⁴	1.34¹	2.06³	7	2	2	2nd	87¹	2.07⁴	1.90*	(TTurJr)	QuebecFleure,ThirdSon,MissFrostyC
8- 7??	Btva	ms	1700	ft	3000 clm	1	.31³	1.03	1.33	2.06³	1	5	5	5³⁴	8¹²³	8.20	(TTurJr)	ThirdSon,MightyKen,QuebecFleure
7-15??	Btva	ms	1800	ft	5000 clm	1	.30²	1.02¹	1.34²	2.07²	6	4	4	4²⁴	85³	2.08²	6.50	(RTurcot)	IndianRuler,Butterknight,MssMargaretEd
7- 1??	Btva	ms	1800	ft	5000 clm	1	.30²	1.02¹	1.34²	2.07²	4	4	3	4³	43	2.08	3.30	(TTurJr)	McIntoshMagic,PearlieChita,RoyalShow
6-24??	B.R.	ms	1900	ft	5000 clm	1	.30¹	1.03²	1.35²	2.06³	5	6	7	76³	5²³	6.20	(TTurJr)	DelLynch,SlippersBoy,IanHill
6-17??	B.R.	ms	1900	ft	5000 clm	1	.30¹	1.03	1.36²	2.09	6	8	7	7²³	7²²	2.08	10.30	(TTurJr)	SargeGunner,ColeHillJohn,Gingham
6- 9??	B.R.	ms	1900	ft	5000 clm	1	.32²	1.04¹	1.35	2.06⁴	3	3	4	3³¹	5³⁴	dh2.07³	22.90	(TTurJr)	Gingham,SargeGunner,BentonBuddy

Trainer: T. Turcotte, Jr.

	1977	10	0	0	0	$ 286
2.05½ Btva	1976	43	7	9	5	10876
						78
						72
						74
						77
						79
						80
						64

8

MISS FROSTY C (8, 2.05) — $32071)
DRIVER—FRED HASLIP—Blue, White and Gold

ch. m. 6, by Cardinal G—Stan Dream
Sweetland Stables, Stafford, N.Y.

8-12??	Btva	ms	1700	ft	3600 clm	1	.30²	1.02¹	1.34	2.07	8	5	5²³	52³	2.07³	6.50	(TTurJr)	MissMove,JJByrd,CopperTLite
8- 3??	Btva	ms	1600	ft	3600 clm	1	.31¹	1.04²	1.35¹	2.07⁴	4	4	2	2nd	32¹	2.07⁴	10.00	(TTurJr)	QuebecFleure,ThirdSon,MissFrostyC
7-25??	Btva	ms	1600	ft	3600 clm	1	.32¹	1.05¹	1.37	2.09⁴	6	3	2o	4²⁴	42⁴	2.10	10.00	(TTurJr)	ThirdSon,MightyKen,QuebecFleure
7-	Btva	sy	1700	ft	3600 clm	1	.31	1.04¹	1.36⁴	2.09⁴	4	4	2o	4²¹	4⁹²	2.10	4.50	(FHaslip)	Edstime,DreamerLobell,MightyMcKiyo
7- 6??	Btva	my	1400	ft	3600 clm	1	.33	1.06³	1.39²	2.10	8	8	8	66	55	2.11	4.90	(TTurJr)	MichaelsEdict,MightyMcKiyo,ThirdSon
6-27??	Btva		1400	ft	3600 clm	1	.31	1.03¹	1.36¹	2.09	6	8	40	44	77³	2.09⁴	3.70	(TTurJr)	Twila,Sallimar,LastWii
6-14??	B.R.	cs		ft	Qua	1	.31⁴	1.04	1.36²	2.07²	2	2	2	3¹	43	2.08	NB	(DDiogua)	GlendalePisa,McIntoshMagic,FrostClns

Trainer: D. Dioguardi

	2.05 B.R.	1977	6	0	0	1	$ 723
		1976	41	5	10	6	9913
							71
							75
							72
							80
							63
							78
							79

Batavia Downs 4th Race August 25, 1977

1 Lively Gene
Current form	0
Consistency	3
Class	0
Driver	1
Post position	3
Total	7

2 Genesee Cheryl
Current form	3
Consistency	2
Class	0
Driver	2
Post position	3
Total	10

3 Heza Money
Current form	1
Consistency	2
Class	0
Driver	1
Post position	2
Total	6

4 Copper T Lite
Current form	0
Consistency	0
Class	0
Driver	1
Post position	2
Total	3

5 Barbs Tuffy
Current form	2
Consistency	3
Class	0
Driver	1
Post position	1
Total	7

6 Glenda Mahone
Current form	0
Consistency	2
Class	0
Driver	2
Post position	1
Total	5

7 Poplar Tuxedo
Current form	0
Consistency	0
Class	2
Driver	1
Post position	0
Total	3

8 Miss Frosty C
Current form	0
Consistency	0
Class	0
Driver	2
Post position	0
Total	2

Contenders:
2	Genesee Cheryl	10
5	Barbs Tuffy	7
1	Lively Gene	7
3	Heza Money	6
6	Glenda Mahone	5

Analysis. Glenda Mahone and possibly Poplar Tuxedo will go for the lead, resulting in a fast pace. Genesee Cheryl could move at the half, in front of Heza Money. Or driver Dineen might save Genesee Cheryl until the stretch. Either way, Genesee Cheryl has the best chance of winning this one because of post-position advantage and one respectable move during the race.

Results.

FOURTH RACE — 1 Mile					$3000 Claiming Pace				$1700
Barbs Tuffy ms	5	1⁰	1	1	1²	1¹½	D. Holmes		5.00
Genesee Cheryl ms	2	3	5	4⁰²	2¹	2¹¾	B. Dineen		*2.10
Glenda Mahone ms	6	6	4	5	5¾	3½	B. Altizer		12.20
Miss Frosty C	8	8	8	6	4nk	4½	F. Haslip		6.50
Copper T Lite ms	4	5	6	7	7¾	5²	T. Eichas		5.20
Lively Gene‡	1	2	3	2	3¹¼	6¹¼	A. MacRae		9.60
Poplar Tuxedo ms	7	7	7	8	8	7³	T. Turcotte, Jr.		20.10
Heza Money ms	3	4	2	3⁰	6½	8	L. Manges		3.70

$2 MUTUEL PRICES	5. Barbs Tuffy	12.00	5.60	4.80
Official Program Nos.	2. Genesee Cheryl		3.80	3.20
	6. Glenda Mahone			8.40

Time — .30⅖   1.04⅖   1.35⅖   2.07⅖
EXACTA — 5 AND 2 $52.60

Batavia Downs 6th Race August 25, 1977

1 Rowmars Angel

Current form	5
Consistency	2
Class	0
Driver	1
Post position	3
Total	11

3 Top Skipper

Current form	2
Consistency	3
Class	0
Driver	1
Post position	2
Total	8

2 Arnies Betsy

Current form	5
Consistency	3
Class	−2
Driver	1
Post position	3
Total	10

4 Scott Meadow

Current form	2 (omit 7/23
Consistency	3 race)
Class	0
Driver	1
Post position	2
Total	8

(6) PACE CLAIMING

1 Mile — Purse $2400

EXACTA Wagering This Race

Claiming Price $5000
Mares allowed 20%.

"KNIGHTS OF ST. JOHN"

ASK FOR HORSE BY PROGRAM NUMBER

Saddle Cloth
BLUE

---

1 — ROWMARS ANGEL ‡ 6000
(6, 2.09) (½) — $2576)
DRIVER—TERRY EICHAS—Red, Gold and Black

b. m. 7, by Hartack Hanover—Little Fox
Pritchard Anderson, No. Tonawanda, N.Y.

Trainer: N. Bauch

			1977	28	5	4	3	$ 7763
2.06½ B.R.			1976	18	5	3	2	$ 2310
2.09 Hamb								

8-16⁷⁷ Btva mst2400 ft 6000 clm 1 .30³1.02¹1.33 2.06³ 6 6 6 6 6⁰ 2.30* (TEichas) RwmarsAngel,HonorKennedy,ScottMeadow 75
8- 9⁷⁷ Btva mst2300 ft 6000 clm 1 .30¹1.02²1.34 2.06¹ 5 3 3 2¹ 3³½ 1.70* (TEichas) ButlerAbbot,IanHill,RowmarsAngel 72
8- 2⁷⁷ Btva mst2300 ft 6000 clm 1 .30¹1.02¹1.32²2.06 2 2 2½ 2¹ 2½ .70* (TEichas) HonorKennedy,RowmarsAngel,Goodluck 76
7-25⁷⁷ Btva mst2300 ft 6000 clm 1 .31³1.03³1.35²2.06⁴ 2 3 1 1⁴ 1⁴ 1.80* (TEichas) RowmarsAngel,BckeyeKnight,BradleysGay 72
7-19⁷⁷ Btva mst2400 ft 6000 clm 1 .30²1.03¹1.34⁴2.07⁴ 3 8 7 7⁵³ 7⁵³ 20.10 (TEichas) SctchChaser,BckeyeKnight,WalleyedWillie 79
7-12⁷⁷ Btva mst2400 ft 6000 clm 1 .31 1.04¹1.36 2.07 10 10 3⁰ 1ⁿˢ 1¹½ 1.70* (TEichas) RowmarsAngel,IanHill,RowmarsAngel 84
7- 9⁷⁷ Btva mst1900 ft 6000 clm 1 .30³1.03 1.33 2.05⁴ 7 7 6⁰ 6⁵³ 6⁵³ 3.50 (TEichas) MyBrothersHorse,AdiosWilla,SamC 77

2 — ARNIES BETSY 6000
(6, 2.09½) (½) — $7077)
DRIVER—JIM RANKIN—Red, Blue and White

b. m. 7, by Smash Hit—Ritas Betsy
Betty Price, Toronto, Ont., Can.

Trainer: C. Bitulco

			1977	24	5	4	4	$ 4764
2.06½ FlmD			1976	31	7	5	5	$ 4407
2.09½ Wodsk								

8-14⁷⁷ FlmD 1100 ft c-4000 clm 1 .32 1.03 1.34²2.07 4 20 2⁰ 2³ 1³ 1.50* (RMcLean) ArniesBetsy,DarlingJ,AbideN
8- 7⁷⁷ FlmD 1100 ft 4000 clm 1 .29 1.02²1.34²2.04¹ 6 5 2⁰ 2² 2² 1.30* (RMcLean) WatchsPride,ArniesBtsy,HighMoraleN
7-31⁷⁷ RidC⁵⁸ 1100 ft 4000 clm hcp 1 .30³1.03 1.35²2.07³ 4 3 3² 3² 3¹ 1.20* (GPayne) OldZero,JayDeeLonesome,ArniesBetsy
7-24⁷⁷ FlmD 1100 ft 4000 clm 1 .29⁴1.01³1.34 2.06² 5 5 4 4 4 2.50 (RMcLean) ArniesBtsy,MajstGratin,DirctCause
7-12⁷⁷ Wodsk 500 ft 3500 clm 1 .33 1.07 1.38³2.10 2 1 1¹ 1¹ 1¹ 4.25 (DHepbur) ArniesBetsy,Kelann,PrimaDaisy
6-22⁷⁷ Lon 800 ft 3500 clm 1 .31⁴1.04³1.36 2.08 3 3 3 3² 3²³ 2.35 (BWilson) ClaybrkCopper,ArnesBtsy,DchssStein
6- 8⁷⁷ Lon 750 ft 3000 clm 1 .31 1.04 1.36 2.08³ 7 7 5 5²⁰ 2ⁿᵏ 2.00* (BWilson) ArniesBetsy,BluePence,AlexChoice

3 — TOP SKIPPER 5000
(4, 2.03½) (¾) — $10352)
DRIVER—YVON DEMERS—White, Black and Red

b. g. 5, by Meadow Skipper—Schatzie
Gerald M. Richmond, Windsor, Ont., Can.

Trainer: Y. Demers

			1977	14	3	3	3	$ 6898
2.05½ B.B.'s			1976	18	5	7	4	$ 8898
2.03½ V.D. ¾								

8-17⁷⁷ Btva ms 2400 ft 5000 clm 1 .30⁴1.01¹1.35¹2.07² 5 5 4 4⁰ 3²³ 2.40* (YDemers) Audit,GraysPat,TopSkipper
8- 9⁷⁷ Btva ms 2300 ft 5000 clm 1 .31²1.03 1.35⁴2.07¹ 2 2 2¹ 2¹ 2¹ 3.00 (GGuindo) TrueProject,TopSkipper,DalePro
7-31⁷⁷ RidC⁵⁸ 950 gd 5000 clm hcp 1 .30³1.03 1.35 2.08⁴ 4 8 8x 8dis 8dis 1.70 (YDemers) LelandCreed,Earline,JsBonnie
7-24⁷⁷ RidC⁵⁸ 950 ft 5000 clm 1 .30¹1.03¹1.34³2.06⁴ 5 7 5⁰ 7⁴ 2nd 4.05 (YDemers) ChoreBoyPat,TopSkipper,TrueTom
7-17⁷⁷ RidC⁵⁸ 950 ft 5000 clm 1 .31²1.04³1.37³2.09² 1 1 1 1¹ 1ⁿˢ 5.85 (YDemers) EzraQuick,ChoreBoyPat,TopSkipper
3-29⁷⁷ W.R.⁵⁸ 3500 sl 5000 clm 1 .31 1.03¹1.32²2.04 5 5²³ 3³ 3³ 2.10 (NDessur) AquariousTime,TimePatchen,Elyar
3-19⁷⁷ W.R.⁵⁸ 3000 ft 12500 clm hcp 1 .30⁴1.02¹1.33 2.04² 7 7x 7 be 5dis NB (NDessur) ReplicaPace,FleetwoodBob,LindaBTip

4 — SCOTT MEADOW 5000
(4, 2.05½) (¾) — $33517)
DRIVER—JIM WETZEL—Brown, Gold and Green

br. g. 10, by Meadow Battles—Sweet Alice
Richard J. Gryczynski, Depew, N.Y.

Trainer: G. Neamon

			1977	28	3	9	3	$ 7579
2.08½ B.R.			1976	40	7	6	5	$ 5857
2.08½ B.R.								

8-16⁷⁷ Btva ms 2400 ft 5000 clm 1 .30³1.02¹1.33³2.06³ 6 6 7⁴¹ 3⁴ 5⁴ 5.90 (GSarama) RwmarsAngel,HonorKennedy,ScottMeadow 75
8- 9⁷⁷ Btva ms 2300 ft 5000 clm 1 .30⁴1.03 1.34 2.07² 6 6 5⁹¹ 5⁷¹ 3⁴½ 13.20 (JWetzel) ButlerAbbot,TopSkipper,DalePro 72
7-30⁷⁷ Btva ms 2300 ft 5000 clm 1 .30¹1.01²1.32⁴2.05⁴ 5 4 2⁸ 2² 2² 9.20 (JWetzel) BrackenField,ScottMeadow,MarysPenn 77
7-23⁷⁷ Btva ms 2400 ft 5000 clm 1 .30⁴1.04³1.36 2.08¹ 8 6⁶ 6⁶ 5⁴ 31.40 (JWetzel) ButlerKnight,TrueProject,IndianRuler 76

5 · 5000

(6, 2.04¾) (¾) — $16900)
NOBLE STEIN
DRIVER—JULIEN JOANISSE—Blue and Gold
br. g. 10, by Direct Nobel—Miss Doreen Grattan
Rene Nadon, Templeton, Que., Can.
Trainer: J. Joanisse

8-14⁷⁷ Btva	ms 1900 ft 5000 clm	1	.31¹1.05	1.37⁴2.08¹	2	1	1	1¹	2.08¹	7.10	(GSarama)	BethOregon,ScottMeadow,GraysPat	80
7- 6⁷⁷ Btva	ms 1700 gd 4000 clm	1	.33¹1.06¹	1.38¹2.09²	7	1	1	1¹	2.09²	3.80	(JWetzel)	ScottMeadow,ChesterDevil,BentonBlue	63
6-24⁷⁷ B.R.	ms 1700 ft 4000 clm	1	.32¹1.05¹	1.37¹2.08⁴	7	10	11	1³	2.08⁴	5.80	(JWetzel)	ScottMeadow,EvamarieMaeWin,SuperLaird	79

2.06½ FlmD   2.10⁴ Lon
Trainer: J. Joanisse
	1977	1976				$
	22	7	1	4	$ 4464	
	26	5	4	4	$ 2303	

6 · 5000

(7, 2.08¾) (¾) — $2391)
BRACKEN FIELD
DRIVER—RALPH KAUFMAN—Brown, Gold and Green
b. g. 8, by Canny Scot—Bonny Roto
Poverty Stables, Batavia, N.Y.
Trainer: N. Kaufman

8-16⁷⁷ Btva	ms 2700 sy 7000 clm	1	.30³1.03¹	1.35²2.09¹	7x	x8x	be		DNF	14.90	(RKaufma)	JustASpinner,SirAladdin,NotableBaron	75
8- 5⁷⁷ Btva	ms 2800 ft 7000 clm	1	.30 1.02¹	1.33²2.05⁴	5	2	3	6²	2.06¹	6.50	(RKaufma)	SirAladdin,CFGuy,RacingGene	79
7-30⁷⁷ Btva	ms 2300 ft 5000 clm	1	.30¹1.01²	1.31 1.34	3	1	1	1⁴⁰	1.40*	(RKaufma)	BrackenField,ScottMeadow,MarysPenn	76
7-23⁷⁷ Btva	ms 2400 ft 5000 clm	1	.31 1.03	1.35²2.06²	6	5	5	5¹⁰	2.08	6.35	(RKaufma)	IrtonPrince,BrackenField,RoughLaneH	77
7-15⁷⁷ Btva	ms 2100 sy 4000 clm	1	.31⁴1.05	1.37 2.09¹	2	2	2	2¹³	2.09¹	5.40	(RKaufma)	BrackenField,ChesterDevil,LivelyGene	80
7- 6⁷⁷ Btva	ms 1400 ft 3000 clm	1	.31¹1.04²	1.37 2.10¹	5	4	4	5⁴¹	2.10¹	11.70	(RKaufma)	BrackenField,QuebecFleurie,JLByrd	63
6-24⁷⁷ B.R.	ms 1400 ft 2500 clm	1	.31¹1.02⁴	1.34²2.08¹	2	2	2	2¹	2.08²	4.70	(RKaufma)	BrackenField,MaryAWil	79

2.05¾ Btva   2.05% L.B. ½
Trainer: N. Kaufman
	1977	1976				$
	14	3	3	1	$ 4344	
	21	1	0	0	$ 2391	

7 · 5000

(7, 2.06½) (½) — $13017)
SPEEDY STRUT
DRIVER—ANTHONY MacRAE—Maroon, Gold and White
br. g. 8, by Lieutenant Gray—Princess Strut
Irene J. Boyd, Clarence, N.Y.
Trainer: H. MacMillan

8-16⁷⁷ Btva	ms 2400 ft 5000 clm	1	.30³1.02¹	1.33²2.06³	5	5	5	6³⁴	2.07²	10.60	(AMacRae)	RwmarsAngel,HonorKennedy,ScottMeadow	75
8- 9⁷⁷ Btva	ms 2300 ft 5000 clm	1	.30⁴1.03²	1.34²2.05¹	6	7	7	7¹⁰³	2.07²	29.70	(AMacRae)	ButlerAbbot,IanHill,RwmarsAngel	72
8- 3⁷⁷ Btva	ms 2300 ft 5000 clm	1	.30¹1.01²	1.34²2.04²	6	8	8	6⁴²	2.05	17.90	(AMacRae)	EqualKash,PearlieChita,SargeGunner	74
7-19⁷⁷ Btva	ms 2400 ft 5000 clm	1	.30²1.03¹	1.34²2.06³	1	2	2	2¹³	2.06⁴	8.60	(AMacRae)	SctchChsr,BckyKnght,WilleyedWillie(Pl 4)	79
7-12⁷⁷ Btva	ms 1900 ft 5000 clm	1	.29²1.00	1.31²2.04⁴	4	4	4	4¹⁰⁴	2.07²	11.90	(AMacRae)	GigiLamour,BredByrd,SpeedyStrut	84
7- 6⁷⁷ Btva	ms 1400 ft 5000 clm	1	.32 1.04³	1.37 2.04⁴	4	3	3	3²¹	2.05¹	NB	(PSorge)	RitzyGirl,SpeedyStrut,GeneseeCheryl	70
11-26⁷⁶ Btva	my 5000 clm CD	1	.30⁴1.04	1.35²2.08	1	3	3	1ⁿˢ	2.08	2.70*	(PSorge)	SpeedyStrut,FriscoBennie,DeluxeModel	53

2.07½ Btva   2.07 B.R.
Trainer: H. MacMillan
	1977	1976				$
	21	3	5	4	$ 4855	
	18	4	2	4	$ 4918	

8 · 5000

(5, 2.06¾) (½) — $31796)
JEFFERSON SLO POKE
DRIVER—DON HOLMES—Lt. Blue and White
br. g. 10, by Meadow Skipper—Kitty Spangler
Out In The Country Stable, Darien, N.Y.
Trainer: J. Beszczynski, Jr.

8-16⁷⁷ Btva	2400 ft 5000 clm	1	.30³1.02¹	1.33²2.06³	8	8	8	8⁹⁴	2.08³	38.70	(DHolmes)	RwmarsAngel,HonorKennedy,ScottMeadow	75
8- 3⁷⁷ Btva	2400 ft 5000 clm	1	.30²1.03²	1.34²2.05¹	6	6	7	5⁶	2.06²	36.50	(JBesIII)	IrtonPrnce,RusslTorrence,PearlieChita	75
7-28⁷⁷ Btva	2400 ft 5000 clm	1	.29⁴1.02¹	1.34²2.07¹	6	6	7	6⁴²	2.06²	15.20	(JBesIII)	BredByrd,IrtonPrince,ScooterJones	77
7-21⁷⁷ Btva	2400 ft 5000 clm	1	.31¹1.04	1.35 2.07¹	10	10	12	12¹	2.07¹	5.10	(JBesIII)	JeffersonSloPoke,ScottLobell,GraysPat	78
7-13⁷⁷ Btva	1700 ft 4000 clm	1	.31¹1.06	1.37²2.08²	2	2	2	1¹¹	2.08²	4.20	(JBesIII)	JeffersonSloPoke,EstrnQueen,MoonMssin	70
7- 4⁷⁷ Btva	1700 ft 4000 clm	1	.32¹1.03⁴	1.34²1.37	3	3	3	4⁴¹	4.90	(JBesIII)	GVGrattan,Peetong,CaptainCrunch	81
6-24⁷⁷ B.R.	cs 1700 ft 4000 clm	1	.32²1.05¹	1.37 2.08⁴	4	5	20	7⁵³	2.10*	(JBesIII)	ScottMdw,EvamarieMaeWin,SprLaird(Pl 6)	79

2.06¾ Btva
Trainer: J. Beszczynski, Jr.
	1977	1976				$
	5	0	0	1	$ 796	
	29	4	2	4	$ 3939	

5 Noble Stein

Current form	0
Consistency	2
Class	0
Driver	1
Post position	1
Total	4

7 Speedy Strut

Current form	0
Consistency	0
Class	0
Driver	1
Post position	0
Total	1

6 Bracken Field

Current form	3
Consistency	3
Class	0
Driver	1
Post position	1
Total	8

8 Jefferson Slo Poke

Current form	2
Consistency	1
Class	0
Driver	1
Post position	0
Total	4

Comments. 7 Speedy Strut and 8 Jefferson Slo Poke can be eliminated from consideration immediately. 5 Noble Stein has shown too little recent form to be playable. Arnies Betsy is moving up in class after a change of barn—insufficient information to be playable.

This leaves the following contenders:

1 Rowmars Angel	11
3 Top Skipper	8
6 Bracken Field	8
4 Scott Meadow	8

Analysis. Scott Meadow and Bracken Field are front-runners. The latter is coming into this race after two tough starts. Scott Meadow, however, has the inside and will probably get the lead first, parking Bracken Field in a fast first half. The likelihood is that Rowmars Angel or, less likely, Top Skipper will overhaul Bracken Field in the stretch.

Result.

SIXTH RACE — 1 Mile								$5000 Claiming Pace				$2400
Rowmars Angel‡ ms	1	2	2	2	2^3	1nk	T. Eichas	2.70
Top Skipper ms	3	4	4	4	3^6	2nk	Y. Demers	2.00
Scott Meadow ms	4	1	1	1	1hd	$3^5{}_{\frac{1}{2}}$	J. Wetzel	16.90
Bracken Field ms	6x	6	7	6	6^2	$4^3_{\frac{3}{4}}$	R. Kaufman	7.10
Speedy Strut ms	7	7	6	5	5nk	$5\frac{1}{2}$	A. MacRae	41.60
Jefferson Slo Poke	8	8	8	7	7	6^{16}	D. Holmes	32.30
Arnies Betsy ms	2	3	3	3	$x4x\frac{1}{2}$	$7^3\frac{1}{2}$	J. Rankin	*1.80
Noble Stein ms	5	5	5	ex8	8	ex8	J. Joanisse	47.60

$2 MUTUEL PRICES	1. Rowmars Angel	7.40	3.80	2.60
Official Program Nos.	3. Top Skipper		3.60	3.00
	4. Scott Meadow			4.60

Time — .33   1.05   1.36   2.07⅗
EXACTA — 1 AND 3 $25.00

6

Overlay and Underlay Betting

What Are Overlays and Underlays?

The odds on a horse are determined, as we have seen, by the amount of money wagered on it. Since the state and race track deduct 20 percent of the total pool, your racing dollar is worth only 80 cents. But you can reduce the odds against yourself by betting horses that go off at a good price.

It is important for you not only to get your share of winners, but to get them at acceptable or more than acceptable prices. When a horse you consider a respectable bet at 3 to 1 goes off at odds of 6 to 1, the result is what professional bettors call an overlay. When a horse that is a worthwhile bet at 2 to 1, but not at higher odds, goes off at 6 to 5, the result is an underlay—a poor risk. In principle, underlays are not worth betting.

So it is not enough for you to select the winner of a race—it is also essential that you select horses that go off at good prices. Just as you will not, if you are a good shopper, buy the first automobile you see at the dealer's price, so you will not bet a horse you like at a prohibitive price. You will look for overlays and realize your margin of profit at the races by betting them on a steady basis while laying off races in which your horse is an underlay.

How to Increase Your Chances of Winning by Finding True Overlays

How do you decide whether a horse is a good bet? Since the public is not infallible in its selections and sometimes permits a solid contender to go off at far higher odds than a good handicapper would give it, you can realize a nice profit by betting clear-cut overlays.

You must be an astute handicapper to determine what the odds on a horse should be. If you are not a good handicapper, the odds you assign will be either too high or too low for the horse you bet. In

PACE CLAIMING

1 Mile — Purse $1900

EXACTA Wagering This Race

Claiming Price $3500
Mares allowed 20%, 4 year old horses allowed 30%.

ASK FOR HORSE BY PROGRAM NUMBER

Saddle Cloth
BLACK

---

1 — LADY COLD FRONT

MS 4200

(8, 2133/4) Mat (1/2) — $81

DRIVER-

Green, White and Gold

b m 9, by Cold Front—Aurelias Pride
Frank Santucci, Honeoye Falls, N.Y.

Trainer: F. Santucci

8- 4⁷⁷	Btva	ms	1800	ft	4200 clm	1 30⁴ 1 02¹ 1 34² 2 07	8	8	8	7⁰	6⁹¹	6⁷	2 08³	26 90	(TLanphe)	MisFreeFlo,Cdarwood,Judge,SetlandAags
7-28⁷	Btva	ms	1500	ft	3000 clm	1 31⁴ 1 04 1 34 2 07⁴	2	2	3¹¹	2³	1 2¹	1 2¹	2 08	7 60	(TLanphe)	HppyAcrsSuse,LdyCldFrnt,Sratoga⁰⁴

2 08⅕ Btva Q   2 08⅕ B.R.   2 13⅕ Hmlok Mat

---

2 — C. C. TEMPO

MS 3500

(4, 2.06⅗)(⅗) — $15567

DRIVER-CINDY STEVENS—Red, White and Blue

b g 8, by Ritzy Don—Ambro Frolic
Cynthia Stevens, Lancaster, N.Y.

Trainer: H. Stevens

2 08⅕ B.R.   2 07⅗ Ornvl

---

3 — A Q EQUADOR ᴺʸ

3500

(4, 2.04 (¹⁄₅) — $20421

DRIVER—PHIL SORGE—Sand and Brown

b h 8, by Terry C—May Chief
Robert & Anthony DiSarno, Buffalo, N.Y.

Trainer: R. DiSarno

---

4 — QUEBEC FLEURIE

MS 3500

(3, 2.08⅗)(⅗) — $6326)

DRIVER—RICHARD BLAUN—Gold, Red and Blue

b h 4, by Val Fleure—Quebec Chief
Thomas Buzzee, Buff.''

Trainer: J. Zangara

4550

5 MS 3500

6 MS 4200

7 MS 3500

8 MS 4200

JEFF W
DRIVER—TERRY EICHAS—Red, Gold and Black
(9, 2.05¾ (½) — $19321)
b. g. 10, by Meadow Lands—Indian Gal
Joyce A. Anderson, No. Tonawanda, N.Y.
Trainer: N. Bauch

6-23⁷⁷	B.R.	ms	1600	ft	4375	clm	1	.31	1.03⁴	1.36	2.06²	6	7	7	7¹⁴¹	7¹⁵	2.092	31.10	(JZangar)	CptainCrunch,DreamerLbell,BuddyVelbob	75
6-13⁷⁷	B.R.	ms	1500	ft	3750	clm	1	.31⁴¹	1.04¹	1.37	2.09	4	7	7	4²¹	2³	2.09¹	16.70	(JZangar)	AmyJo,QuebecFleurie,Becket	72
6- 2⁷⁷	B.R.	ms	1600	sy	4375	clm	1	.32	1.06¹	1.39³	2.12²	8	8	8	7⁶³	6⁶³	dh2.134	51.80	(JZangar)	Tonvar,FarmTaara,NorasLastBoy	49

2.12¼ B.R. Q gd   1977   10   0   3   2 $ 1852
2.05¾ Btva   1976   28   4   2   1 $ 3921

MELS FREE FLO
Blue, White and Gold
(3, 2.07½ Q (¼) — $3321)
br. m. 7, by Forever Hanover—Meadow Girl
Flossie S. & Nelson M. Mason, Avon, N.Y.
Trainer: F. Haslip

6-28⁷⁷	Btva	ms	1600	ft	4000	clm	1	.30⁴¹	1.02¹	1.34⁴	2.07¹	3	4	4	2ⁿᵈ	4³	2.074	3.10	(FHaslip)	MlsFreeFlo,CdarwoodJudge,SctlandAgns	82
6-16⁷⁷	B.R.	ms	1700	ft	4000	clm	1	.32	1.04¹	1.36¹	2.07¹	5	6	6	8⁸	8⁸	2.091	8.70	(FHaslip)	BannersPrince,RogerFarr,LarryLinn	77
6-29⁷⁷	Btva	ms	1700	ft	4000	clm	1	.30⁴¹	1.03¹	1.35³	2.07²	5	5	2x	8x¹⁵,x8⁴¹³⁻²	2.112	2.10*	(FHaslip)	LivelyGene,MarysPenn,Governorette	67
6-10⁷⁷	B.R.	ms	1500	ft	3000	clm	1	.32¹	1.05³	1.37³	2.07⁴	3	2	2	6⁸	6⁸	2.08	10.90	(FHaslip)	Spohn,GoldPrize,ChesterDevil	80
							1	.32¹	1.04¹	1.36¹	2.07⁴	5	2	1	.1x⁰,x8x	x8xdis	4.60	(TEichas)	SlipperBoy,Sanction,JeffW	77
							1	.31³	1.05³	1.37²	2.10³	3	3	3¹⁴	3⁴⁴	2.10¹	2.80	(TEichas)	IndianRuler,CaptainCrunch,JeffW	62
5-30⁷⁷	B.R.	ms	1700	ft	4000	clm	1	.32¹	1.05¹	1.37³	2.07¹	6	2⁰²	2¹⁴	2ⁿᵈ	2.07¹	2.90	(TEichas)	TThree,JeffW,CharlieDoubleE	75

2.07½ Btva   1977   6   0   0   0 $ 000

CEDARWOOD JUDGE
DRIVER—RICK TURCOTTE (P)—Yellow and Red
(5, 2.04½ (½) — $61755)
b. g. 10, by Painter—Our Frechi
Rita H. Thorpe, Rochester, N.Y.
Trainer: T. Turcotte, Jr.

8- 4⁷⁷	Btva	ms	1800	ft	4200	clm	1	.30⁴¹	1.02¹	1.34⁴	2.07¹	7	7	7	5²⁴	2¹	2.072	6.40	(TTurcln)	MlsFreeFlo,CdarwoodJudge,SctlandAgns	82
7-28⁷⁷	Btva	ms	1800	ft	3500	clm	1	.30¹	1.03¹	1.35	2.06²	4	5	7⁸	7⁷³	2.08	4.20	(TTurcln)	Edstime,WorthyRoger,LittleEtta	77
7-21⁷⁷	Btva	ms	1700	ft	4200	clm	1	.32³¹	1.03¹	1.36³	2.07	5	1	3²	3²	2.08⁴	5.30	(TTurcln)	ShdyHillDasy,EastPresent,MlsFreeFlo	79
7-12⁷⁷	Btva	ms	1500	ft	4200	clm	1	.31	1.03	1.34	2.06	7	4	4²	7⁷³	2.074	5.60	(TTurcln)	d-NannaCollins,StanleyPick,WorthyRoger	84
							1	.31¹	1.03¹	1.35³	2.09¹	7	1	6⁸	6⁸	2.08	10.90	(TTurcln)	CedarwoodJudge,MissMove,AndyM	80
7- 5⁷⁷	Btva	ms	1300	ft	2500	clm	1	.31⁴	1.04¹	1.36¹	2.07¹	6	2¹	3¹⁴	3¹⁴	2.072	8.70	(TTurcln)	DocsDuke,HawthorneFran,CedarwoodJudge	77
6-20⁷⁷	Btva	ms	1500	ft	2500	clm	1	.31	1.04¹	1.37¹	2.11¹	6	2	4¹³	3¹²	2.112	8.00	(TTurcln)	TarSanbra,(NossiBe,HappyAcres)Susie)	74
6-13⁷⁷	B.R.	ms	1500	ft	3000	clm	1	.31⁴	1.04¹	1.36⁴	2.08	5	4	4⁰	7⁷⁴	2.092	15.80	(TTurcln)	Cedarwoodjudge,DremrsLobil,BinnersPrnce	78
							1	.31¹	1.04¹	1.37	2.09	6	4	6³	6⁴	2.094	3.50	(TTurcln)	AmyJo,QuebecFleurie,Becket	72

2.07¾ Btva   1977   23   3   2   3 $ 3482
2.07½ Btva   1976   47   5   6   4 $ 8882

GENESEE CHERYL (W)
DRIVER—, Red and Green
(6, 2.06 (½) — $18665)
b. m. 9, by John A. Hanover—Grand Girl
Bruce J. Dineen, Ellicottville, N.Y.
Trainer: B. Dineen

8- 3⁷⁷	Btva	ms	1600	ft	3600	clm	1	.32¹	1.04³	1.36³	2.08⁴	4	5	5³⁰	2¹	2.084	3.70	(BDineen)	AmyJo,GeneseeCheryl,BabyArizona	75
7-25⁷⁷	Btva	ms	1600	ft	3600	clm	1	.31	1.03¹	1.36	2.08¹	4	4	4⁰	1¹	2.081	4.30	(BDineen)	GeneseeCheryl,SuccessGrnt,VictriaString	72
7-18⁷⁷	Btva	ms	1700	ft	3600	clm	1	.31¹	1.04²	1.36	2.07	7	4	4³²	2ⁿᵈ	2.073	33.60	(BDineen)	DRsRhythm,Sallimar,ThirdSon	90
7- 7⁷⁷	Btva	ms	1400	my	3600	clm	1	.33	1.06³	1.39¹	2.10	3	3	3¹	4³²	2.104	12.20	(BDineen)	MichaelsEdict,MightyMcKyo,ThirdSon	63
6-28⁷⁷	Btva	ms			Qua	tp		1	.32	1.03	1.37	2.084	2	2	2⁵	2.094	NB		(BDineen)	RitzyGirl,SpeedyStrut,GeneseeCheryl	70
6-20⁷⁷	Btva	ms			Qua	tp		1	.31⁴	1.05²	1.38¹	2.10¹	6	5	3⁵¹	1¹³	2.10¹	NB		(BDineen)	GeneseeCheryl,GreatSullivan,EmilyC	78
6-13⁷⁷	B.R.	ms			3000	clm		1	.33¹	1.05³	1.38	2.104	2	1	1³	4¹¹	2.103	4.60	(BDineen)	MissKatByrd,CaptainRed,RobbyCarLith	74

2.08½ Btva   1977   22   3   4   1 $ 4221
2.06½ B.R.   1976   23   1   1   1 $ 1906

either case you will lose in the long run. If the odds you assign are too high, you will probably not bet the horse, believing it an underlay when it's really an overlay. If the odds you assign are too low, your wager will be a badly calculated risk, for you will believe that an underlay is actually an overlay.

Suppose there are two or more overlays in a race. Then you have the choice of either betting the horse you think is most likely to win or betting on two (or all) of the overlays. Naturally, the more overlays you bet in a race, the more you reduce your margin of profit. Good handicapping is therefore a prerequisite for using the rule that you should bet overlays.

A useful way to deal with overlay betting is to assign a percentage to each horse, according to what you consider its chance to win the race. The following chart makes the percentages clear.

Horse	Chance of winning	Minimum acceptable odds	Actual odds in race	Overlay
1 Lady Cold Front	10%	9 to 1	6.20	no
2 C. C. Tempo	20	4 to 1	2.40	no
3 A Q Equador	0	0	29.10	no
4 Quebec Fleurie	40	3 to 2	3.70	yes
5 Jeff W	0	0	6.80	no
6 Mels Free Flo	20	4 to 1	3.40	no
7 Cedarwood Judge	10	9 to 1	6.20	no
8 Genesee Cheryl	0	0	20.70	no

Clearly, Quebec Fleurie was the overlay in this race and in fact won, paying $9.40 for a $2.00 win ticket.

Results.

FIFTH RACE — 1 Mile					$3500 Claiming Pace				$1900
Quebec Fleurie ms	4	5	5	3	3¹	1¾	R. Blaun		3.70
C C Tempo ms	2	2	3	2º	2¹¼	2nk	C. Stevens		*2.40
Lady Cold Front ms	1	1	1	1	1¹	3½	T. Lanpher		6.20
Cedarwood Judge ms	7	8	8	4	4hd	4½	Ri. Turcotte		6.20
Mels Free Flo ms	6	7	7	6	5⁵	5²½	F. Haslip		3.40
Jeff W ms	5	6	6	8	7¹	6²½	T. Eichas		6.80
Genesee Cheryl ms	8	3º	2º	5	6½	7½	B. Dineen		20.70
A Q Equador	3	4	4	7	8	8	P. Sorge		29.10

$2 MUTUEL PRICES   4. Quebec Fleurie   9.40   4.80   5.00

Official Program Nos.   2. C C Tempo   4.00   3.40

                         1. Lady Cold Front   5.00

Time — .32⅖   1.04⅖   1.36   2.08⅖

EXACTA — 4 AND 2 $33.20

ATTENDANCE: 3,245

HANDLE: $263,884

                                      (Order of finish and beaten lengths·

If you think a horse has no chance to win, assign it 0 percent. If you believe it has a 10 percent chance of winning, then it will be a respectable bet only if it goes off at odds of 9 to 1 or higher. The reason is that you give it one chance in ten of winning, so that you will require that at least nine out of ten dollars (after deductions) be bet against it. If you think that a horse has a 20 percent chance of winning, then you will require odds of 4 to 1 or higher.

Before we handicap a sample race to look for overlay betting, one important point needs to be emphasized. Even if a horse seems a good overlay bet, you will probably be better off not to play it unless you really like it. Stick to betting overlays you believe will win. If you can't get a fair price on a horse you really like, I recommend that you not wager on that race.

Examples of Races: How the Point System Yields Overlay Bets

Let's look at a few races in terms of overlay possibilities. Keep in mind that the total percentage of possibilities to win will be one hundred and that we want to divide the chances of the eight horses in each race on this basis. In each race we will begin by excluding horses our system rules out and restrict our betting to the apparent contenders.

PACE

CLAIMING
1 Mile — Purse $2100

Saddle Cloth
BROWN

Claiming Price $5000
Mares allowed 20%, 4 year old horses allowed 30%.
FIRST HALF OF DAILY DOUBLE

ASK FOR HORSE BY PROGRAM NUMBER

---

1 — TRUE PROJECT (6, 2.07¾ (½) — $8842)
DRIVER—ED McNEIGHT, JR.—Orange, Black and White
b. m. 7, by Project Apollo—True Blue
Jerome Nugent, E. Pembroke, N.Y.

Trainer: Jer. Nugent (McNeight, Jr. Stable)

| | | | | | | | | | | | | | | 1977 30 8 6 4 $11650 |
| | | | | | | | | | | | | | | 1976 31 7 11 7 $5253 |

8-17 77	Btva	ms 2500	ft 7200	clm	1	.29¹	1.02	1.33²	2.04²	7	6	6	4⁷³	5⁷¹	2.05⁴	31.00 (EMcNeJr) IronPrince,ProTestor,ButlerAbbot
8- 9 77	Btva	ms 2300	ft 6000	clm	1	.31²	1.03¹	1.35⁴	2.07¹	5	5	3¹⁴	½²	2.07¹	1.40* (EMcNeJr) TrueProject,TopSkipper,DalePro
8- 2 77	Btva	ms 2600	ft 7200	clm	1	.30³	1.02⁴	1.34²	2.05²	5	4	4¹³	1½	2.05⁴	3.20 (EMcNeJr) SctchChasr,MjesticBrewer,OldeSoftShoe
7-29 77	Btva	ms 2600	sy 7200	clm	1	.30²	1.02¹	1.34¹	2.07¹	5	5	8	3⁴½	3²	2.07⁴	5.20 (EMcNeJr) CfGuy,FreightBaron,TrueProject
7-23 77	Btva	ms 2400	ft 6000	clm	1	.30²	1.02	1.34¹	2.07	5	5	5	6⁴	3²⁴	2.07²	2.00* (EMcNeJr) ButlerKnight,TrueProject,IndianRuler
7-16 77	Btva	ms 2400	ft 6000	clm	1	.30⁴	1.04¹	1.35²	2.06²	1	3	3²²	2ns	2.06³	1.90* (EMcNeJr) RussellTorrence,TrueProject,BradleysGay
7-12 77	Btva	ms 2200	ft 7200	clm	1	.30²	1.03¹	1.33	2.05	6	7	7	7⁴⁴	5⁴²	2.05⁴	9.50 (EMcNeJr) ProTestor,FamousJulie,Quickem

---

2 — MIGHTY OTTO (3, 2.06⅓ (½) — $1484)
DRIVER—JIM RANKIN—Red, Blue and White
br. h. 4, by Meadow Paige—Eve Tide
James Rankin & Burley Brown, St. Catharines, Ont. Can. & Lkpt. N.Y.

Trainer: T. Dunlap (Rankin Stable)
2.05 B.R.
2.06⅓ Hamb
1976 13 1 1 4 $1484

8-17 77	Btva	ms 2500	ft 7800	clm	1	.31²	1.03	1.33²	2.06¹	6x	8	2°	7⁹	be⁷¹⁰⁴	2.08²	2.00* (JRankin) RaiseHobb,FreightBaron,MightyYankee
8-11 77	Btva	ms 2600	ft 7800	clm	1	.30¹	1.02⁴	1.34	2.05⁴	7	7	6⁵	5⁶³	2.07¹	2.071	3.00 (JRankin) IronPrince,FreightBaron,MightyYankee
8- 2 77	Btva	ms 2800	ft 7800	clm	1	.29¹	1.01¹	1.32²	2.05²	5	4	3¹⁴	3¹⁴	2.054	2.30* (JRankin) RacingGene,MightyOtto,BredByrd
7-16 77	Btva	ms 2100	ft 9100	clm	1	.32²	1.04	1.34³	2.05²	3	1	3³⁴	2¹⁴	2.051	4.30 (AWaddel) MightyOtto,OldeSoftShoe,EllayJoe
7- 2 77	Btva	ms 2100	ft 7800	clm	1	.30¹	1.02	1.34³	2.05²	3	1	1⁵	1²	2.05²	4.20 (JRankin) MightyOtto,BeverlysJune,StarG
6-28 77	Btva	ms 2100	ft 7800	clm	1	.31¹	1.03¹	2.06²	1	5	6¹⁴²	6⁸	2.06²	5.40 (JRankin) BurleyGuy,HosiGuy,KeystoneWhiz
6-22 77	B.R.	ms 2250	ft 8750	clm	1	.31³	1.03²	1.35²	2.05³	1	3	4²	6¹⁴³	2.08¹	1.90* (JRankin) RedArgotKid,JohnWAdios,BidingTime
6- 9 77	B.R.	ms 2550	ft 10000	clm	1	.31⁴	1.03⁴	1.35³	2.05³	6	6	2	2¹⁴	2.10	15.60 (JRankin) BeverlysJune,MightyOtto,MissMaryDi

---

3 — ADIOS PETER COOPER (5, 2.07 (½) — $5585)
DRIVER—JOE HODGINS—Maroon and White
b. g. 6, by Michael Lynn—Annabel Adios
Karl J. & Terry Anne Ortner, Cattaraugus, N.Y.

Trainer: T. Ortner

| | | | | | | | | | | | | | | 1977 16 0 2 3 $1790 |
| | | | | | | | | | | | | | | 1976 32 3 4 3 $4976 |

8-18 77	Btva	ms 2400	ft 5000	clm	1	.30²	1.03	1.34¹	2.07²	7	5	5²	5²⁴	5¹⁴	2.07³	15.40 (JHodgin) MyBrothersHorse,Cuba,SamC
8-10 77	Btva	ms 2000	ft 4000	clm	1	.30²	1.01³	1.33²	2.05³	2	1	4⁷	2⁵²	2.063	3.00 (JHodgin) EdstIme,AdiosPeterCoopr,MichaelsEdct
8- 1 77	Btva	ms 2000	ft 4000	clm	1	.30	1.01⁴	1.34²	2.06¹	4	4	3³¹	3³¹	2.06⁴	17.60 (JHodgin) Acropolis,DalePro,AdiosPeterCooper
7-26 77	Btva	ms 2000	ft 4000	clm	1	.31¹	1.04¹	1.35²	2.07⁴	1	6	6⁵³	6²²	2.08¹	5.20 (JHodgin) DrIngDrxel,JIffrsonVictry,SndyHillDasy
7-18 77	Btva	ms 2000	ft 4000	clm	1	.31¹	1.04¹	1.34	2.06³	5	6	6⁴	6⁸	2.08¹	7.60 (JHodgin) EbenJones,DalePro,CCTempo
7-11 77	Btva	ms 1400	fs 76-7nw150ps		1	.30⁴	1.02¹	1.34²	2.07	2	3	3²⁴	6³¹	2.07⁴	4.10 (JHodgin) RedArgotKid,JohnWAdios,BidingTime
6-28 77	Btva	ms 1600	ft 76-7nw175ps		1	.32⁴	1.05¹	1.37	2.08	6	6	x6⁸²	6⁹³	2.10	15.60 (JHodgin) MaryG,WeeChance,RedArgotKid

---

4 — ROWDY G. TIME (5, 2.06 (½) — $9478)
DRIVER—BOB BOMAR—White and Gold
b. g. 6, by Good Time Boy—Miss Tiny G.
Thomas Agosti, Tonawanda, N.Y.

Trainer: T. Agosti (Griffin Stable)
2.06½ Btva
2.06 Stga
1977 22 2 7 2 $5429
1976 17 1 3 2 $2487

8-17 77	Btva	ms 2100	ft 4000	clm	1	.31	1.02¹	1.34²	2.05³	3	2	2	2²	2.06	1.00* (FGrifti) Peetong,RowdyGTime,BarbVolo
8- 8 77	Btva	ms 2000	gd 4000	clm	1	.30³	1.02¹	1.34²	2.06⁴	2	2	2ns	2ns	2.06⁴	2.20 (FGrifti) EasternQueen,RowdyGTime,IndianRuler
7-29 77	Btva	ms 2100	sy 4000	clm	1	.31¹	1.03	1.35	2.07⁴	6	7	4³	3¹	2.08	9.80 (FGrifti) PetronBetsy,LisasLucky,RowdyGTime
7-27 77	Btva	ms 2000	ft 4000	clm	1	.31¹	1.02¹	1.35	2.06¹	4	1	1³	1²²	2.06¹	2.10* (GSarama) RowdyGTime,CCTempo,BarbVolo

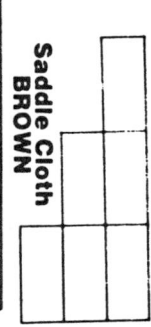

5 — SONNY DIRECT

DRIVER—FRED HASLIP—Blue, White and Gold

(3, 2.06¼) (½) — $19059)

b. g. 7, by Direct Noule—Trivue

Richard Culotta & Stephen L. Joy, Rochester, N.Y.

Trainer: F. Haslip

7-15	77	Btva	ms	1700	sy	c-3000 clm	1	.31¹	1.04⁴	1.36⁴	2.08¹	8	8	8	7⁶⅜	7¹⁴	2.10³	24.70	(DMcNeig)	Edstime,Dreamer,Lobell,MightyMcKyo	80
7- 4	77	Btva	ms	1400	ft	3000 clm	1	.30¹	1.02²	1.34⁴	2.06⁴	4	5	2¹	2¹	2½	2.07	6.20	(WJensen)	ShadyHillDaisy,RowdyGTime,PannArtic	81
6-23	77	B.R.	ms	1600	ft	3500 clm	1	.31	1.03¹	1.35²	2.06³	6	7	7	7½	5⁴⁄	2.07²	18.80	(WJensen)	EbenJones,LarryLinn,JohnSilver	75

Trainer: F. Haslip   1977   0   0   0   0 $ 000
2.08¼ Btva Q   1976   12   3   0   0 $ 2957

6 — PEETONG

DRIVER—CHRIS CHRISTOFOROU—Blue, White and Gold

(5, 2.06) — $12096)

b. g. 7, by Greenie Desota—Skys Dream

Frank Mele, Mississauga, Ont., Can.

Trainer: C. Christoforou

8-13	77	Btva	ms		Qua		1	.31¹	1.04	1.36	2.08²	1	1	1	1²	1⁴½	2.08²	NB	(FHaslip)	SonnyDrect,CptnCutlass,PnutsBrewstr	
8- 9	77	Btva	ms		Qua		1	.31¹	1.03	1.36¹	2.09	2	1°	1¹	3⁷	3⁷	2.10²	NB	(FHaslip)	HudatDare,PrettyBoyDon,SonnyDirect	
8- 2	77	Btva	ms		Qua		1	.31	1.03¹	1.35⁴	2.07¹	7	4°	7dis	7dis	6dis		NB	(FHaslip)	MrSuprCrn,WindmlAngl,MyBrthrsHrse	
4-14	76	B.R.	ms	1500	ft	4500 clm	1	.30⁴	1.02	1.33⁴	2.06¹	5	7	8	8dis	8dis		7.90	(DSpazia)	Reeds,TarHeel,TopCaliber,JennferAdios	
3-22	76	B.R.	ms	1550	ft	5000 clm hcp	1	.30¹	1.02²	1.34¹	2.07²	3	3²⅜	3²⅜	7²⅜	6¹³	2.07²	7.90	(DSpazia)	HighJimmy,ArmbroOshawa,CallMeGenrl	
3-15	76	B.R.	ms	1700	ft	5000 clm hcp	1	.31³	1.01³	1.33	1.36	4	4¹³	4¹³	7⁴¼	7⁴¼	2.07²	6.60	(DSpazia)	MarysDream,JennfrDawn,LettuceDrm	
3- 8	76	B.R.	ms	1700	ft	5500 clm	1	.31¹	1.02⁴	1.36¹	2.06	1	5⁴	5⁴	6⁵⁴	6⁵⁴	2.07	4.00	(GGibson)	CapeCharles,MissZipadoo,MurphsPride	

Trainer: C. Christoforou   1977   25   3   4   2 $ 5318
2.06½ Btva   1976   21   1   2   3 $ 4086
2.06½ B.R.

7 — AUDIT

DRIVER—BRUCE DINEEN—Gray, Red and Green

(3, 2.07) — $3547)

b. m. 6, by Clay—Avalon Audrey

Annie Collins, Niagara Falls, N.Y.

Trainer: R. Chase

8-16	77	Btva	ms	2400	ft	6000 clm	1	.32	1.04¹	1.35¹	2.06¹	3	2¹	1²	1¹	1nk	2.06¹	2.80	(BDineen)	Audit,GraysPat,TopSkipper	76
7-30	77	Btva	ms	2000	ft	4800 clm	1	.30²	1.02³	1.34	2.06³	2	1¹	2°	3¹¹	2nk	2.06³	1.30*	(BDineen)	Three,Audit,Peetong	77
7-22	77	Btva	ms	2000	ft	4800 clm	1	.30²	1.04	1.34¹	2.06³	2	6	3³	3⁵¼	2⁵⁴	2.06³	3.90	(BDineen)	ChesterDevil,Audit,MichaelsEdict	74
7-15	77	Btva	ms	1400	ft	c-3600 clm	1	.31¹	1.04³	1.35⁴	2.07⁴	6	6	4⁵⁴	4³²	1ns	2.07⁴	1.20*	(DRothfu)	Audit,EasterPresent,CopperTLite	70
7-11	77	Btva	ms	1600	ft	76-7nw3000CD1	1	.30¹	1.02⁴	1.33⁴	2.04³	8	10	7²⅜	5⁷	5⁷	2.06	10.20	(DRothfu)	DustyLehigh,StarettaCharm,CoalKat	77
6- 7	77	Btva	ms	4200	clm		1	.30¹	1.03	1.35	2.06¹	4	1	1³	1⁶½	1⁶½	2.06¹	3.80	(DRothfu)	Audit,SingleJohnnie,Twila	55
5-25	77	B.R.	ms	1700	ft	76-7nw3000CD1	1	.31⁴	1.04²	1.36¹	2.06³	2	6	6	6⁵⁴	6⁵⁴	2.07³	13.30	(BSlade)	Perquimansindian,ArticLad,CoTarGrattn	74

Trainer: R. Chase   1977   9   3   2   0 $ 3865
2.06½ B.R.   Last Raced in 1975

8 — ADIOS WILLA (NY)

DRIVER—RON CHASE—Blue, Yellow and Lt. Blue

(5, 2.03¼) (¼) — $36055)

br. m. 10, by Adios Boy—Willolas Counsel

Ronald & Sue Chase, Schoharie, N.Y.

Trainer: R. Chase

8-17	77	Btva	ms	2500	ft	7200 clm	1	.31²	1.01	1.33	2.06¹	1	5	6	6⁷	5³	2.07	20.90	(RChase)	RaiseHobb,FreightBaron,MightyYankee	67
8- 4	77	Btva	ms	2600	ft	7200 clm	1	.31	1.34²	1.34²	2.05⁴	8	8	4⁰	5⁵⁴	4⁴⁴	2.06³	25.10	(RChase)	EljayJoe,RaiseHobb,KennyYankee	77
7-29	77	Btva	ms	2600	ft	7200 clm	1	.30³	1.34³	2.06	1	6	6	2	3	3²³	2.06³	3.60	(RChase)	Beverly&June,RaiseHobb,AdiosWilla	82
7-20	77	Btva	ms	2600	sy	7200 clm	1	.30¹	1.34¹	2.04¹	6	6	3	4³	4³⅜	4³⅜	2.07⁴	38.30	(RChase)	CFGuy,FreightBaron,TrueProject	73
7-20	77	Btva	ms	1900	ft	6000 clm	1	.31¹	1.34	1.33³	2.05⁴	7	1	2²	2²	4⁷	2.07¹	37.40	(RChase)	Quickem,RaiseHobb,CoTarGrattan	88
7- 9	77	Btva	ms	2100	ft	7200 clm	1	.30³	1.01⁴	1.33²	2.05⁴	6	1	1³	1⁶⅜	1⁶⅜	2.06	8.90	(RChase)	MyBrothersHorse,AdiosWilla,SamC	77
7- 2	77	Btva	ms	2100	ft	7200 clm	1	.31¹	1.03¹	1.34¹	2.06	6	6⅜	6	6⁶⅜	7⁴³	2.07	13.10	(RChase)	TiogaCrdigan,GrayEdna,PeerissLobell	65

Trainer: R. Chase   1977   14   2   1   5 $ 4353
2.06¾ B.R.   1976   26   6   4   1 $ 5473
2.07½ Btva Q

Batavia Downs 1st Race October 27, 1977

1 True Project

Current form	3
Consistency	2
Class	2
Driver	2
Post position	3
Total	12

4 Rowdy G. Time

Current form	4
Consistency	1
Class	−2
Driver	1
Post position	2
Total	6

2 Mighty Otto

Current form	0
Consistency	2
Class	2
Driver	2
Post position	3
Total	9

5 Sonny Direct

Not a contender
(Horse's first
start in 1977.)

3 Adios Peter Cooper

Current form	1
Consistency	0
Class	0
Driver	1
Post position	2
Total	4

Not a Contender

6 Peetong

Current form	3
Consistency	1
Class	−2
Driver	2
Post position	1
Total	5

7 Audit

Current Form	4
Consistency	3
Class	0
Driver	1
Post Position	0
Total	8

8 Adios Willa

Not a contender.
(Poor recent form,
post position)
and driver.)

Let's turn now to the contenders in this race.

1 True Project

This horse won its last start in this class on August 9 and was second in close races on July 23 and July 16 in $5,000 claimers. The races on August 17, August 2, and July 29 should not be counted against the horse. They were higher-class claimers in which horse fell back by the three-quarter mark and made up some ground in the stretch.

2 Mighty Otto

After nearly a month's layoff, Mighty Otto showed he was not in shape in his races on August 11 and August 17. Mighty Otto is a risky bet, considering that he will be the favorite and ran poorly in his last two starts.

4 Rowdy G. Time

This horse is moving up in class after having placed in his last two starts. There is no reason to bet this horse considering that he is moving up after failing to win in $4,000 claimers.

6 Peetong

This horse ran very well in its last start but is going up in class and is too far back to be a real threat in this race. The three races on July 15, July 22, and July 30 should be discounted because the horse had a catch driver.

7 Audit

A front-runner, Audit will be in trouble if Rowdy G. Time, also a front-runner, goes for the lead. To win this race, Audit must get the lead easily and this is very unlikely. Note that Audit's races on July 22 and July 30 were $4,000 claimers and that Audit had an easy race on August 16.

Overall ranking in race:

Horse	Point total	Chance of winning	Minimum acceptable odds	Actual odds
True Project	12	40%	3 to 1	3.70 to 1
Mighty Otto	9	25	3 to 1	6 to 5
Rowdy G. Time	6	15	6 to 1	11 to 1
Peetong	5	10	9 to 1	5 to 1
Audit	8	10	9 to 1	9 to 1

Analysis. The pacing of the race will probably be slow. Rowdy G. Time and Audit are the front-runners here, but they will probably not battle for the lead in a fast first quarter. Most likely, either or both will go to the front and slow the pace. This will provide an excellent opportunity for True Project, the horse with the best current form in this race, to win going away in the stretch. Odds of 7 to 2 make True Project a good bet in this race.

Results.

BATAVIA DOWNS RESULTS CHARTS

FIRST RACE — 1 Mile							$5000 Claiming Pace			$2100
True Project ms	1	3	3	3	$3\frac{3}{4}$	$1^{1\frac{3}{4}}$	E. McNeight, Jr.			3.70
Peetong ms	6	7	8	6	$6^{1}\frac{1}{4}$	$2\frac{1}{2}$	C. Christoforou			4.90
Mighty Otto ms	2	4	4	4^{0}	4^{2}	3hd	J. Rankin			*1.20
Audit ms	7	1^{0}	1	1	$1\frac{1}{2}$	$4^{1}\frac{1}{4}$	B. Dineen			9.00
Adios Peter Cooper ms	3	5	5	5	$5\frac{1}{2}$	$5\frac{3}{4}$	J. Hodgins			11.00
Rowdy G Time ms	4	2	2	2^{0}	2^{1}	6nk	B. Bomar			11.30
Adios Willa ms	8	8	6	7^{0}	7^{10}	$7^{17}\frac{1}{2}$	R. Chase			23.10
Sonny Direct ms	5	6	7	8x	8	8	F. Haslip			14.80
$2 MUTUEL PRICES		1. True Project					9.40	4.80	2.60
Official Program Nos.		6. Peetong						5.60	3.20
		2. Mighty Otto							2.40

Time — .30¾   1.03⅔   1.35⅓   2.06¾

Batavia Downs   7th Race   October 25, 1977

Eliminate these horses from contention:

2 Count Adios A

Out for the past three weeks, Count Adios A has not turned in a good effort since July 21, three months ago. No current form.

5 Suzies Son

Moving up in class, Suzies Son does not appear to be a threat in this race. He is outclassed by the tough competition here.

7 C F Guy

No current form to speak of. C F Guy's last good showing dates back to August 5, two and a half months ago. Also hindered by an outside post.

8 Just a Spinner

Raced well on October 15 after several mediocre efforts but cannot be expected to threaten here. The 8 hole is too big a handicap for this horse to overcome against this field.

The contenders shape up as follows: ·

1 Pearlie Chita

After a fine effort on October 4, Pearlie Chita didn't run at all in her next start on October 11, perhaps hindered by the off track. But tonight the track is fast and Pearlie Chita must be considered a contender, especially from the rail.

3 Parkwood

The class of this race. After three seemingly easy victories in $7,000 claimers, Parkwood is moving *down* in class. Why Parkwood is stepping down is a mystery, but that should not deter us from betting on this horse if the odds are favorable.

4 Sonny Direct

Moving up in class after easy back to back wins in $5,000 claimers. We will find out how good Sonny Direct is in this race, for his competition is formidable.

6 Briar Lea Dwight

Is this horse even a contender here? Yes, Briar Lea Dwight has run consistently well in his last three starts and can't be counted out of this one. But from an outside post, Briar Lea Dwight cannot be accorded a good chance to beat this field.

Point Assignments:

1 Pearlie Chita

Current form	4
(disregard Oct. 11 race)	
Consistency	2
Post position	3
Driver	2
Total	11

3 Parkwood

Current form	4
Class	2
Post position	2
Driver	3
Total	11

4 Sonny Direct

Current form	4
Consistency	2
Class	−2
Post position	2
Driver	3
Total	9

6 Briar Lea Dwight

Current form	4
Consistency	1
Class	0
Post position	1
Driver	3
Total	9

CLAIMING
1 Mile — Purse $2000

Claiming Price $6000
Mares allowed 20%, 4 year olds allowed 30%.

ASK FOR HORSE BY PROGRAM NUMBER

Saddle Cloth
RED

---

1 MS **9000** **-10**
(3, 2.04⅖ (¾) — $5827)
PEARLIE CHITA
DRIVER—JOHN SCHROEDER—Blue, Gold and White
b. m. 4, by Chita Can—Pearlie Whirry
Juniors III, Buffalo, N.Y.

Trainer: M. Striegl, Jr.
2.04⅖ V.D. ¾   1977 33 7 5 6 $10183
2.04⅖ Btva   1976 30 2 7 6 $ 5353

10-11⁷⁷	Btva	ms 2300 sy	9000 clm	1.31³	1.05³	1.37	2.10	1	3	2	89	2.11⁴	1.50⁵ (JSchroe)
10-4⁷⁷	Btva	ms 2300 ft	9000 clm	1.29³	1.04³	1.34⁴	2.06³	6	6	3⁰	1²³	1.2³	15.90 (JSchroe)
9-27⁷⁷	Btva	ms 2300 ft	9000 clm	1.30	1.04	1.34²	2.06²	6	5⁰	5⁴³	6²³	2.07	3.80 (JSchroe)
9-15⁷⁷	Btva	ms 2100 ft	7500 clm	1.31³	1.04	1.35⁴	2.06²	4	4	1¹²	1¹²	2.06²	1.60⁶ (JSchroe)
9-5⁷⁷	Btva	ms 2100 ft	7500 clm	1.31³	1.04²	1.35³	2.06	8	7	7	5⁴	dh2.06²	6.70 (JSchroe)
8-29⁷⁷	Btva	ms 2100 ft	7500 clm	1.31³	1.04²	1.35¹	2.06³	3	3	1	1²	2.06³	1.60⁶ (JSchroe)
8-13⁷⁷	Btva	ms 2400 ft	7500 clm	1.29³	1.01²	1.33²	2.05	4	4	3²¹	3²	2.05¹	3.90 (JSchroe)

Trainer: G. Guindon
2.06 B.R.   1977 12 2 0 1 $2478
                    1976 14 1 0 0 $4045

PearlieChita,TiogaCardigan,FaysThunder 55
PearlieChita,TiogaCardgan,FaysThundr   55
BriarLeaDwight,Kenwoodjim,RaiseHobb   60
PearlieChita,DalePro,ChesterDevil   73
TerrAdios,EasternQueen,WinnieSong   70
PearlieChita,SuccessGrant,TerrAdios   75
PetronBetsy,ScooterJones,PearlieChita   77

---

2 MS **9000**
(9, 2.02⅖) — $5990)
COUNT ADIOS A
DRIVER—GASTON GUINDON—Brown and Gold
br. g. 10, by Seven Brothers (F)—Queen Adios
Jamison Acres, Elma, N.Y.

Trainer: Y. Demers
2.02⅖ Y.R.   1977 15 6 3 3 $9232
                    1976 14 3 2 2 $5194

10-4⁷⁷	Btva	ms 2300 ft	6000 clm	1.29¹	1.02⁴	1.34⁴	2.06³	7	7	6⁰	7¹¹³	7¹¹³	50.40 (GGuindo)
9-20⁷⁷	Btva	ms 2500 gd	7000 clm	1.29	.59⁴	1.32²	2.05²	4	6	7	7²⁴	7²⁴	15.50 (GGuindo)
9-12⁷⁷	Btva	ms 2700 ft	8000 clm	1.31¹	1.04	1.36	2.07²	4	4	3	7⁸	7⁸⁴	20.10 (GGuindo)
9-2⁷⁷	Btva	ms 2700 ft	8000 clm	1.31¹	1.05	1.36³	2.06¹	1	1	1⁵	1⁵²	2.06¹	NB (GGuindo)
7-21⁷⁷	Btva	ms 2400 ft	Qua	1.31²	1.03	1.36	2.08³	5	60	6⁴	3¹	2.08³	4.40 (GGuindo)
7-11⁷⁷	Btva	ms 2800 ft	8000 clm	1.30	1.02⁴	1.34	2.05²	2	2	1¹	3²	2.05⁴	19.50 (GGuindo)
7- 1⁷⁷	Btva	ms 3000 ft	9000 clm	1.30²	1.03¹	1.33²	2.04³	3	4	5²⁴	8⁹²	2.06²	33.10 (GGuindo)

NotableBaron,MarkMinBar,AvonFairline   58
LincolnsValor,MerryJohnA,Parkwood   68
CountAdiosA,CuriosityA,FaitAccompli   78
CountAdiosA,ClaudsTown,MartyG   78
ColeHillJohn,MerryJohnA,CountAdiosA   70
ArmbroProfit,ErindeleRbin,LincinsValor   77

---

3 MS **6000** **5-2**
(6, 2.03⅖ (¾) — $25128)
PARKWOOD
DRIVER—YVON DEMERS—White, Black and Red
b. h. 7, by Shadow Wave—Gay Bett
Guy Joanis, Montebello, Que., Can.

Trainer: Y. Demers
2.04½ Btva ¾   1977 15 6 3 3 $9232
2.02¾ B.B. ¾   1976 14 3 2 2 $5194

10-15⁷⁷	Btva	ms 2200 ft	7000 clm	1.31¹	1.03²	1.35¹	2.08	4	3⁰	3⁰	4²½	2.08	.90⁴ (YDemers)
10-8⁷⁷	Btva	ms 2500 sl	7000 clm	1.31³	1.04¹	1.37¹	2.10¹	8	4	5	5³½	2.10¹	5.80 (YDemers)
10-1⁷⁷	Btva	ms 2500 ft	7000 clm	1.31¹	1.02⁴	1.35¹	2.08²	2	4	5	2½	2.08²	1.40⁰ (YDemers)
9-22⁷⁷	Btva	ms 2700 ft	8000 clm	1.31¹	1.04¹	1.36³	2.08¹	2	1	1¹	1½	2.08¹	5.90 (MBouvre)
9-12⁷⁷	Btva	ms 2700 ft	8000 clm	1.31¹	1.04	1.36	2.07²	8	8	6⁴½	6⁷½	2.07⁴	10.60 (MBouvre)
9- 1⁷⁷	Btva	ms 2100 ft	c-6000 clm	1.29¹	1.02	1.33²	2.07²	8	8	8	3²½	2.07²	.85⁰ (JDemers)
8-18⁷⁷	Btva	B.B.⅝	6000 clm	1.29¹	1.02³	1.33²	2.04³	2	4⁰	2⁰	2½	2.04³	2.95 (JHerber)

Parkwood,JustASpinner,GoldenJuelka   60
Parkwood,MarysHeel,TerrAdios   50
Parkwood,ScotchChaser,GoldenJuelka   52
Squall,ArmbroProfit,LincolnsValor   68
LincolnsValor,MerryJohnA,Parkwood
Parkwood,JustaplainLady,DuanesJane
ArmbroMcKee,Prkwood,BaronMichael

---

4 **3** **6000** **6**
(3, 2.02⅖ (¾) — $19059)
SONNY DIRECT
DRIVER—FRED HASLIP—Blue, White and Gold
b. g. 7, by Direct Noble—Trivue
Richard Cuiotta & Stephen L. Joy, Rochester, N.Y.

Trainer: F. Haslip
2.06⅖ Btva   1977 8 2 0 0 $2208
2.10½ B.R.   1976 12 3 0 0 $2867

10-15⁷⁷	Btva	ms 1800 ft	5000 clm	1.30¹	1.03²	1.35⁴	2.06⁴	5	1	1	1³	2.06⁴	3.70 (FHaslip)
10- 6⁷⁷	Btva	ms 2100 ft	5000 clm	1.30¹	1.03¹	1.34²	2.06⁴	2	3	3	1	2.06⁴	1.90⁰ (FHaslip)
9-27⁷⁷	Btva	ms 2100 ft	5000 clm	1.30¹	1.04¹	1.34²	2.06²	7	7	6	4⁰	2.07¹	17.40 (FHaslip)
9-17⁷⁷	Btva	ms 2100 ft	5000 clm	1.29¹	1.02	1.34²	2.06²	6	4	4	4²½	2.06⁴	14.50 (FHaslip)

SonnyDirect,SuccessBoy,FreightBaron   60
SonnyDirect,SuziesSon,SlippersBoy   53
TorpidsAytch,SuccessGrant,KittysHope   60
SuccessGrant,TorpidsAytch,BigFrosty   70

JUST A SPINNER

(4, 2.00) — $89953)

DRIVER—AL MARIACHER—White, Gold and Red

b. g. 10, by Justly Worthy—Josedale Spun Silk

Daniel Mees, Lackawanna, N.Y.

Trainer: A. Mariacher

| | | | | | | | | | | | 2.07½ B.R. gd | | 1977 | 34 | 3 | 2 | 4 | $ 6279 |
| | | | | | | | | | | | 2.04½ R.R. | | 1976 | 25 | 5 | 5 | 1 | $18522 |

10-15⁷⁷ Btva ms 2200 ft 7000 clm 1 .31¹ 1.03² 1.35¹ 2.08 6 7 7³³ 2.08 19.40 (AMariac) Parkwood,JustASpinner,GoldenJuelka 60
10- 8⁷⁷ Btva ms 2500 sl 6000 clm 1 .32 1.06³ 1.39⁴ 2.12⁴ 8 8 8 25.30 (AMariac) Sphrunia,MyBrothersHorse,ScotchChaser 50
9-27⁷⁷ Btva ms 2300 ft 6000 clm 1 .30 1.03¹ 1.34² 2.06² 8 6 6⁵ 37.00 (AMariac) BriarLeaDwight,Kenwoodjim,RaiseHobb 60
9-19⁷⁷ Btva ms 2300 ft 6000 clm 1 .32⁴ 1.05¹ 1.36⁴ 2.09³ 7 7 6⁶⁴ 11.60 (AMariac) RitzyGirl,RaiseHobb,FamousJulie 66
9- 9⁷⁷ Btva ms 2500 ft 7000 clm 1 .30² 1.01⁴ 1.33⁴ 2.05 4 3 2½ 9.10 (AMariac) KeystoneWhiz,AvonFairline,MarysHeel 63
9- 1⁷⁷ Btva ms 2500 ft 7000 clm 1 .33² 1.06² 1.37¹ 2.07 7 2½ 17.00 (AMariac) GoldenJuelka,MissMaryDi,MarysHeel 80
8-24⁷⁷ Btva ms 3100 ft 9000 clm 1 .31¹ 1.04 1.35¹ 2.06⁴ 3 4 5 9.60 (AMariac) MerryJohnA,ConchoByrd,BuddyFerndale 62

C F GUY

(6, 2.03½ (1) — $42114)

DRIVER—BRUCE TUBIN (P)—Blue, White and Red

ch. g. 8, by Greatheart Pick—Piper Day

Robert Moser & Rene Robert, Buffalo, N.Y. & Trois Rivieres, Que, Can.

Trainer: N. Fluet (Tubin Stable)

| | | | | | | | | | | | 2.06% N.E. % | | 1977 | 33 | 2 | 4 | 5 | $ 7825 |
| | | | | | | | | | | | 2.05% Fox % | | 1976 | 42 | 5 | 6 | 3 | $ 8955 |

10-15⁷⁷ Btva ms 2200 ft 7000 clm 1 .31 1.03¹ 1.35¹ 2.08 6 6 6 9.00 (BTubin) Prkwood,JustASpnner,GoldenJuelka(Pl 5) 60
10- 8⁷⁷ Btva ms 2500 sl 7000 clm 1 .31³ 1.04¹ 1.37¹ 2.10¹ 7 8 7⁸ 49.80 (NFluet) Parkwood,MarysHeel,TerrAdios 50
10- 1⁷⁷ Btva ms 2300 ft 6000 clm 1 .31³ 1.04 1.34² 2.06² 5 6 6⁵ 18.40 (NFluet) TerrAdios,JimmieCollins,MEPoplar 53
9-22⁷⁷ Btva ms 2700 ft 8000 clm 1 .30¹ 1.03¹ 1.34² 2.05⁴ 7 7 6⁶⁴ 17.50 (BTubin) Squall,ArmbroProfit,LincolnsValor 52
9-12⁷⁷ Btva ms 2700 ft 8000 clm 1 .31¹ 1.04 1.36 2.07² 6 6 4³¹ 44.10 (NFluet) LincolnsValor,MerryJohnA,Parkwood 68
8- 7⁷⁷ Btva ms Qua 1 .33² 1.06² 1.37⁷ 3 1 1½ NB (BTubin) CFGuy,MyBrothersHorse,SharpiesBeta 68
8- 5⁷⁷ Btva ms 2800 ft 7000 clm 1 .30 1.02¹ 1.33⁴ 2.05⁴ 2 2 2nk 30.00 (BTubin) SirAladoth,CFGuy,RacingGene 79

BRIAR LEA DWIGHT

(6, 2.03½) — $44564)

DRIVER—PERRY SMITH—Maroon and Gold

br. g. 8, by Major Goose—Febe

Perry Smith & William Lupton, Painesville & Lakewood, Ohio

Trainer: P. Smith

| | | | | | | | | | | | 2.04½ Nfld | | 1977 | 23 | 3 | 4 | 3 | $ 6377 |
| | | | | | | | | | | | 2.03% Nfld | | 1976 | 40 | 4 | 5 | 4 | $ 9165 |

10-14⁷⁷ Btva ms 2000 ft 6000 clm 1 .31 1.03 1.34 2.06³ 6 6 4⁴⁴ 2.40* (PSmith) FaysThundr,BriarLeaDwght,TorpidsAytch 40
10- 6⁷⁷ Btva ms 2500 ft 7000 clm 1 .30 1.01⁴ 1.33 2.06 8 7 6³¹ 28.40 (PSmith) MarkMinbar,MerryJohnA,Baratony 53
9-27⁷⁷ Btva ms 2300 ft 6000 clm 1 .31 1.03¹ 1.34² 2.06² 5 5 7⁴³ 5.60 (PSmith) BriarLeaDwight,Kenwoodjim,RaiseHobb 60
9-17⁷⁷ Nfld ms 1500 ft 5000 clm 1 .30¹ 1.02 1.34 2.06 5 5 5³¼ 2.00 (LWard) AnotherRporter,BriarLeaDwght,GoodRecord 72
9-10⁷⁷ Nfld ms 1500 ft 5000 clm 1 .30² 1.01⁴ 1.32⁴ 2.05³ 6 5 3³ 2.40 (LWard) BriarLeaDwght,OhOhHenry,Promoted 61
9- 1⁷⁷ Nfld ms 1500 ft 5000 clm 1 .31 1.03¹ 1.33² 2.05 1 1 1½ 3.90 (LWard) LhgtHowie,BriarLeaDwght,AntherRporter 80
8-25⁷⁷ Nfld ms 2400 ft 5000 clm 1 .31³ 1.35 2.06⁴ 4 3 2½ 2.70 (DirviJ) MrshallBoy,BriarLeaDwght,OhioDenMar 56

SUZIES SON

(5, 2.05% (½) — $14919)

DRIVER—FRANK KRYSTOFIK—White and Purple

br. g. 7, by Leos First—Susan Wick

Purple K Stable, Lancaster, N.Y.

Trainer: F. Krystofik

| | | | | | | | | | | | 2.06% QCD % | | 1977 | 32 | 4 | 7 | 6 | $ 8411 |
| | | | | | | | | | | | 2.06 Cka % | | 1976 | 27 | 2 | 9 | 4 | $ 5933 |

10- 6⁷⁷ Btva ms 2100 ft c-5000 clm 1 .30² 1.03¹ 1.34¹ 2.06⁴ 5 5 7 7⁴³ 14.70 (FHaslip) SonnyDirect,SuziesSon,SlippersBoy 66
9-29⁷⁷ Btva ms 2100 ft 5000 clm 1 .30¹ 1.03¹ 1.36 2.08⁴ 7 1 1½ NB (FHaslip) SonnyDirect,DellLynch,GrandPro 75
9-17⁷⁷ Btva ms 2100 ft 5000 clm 1 .31¹ 1.03³ 1.35² 2.07² 4 2 1½ 14.80 (FHaslip) TrueProject,Peetong,MightyOtto 82
8-30⁷⁷ Btva ms 2100 ft 5000 clm 1 .31² 1.04¹ 1.36 2.07⁴ 2 3 2½ (JWetzel) BredByrd,THAlmighty,SuziesSon 69
8- 9⁷⁷ Btva ms 1800 ft c-4000 clm 1 .31¹ 1.05 1.36¹ 2.08 8 7 8²¾ 23.60 (PSmith) MissMargaretEd,IndianRuler,LarryLinn 69
8-19⁷⁷ Btva ms 2100 ft 4000 clm 1 .31¹ 1.04¹ 1.36¹ 2.06¹ 7 10 9 28.40 (JWetzel) SuziesSon,BeckysAdora,LuckyLang 60
8-13⁷⁷ Btva ms 2400 ft 5000 clm 1 .30³ 1.03¹ 1.35¹ 2.06² 5 7 7⁴¼ 25.90 (BSmith) EqualKash,MyBrothrsHrse,SteadyMoran 77

Analysis. Sonny Direct will go to the front but may be parked in a fast quarter by Pearlie Chita. Pearlie Chita will probably pull out at the half, if not earlier. Parkwood may be saved for the stretch. Ditto for Briar Lea Dwight. The pacing of this race seems to favor Parkwood and Pearlie Chita. Parkwood must be our choice.

Now let us construct a chart showing overlays and underlays in this race.

Horse	Point total	Chance of winning	Minimum acceptable odds	Actual odds	Overlay
Parkwood	11	40%	3 to 2	4.30	yes
Pearlie Chita	11	25	3 to 1	2.00	no
Sonny Direct	9	20	4 to 1	2.30	no
Briar Lea Dwight	9	15	6 to 1	3.30	no

Results.

SEVENTH RACE — 1 Mile								$6000 Claiming Pace		$2000
Parkwood ms	3	2⁰	1	1	1¹⅄	1½	Y. Demers		4.30
c Briar Lea Dwight ms	6	6	6	4	4½	2¹	P. Smith		3.30
Pearlie Chita ms	1	3	3	3	3¹	3hd	J. Schroeder		*2.00
CF Guy ms	7	7	7	6	7¹½	4½	B. Tubin		6.60
Just A Spinner ms	8	8	8	7	6hd	5¹	A. Mariacher		23.50
Sonny Direct ms	4	1⁰	2	2	2¾	6¹	F. Haslip		2.30
Count Adiois A ms	2	4	4	5	5¾	7²¾	G. Guidon		12.80
Suzies Son ms	5	5	5	8	8	8	F. Krystofik		22.30
$2 MUTUEL PRICES		3. Parkwood					10.60	5.00	3.20
Official Program Nos.		6. Briar Lea Dwight						4.20	2.80
		1. Pearlie Chita							3.60

Batavia Downs   1st race   October 8, 1977

How is it possible to determine the appropriate percentage to assign the contenders in this next race? First, we should point out that only one horse, Neda Sal, has more than eight points, which is the absolute minimum our system requires for a horse to be played. Neda Sal, with eleven points, is therefore the only playable animal in this race.

I do not suggest that Neda Sal be assigned a percentage in relation to the points of any other horses in this race. Instead, we can use a formula to determine what odds are acceptable on the only playable horse in a race: Multiply the number of points assigned to the horse by 5 percent. This means that Neda Sal will be given 55 percent probability, according to our "book," of winning this race.

The same formula can be applied to any horse that earns eight points or more. Thus, a horse with exactly eight points, if it is the only contender in its race, will be assigned a 40 percent chance of winning, which translates to odds of 3 to 2. On this basis, Neda Sal's chances of winning are 4 to 5, and since Neda Sal's track odds are 7 to 5, this horse is a definite overlay.

We begin by eliminating the following horses from consideration:

1 Ambro Oshawa
Poor recent form.

3 J's Jane
After a three-month layoff, J's Jane has not returned to earlier form. With a weak driver, she does not appear to be a factor in this race.

5 Game Guy Pick
Erratic; has had only one good race in last six starts.

6 Culver's Andy
No recent form.

8 Arnies Betsy
Has not run since changing to new barn. Outside post position also a factor.

2 Neda Sal

Current form	4
Consistency	2
Class	0
Driver	2
Post position	3
Total	11

7 Becky's Adora

Current form	1
Consistency	3
Class	0
Driver	2
Post position	0
Total	6

4 Noble Stein

Current form	1
Consistency	2
Class	0
Driver	1
Post position	2
Total	6

CLAIMING
1 Mile — Purse $1800

Claiming Price $4000
Mares allowed 20%, 4 year olds allowed 30%.
FIRST HALF OF DAILY DOUBLE

ASK FOR HORSE BY PROGRAM NUMBER

Saddle Cloth
BROWN

---

1 ARMBRO OSHAWA
(4, 2.07⅗ (½) — $10570)
DRIVER—DON HOLMES—Lt. Blue and White
br. g. 6, by Overtrick—Armbro Adios
Don J. Holmes, Darien, N.Y.
MS
4000

Trainer: D. Holmes

| | | | | | | | | | | | | | | | | 1977 | 28 | 1 | 3 | 2 | $ | 2871 |
| | | | | | | | | | | | | | | | | 1976 | 28 | 2 | 4 | 1 | $ | 4686 |

9-29⁷⁷ Btva ms 1900 ft 4000 clm 1 .31² 1.03¹ 1.35² 2.07² 1 6 5 6 8⁵² 2.09² 8.20 (DHolmes) MssMargtEd,BluejayJnet,SaratogaBrbra 55
9-21⁷⁷ Btva ms 1800 gd 4000 clm 1 .31⁴ 1.06³ 1.37² 2.08⁴ 8 8 8 7⁷·¹ 7⁵⁴ 24.50 (DHolmes) DaringDrexel,NobleStein,KittyHal 52
9-9⁷⁷ Btva ms 1800 ft 4000 clm 1 .30³ 1.06² 1.36¹ 2.07⁴ 5 60 5 5⁵·¹ 4⁵⁴ 23.50 (DHolmes) TorpidsAytch,LarryLinn,LuckyLang 74
8-30⁷⁷ Btva 1800 ft 4000 clm 1 .31⁴ 1.04¹ 1.35 2.08 5 70 6 6⁶·¹ 7⁵³ 20.60 (DHolmes) MissMargaretEd,IndianRuler,LarryLinn 69
8-19⁷⁷ Btva 2100 ft 4000 clm 1 .31¹ 1.06 1.35 2.06² 4 4 4 4³·¹ 7¹·³ 19.80 (DHolmes) IndianRuler,LarryLinn,Cedarwooddudge 71
8-12⁷⁷ Btva 2100 ft 4000 clm 1 .30⁴ 1.03 1.33 2.08² 2 3 4 4² X6X1³·¹ 22.70 (DHolmes) SuperLaird,MissMargaretEd,WorthyRoger 71
8-5⁷⁷ Btva 2000 ft 4000 clm 1 .30¹ 1.01⁴ 1.34¹ 2.07 2 6 5 5⁴ 6³ 14.20 (DHolmes) BeckysAdora,TerrAdios,CaptainCrunch 79

---

2 NEDA SAL (N)
(6, 2.05 (¼) — $31943)
DRIVER—JOE RICH, JR.—Red, Black and White
b. m. 8, by Adios H—Sal Win
Robert Claus, Buffalo, N.Y.
MS
4800

Trainer: R. Claus

| | | | | | | | | | | | | | | | | 1977 | 35 | 4 | 6 | 4 | $ | 6672 |
| | | | | | | | | | | | | | | | | 1976 | 46 | 2 | 8 | 12 | $ | 8655 |

9-28⁷⁷ Btva ms 1800 sl 4800 clm 1 .31² 1.01³ 1.34³ 2.08⁴ 6 6 4 4 3¹·¹ 3.00 (JRichJr) NedaSal,Three,JsJane 55
9-16⁷⁷ Btva ms 1800 my 4800 clm 1 .31¹ 1.03⁴ 1.36 2.09² 7 1⁰ 2 2¹·¹ 1³ 9.10 (JRichJr) JeboroExpress,NedaSal,JiByrd 63
9-2⁷⁷ Btva ms 1800 ft 4800 clm 1 .32² 1.04¹ 1.35² 2.06⁴ 1 2 2 2¹·¹ 2¹·¹ 5.90 (JRichJr) RowdyGTime,NedaSal,Spohn 67
8-23⁷⁷ Btva ms 2100 ft 4800 clm 1 .31³ 1.05 1.35⁴ 2.07⁴ 6 5 6 4² 2¹·⁴ 10.50 (JRichJr) VeracityN,NedaSal,Goodjudge 75
8-15⁷⁷ Btva ms 2100 ft 4800 clm 1 .31³ 1.04¹ 1.35² 2.07¹ 3 1 3 3⁰·² 7¹·³ 10.50 (JRichJr) MissMargaretEd,IndianRuler,LarryLinn 71
8-8⁷⁷ Btva ms 2000 gd 4800 clm 1 .30³ 1.02¹ 1.34² 2.06⁴ 6 6 6 5³·¹ 5³ 22.90 (JRichJr) WinnieSong,EasternQueen,LisasLucky 70
7-30⁷⁷ B.R. ms 2300 ft 6000 clm 1 .30¹ 1.01² 1.32² 2.05⁴ 2 3 6 7¹³·¹ 7¹⁸ 3.10 (JBesIII) EasternQueen,RowdyGTime,IndianRuler 77

---

3 J'S JANE
(5, 2.06½ (½) — $19553)
DRIVER—LESTER TOURVILLE—Purple, White and Gold
b. m. 8, by Meadow Battles—Lively Gen
M. D. P. Stables, Hamburg, N.Y.
MS
4800

Trainer: J. Giair

| | | | | | | | | | | | | | | | | 1977 | 26 | 7 | 4 | 4 | $ | 5234 |
| | | | | | | | | | | | | | | | | 1976 | 26 | 5 | 4 | 4 | $ | 2303 |

9-28⁷⁷ Btva ms 1800 sl 4800 clm 1 .30³ 1.01³ 1.34³ 2.08⁴ 2 5 5 4²·³ 3¹·¹ 8.10 (BAltize) NedaSal,Three,JsJane 55
9-12⁷⁷ Btva ms 1800 ft 4800 clm 1 .32 1.03¹ 1.36 2.07 3 4 5 7 6¹·¹ 5.20 (BAltize) MyBrothersHorse,Gingham,RichlandNancy 68
9-1⁷⁷ Btva ms 1800 ft 4800 clm 1 .30⁴ 1.03 1.34¹ 2.05⁴ 7 7 7 7¹·³ 7¹·³ 6.60 (BAltize) JffersnVictory,MicheByrd,RchlandNncy 80
8-19⁷⁷ Btva 1800 ft Qua 1p 1 .31² 1.06 1.36 2.08 1 1hd 1¹·² 1² NB (BAltize) JsLane,Khadir,InTime 70
6-27⁷⁷ B.R. ms‡1900 sy 5000 clm 1 .30² 1.02¹ 1.36² 2.08² 7x 7 1 8dis 8¹·² 9.70 (JGosman) PeerlessLobii,RusselTorrence,MarysHeel 49
5-24⁷⁷ B.R. ms‡2150 ft 6000 clm 1 .31² 1.04 1.36 2.04 8 8 8 7dis 8⁷·⁴ 14.50 (JGosman) BeverlysJune,Quickem,KeystoneWhiz 80
5-17⁷⁷ B.R. ms‡1900 ft 5000 clm 1 .30¹ 1.00⁴ 1.32⁴ 2.05² 4 2 2 2¹ 1¹·² 4.60 (JGosman) JsJane,Gingham,BardellaN 79

---

4 NOBLE STEIN
(6, 2.04½ (½) — $16900)
DRIVER—JULIEN JOANISSE—Blue and Gold
br. g. 10, by Direct Nobel—Miss Doreen Grattan
Julien Joanisse & Ralph Deperno, Que., Can. & N.Y.

Trainer: J. Joanisse

| | | | | | | | | | | | | | | | | 1977 | 15 | 2 | 1 | 2 | $ | 2544 |
| | | | | | | | | | | | | | | | | 1976 | 35 | 4 | 6 | 3 | $ | 6950 |

9-29⁷⁷ Btva 1900 ft 4000 clm 1 .31² 1.03¹ 1.35² 2.07² 7 4 4 4 5 16.10 (JJoanis) MssMargtEd,BluejayJnet,SaratogaBrbra 55
9-21⁷⁷ Btva 1800 gd 4000 clm 1 .31⁴ 1.06³ 1.37² 2.08⁴ 2 2 3 4 5 7.80 (JJoanis) DaringDrexel,NobleStein,KittyHal 52
9-8⁷⁷ Btva 2100 ft 5000 clm 1 .31² 1.04² 1.36 2.07⁴ 3 4 3 4³ 12.60 (JJoanis) BredByrd,THAlmighty,SuziesSon 66
8-25⁷⁷ Btva ms 2400 ft 5000 clm 1 .33 1.05 1.36 2.07³ 5 5 5 5 ex8 8dis ex8dis 47.60 (JJoanis) RowmarsAngel,TopSkipper,ScottMeadow 65

5 MS 4000

(None — $418) **GAME GUY PICK**
DRIVER—ROBERT BOMPCZYK (P)—Brown, Gold and White
b. g. 6, by Dam Flashy—Sultry Rose
Raymond Bompczyk, Blasdell, N.Y.

Trainer: Ro. Bompczyk

8-14⁷⁷	RidC⅝		1000 ft	5500 clm hcp	1	.30³	1.01³	1.33⁴	2.05¹	6	6	7⁹²	7¹⁴²	2.08	10.70	(RBompcz)	NedaSal,TThree,JsIane		55
8-10⁷⁷	RidC⅝		900 ft	c-4000 clm hcp	1	.30³	1.03²	1.34²	2.06³	7	6⁰	4³	3¹⁴	2.064	12.20	(RCoulte)	EagleDaleN,ColoredArtist,NobleStein
8- 3⁷⁷	RidC⅝		850 ft	3500 clm hcp	1	.30¹	1.01⁴	1.33	2.04²	1	3	5	6²³	2.05	6.35	(RCoulte)	CheckMark,YLBlaze,MorleySChoice

6 MS 5200

(3, 2.09¾ (½)) **CULVERS ANDY**
DRIVER—DICK WILCOX—Blue, Red and White
b. g. 4, by Bye Bye Andy—Lady Culver
Jesse & Charlotte Iatonna, Cheektowaga, N.Y.

Trainer: D. Wilcox   2.09¾ Bucy

9-29⁷⁷	Btva	ms	1900 ft	5200 clm	1	.31²	1.03¹	1.35²	2.07²	6	7	7⁵	7³³	2.08¹	17.50	(DWilcox)	MssMargrtEd,Bluejaynet,SaratogaBrbra	55
9-21⁷⁷	Btva	ms	1800 gd	5200 clm	1	.31⁴	1.06³	1.37²	2.08⁴	4	3	3	6³³	2.093	11.90	(DWilcox)	DaringDrexel,NobleStein,KittyHal	52
9- 5⁷⁷	Btva	ms	1600 ft	nw1500LtCD	1	.31	1.02¹	1.33⁴	2.05	5	5	20²	38¹	2.12	12.10	(DWilcox)	TripleShot,JaiLaiGale,CulversAndy	73
8-20⁷⁷	Btva	ms	1800 ft	wRLtCD	1	.30²	1.02³	1.35	2.06⁴	3	20	25	54	2.073	25.00	(DWilcox)	AvonFairline,AvonJester,Fortunato	65
8- 9⁷⁷	Btva	ms	1500 ft	76-7nw150ps	1	.31¹	1.04¹	1.35³	2.06³	7	5	6³	6¹⁰	2.081	31.90	(DWilcox)	Vatican,KingMacMillan,Lady8There	72
8-12⁷⁷	Btva	ms	1500 ft	76-7nw150ps	1	.30¹	1.02³	1.35	2.07¹	7	7	5²	5³²	2.081	41.00	(DWilcox)	SterlingsAugh,Romero,KeystoneDebut	72
7-26⁷⁷	Btva	ms	1500 ft	76-7nw150ps	1	.31²	1.02²	1.34¹	2.07	6	8	7	5⁷³	2.082	82.10	(DWilcox)	Romero,JffrsonPlayboy,KeystoneGlamour	68

7 MS 4800

(5, 2.07% (½)) **BECKY'S ADORA**
DRIVER—ED McNEIGHT, JR.—Orange, Black and White
b. m. 6, by Adoras Dream—Becky Belle
James Helfeldt, Buffalo, N.Y.

Trainer: J. Helfeldt   2.05% B.R.   2.07% B.R.

9-29⁷⁷	Btva	ms	1900 ft	4800 clm	1	.31²	1.03¹	1.34²	2.06²	5	3⁰²	7⁵	6³¹	2.08	3.60	(EMcNeJr)	MssMargrtEd,Bluejaynet,SaratogaBrbra	55
9-19⁷⁷	Btva	ms	1800 sy	4800 clm	4	.31³	1.04	1.36⁴	2.09⁴	4	3	5	56²	2.11	4.00	(EMcNeJr)	ViCon,MissMargaretEd,TThree	66
9- 7⁷⁷	Btva	ms	1800 ft	4800 clm	2	.31¹	1.03¹	1.34	2.07⁴	7	5	202	31³	2.08¹	7.50	(EMcNeJr)	GameGuyPick,BckysAdora,EvamarieMaeWin	63
8-29⁷⁷	Btva	ms	1800 ft	4800 clm	5	.31	1.03	1.35	2.06⁴	3	4³⁰	3²	54	2.073	2.90	(LMcNeig)	Tonivar,AdiooRepDoll,BeckysAdora	75
8-19⁷⁷	Btva	ms	2100 ft	4800 clm	1	.31³	1.04²	1.36¹	2.08³	3	3	3¹	62¹	1.90*	(GSarama)	SuzieSSon,BeckysAdora,LuckyLang	60
8-12⁷⁷	Btva	ms	2100 ft	4800 clm	1	.30³	1.03	1.35²	2.08²	5	3	2²	5¹	2.083	3.30	(JRankin)	SuperLand,BeckysAdora,WorthyRoger	71
8- 5⁷⁷	Btva	ms	2000 ft	4800 clm	1	.31²	1.01⁴	1.34³	2.07	4	3	2	1¹	2.07	3.80	(EMcNeJr)	BeckysAdora,TerrAdios,CaptainCrunch	79

8 MS 4800

(6, 2.09¾ (½)) **ARNIES BETSY**
DRIVER—JIM RANKIN—Red, Blue and White
b. m. 7, by Smash Hit—Ritas Betsy
Thomas P. Cirincione & Carmen Bifulco, Buffalo, N.Y.

Trainer: C. Bifulco   2.06¾ FlmD   2.09% Wodsk

9-27⁷⁷	Btva	ms	2100 ft	6000 clm	1	.30⁴	1.04¹	1.34	2.06²	5	6	57⁴	56⁴	2.073	15.10	(TTurclJ)	TorpidsAytch,SuccessGrant,KittysHope	60
9-17⁷⁷	Btva	ms	2100 ft	6000 clm	1	.31¹	1.03	1.35²	2.07²	3	4	4²	42³	2.08	9.40	(TTurclJ)	SuzieSSon,RussellTorrence,BeverlysJune	70
9-10⁷⁷	Btva	ms	2100 ft	6000 clm	1	.31	1.03⁴	1.35³	2.07²	2	10	3⁴	37	2.09¹	2.70*	(JRankin)	SpeedyStrut,ButterKnight,ArniesBetsy	62
9- 3⁷⁷	Btva	ms	2400 ft	6000 clm	1	.31¹	1.02	1.35	2.06²	3	4	3⁴	64³	3.40	(JRankin)	IanHill,RussellTorrence,Peetong	70
8-25⁷⁷	FlmD		1100 ft	c-4000 clm	1	.33	1.05	1.36	2.07³	2	2	1²¹	72³⁴	1.80*	(JRankin)	RowmarsAngel,TopsSkipper,ScottMeadow	60
8-14⁷⁷	FlmD		1100 ft	6000 clm	1	.30²	1.03	1.34²	2.07	5	5	1³	13	1.50*	(RMcLean)	ArniesBetsy,Darling,AbidenN	71
8- 7⁷⁷	FlmD		1100 ft	4000 clm	1	.29	1.00²	1.32¹	2.04¹	6	5	2⁰	2²	2.043	1.30*	(RMcLean)	WatchrsPride,ArniesBtsy,HighMoraleN	65

	1977				1976				
	18	2	1	1	$ 2824
	0	0	0	0	$ 000
	33	9	4	6	$ 9290
	37	4	8	4	$ 6788

Analysis. Neda Sal is clearly the play in this race unless the odds are prohibitive. The best way to decide whether the odds make Neda Sal a favorable play is to make up a "book," assigning a percentage to the three contenders according to their chances of winning.

Horse	Points	Chance of winning	Minimum acceptable odds	Actual odds	Overlay
2 Neda Sal	11	60	4 to 5	1.30	yes
4 Noble Stein	6	20	4 to 1	3.00	no
7 Becky's Adora	6	20	4 to 1	8.60	yes

Neda Sal was a definite overlay at 1.30 to 1 in this race.

Results.

FIRST RACE — 1 Mile				\$4000 Claiming Pace				\$1800
Neda Sal ms	2	2	2	1^0	1^2	1^1	J. Rich, Jr.	*1.30
Armbro Oshawa ms	1	x5	5	3^0	3^1_4	2^2	D. Holmes	13.60
Beckys Adora ms	7	7	6	5^0	5^1	3nk	E. McNeight, Jr.	8.60
Noble Stein	4	1^0	1	2	2^1	4ns	J. Joanisse	3.00
Game Guy Pick ms	5	4^0	4	6	6^1_4	5^1_4	R. Bompczak	10.30
J's Jane ms	3	6	7	8	7^2	6nk	L. Tourville	7.20
Culvers Andy ms	6	3	3	4	4^1_2	7^6	D. Wilcox	12.50
Arnies Betsy ms	8	8	8	7^0	x8x	8	J. Rankin	10.90

\$2 MUTUEL PRICES	2. Neda Sal	4.60	3.40	2.20
Official Program Nos.	1. Armbro Oshawa		8.00	4.00
	7. Beckys Adora			3.00

Time — .33⅕   1.08⅕   1.42   2.15

7

Applying the System at Other Raceways

In this chapter we will extend our handicapping system to two additional tracks, Pompano Park and the Meadowlands, to illustrate its applicability to tracks of different sizes. Pompano Park, a ⅝-mile track, is of much the same caliber as Batavia Downs. The Meadowlands is a premier 1-mile track. The purses offered at the Meadowlands compare favorably with those offered anywhere in America.

Pompano Park

Because Pompano is a ⅝-mile track, horses start in the backstretch ⅜ mile before the finish line. Once the field hits the finish line, they have one complete turn around the track to go. This means that a mile race involves only three turns rather than the four taken on a ½-mile track, and the turns are not as sharp. Moreover, there is room for nine starters on a ⅝-mile track, instead of the eight common to ½-milers. The outside post positions are not as disadvantageous on a ⅝-mile track because the turns are fewer and not as sharp. For this reason, it is necessary to revise our point assignment for post positions as follows:

1 or 2—3 points
3 to 6—2 points
7 to 9—1 point

Notice that the Pompano program, unlike those of other tracks, includes records of leading trainers as well as drivers. We can take advantage of this by assigning points for the trainer as follows: A trainer whose horses win more than 25 percent of their races receives 3 points; a trainer successful 20 to 25 percent of the time gets 2 points; and one who produces winners in 15 to 20 percent of his

stable's starts is assigned 1 point. These are *not* bonus points in addition to points assigned to drivers. We will assign points either to the driver or to the trainer, whichever is higher, but not to both.

Pompano Park Statistics

A final question concerns our scoring of a horse's consistency at Pompano. It was still very early in 1978 when this was written, and most horses at the track had not accumulated nearly enough starts to be assigned points on their overall percentage of win and place finishes for 1978. (A minimum of ten starts in a year is a fair test of consistency.) For this reason, we propose to ignore consistency entirely in assigning points to each horse in a race. Instead, we will require at least six points overall (not eight) for a horse to be considered a genuine contender in its race. This will give us more close decisions than previously in our sample races.

Reading the Pompano Program

Now let us note some differences between the Pompano program and that of Batavia Downs. We have already seen that Pompano's program contains useful information on trainers at the track. In addition, the Pompano Program clearly states whether a horse is moving up, dropping down, or remaining in the same class as its last race. A + means a horse is moving up in class; a − means that it is stepping down; and an = means that its class is unchanged from its last start. This valuable information is stated directly under the horse's program number.

Second, the mean temperature for a given evening is stated after the condition of the track for that date. This may be useful, since times vary slightly with temperature, hotter nights producing faster races.

Third, the Pompano program states the year of a horse's birth date instead of simply stating the horse's age as of January 1.

Last, Pompano has a *standard* set of allowances for horses running in claiming-allowance races. For example, in a $3,000 claiming-allowance race, a three-year-old filly can be claimed only for an additional 60 percent, or a total of $4,800.

TEMPERATURE DATA

The mean temperature for a given race date at Pompano Park will appear in the past performance lines directly following the track condition.

EXAMPLE: ft 81½° or gd 77°

In the first example, the track was rated "fast" by the judges, and the mean temperature was 81°; in the second example, the track condition was "good", and the mean temperature was 77°.

The temperatures in the past performances lines will include not only those at Pompano Park, but also those from other racetracks (provided the information was made available).

CLAIMING ALLOWANCES

Unless specifically stated otherwise in the claiming conditions, all claiming races at Pompano Park will have the following age and sex allowances calculated off the base claiming price:

3-YEAR-OLD FILLIES	60%
3-YEAR-OLD COLTS & GELDINGS	50%
4-YEAR-OLD MARES	50%
4-YEAR-OLD COLTS & GELDINGS	30%
4-YEAR-OLD COLTS & GELDINGS	25%
AGED MARES (5 Years Old & Up)	20%

DISTANCE RACED

ALL RACES — unless otherwise stated — are ONE MILE in distance.

LEADING DRIVERS

THROUGH WEDNESDAY, FEBRUARY 8, 1978

WIN — 9 Points   Second — 5 Points   Third — 3 Points   47 STARTS OR MORE

	Driver	Sts.	1st	2nd	3rd	Pts.	Avg.
1	STEVE WARRINGTON	48	13	7	5	167	.387
2	RICHARD MACOMBER	57	16	5	5	178	.347
3	STERLING BUCH	56	10	8	12	166	.329
4	BERNARD GERVAIS	73	15	8	8	199	.303
5	DOUG HIE	82	11	11	11	223	.302
6	DON BRAINARD	75	13	8	12	193	.286
7	J. (CARL) SMITH	47	9	8	8	120	.284
8	MICKEY McNICHOL	171	29	23	17	427	.271
9	FRANK O'MARA	71	11	10	8	173	.271
10	TED TAYLOR	156	22	19	26	371	.264

LEADING TRAINERS

THROUGH WEDNESDAY, FEBRUARY 8, 1978

	Trainer	Sts.	1st	2nd	3rd
1	ALLEN SAUL	44	14	2	7
2	TERRY EICHAS	52	14	9	11
3	MICKEY McNICHOL	58	14	8	8
4	ROBERT MILLER, JR.	35	13	3	3
5	CLIFF HUNER	37	13	4	4
6	BILL NELSON	70	13	11	12
7	DON BRAINARD	74	13	7	11
8	CHARLES JENKINS	21	12	4	2
9	BILL LAMBERTUS	136	12	15	22
10	RICHARD MACOMBER	30	11	4	0

POMPANO PARK WINNING POST POSITIONS — THRU WEDNESDAY, FEBRUARY 8, 1978

Post Positions	1	2	3	4	5	6	7	8	9
Starts	509	509	509	509	509	509	504	478	364
Wins	83	74	73	73	71	71	49	34	23
Percentage	16	15	14	14	14	14	10	7	6

Percentage of Winning Favorites 34%
Percentage of Favorites in the Money 61%

Printed by Colonial Press, Inc.

WARMUP SADDLE CLOTH—GREY
ONE MILE

QUINIELA & TRIFECTA RACE

CLAIMING PACE

Claiming price $4500. With allowances.

Purse $1800

	QUINIELA & TRIFECTA		

Morning Line, PP Hd. No.	Date Trk	Cond & Temp	Class	Dist 1/4	Leader's Time 1/2	3/4	Winner's Time	PP 1/4 1/2 3/4	Str	Fin	Ind. Time	Odds		Driver	First	Second	Third

RED $4500

1 — Morning Line 9-2

FLEETWOOD KNOX

Lifetime—$8,219—3, 2:07.3

Driver—TOM WANTZ, White-Brown-Gold   R g 1973, by Knox Hanover—Aggi Dale—Ross Hanover.   Breeder: J. A. Konen
Tr.—M. Goldschmidt, Jr.   Owner: Joseph A. Konen, Croswell, Mich.

1-24 PPk⅝ ft 72° 4500clm	:29⁴ 1:00¹ 1:32¹ 2:02¹	8 2o 2o 2o	3⁹¾	3⁹¾	(2:04¹)	11.40	1978 4 0 1 1 $ 719
1-18 PPk⅝ ft 70° 5000clm	:32 1:02³ 1:33⁴ 2:05	8 2o 2o 2o	7⁵¼	7⁵¼	(2:06)	10.70	1977 14 2 2 2 $ 3180 (2:09² Nor)
1-11 PPk⅝ ft 65° 5000clm	:30² 1:01³ 1:32² 2:03³	4 4 4 4	4⁷¼	4⁷¼	(2:04¹)	4.50	T.Wan) ScottFashion FittyGs FleetwoodKnox
1-4 PPk⅝ ft 68° 6250clm	:29⁴ 1:03 1:33³ 2:05²	4 2 3 3	2³⁄₄	2³⁄₄	(2:04)	5.10	T.Wan) MrTrapp SkygoBoy MyBonnieLad
12-28 PPk⅝ ft 55° 6250clm	:29⁴ 1:01² 1:33² 2:05	5 4 4o 4²	2¹¾	2¹¾	(2:05²)	6.00	T.Wan) UnclesGirl FleetwoodKnox SantasGirl
12-23 PPk⅝ ft 68° 7500clmhcp	:31² 1:03¹ 1:34¹ 2:04¹	1 5o 5o 4²	6⁶	6⁶	(2:06)	3.80	T.Wan) BarbaraButler FleetwoodKnox LadyBillie
							T.Wan) UnclesGirl PeterRobin Sheepshead

BLUE $4500

2 — Morning Line 6

D W P

Lifetime—$17,897—4, 2:04.2

Driver—A. "TONY" MANNINO, White-Green-Orange   B g 1972, by Greentrees Pride—Miss McGuinea—McGuinea.   Breeder: D. W. Parr
Tr.—A. Mannino   Owner: Ann Nunziata, Douglaston, N.Y.

1-18 PPk⅝ ft 70° 5000clm	:32 1:02³ 1:33⁴ 2:05	3x 4 3o 4	5⁴¹⁄₂	5⁴¹⁄₂	(2:06)	15.70	1978 3 0 1 0 $ 375
1-10 PPk⅝ ft 55° 4500clm	:30⁴ 1:03⁴ 1:34³ 2:05²	6 4 4 4	2¹¾	2¹¾	(2:06)	16.70	1977 23 1 6 1 $ 2795 (2:06¹ MR)
1-3 PPk⅝ ft 59° 4500clm	:30⁴ 1:04³ 2:06¹	8 3 4 5	7⁷¼	7⁷¼	(2:08)	23.50	A.Man) MrTrapp SkygoBoy MyBonnieLad
12-16 PPk⅝ ft 72° cdnw1550L8	:30¹ 1:02² 1:32⁴ 2:05	8 4 2 2	7⁹¾	7⁹¾	(2:08¹)	22.40	A.Man) FittyGs DWP ScottFashion
12-16 PPk⅝ ft 72° cdnw350L5	:30¹ 1:01² 1:31⁴ 2:03⁵	1 o 1 1	7⁹½	7⁹½	(2:05²)	22.40	A.Man) CBDuane SlickWave MissBanker
11-26 DD⅝ ft 30° 500clm	:32⁴ 1:04¹ 1:35 2:08²	5 9 9 9	6²³⁄₄ 7	6²³⁄₄ 7	(2:13)	2.40	A.Man) SpikedTime DWP Jorobasfack
11-18 DD⅝ ft 6000clm	:31 1:02³ 1:33² 2:06	x1x 8 7	6⁴¾	6⁴¾	(2:06¹)	5.30	F.GalSr) MissDove MyMainMandta AftonFrtunetdq
							F.GalSr) Kimbr'tsDuane GriggBEasy MgnoliasVnon

WHITE $4500

3 — Morning Line 10

BAY B. ECHO

Lifetime—$8,009—5, 2:04.4

Driver—R. W. DeSANTIS, Gold-Blue   B h 1972, by Smith Cress—Hopeful Elise—Adios Harry.   Breeder: H. F. Harp
Tr.—R. W. DeSantis   Owner: Sandra & David Shein, Schenectady, N.Y.

1-21 PPk⅝ ft 59° 5000clm.imhcp	:30¹ 1:02 1:33 2:05	7 7o 7o 7o	8²²¾	8²²¾	(2:07)	62.20	1978 1 0 0 0 $ 00
1-22 PPk⅝ ft 55° 5000clm	:30¹ 1:02 2:05¹	7 8 8o 8o	6¹³	6¹³	(2:07¹)	62.20	1977 27 2 2 5 $ 4012 (2:04¹ Stga gd)
12-10 PPk⅝ ft 70° 6500clm	:30² 1:01² 1:32² 2:04²	3x 9 9	9dis	9dis		21.60	R.W.DeS) RecordClip Temperamental DizlingShadow
11-16 Stga hy 5000clm	:36³ 1:14³ 1:50² 2:25³	7 8 7o 7	3⁸	3⁸	(2:27¹)	9.40	R.W.DeS) Temperamental MrTrapp KammysDrmHigh
10-24 Stga gd cdnw1000L5	:31¹ 1:03 1:35 2:07⁴	7 7 7 5	5⁴¾	5⁴¾	(2:08²)	5.70	R.W.DeS) GuyKent TedMacGrattan AvonKnave
							K.Cra) SnapJudgement SaratogaStan BayBEcho
							R.W.DeS) Namahana SpdyChrisTime SuperVallyBlle
							R.W.DeS) PlymouthPrincess PrettyLisa Keith

GREEN $4500

4 — Morning Line 8

PLEASANT RHYTHM

Lifetime—$23,841—5, 2:03.4 (⅝)

Driver—EUGENE WASZAK, Blue-Gold-White   B h 1971, by Rhythm Mite—Quick Sue—Quick Pick.   Breeder: M. A. Miller
Tr.—E. Waszak   Owner: Eugene Waszak (lessee), Clarendon Hills, Ill.

1-24 PPk⅝ ft 72° 4500clm	:30² 1:02¹ 1:33² 2:04¹	4 7 7 8	6³¹⁄₂	6³¹⁄₂	(2:04¹)	12.90	1978 33 4 0 0 $ 357
1-19 PPk⅝ ft 72° 5000clm	:29¹ 1:01² 1:32² 2:04²	7 8o 9 9³¾	5¹⁰¼	5¹⁰¼	(2:06²)	23.30	1977 33 2 2 3 $ 8456 (2:06² May)
1-13 PPk⅝ gd 65° 6000clmhcp	:29⁴ 1:02 1:33 2:05²	5 5 5 5	8⁹½	8⁹½	(2:07)	5.90	E.Was) HopefulOne CoachApril LynwoodsMajor
1-6 PPk⅝ ft 70° 6000clm	:30 1:02³ 1:32⁴ 2:04³	6 6o 6o 6¹	4¹³⁄₄	4¹³⁄₄	(2:05)	32.60	E.Was) HighChance SantasGirl HappyCreed
12-15 Arl 1⅛ ft 6000clm	:31³ 1:04³ 1:38² 2:03	4 4 4 3	6⁴	6⁴	(2:11²)	32.60	E.Was) SteadyHostess AdahiDream HaloJackson
12-10 Arl 1⅛ ft 6000clm	:33² 1:07 1:40 2:12	1 3 3 2o	3³⁄₄	3³⁄₄	(2:13²)	4.70	E.Was) RompinRita SteadyHostess HaloJackson
							E.Was) RcewayThndor RustyForbes CraigWorthy
							E.Was) WinMike MajesticMack PleasantRhythm

5
BLACK $5400 + 3

Lifetime—$31,037—6, 2:02.3 (⅞)

Driver—ED TAYLOR, Red-White-Blue

Tr.—E. Taylor   Breeder: P. B. Dennis

1-23 PP⅞ ft 72⁰ 4200clm	:29¹	1:00⁴	1:32²	2:03³	4	1	1	1½	1½	(2:03⁴)	4.40
1-18 PP⅞ ft 70⁰ 3600clm	:30¹	:02⁴	:34	2:05¹	8	1	1	1½	1½	(2:05¹)	12.20
1-11 PP⅞ ft 65⁰ 3600clm	:30¹	:02⁴	:34	2:07²	4	4o	3	1	1	(2:07²)	7.50
1- 2 PP⅞ ft 65⁰ 4200clm	:30⁴	:02¹	:34²	2:05³	5	5	2½	9⅝	(2:05³)	12.30
12-28 PP⅞ ft 65⁰ 3600clm	:30²	1:03	1:34	2:08	5	3o	3	5	5½¼	(2:08)	5.90
12- 9 PP⅞ sy 68⁰ cdnw350L5	:30³	:03¹	:35²	2:07³	6	5	6o	5⅗⁴	5⅜⁴	(2:08³)	8.70

1978   4   2   1   0 $ 1525   (2:03⁴ PP⅞)
1977   16   2   2   0 $ 1851   (2:07¹ Har)

(G.Bru) StrlingsCpe DugoClverWon Accountable
(E.Tay) DugoCleverWon Bill;yMahone SassyDevil
(E.Tay) DugoClvrWon CnstgaDaniel OcalaStrRae
(E.Tay) TennesseeSinger ArmbroRscal Shiaway1Frsty
(E.Tay) DugoCleverWon PeccaTrubble JustLeigh
(E.Tay) NblieFrbes BpniesSr4yBoy HntngdnChoice

6
GREY $4500 + 4

Lifetime—$73,838—5, 2:00.2 (1)

Driver—GAETAN BRUNET, Green-Red-White

Owner: Joe D'Amato, Fort Lauderdale, Fla.

Tr.—G. Brunet

1-21 PP⅞ ft 59⁰ 4000clm	:30	:01³	1:33	2:05⁴	2	4	4½¼	2½	(2:05⁴)	2.50
1-14 PP⅞ ft 59⁰ 5500clmhcp	:29¹	:03	1:31²	2:04²	9	4	5⅝⁴	5⅝⁴	(2:05²)	12.30
1- 7 PP⅞ ft 72⁰ 5000clmhcp	:30	:02	1:32²	2:04	9	4	4	2⅜⁴	3⅜⁴	(2:04)	8.70
1- 9 PP⅞ ft 49⁰ 3500clm	:30³	:01¹	1:31⁴	2:06³	9	7	8	6⅝⁴	4⁶	(2:06³)	12.70
12-29 PP⅞ ft 72⁰ 6000clmhcp	:29¹	:01	1:31¹	2:03¹	9	4	4	8	2½	(2:03¹)	2.50
12-28 PP⅞ ft 55⁰ 5000clm	:29	1:01	:32	2:07	9	9	9o	8½	4⁶	(2:07²)	*2.40
12-22 PP⅞ ft 55⁰ 5000clm	:31	:04	:34²	2:07	2	5	5	4⁶	2²	(2:07²)	1.60
10-26 VD¾ ft 60⁰ 6000clmhcp	:28⁴	:01	:32²	2:03¹	3	5	5	6o	5⅞½¼	(2:03)	5.20

1978   36   4   5   4 $ 7617   (2:02⁸ VD¾)
1977   22 $ 6392   (2:04² MR)

(G.Bru) BoGator TeeniTime RockvilleChris
(G.Bru) RJYankee SamBengazi Kerry
(G.Bru) VMarJ JuneOvertrack TeeniTime
(G.Bru) BarRTar MeadowMechanic Fahrenheit
(G.Bru) TJMac TeeniTime SpecialByrd
(G.Bru) MyMyBrooklyn JDKat MissBettingTime

7
PINK $5625 —

Lifetime—$118,874—5, 2:02.1

Driver—RICHARD MACOMBER, Maroon-Gold

Owner: Vincent Tancredi, Coconut Creek, Fla.

Tr.—R. Macomber   Breeder: J. Walters

1-25 PP⅞ ft 76⁰ 5000clm	:29²	1:00⁴	1:31³	2:02	6	9	9be8o	8¹²	4¹¹¼	(2:05¹)	*1.00
1-17 PP⅞ ft 72⁰ 4500clm	:30	:01⁴	:33²	2:04²	6	7	7o6o	1¹¼	1⁴¾	(2:04²)	1.80
1- 7 PP⅞ ft 72⁰ 8250clmhcp	:29⁴	:01	:32²	2:04¹	5	5	5o5o	7⁷¼	5⅞⁴	(2:05²)	*1.50
12-31 PP⅞ ft 80⁰ 7500clmhcp	:29³	:01²	:32³	2:03	2	3	3o	3	2³¾	(2:03³)	*1.20
12-12 Nor gd 6000clm	:31³	:03	:43	2:07	4	4o	4o	4½²	4¹²	(2:07²)	*1.60
11-26 Nor ft 7500clm	:31²	:04	1:36²	2:09¹	8	7	7	6⅝½	5³	(2:09¹)	*1.70

1978   4   3   0   0 $ 2102   (2:04¹ PP⅞)
1977   22 $ 2348

(R.Mac) MyBonnieLad OpalPark ForeversPride
(W.Lam) HopefulOne CoachApril LynnwoodsMajor
(R.Mac) TennesseeSinger KootneyBrown LittleEtta
(R.Mac) TennesseeSinger ArmbroRscal ShiawayFrsty
(R.Mac) BarbaraBButler FleetwoodKnox LadyBillie
(R.Mac) TnnsseeSinger RntreesCharity Accountble

8
ORANGE $4500 =

Lifetime—$7,930—2, 2:14.2

Driver—W. "BILL" LAMBERTUS, Gold-White-Black

Owner: Terrigno Stables, Loxahatchee, Fla.

Tr.—W. Lambertus

1-24 PP⅞ ft 72⁰ 5625clm	:30¹	:01²	:33¹	2:04¹	4	4	4o	5	4²	(2:05)	7.60
1-17 PP⅞ ft 72⁰ 5625clm	:30	:01⁴	:33²	2:05	4	4o	2o	2¹¼	2⁴¾	(2:06)	2.80
1- 7 PP⅞ ft 72⁰ 6250clmhcp	:29⁴	:01	:32²	2:03²	1	5	5o	5½	7⁷½	(2:04⁴)	*2.40
12-31 PP⅞ ft 80⁰ 3000clm	:29³	:01²	:33	2:03³	1	5	5	2³¾	2³¾	(2:04¹)	11.20
12-12 Nor gd 6000clm	:31³	:03	:43	2:09¹	7	7	7	6⅝½	4¹²	(2:10)	2.80
11-26 Nor ft 7500clm	:31²	:04	1:36²	2:07³	6	6	6⅜½	5³	(2:09¹)	17.50

1978   3   0   1   1 $ 591
1977   13   1   3   3 $ 817   (2:06⁴ ScD⅝)

(W.Lam) TennesseeSinger LynnwoodsMajor FiftyGs
(L.Sam) VMarJ JuneOvertrack TeeniTime
(L.Sam) PollyPrior LynnwdkMajor MadamCamaro
(L.Sam) Bahama HastyBelle McKinneyAbby
(L.Sam) RoyalPaceAndy LittleBigMan MajorLloyd

9
ORANGE $4500 + 8

Driver—AL JASPERSON, Green-Black-White

Lifetime—$3,379—5, 2:06.4 (⅞)

Owner: Rob Howell, Mark Steele, Wm. F. Hartman & Brett Merkle, Lancaster, Ohio
Breeder: B. McKinney

Tr.—M. Ferguson

1-25 PP⅞ ft 76⁰ 2500clm	:29¹	:03	1:33	:34²	2:05¹	9	4o	5	4o	3¾	(2:05¹)	*2.40
1-18 PP⅞ ft 70⁰ 2500clm	:30	:02	:34²	2:05	2	2	2½	1½	1¼	(2:05)	4.90
1-11 PP⅞ ft 65⁰ 3000clm	:30¹	:01¹	:32²	2:06⁴	5	5	6o6¼¼	5⁴¾	(2:08²)	3.50
12-31 PP⅞ ft 80⁰ 3000clm	:30¹	:01¹	:32²	2:06⁴	6	4	4o	3⅜¼	4³	(2:05¹)	3.40
12-15 PP⅞ ft 78⁰ 3500clm	:30⁴	:04	1:36⁴	2:07³	5	6	6	9o8¹²¼	8¹³	(2:10)	10.40
10-14 Lancaster ft cdnw1000			Race in 2:16³, dnf.								

1978   3   3   1   3 $ 1207

(A.Jas) MeigsMarauder PioneerSpirit Chrissie
(A.Jas) MeigsMarauder QuickNCfty YankeeHobo
(A.Jas) DugoClvrWon CnstgaDaniel OcalaStrRae
(A.Jas) MaysTar-Baby FlashinKash BlossomBelle
(A.Jas) IkesImpression SummerYankee SalC
(R.Har) BatWish LittleDrop HiddenChoice

Trackman's Selections: 7—5—6—1

Examples of Races at Pompano

Pompano Park   7th Race   January 28, 1978

Eliminate the following horses because of poor recent form: 2 D W P, 3 Bay B. Echo, 4 Pleasant Rhythm, 8 Lynnwoods Major. 9 Meigs Marauder is going up too much in class and is too far back. D W P and 6 Teenie Time have not been consistent enough. This leaves us with:

1 Fleetwood Knox

Current form	2
(disregard races on	
1/18 and 1/24)	
Class	0
Post position	3
Driver	1
Total	6

7 Tennessee Singer

Current form	4
Class	0
(omit 1/25 race)	
Post position	1
Driver	3
Total	8

5 Dugo Clever Won

Current form	5
Class	−2
Post position	2
Driver	2
Total	7

Close Decision

Let's assign bonus points to each of the three contenders on the basis of their recent good races.

Fleetwood Knox: 1 bonus point for roughing it in December 28 race. Total: 1 point.

Dugo Clever Won: 2 points for roughing it for two quarters in January 11 race. Total: 2 points.

Tennessee Singer: 2 points for roughing it and 1 for the stretch gain in the January 17 race; 1 point for each in the January 9 race. Total: **5** points.

Analysis. Tennessee Singer is the horse to beat but could have a tough race if he gets too far back. Fleetwood Knox is a threat from the

rail; Dugo Clever Won has an outside shot. At 1.10 to 1, however, Tennessee Singer is no bargain.

Result (chart shows number of lengths each horse finished behind the winner).

```
7th RACE  —  CLAIMING PACE  —  1 MILE
Quarter Times—:30³ 1:02² 1:33¹ 2:05²
6 Teeni Time            6  4  4  4   4²     1ⁿˢ    (2:05²)   7.00    (G.Bru)
7 Tennessee Singer      7  8  6o 6o 5³½    2ⁿˢ    (2:05²)  *1.10    (R.Mac)
1 Fleetwood Knox        1  2  3  3o 2½     3ⁿˢ    (2:05²)   3.30    (T.Wan)
9 Meigs Marauder        8  5  5  5   6⁴     4¾     (2:05³)  19.00    (A.Jas)
5 Dugo Clever Won       5  3  1  1   1½     5¹¼    (2:05³)   3.10    (E.Tay)
4 Pleasant Rhythm       4  7  8o 7  7¹½     6³     (2:06 )  18.70    (E.Was)
2 DWP                   2  1  2  2   3¹¾    7³     (2:06 )  21.90    (A.Man)
3 Bay B Echo            3  6  7  8  8⁺³⁴    8⁺³⁴   (2:06²)  74.50    (R.W.DeS)
8 Lynwoods Major            Scratched
Mutuels:    (6)—16.00 5.60 3.40     (7)—3.40 2.60     (1)—2.60          •
TRIFECTA—6-7-1—$187.80                        QUINIELA—6 and 7—$20.40
```

Pompano Park   9th Race   January 28, 1978

Eliminate the following horses because of poor recent form: 1 Bluegum, 2 Douro Lobell, 3 Mark William, 7 Windy David, and 8 Steady Brookdale. 9 Bo Gator, moving up in class, is too far back.

The contenders are:

4 Coach April

Current form	3
Class	−2
Post position	2
Driver	2
Total	5

6 Rompin Risa

Current form	2
Class	0
Post position	2
Driver	2
Total	6

5 Coolup Way

Current form	1
Class	0
Post position	2
Driver	1
Total	4

Close Decision

Coach April: 1 point for being parked in race on January 24; ditto for January 4 race. Total: 2 points.

NINTH RACE

WARMUP SADDLE CLOTH—ORANGE

ONE MILE

QUINIELA & TRIFECTA RACE

CLAIMING PACE

Claiming price $6000. With allowances.

Purse $2000

	QUINIELA & TRIFECTA		
	First	Second	Third

Morning Line, PP Hd. No.	Date Trk	Cond & Temp	Class	Dist 1/4	Leader's Time 1/2	3/4	Winner's Time	PP 1/4 1/2 3/4	Str	Fin	Ind. Time	Odds	Driver

RED $6000

1 —

6

BLUEGUM

B g 1968, by Van Hanover—Van Kitty—Van Dieman. Breeder: C. C. Devine

Lifetime—$28,255—8, 2:03.4

Driver—CHRIS CUSIMANO, Green-White-Gold

Owner: Christopher Cusimano, Lake Ronkonkoma, N.Y.

Tr.—C. Cusimano

													1978	2	0	0	0	$	70
													1977	23	1	1	2	$	2430	(2:05² Fhld)
1- 24	PP5⁄8	ft 72°	7500c/mhcp	:30¹	1:02	1:32³	2:02⁴	7	2o 1	4½	9¹⁷	(2:06¹)	49.70	(C.Cus)	ShiawayDale	Rebel	Grttandq	PeterHop⁴dq
1- 4	Fhld	ft 35°	cdnw150ps	:31	1:01	1:34²	2:05	6	5	4o	5⁶½	5¹⁷	(2:08²)	11.10	(O.Pis)	Deso⁴q	GB	TheJokerA	DoubleCopy
12- 27	Fhld	ft 30°	10000c/m	:31	1:01	1:33	2:05¹	7	2o	2o	8⁸	8¹⁷⁴	(2:08⁴)	133.80	(C.Cus)	Deakon	NeverKnowA	Fullapoleon
12- 19	Fhld	gd 45°	10000c/m	:30³	1:03	1:35	2:07³	3	4	4⁷	8⁶	7⁷⁴	(2:08³)	6.90	(C.Cus)	RawlingsStreet	RomanA	Augustun
12- 12	Fhld	ft 25°	10000c/m	:31¹	1:02	1:34²	2:07²	6	2o	2o	3¹	7⁵	(2:08²)	12.70	(C.Cus)	MiteMarvel	FortWaikato	OneAndAll
12- 5	Fhld	sy 40°	10000c/m	:31²	1:04	1:36⁴	2:08¹	2	2o	3o	3¹	8⁷⁵	(2:03)	56.30	(C.Cus)	NorasFirst	DukesGldnImage	NeverKnowA

WHITE $6000

2 +

6

DOURO LOBELL

B h 1969, by Torpid—High Rock—Tar Heel. Breeder: Lana Lobell Farms

Lifetime—$88,241—4, 2:02.4

Driver—CHARLES DEL GATTO, Orange-White

Owner: Arthur G. Grodner & Harvey R. Goldberg, Forest Hills & Yonkers, N.Y.

Tr.—C. Del Gatto

													1978	0	0	0	0	$	1214	(Q 2:08¹ PP5⁄8)
													1977	18	3	0	0	$	4375	(2:02² NE5⁄8)
1- 18	PP5⁄8	ft 70°	cdnw800L9	:29⁴	:59¹	1:31⁴	2:04	9	1o	1	1¹	5⁷½	(2:05²)	34.40	(C.Del G)	SteadyWynnah	BonieBetty	SteadyMrLady
1- 11	PP5⁄8	ft 65°	cdnw800L10	:30⁴	1:01²	1:31³	2:05³	8	7o 4o	4⁶½	6¹⁸¼	(2:09¹)	34.60	(C.Del G)	OcalaStarPrince	JrbelJack	KystneArdmre
1- 5	PP5⁄8	ft 71°	7500c/m	:29¹	1:01²	1:33²	2:05	4	9o	9o	9¹⁸	9¹⁶	(2:06³)	17.70	(D.Rob)	LongTime	GrunkosBoy	ByrdBobby
12- 29	PP5⁄8	ft 65°	7500c/m	:29²	:59¹	1:31	2:03²	9	2o	2o	8¹⁶	8¹⁶	(2:05⁴)	9.80	(C.Del G)	GreenwdMuffey	SteadyDanny	PeterRobin
12- 22	PP5⁄8	ft 55°	7500c/m	:31¹	1:01²	1:31	2:05	8	8¹	7o 6	6⁶½	4⁷½	(2:06²)	33.00	(C.Del G)	GuyKent	AvonKnave	LongTime
12- 17	PP5⁄8	gd 75°	qua	:31	1:03	1:36²	2:08¹	3	3	3	1⁴	1⁸¼	(2:08¹)	NB	(C.Del G)	DouroLobell	BoldInvader	MarchWay

BLUE $6000

3 =

6

MARK WILLIAM

B h 1970, by Knight Time—Margo Hill—Hoot Mon. Breeder: Hill Distributing Co.

Lifetime—$34,515—7, 2:02.2 (⅝)

Driver—J. (CARL) SMITH, Maroon-Tan

Owner: Arthur Brewer II, Haverhill, Mass.

Tr.—J. Carl Smith

													1978	1	0	0	0	$	00	
													1977	43	8	5	8	$ 10517	(2:02² PP5⁄8)
1- 24	PP5⁄8	ft 72°	6000c/m	:31	1:03	1:32⁴	2:03¹	2	2o 1	1¹	7⁴½	(2:04)	28.70	(J.Smi)	RCQuestor	CredibleVon	CoolupWay
12- 26	PP5⁄8	ft 58°	6500c/m	:30¹	1:00⁴	1:32⁴	2:05⁴	5	4o 5o	8³	7⁷½	(2:06)	11.10	(J.Smi)	ShadyHillDaisy	BigFire	HeatherRuss
12- 15	PP5⁄8	ft 78°	7500c/m	:29²	1:01²	1:32²	2:03	6	7	7	7⁴¼	7⁷½	(2:04⁴)	54.10	(J.Smi)	FerRusPrincess	OzrkChief	SilentAdventure
11- 23	Rock	ft 8000c/m		:30⁴	1:02³	1:34¹	2:05	7	4	5	6⁵½	4⁵½	(2:06)	75.10	(J.Smi)	GreatReturn	BlazinLace	NickelBeer
11- 17	Rock	sy 8000c/m		:30	1:02	1:35²	2:07³	2	2o	2o	5⁵¾	6⁵	(2:08³)	38.50	(J.Smi)	MountnGeneral	GreatReturn	BoldRhythm
11- 10	Rock	ft 8000c/mhcp		:31¹	1:03	1:35	2:05³	4	2o	2	2¹½	3⁴¼	(2:06²)	6.10	(J.C.Smi)	GreatReturn	GoldEnzyme	MarkWilliam

GREEN $7500

4 +

4

COACH APRIL

B g 1974, by Tempered Yankee—Madam Napoleon—Irish Napoleon. Breeder: Heritage Stud Farm Ltd.

Lifetime—$2,837—3, 2:05.1 (⅝)

Driver—LARRY SAMPLES, White-Maroon

Owner: Robert & Fanny Kalish, Pompano Beach, Fla.

Tr.—L. Samples

													1978	3	1	1	0	$	1000	(2:06³ PP5⁄8)
													1977	11	1	1	0	$	2837	(2:05¹ Lau5⁄8)
1- 30	PP5⁄8	ft 72°	c5625c/m	:30²	1:02¹	1:33²	2:04¹	7	2o 1	2¹	2¹¾	(2:04³)	13.60	(G.Bru)	HopefulOne	CoachApril	LynwoodMajor
1- 16	PP5⁄8	ft 65°	c4375c/m	:30²	1:01³	1:33³	2:05³	6	2o	2o	3	6³¼	(2:06¹)	*.90	(S.War)	MaysTarBaby	Esplanade	KootneyBrown
1- 4	PP5⁄8	ft 68°	4500c/m	:30	1:02¹	1:34⁴	2:06³	1	2o 1	2o	2¹	2³⁴	(2:06³)	*2.40	(S.War)	CoachApril	TarportBryn	KKAdios
12- 29	PP5⁄8	ft 65°	5250c/m	:30	1:01¹	1:33²	2:05	6	2	2	2	5²½	(2:05²)	3.20	(S.War)	KatuStar	LittleEtta	ScarletAir
12- 17	PP5⁄8	gd 72°	7500c/mhcp	:30	1:02	1:34¹	2:05	4	6	2	2	5⁵¾	(2:09²)	4.40	(S.War)	Goldock	BarbaraBButler	Banyan
12- 8	LB⅝	ft 30°	8000c/m	:30³	1:04	1:34³	2:06²	5	1	1	2²½	2²¼	(2:06⁴)	14.50	(S.War)	TahrenheIt	CoachApril	CheerfulMir

9-2

5 — YELLOW $6000 — 5-2

COOLUP WAY
Lifetime—$105,511—9, 2:02.2
Driver—GARY LEWIS, Purple-White-Green
Owner: Edward C. Abbott, So. Perth, W. Australia
Br g 1964, by Admiral Way—Miverta—Gallantry. Breeder: J. H. Bele
Tr—Marthalou Cavaliere St.—G. Lewis

1-24 PP1⅝ ft 72° 6000clm	:31	1:03	1:32¼	2:03¼	1	1	1	3¾	2:03²	5.50	(G.Lew) RCQuestor CreditableVon CoolupWay
1-17 PP1⅝ ft 72° 6000clm	:31	1:00¹	1:32²	2:04¹	4	2	2	1	2:04²	9.30	(G.Lew) UnclesGirl CoolupWay CreditableVon
1-2 PP1⅝ ft 65° 6000clm	:31	1:00¹	1:32²	2:04¹	5	1	1	1¼	2:04⁴	1.80	(G.Lew) BigChase ScottKeyStar LuckyNiftyDean
12-23 PP1⅝ ft 68° 8000clm	:28¹	1:01²	1:32²	2:04³	3	2	2	2¾	2:05	*1.80	(G.Lew) HMJets CoolupWay PeterHop
1-6 PP1⅝ ft 70° 8000cimhcp	:30¹	1:04³	1:34⁴	2:05	7	1	1	4⁹¼	14.60	(G.Lew) RompinRisa SteadyHostess HaloJackson
10-2 MR gd 55° 8000clm	:29³	1:02	1:33¹	2:05⁴	3	2	3	2¹	2:05⁴	3.80	(J.Gil) CoolupWay Nonni HempsteadMurray

6 — BLACK $7200 — =

ROMPIN RISA
Lifetime—$25,217—2, TT 2:02.4 (1)
Driver—GEORGE FOLDI, Green-Red-White
Owner: J.A.A.W. Stable, So. Fallsburg, N.Y.
Br m 1970, by Sampson Direct—Pizzeria—Knight Star. Breeder: M. G. Westfall
Tr—H. Purdy

1-24 PP1⅝ ft 72° 6000clm	:31	1:03	1:32¼	2:03¹	5	5	5	5²¼	2:03³	5.50	(G.Fol) RCQuestor CreditableVon CoolupWay
1-17 PP1⅝ ft 72° 6000clm	:31	1:00¹	1:32²	2:04¹	4	2	2	2¼	2:04²	9.30	(G.Fol) UnclesGirl CoolupWay CreditableVon
1-10 PP1⅝ ft 55° 7200clm	:31	1:04²	1:34⁴	2:05⁴	7	6	6o	2¼	2:05	*1.40	(G.Fol) AndysCoho HatfieldChuck RompinRisa
1-6 PP1⅝ ft 70° 7200cimhcp	:30	1:02²	1:34⁴	2:04³	1	1	1	1½	2:05	7.60	(G.Fol) RompinRisa SteadyHostess HaloJackson
12-30 PP1⅝ ft 58° 6250clm	:29³	1:01³	1:31⁴	2:03¹	7	7	7o	9⁹¼	15.00	(G.Fol) BarRTar MeadowMechanic Fahrenheit
12-17 PP1⅝ gd 72° 6250cimhcp	:31	1:04¹	1:34²	2:05⁴	7	7o	7o	5⁵	2:07⁴	27.00	(G.Fol) GoodCustomer BigFire ShadyHillDaisy

7 — GREY $6000 — =

WINDY DAVID
Lifetime—$10,931—4, 2:05.3 (⅝)
Driver—STERLING BUCH, Red-White-Black
Owner: Virginia Shell, Pompano Beach, Fla. Breeder: B. R. & P. W. Mathewson
Tr—R. Shell

1-24 PP1⅝ ft 72° 6000clm	:31	1:03	1:32¼	2:03¹	3	3	3	3½	2:03⁴	44.40	(S.Buc) RCQuestor CreditableVon CoolupWay
1-17 PP1⅝ ft 72° 6000clm	:31	1:00¹	1:32²	2:04¹	3	5	5	5³	2:04³	1.40	(S.Lev) UnclesGirl CoolupWay CreditableVon
1-7 PP1⅝ ft 72° 7000cimhcp	:30¹	1:01	1:32¹	2:03	9	9	9o	4⁵	25.10	(S.Lus) UnclesGirl TJMac Ancindy
12-18 NE⅝ ft s/7000clm	:31	1:05²	1:32²	2:08	4	2	2	7⁸¼	10.10	(J.Ken) MnyMkrMadman MjesticBrwr RylBellows
12-26 PP1⅝ ft 58° 6250clm	:29³	1:03¹	1:34⁴	2:06	4	4	4	8⁴¾	8.70	(J.Ken) MajesticBrwr RoyalBellows MyBonnieLad
12-17 PP1⅝ gd 72° 6250cimhcp	:31	1:04¹	1:34²	2:05⁴	2	3	3	3¹¼	2:06¹	7.80	(J.Ken) RoyalBellows WindyDavid MajesticBrewr

8 — PINK $6000 — =

STEADY BROOKDALE
Lifetime—$30,894—4, 2:04
Driver—SAM LUSSIER, Green-Red-White
Owner: M. E. & S. J. Lussier, R. D. Jones, No. Amherst & Sunderland, Mass. Breeder: J. R. Colvin
Tr—S. Lussier

1-23 PP1⅝ ft 72° 6500clm	:30	1:04¹	1:31²	2:02²	7	7	7o	6⁵	2:03²	29.10	(S.Lus) MullettStreet Challenge General/Burlar
1-14 PP1⅝ ft 59° 7000cimhcp	:29²	1:02	1:32¹	2:03	9	9	9⁵¾	7¹²¼	153.50	(S.Lus) JBDirect OK5Breeze BigFire
1-7 PP1⅝ ft 72° 7000cimhcp	:30¹	1:01	1:32¹	2:03	8	9	9⁹¾	8⁹¾	91.90	(S.Lus) PllyPrior MnneyMkerMdmn Mechanic
12-18 NE⅝ ft s/7000clm	:31	1:05²	1:32²	2:08	3	3	3	4⁴	4.60	(S.Lus) MasterProof JustWite BullRun
1-27 Rock ft 7000clm	:31¹	1:03	1:35	2:07²	7	7	4o	5⁴¾	18.70	(S.Lus) BestBye BullRun Kwajalein
11-18 Rock ft 7000clm	:30¹	1:03²	1:33²	2:05⁴	2	2	2	2 ʰᵈ	22.20	(S.Lus) EasyDirect Bullye Goudron

9 — ORANGE $7500 — +

BO GATOR
Lifetime—$3,712—3, 2:07
Driver—GUY LaBELLE, Red-Green-Yellow
Owner: Guy LaBelle & Anthony Marro, Montreal, Que., Can. & Troy, N.Y. Breeder: R. M. Whitcomb
Tr—G. LaBelle

1-21 PP1⅝ ft 59° 5000clm	:30	1:13	1:33¹	2:05⁴	3	7	7o	1½	2:05⁴	(G.LaB) BoGator TeeniTime RockvilleChris
1-13 PP1⅝ gd 65° 5000clm	:31²	1:05	1:33¹	2:07⁴	2x	9o	9⁰¾	9¹⁸¼	15.30	(G.LaB) RecordClip DzzlingShadow WildwdStorm
1-9 PP1⅝ ft 49° 4375clm	:31⁴	1:03²	1:34²	2:06³	5	1	4²¾	2¹	4.60	(G.LaB) TimeWay BoGator ShiawayFrosty
1-2 PP1⅝ ft 65° cdnw510L8	:30	1:04¹	1:32¹	2:04	4	6	7	5⁹	37.50	(G.LaB) Kreuma MiniPower CurlJubilee
12-28 PP1⅝ ft 55° 4500clm	:30	1:01⁴	1:33¹	2:06¹	4	4	4¹²¼	₄¹²¾	30.30	(G.LaB) BafTime SandMonarch ShiawayFrosty
12-15 PP1⅝ ft 79° 5250clm	:30⁴	1:04	1:36⁴	2:07³	9	8	7o	5⁷⅝ˣ	54.60	(G.LaB) IkesImpression SummerYankee SalC

Trackman's Selections: 5—6—4—3

Coolup Way: No bonus points.

Rompin Risa: 2 points for roughing it and 1 for the stretch gain in the January 6 race. Total: 3 points.

Analysis. Coach April is moving up in class after a change in barns—too many imponderables. Coolup Way stops in the stretch. Rompin Risa looks best here, considering that Coach April and Coolup Way are front-runners and may have to battle for the lead, thereby setting a fast pace. Bo Gator, moving up in class, is disadvantaged by post position. At odds of 9 to 2, Rompin Risa is a good bet.

Results.

```
9th RACE  —  CLAIMING PACE  —  I MILE
Quarter Times—:30² 1:02¹ 1:33³ 2:04³
6 Rompin Risa        6  6  6o 4o 4¹¹⁄₂    1²¹⁄₂   (2:04³)   4.60   (G.Fol)
7 Windy David        7  7  7  6o 5³       2²¹⁄₂   (2:05 )  10.70   (S.Buc)
8 Steady Brookdale   8  8  8  8o 8⁴³⁄₄    3⁵     (2:05³)  29.40   (S.Lus)
5 Coolup Way         5  1  1  1  1 ⁿᵏ     4⁵³⁄₄   (2:05⁴)  *1.20   (G.Lew)
2 Douro Lobell       2  2  3  3  3¹¹⁄₄    5⁷¹⁄₂   (2:06 )  21.30   (C.DelG)
4 Coach April        4  3o 2o 2o 2 ⁿᵏ    6ᴿ     (2:06¹)   3.60   (L.Sam)
1 Blue Gum           1  4  4  5  6³¹⁄₄    7⁸     (2:06¹)  35.90   (C.Cus)
3 Mark William       3  5  5  7  7⁴¹⁄₂    8⁹     (2:06²)   6.30   (J.Smi)
9 Bo Gator  ·        9  9  9  9  9⁶³⁄₄    9¹¹    (2:06⁴)  17.70   (G.LaB)
Mutuels:    (6)—11.20  7.80  7.00     (7)—8.00  6.00     (8)—11.20
TRIFECTA—6-7-8—$1,617.00                    QUINIELA—6 and 7—$53.80
```

Pompano Park   4th Race   February 2, 1978

Eliminate 2 Rebellion, 3 April Lorr, 4 TNT Freight, 7 Lucky Mr G, and 8 Golda Herbert for poor recent form. 5 Kanaka Boy is a quitter going *up* in class. 1 Miss Spinning Song has not won since December 29, although her last effort was respectable.

The contenders:

6 Riddle		**9 Jades Dream**	
Current form	3	Current form	2
Class	0	Class	0
Post position	2	Post position	1
Driver	1	Driver	3
Total	6	Total	6

Close Decisions. Riddle: no bonus points. Jades Dream: 1 point for

roughing it on January 19.

Analysis. Jades Dream can win this race if he is not parked for all or most of the mile going for the lead. Riddle stops in the stretch. Miss Spinning Song could be dangerous in this one. But at odds of 8 to 1, Jades Dream is a definite overlay despite his outside post.

Result. Jades Dream won, paying $17.60, $6.40, and $3.80. Miss Spinning Song was second, and Riddle showed.

Pompano Park   Sixth Race   February 6, 1978

We can eliminate 2 Wildwood Earl, 4 Little Etta, 6 Time Way, and 8 Pleasant Rhythm on grounds of poor recent form. 1 Katu Star, moving well up in class after a second-place finish in a $2,500 claimer, can be discounted. 9 Fleetwood Knox is too handicapped by an outside post to be dangerous.

Three horses remain:

3 Threat

Current form	2
Class	0
Post position	2
Driver	2
Total	6

7 Esther Herbert

Current form	2
Class	0
Post position	1
Driver	2
Total	5

5 Meigs Marauder

Current form	4
Class	1
Post position	2
Driver	2
Total	9

Analysis. Meigs Marauder gets off well and should be in striking position going into the stretch. Esther Herbert, off her last race, is a genuine possibility. Threat has a chance but is a poor bet as favorite, at odds of 2 to 1. Meigs Marauder is the play.

FOURTH RACE

WARMUP SADDLE CLOTH—GREEN

ONE MILE

QUINIELA & TRIFECTA RACE

CLAIMING HDCP. TROT

Claiming price $6000-$8000. With allowances.

Purse $2050

Morning Line, PP Hd. No.		Date Trk	Cond & Temp	Class	Dist 1/4	Leader's Time 1/2	3/4	Winner's Time	PP 1/4 1/2 3/4	Str	Fin	Ind. Time	Odds		Driver	First	Second	Third

1 — RED $7700

MISS SPINNING SONG

Lifetime—$42,390—9, 2:05.3 (⅝)

Driver—MARK O'MARA, Green-White

B m 1968, by Spinning Song—Battle Red—Ronald Scot.
Owner: Leonard Fancher, Pompano Beach, Fla.

Tr.—M. O'Mara   Breeder: D. D. Bedwell

1-25	PPk⅝ ft 76°	7200clmhcp	:31	:29¹ 1:01	:32² 2:03³	5	5o 5o 5½	3¹¾	(2:04)	5.70	1978	(M.O'Ma) GranbyHope Riddle MissSpinningSong
1-19	PPk⅝ gd 72°	7800clmhcp	:29²	:29¹ 1:03¹	1:31¹ 2:07¹	3	6o 6o 5¾	5½	(2:08²)	*1.80	1977	(M.O'Ma) JadesDream Plunter Riddle
1-11	PPk⅝ ft 68°	7200clmhcp	:31²	:30¹ 1:03¹	1:35² 2:07²	7	8o 8o 8¼	5⅔	(2:08)	3.90	(J.All) Riddle GranbyHope EdgewoodGrania
1- 4	PPk⅝ ft 68°	8400clmhcp	:31²	:31 1:01	1:34¹ 2:06³	4	2o 1 1nk	7¹¹	(2:08¹)	3.50	(J.All) Arm5roMiami PanLadyJ ReliableGordon
12-29	PPk⅝ ft 65°	7200clmhcp	:31¹	:31 1:02¹	1:33¹ 2:03³	4	2 2 3¹¼	1¹½	(2:05³)	2.40	(J.All) MissSpinningSong PanLadyJ Riddle
12-16	PPk⅝ ft 72°	6600clmhcp	:30	1:03²	1:34³ 2:05¹	9	2 2 2o 2½	2¹¾	(2:06¹)	4.90	(J.All) Riddle MissSpinningSong EdsBuddy

3 — WHITE $6000

REBELLION

Lifetime—$66,554—8, 2:02.1 (1)

Driver—WARREN McILMURRAY, Green-Gold-Brown

Ch g 1966, by Florlis—Rosadean—Dean Hanover.
Owner: Edsel W. Johnson, Detroit, Mich.

Tr.—W. McIlmurray   Breeder: Almahurst Farm Inc.

1-25	PPk⅝ ft 76°	7000clmhcp	:29¹	:29¹ 1:01	:32¹ 2:03¹	4	7 6o 6¹²	6³²	(2:04¹)	15.40	1978	(W.Mcl) GranbyHope Riddle MissSpinningSong
1-19	PPk⅝ gd 72°	7000clmhcp	:29²	:29¹ 1:03¹	1:34² 2:07¹	6	6o 6¹⁴	6o⁵	(2:08²)	6.90	1977	(W.Mcl) JadesDream Plunter Riddle
12-20	Nor sl 6500clmhcp	:32⁴	:30¹ 1:03¹	1:38² 2:11¹	2	6 7 4⁴½	4½	(2:12¹)	4.70	(G.Ban) OHJohnnie DoubleBubble ElbysPrince
12- 6	Nor gd 6500clmhcp	:39²	1:33 1:49	2:22¹	6ix3 3¹²	2½	(2:22¹)	8.10	(H.Wat) JanetKayFarley Rebellion PrinceDiller
11-28	Nor gd 10000clmhcp	:31²	1:05 1:38¹	2:10¹	9 8 8o¹½	7⁹½	(2:12)	16.60	(H.Wat) DougsAlibi Khartoum SparkyReid
11- 8	Nor gd 7500clmhcp	:30¹	1:04³ 1:36³	2:08¹	8 8 8 8o⁵²	2¹¾	(2:06¹)	47.40	(H.Wat) MissEmpiresEcho Rebellion MarConFrisky

4 — BLUE $7200

APRIL LORR

Lifetime—$19,701—8, 2:06.2

Driver—LEONARD ABBRUZZIO, Red-Gold

B m 1969, by Argyle Hanover—Miss Treat—Blaze Hanover.
Owner: Michael J. McCarthy & Leo T. Doran, Troy & Watervliet, N.Y.

Tr.—L. Abbruzzio   Breeder: P. V. Sanguinet

1-26	PPk⅝ ft 62°	5400clmhcp	:31	1:03	1:34³ 2:06¹	3	3x3x7 7 7dts	7dls	2.20	1978	(L.Abb) EdsBuddy Wildwood5Intruder WeDoGrald
1-20	PPk⅝ ft 66°	4800clmhcp	:31	1:05³ 1:36	2:07³	3	2 2 2²	1¹¼	(2:07³)	9.90	(L.Abb) AprilLorr KanakaBoy ReliableGordon
12-28	MR ft 10°	2500clm	:31³	1:04 1:38³	2:09¹	2	2 2o 2nk	1nk	(2:09¹)	3.00	1977	(J.RamJr) AprilLorr FlowerPower MelissaDear
12-26	MR ft 9o°	2500clm	:31⁴	1:05¹ 1:38¹	2:12¹	8	x3o 2o 1²	4⁶¹²	(2:13³)	3.60	(J.RamJr) EmbaMelody Audible WorthyReward
12-21	MR ft 32°	4000clm	:32	1:04 1:37	2:09⁴	4	5 5 4⁶½	4¹½	(2:10)	6.10	(J.RamJr) LainiesDeb DukeReturn StandardSong
12-17	MR ft 28°	4000clm	:31	1:04¹ 1:36²	2:10	5	3 2 2¹²½	2¹²½	(2:11)	5.20	(R.Faw) LainiesDeb FastStreak Luport

8 — GREEN $6000

TNT FREIGHT

Lifetime—$26,514—5, 2:05.4 (⅝)

Driver—LARRY SAMPLES, White-Maroon

B g 1972, by Perfect Freight—Trim Rodney—Rodney.
Owner: Robert & Fanny Kalish, Pompano Beach, Fla.

Tr.—L. Samples   Breeder: ABC Stables Inc.

1-28	PPk⅝ ft 60°	qua	:32¹	1:03³ 1:34²	2:05⁴	4	4	1²½	1¹¼	NB	1978	(L.Sam) TNTFreight DownTheHatch AteAMile
1-25	PPk⅝ ft 76°	6000clmhcp	:29¹	1:01 1:32²	2:03³	8	8x8 8dts	8¹⁻¾	(2:05¹)	10.80	(L.Sam) GranbyHope Riddle MissSpinningSong
1-17	PPk⅝ ft 76°	qua	:29¹	1:03 1:33⁴	2:06¹	3o	3o 3¹0	8¹⁻⁴	(2:07⁴)	NB	1977	(L.Sam) BreezingSpeed SpeedRally TNTFreight
1-11	PPk⅝ gd 76°	qua	:31²	1:03 1:32¹	2:04³	4o3 3 x2¹x	x9²·⁴³x	(2:12²)	4.80	(L.Sam) Riddle GranbyHope EdgewoodGrania
1- 4	PPk⅝ gd 60°	qua	:32¹	1:04³ 1:36	2:07³	5	2 3x4 4¹0	1½	(2:07³)	NB	(L.Sam) TNTFreight MyGalGussie SpecialJoe
11-15	Nor sy qua	:34¹	1:07² 1:41²	2:15²	2	3x4 4¹0	4¹0	(2:17²)	NB	(L.Sam) DavisonMiss SpclProduct SaltAndPepper

		QUINIELA & TRIFECTA		
	Driver	First	Second	Third

5 YELLOW $6000

KANAKA BOY
B. g 1968, by Greentree Adios—Friendly Lass—Garrison Hanover.
Owner: Ernest D. Danks, Jr., Pompano Beach, Fla.   Breeder: Rainbow International Inc.
Lifetime—$15,474—7, 2:03.4 (⅝)
Driver—MICKEY McNICHOL, Blue-White-Black   Tr.—E. Danks

1-28 PPK⅝ ft 60° qua	:31³ 1:04¹ 1:35¹ 2:07²	6	1	2¹	2³¹²	23½	[2:08]	NB	1978 3 0 2 0 $ 825	(♥ 2:09² Sem¾)
1-26 PPK⅝ ft 62° 5000clmhcp	:29² 1:01 1:33 1:41	x8x choked down pulled up dnf					[2:08]	21.50	1977 8 0 2 0 564	(♥ 2:07² PPK⅝)
1-20 PPK⅝ ft 66° 4500clmhcp	:31³ 1:03³ 1:36 2:07³	6	1 o 2 2 2¹½			2½	[2:08]	5.30	(M.O'Ma) EdsBuddy WildwoodIntruder WeDoGrald	
1-13 PPK⅝ gd 65° 4500clmhcp	:31³ 1:05 1:36¹ 2:08¹	5	1	1½	2½	2½	[2:07¹]	11.00	(M.McN) AprilLorr ReliableGordon	
1- 7 PPK⅝ ft 78° qua	:31¹ 1:03¹ 1:35¹ 2:07¹	5	1	1	1	1	[2:07¹]	NB	(E.Dan) NeveFlame KanakaBoy ToughShot	
8-11 Sem¾ gd cdnw500	:31² 1:04² 1:38	6	3o 3o 1o 1³			2⁵	[2:13¹]	14.10	(E.Dan) SailBoat KanakaBoy CJRodney	

10 BLACK $7000

RIDDLE
Br. g 1970, by Fairview Ike—Bonnie Eileen—John A Hanover.
Owner: Bud Foster & Beverley Ferris (lessees), Pompano Beach, Fla.   Breeder: M. Dufford
Lifetime—$11,911—7, 2:05.4 (⅝)
Driver—BUD FOSTER, Blue-White   Tr.—Beverley Ferris   St.—B. Foster

1-25 PPK⅝ ft 76° 7000clmhcp	:29¹ 1:01 1:32² 2:03	6	7	8³⁴	7¹⁰¹²	[2:04]	*2.00	1978 4 0 0 0 $ 368		
1-19 PPK⅝ gd 72° 7000clmhcp	:29² 1:03⁴ 1:34¹ 2:07¹	5	6 6o 5o 5¼		4²¹⁴	[2:07³]	3.00	1977 27 3 4 6 8509	(2:05² PPK⅝)
1-11 PPK⅝ ft 65° 10500clmhcp	:30¹ 1:03 1:33 2:05²	1	1	1¾	3¹¾	[2:05¹]	*2.40	(B.Fos) JadesDream Plunker Riddle	
1- 5 PPK⅝ ft 71° 10500clmhcp	:30³ 1:01² 1:32³ 2:05³	4	7	7¹³⁴	6⁵¾	[2:06³]	8.00	(B.Fos) MissCamasB Snackadoo DerbySong	
12-30 PPK⅝ ft 65° 6000clmhcp	:31¹ 1:03¹ 1:33¹ 2:05³	2	x6 7	7	3¹¾	[2:05¹]	*1.00	(B.Fos) MissSpinningSong PanLadyJ Riddle	
12-16 PPK⅝ ft 72° 4500clmhcp	:30 1:03² 2:05⁴	1	1	1½	2⁵	[2:06¹]	*1.30	(B.Fos) Riddle MissSpinningSong EdsBuddy	

7 GREY $7000

LUCKY MR G
B. g 1967, by Duke Rodney—Avalon Holly—Galophone.
Owner: Anthony Giordano, Stratford, Conn.   Breeder: A. Giordano
Lifetime—$159,483—6, 2:03.4
Driver—GEORGE HARP, JR., Green-White   Tr.—G. Harp, Jr.

1-27 PPK⅝ ft 56° 10500clmhcp	:29¹ 1:01 1:33¹ 2:05	3	2	1½	2½	[2:05]	2.20	1978 4 0 0 0 $	
1-20 PPK⅝ ft 66° 10500clmhcp	:31¹ 1:03 1:34¹ 2:05²	1	5 6o 5o 5¼		7¹⁰½	[2:07³]	3.40	1977 14 4 2 2 5625	(2:07¹ KD⅝)
1-12 PPK⅝ ft 67° 10500clmhcp	:30¹ 1:03 2:04⁴	5	2 2 2¹½		3²¼	[2:05¹]	3.90	(G.HarJr) GrandmaWall RedsMrAyres PanLadyJ	
1- 4 PPK⅝ ft 67° 13800clmhcp	:30³ 1:01² 1:33¹ 2:05²	4	4 7 7	7¹¾		[2:05]	*2.50	(G.HarJr) GrandmaWall Tell!tAll AmbroMiami	
1- 5 PPK⅝ ft 71° 10500clmhcp	:30³ 1:01² 1:32³ 2:05³	2	x9	9¹¹	9²³¼	[2:09³]	2.40	(G.HarJr) ArmbroMiami DerbySong Macedonia	
12-30 PPK⅝ ft 65° 10500clmhcp	:30 1:03 1:34³ 2:06²	1	2 x6	7	3½	[2:05¹]	3.90	(G.HarJr) MissCamasB Snackadoo DerbySong	
12-22 PPK⅝ ft 55° 10500clmhcp	:31 1:04³ 1:34³ 2:06⁴	7	4 6 5 5⁵¾		5⁵¾	[2:06³]	8.80	(G.HarJr) MissCamasB LuckyMrG Snackadoo	
12-22 PPK⅝ ft 55° 10500clmhcp		1	2 2o 2o 1½		2²⁵½	[2:06⁴]	9.60	(G.HarJr) MissCamasB LuckyMrG DerbySong	

6 PINK $9600

GOLDA HERBERT
B. m 1973, by Replica Herbert—Goldilock Herbert—Hickory Smoke.
Owner: Van Stables, Ontawa, Ont., Can.   Breeder: Ruth E. Herbert
Lifetime—$98,590—3, 2:07 (⅝)
Driver—DOUG HIE, Blue-Gold   Tr.—D. Hie

1-25 PPK⅝ ft 76° 9600clmhcp	:29¹ 1:01 1:32² 2:03	3	4	4	4³½	[2:04]	10.30	1978 3 0 0 0 $ 286	
1-20 PPK⅝ ft 66° 12600clmhcp	:31¹ 1:03¹ 1:34¹ 2:05²	2	6	5	5⁷¼	[2:06⁴]	21.00	1977 22 4 0 5 3006	(2:07¹ PPK⅝)
1-12 PPK⅝ ft 67° 13800clmhcp	:30³ 1:01² 1:33¹ 2:05²	6	3	3o 2¼	4³¼	[2:05¹]	18.50	(D.Hie) GranbyHope Riddle MissSpinningSong	
1- 4 PPK⅝ ft 60° qua	:32¹ 1:04² 2:07³	7	7o 7 7 7¾			[2:08⁴]	NB	(D.Hie) GrandmaWall Tell!tAll AmbroMiami	
12-30 PPK⅝ ft 65° 14950clmhcp	:30 1:03¹ 1:34³ 2:06²	5	1 2 6¾		5⁶¾	[2:08⁴]	8.60	(D.Hie) TNTFreight MyGalGussie SpecialJoe	
12-22 PPK⅝ ft 55° 14950clmhcp	:31 1:04³ 1:34³ 2:06⁴	1	2 2o 2¹½½		8¹⁹¼	[2:10¹]	3.30	(D.Hie) MissCamasB LuckyMrG DerbySong	

9 ORANGE $8000

JADES DREAM
Br. g 1970, by A Go Viking—Larmon—Hickory Smoke.   Breeder: H. & I. T. Horowitz
Owner: Ruth N. Westmoreland & Nancy Golden, Pompano Beach & Boca Raton, Fla.
Lifetime—$40,352—6, 2:04 (⅝)
Driver—ALLEN SAUL, Gold-Black-White   Tr.—A. Saul

1-25 PPK⅝ ft 76° 8000clmhcp	:29¹ 1:01 1:32² 2:03	8	2o 3 3o 3³¼	5²¼	[2:04]	2.20	1978 4 0 0 2 $ 977	(♥ 2:06³ PPK⅝ gd)
1-19 PPK⅝ gd 72° 7000clmhcp	:29² 1:03⁴ 1:34¹ 2:07¹	6	3 3	3o 2¾	1¾	[2:07¹]	3.80	(A.Sau) GranbyHope Riddle MissSpinningSong	
1-14 PPK⅝ gd 70° qua	:32¹ 1:04³ 1:35¹ 2:06³	1	2	2	1²¹⁵	[2:06³]	NB	(A.Sau) JadesDream Plunker Riddle	
1-11 PPK⅝ ft 65° 7000clmhcp	:31² 1:01² 1:32³ 2:07²	2	4 9 9 9⁹⁶		[2:08⁴]	NB	(A.Sau) JadesDream DecaturBoy TheMarkenMan	
1- 4 PPK⅝ ft 68° 7000clmhcp	:31¹ 1:03¹ 1:34¹ 2:06³	9	9	9 9⁹⁶	8²⁰½	[2:08]	22.30	(A.Sau) Riddle GranbyHope Grania	
1- 1 PPK⅝ ft 65° 7000clmhcp	:31² 1:01⁴ 1:32⁴ 2:03²	6	6 6 8×8¾	9dis	[2:11²]	31.90	(A.Sau) ArmbroMiami PanLadyJ ReliableGordon	
12-29 PPK⅝ ft 65° cdnw5000	:30	5	5 6×8¾	dnf	[2:09]	40.60	(A.Sau) ICHills Inferno BananaPeel	

Trackman's Selections: 6—1—2—9

SIXTH RACE

WARMUP SADDLE CLOTH—BLACK

ONE MILE

QUINIELA & TRIFECTA RACE

CLAIMING PACE — Purse $1900

Claiming price $4000. With allowances.

	QUINIELA & TRIFECTA	First	Second	Third

Morning Line, PP Hd. No.

1 — RED $4000

KATU STAR Lifetime—$19,836—5, 2:01.4 (¾)
Driver—MIKE HARDING, White-Gold-Black
B g 1972, by Newport Tarzan—Grand Opera Star—Ensign Hanover.
Owner: Jeanne D. Harding, Delray Beach, Fla. Tr—M. Harding. Breeder: F. Mays.

Date Trk	Cond & Temp Class	Dist ¼	½	¾	Winner's Time	PP ¼ ½ ¾ Str Fin	Ind. Time	Odds	Driver	First Second Third
1-24 PP⅝	ft 72° c 2500clm	:30	1:01⁴	1:33⁴	2:05²	8 1o I 1¼ 2¼	(2:05³)	*2.40	(G.Bru)	ColinsLady KatuStar RodoMelody
1-17 PP⅝	ft 72° 2500clm	:30	1:02	1:34²	2:07³	9 4 4 4¾ 4¼	(2:08¹)	1.40	(G.Bru)	RodoMelody TexasSpur BudByrd
12-29 PP⅝	ft 65° 3500clm	:30	1:02	1:33²	2:05	6 3 3 4½ 1	(2:05)	*1.60	(G.Bru)	KatuStar LittleEtta ScarletAir
12-17 PP⅝	gd 72° 3000clm	:29	1:01	1:32	2:04	5 2 2 2 1²	(2:04)	*1.40	(G.Bru)	KatuStar Trudy LuddenhamBay
10-27 VD¾	ft 55° 2500clm	:29	1:01	1:32	2:04²	4 2 2 2o 1½	(2:04³)	1.30	(G.Bru)	KatuStar EgyptianRa Kniffen
10-20 VD¾	gd 50° 2500clm	:30	1:02³	1:34¹	2:07¹	8 2 1 1 1½	(2:07⁴)	*1.30	(G.Bru)	KatuStar Keyrupa HereComesGenie

1978 2 0 1 0 $ 384
1977 39 14 7 6 $12037 (2:01⁴ VD¾)

2 — WHITE $4000

WILDWOOD EARL Lifetime—$39,370—3, 2:02.4 (⅝)
Driver—W. "BILL" LAMBERTUS, Gold-White-Black
B g 1972, by Noble Napoleon—Keystone Greta—Bye Bye Byrd.
Owner: H. P. & John C. Skoglund, Minneapolis, Minn. Tr—W. Lambertus. Breeder: Estate of D. L. Brown.

Date Trk	Cond & Temp Class	Dist ¼	½	¾	Winner's Time	PP ¼ ½ ¾ Str Fin	Ind. Time	Odds	Driver	First Second Third
1-30 PP⅝	ft 55° 5000clm	:29²	1:02¹	1:31⁴	2:03¹	7 4 4 3o 3¹¹ 3¹²½	(2:05³)	3.50	(W.Lam)	Kerry RJYankee WildwoodEarl
1-23 PP⅝	ft 55° 5000clm	:31¹	1:02	1:34	2:05¹	4 4 4 5¼ 5¹	(2:05²)	9.20	(W.Lam)	TJMac RythmnsSon Sheepshead
1-16 PP⅝	ft 65° 5000clm	:31¹	1:03	1:34²	2:04⁴	3 5 5 5⁷¼ 3⁸¼	(2:06)	7.10	(R.Gay)	MynaMitzvah Aragon WildwoodEarl
1-9 PP⅝	ft 49° 5000clm	:30³	1:01	1:32²	2:04²	4 5 5 5⁷¼ 6⁸	(2:05²)	3.90	(W.Lam)	UnclesGirl TJMac Ancindy
12-31 PP⅝	ft 80° 6500clm	:30³	1:02²	1:33²	2:04⁴	3 4 4 7 7²¾ 8⁸¼	(2:06²)	8.30	(R.Gay)	Customary DustyLehigh NotoriousTip
12-27 PP⅝	ft 49° 6000clm	:30	1:02³	1:34	2:06	4 6 6 4 4⁹¾ 4²¼	(2:06²)	7.80	(G.Bru)	CreditableVon ByrdBobby Customary

1978 4 0 1 2 $ 515
1977 37 2 2 7 $ 8387 (2:03 Mea⅝)

3 — BLUE $4000

THREAT Lifetime—$60,228—11, 2:04.2 (⅝)
Driver—BRUCE KENNEDY, Maroon-Grey
Ch g 1965, by Reason Why—Lairds Lass—Scotts Way.
Owner: Pat McDonald, Cardinal, Ont., Can. Tr—B. Kennedy. Breeder: S. S. Day.

Date Trk	Cond & Temp Class	Dist ¼	½	¾	Winner's Time	PP ¼ ½ ¾ Str Fin	Ind. Time	Odds	Driver	First Second Third
2-1 PP⅝	ft 66° 4000clm	:30²	1:01	1:32¹	2:04²	4 4o 2o 2 2½ 2½	(2:04²)	2.30	(B.Ken)	Ancindy Threat RockvilleChris
1-27 PP⅝	ft 55° 4000clm	:30¹	1:01	1:33	2:04⁴	5 5 4 5⁴⁴½ 4⁵¼	(2:05¹)	4.50	(B.Ken)	EstherHerbert RockvilleChris MeadowBet
1-20 PP⅝	ft 66° 4000clm	:30²	1:02	1:32²	2:05²	7 7 7o 5³¾ 2ⁿᵈ	(2:05²)	*1.30	(B.Ken)	RaiderCity Threat ShiawayTar
1-10 PP⅝	ft 55° 4000clm	:30⁴	1:03¹	1:34³	2:05²	5 5 5 4⁴¾ 4⁴¾	(2:06³)	4.00	(B.Ken)	FiftyGs DWP ScottFashion
1-3 PP⅝	ft 59° 4000clm	:30¹	1:02²	1:34	2:05²	4 3 2 2½ 1ⁿˢ	(2:05²)	3.00	(B.Ken)	Threat HopefulOne FiftyGs
12-27 PP⅝	ft 49° 4500clm	:30	1:03	1:34	2:07	3 4 4 3o 3⅛¾ 2¹½	(2:07¹)	4.60	(R.Gay)	MoneyMakerMadman Threat LushLife

1978 5 1 2 0 $ 1723 (2:05² PP⅝)
1977 34 7 6 6 $ 9708 (2:05¹ RidC⅝)

4 — GREEN $4800

LITTLE ETTA Lifetime—$11,340—3, 2:05.1 (⅝)
Driver—ROBERT BARELLA, Blue-Gold-Black
Br m 1973, by Lenny Byrd—Ettagraph—Phonograph.
Owner: Mr. & Mrs. Lester T. Vance, Pompano Beach, Fla. Tr—L. Vance. Breeder: C. J. Hussey.

Date Trk	Cond & Temp Class	Dist ¼	½	¾	Winner's Time	PP ¼ ½ ¾ Str Fin	Ind. Time	Odds	Driver	First Second Third
1-30 PP⅝	ft 55° 4200clm	:30⁴	1:02¹	1:33¹	2:05³	4 8 8 7⁵¼ 4¹¾	(2:06)	5.10	(R.Bar)	PartysChoice KtneyBrown BonniesStdyBoy
1-23 PP⅝	ft 72° 4200clm	:29⁴	1:00¹	1:32²	2:03³	9 4 4 4⁴ 4⁴	(2:04²)	26.60	(R.Bar)	StrlingsCpe DugoClverWon Accountable
1-16 PP⅝	ft 65° 4200clm	:30¹	1:02	1:33	2:04⁴	6 7 7 7o⁵³¾ 6⁴¼	(2:05³)	8.20	(R.Bar)	TomMagoo SterlingsCpe DoctorsReef
1-9 PP⅝	ft 49° 4200clm	:30³	1:01³	1:33	2:04¹	7 5 5 5³¼ 3⁹½	(2:05)	6.00	(R.Bar)	TennesseeSinger KootneyBrown LittleEtta
1-5 PP⅝	ft 71° 4200clm	:30⁴	1:01	1:33	2:05	9 5o 5o 7o 6²½ 3²	(2:05³)	17.40	(R.Bar)	KootneyBrown Accountable LittleEtta
12-29 PP⅝	ft 65° 4550clm	:30	1:01	1:33¹	2:05	3 4 4 5o 6²¾ 2¹	(2:05)	9.50	(R.Bar)	KatuStar LittleEtta ScarletAir

1978 38 1 0 2 $ 5875 (2:06 VD¾)
1977 5 1 8 9 $ 512

YELLOW $4000 — **5** – 4

MEIGS MARAUDER

B g 1972, by Ohio Time—Worthy First—Ohio Worthy. Breeder: B. McKinney
Owner: Rob Howell, Mark Steele, Wm. F. Hartman & Brett Merkle, Lancaster, Thornville & Newark, Ohio

Lifetime—$3,379—5, Q 2:06.4 (5/8)

Driver—AL JASPERSON, Green-Black-White — Tr.—M. Ferguson

1978 4 2 0 0 $ 1351 (2:05 PPk5/8)
1977 13 3 1 3 $ 817 (Q 2:06^{4} ScD5/8)

1-31 PPk5/8 ft 65° 4500clm	:30^{3} 1:02^{2} 1:33^{1} 2:05^{2}	8 5 5 5 6^{4}	4¾	(2:05^{3})	19.00	(A.Jas)	TeeniTime TennesseeSinger FleetwdKnox
1-25 PPk5/8 ft 76° 2500clm	:29^{4} 1:03^{3} 1:34^{2} 2:05^{1}	9 4o 5 4o 3¾	1^{2}¾	(2:05^{1})	*2.40	(A.Jas)	MeigsMarauder PioneerSpirit Chrissie
1-18 PPk5/8 ft 70° 2500clm	:30 1:02^{1} 1:33^{3} 2:05	7 2 2 2 2½	1^{1}¼	(2:05)	4.90	(A.Jas)	MeigsMrauder QuickNCrfty YankeeHobo
1-11 PPk5/8 ft 65° 3000clm	:29^{4} 1:02 1:34^{2} 2:07^{2}	2 3 4 6o 6^{4}¼	5^{4}¾	(2:08^{2})	3.50	(A.Jas)	DugoClvrWon CnstgaDaniel OcalaStrRae
12-31 PPk5/8 ft 80° 3000clm	:30^{1} 1:01^{1} 1:32^{2} 2:04^{3}	1 4 4 4 3^{1}½	4^{3}	(2:05^{1})	3.40	(A.Jas)	MaysTarBaby FlashinKash BlossomBelle
12-15 PPk5/8 ft 78° 3500clm	:30^{4} 1:04 1:36^{4} 2:07^{3}	6 5 6 9o 8^{12}¼	8^{13}	(2:10^{1})	10.40	(A.Jas)	IkesImpression SummerYankee SalC

BLACK $4000 — **6** + 10

TIME WAY

Br g 1972, by Waygale—Gale Time—Good Time. Breeder: K. M. Eastin
Owner: Philip Ragozzino, Maitland, Fla.

Lifetime—$27,680—4, 2:05 (5/8)

Driver—TED TAYLOR, Green-Gold-Grey — Tr.—E. Kish

1978 4 1 0 0 $ 660 (2:06^{3} PPk5/8)
1977 25 0 4 3 $ 6573

1-25 PPk5/8 ft 76° c3000clm	:29^{2} 1:01^{2} 1:32^{3} 2:04^{2}	1 4 4 5 7^{7}	6^{8}¾	(2:06^{1})	7.20	(A.Jas)	DougsDandy FlashinKash BlueFibre
1-16 PPk5/8 ft 65° 3500clm	:30^{1} 1:02 1:33^{3} 2:04^{4}	3 4 4 4 7^{4}¼	7^{4}½	(2:05^{3})	7.70	(A.Jas)	TomMagoo SterlingsCape DoctorsReef
1- 9 PPk5/8 ft 49° 3500clm	:31^{4} 1:03^{2} 1:34^{2} 2:06^{3}	4 3o 1 2 1^{1}½	1^{1}	(2:06^{3})	10.70	(A.Jas)	TimeWay BoGator ShiawayFrosty
1- 2 PPk5/8 ft 65° 3500clm	:30^{4} 1:02^{1} 1:33^{4} 2:05^{3}	7 8 8 8 8^{5}¼	5^{8}	(2:07^{1})	16.40	(A.Jas)	TnnesseeSnger ArmbroRscal ShiawayFrsty
12-27 PPk5/8 ft 49° 4500clm	:30^{2} 1:03 1:34 2:07	5 7 8 6o 6^{4}½	5^{3}½	(2:07^{3})	9.40	(A.Jas)	MoneyMakerMadman Threat LushLife
12-22 PPk5/8 ft 55° 5000clm	:31 1:04 1:34^{4} 2:07	3 6 6 6 6^{5}	5^{7}½	(2:08^{2})	14.80	(A.Jas)	TJMac TeeniTime SpecialByrd

GREY $4800 — **7** = 6

ESTHER HERBERT

Ro m 1968, by Cruiser Herbert—Shamrock Esther—Watson E Direct. Breeder: W. H. Herbert Stables Ltd.
Owner: Real Fortin ,St. Paul Ile Aux Noix, Que., Can.

Lifetime—$34,929—6, 2:05.3

Driver—ALFRED LaLONDE, Red-White — Tr.—A. LaLonde

1978 4 1 0 0 $ 975 (2:04^{4} PPk5/8)
1977 37 2 7 7 $ 7678 (2:06^{3} Stga gd)

1-27 PPk5/8 ft 56° 4800clm	:30^{2} 1:01^{3} 1:32^{3} 2:04^{4}	6 6 7 8o 4^{5}¾	1^{1}	(2:04^{4})	12.20	(A.LaL)	EstherHerbert RockvilleChris MeadowBet
1-20 PPk5/8 ft 66° 4800clm	:30^{2} 1:01^{2} 1:32^{2} 2:05^{2}	5 6 6 7o 5^{4}	5^{4}	(2:06^{1})	7.50	(A.LaL)	RaiderCity Threat ShiawayTar
1-10 PPk5/8 ft 55° 5400clm	:30^{4} 1:03^{4} 1:34^{3} 2:05^{2}	9 9 9 9 7^{7}¼	6^{10}	(2:07^{2})	26.00	(A.LaL)	FiftyGs DWP ScottFashion
1- 4 PPk5/8 ft 68° 4800clm	:32 1:03 1:33^{4} 2:05^{4}	7 7 7 6 5^{7}	4^{1}½	(2:06)	19.00	(A.LaL)	Ancindy OpalPark Whizzit
12-28 PPk5/8 ft 55° 6000clm	:29^{4} 1:01^{2} 1:33^{2} 2:05	4 6 6 6o 5^{3}¼	6^{7}¾	(2:06^{3})	32.60	(A.LaL)	BarbaraBButler FleetwoodKnox LadyBillie
12-22 PPk5/8 ft 55° 6000clm	:31 1:04 1:34^{4} 2:07	8 8 8 8 7^{6}	7^{9}¾	(2:09)	24.00	(A.LaL)	TJMac TeeniTime SpecialByrd

PINK $4000 — **8** – 8

PLEASANT RHYTHM

B h 1971, by Rhythm Mite— Quick Sue—Quick Pick. Breeder: M. A. Miller
Owner: Eugene Waszak (lessee), Clarendon Hills, Ill.

Lifetime—$23,841—5, 2:03.4 (5/8)

Driver—EUGENE WASZAK, Blue-Gold-White — Tr.—E. Waszak

1978 5 0 0 0 $ 357
1977 33 2 2 3 $ 8456 (2:06^{2} May)

1-31 PPk5/8 ft 65° 4500clm	:30^{3} 1:02^{2} 1:33^{1} 2:05^{2}	4 7 8o 7 7^{4}½	6^{3}	(2:06)	18.70	(E.Was)	TeeniTime TennesseeSinger FleetwdKnox
1-24 PPk5/8 ft 72° 4500clm	:30^{2} 1:02^{1} 1:33^{2} 2:04^{1}	4 7 7 8 6^{3}½	4^{3}¼	(2:04^{4})	12.90	(E.Was)	HopefulOne CoachApril LynnwoodsMajor
1-19 PPk5/8 gd 72° 5000clm	:29 1:01^{2} 1:32^{3} 2:04^{2}	7 6o 7 8o 9^{5}¾	5^{10}¼	(2:06^{2})	23.30	(E.Was)	HighChance SantasGirl HappyCreed
1-13 PPk5/8 gd 65° 6000clmhcp	:29^{4} 1:02 1:33 2:05^{2}	2 5 4 5 5^{5}	8^{9}½	(2:07^{1})	5.90	(E.Was)	SteadyHostess AdahsDream HaloJackson
1- 6 PPk5/8 ft 70° 6000clmhcp	:30 1:02^{2} 1:32^{4} 2:04^{3}	5 6 6o 6o 6^{4}	4^{1}¾	(2:05)	32.60	(E.Was)	RompinRisa SteadyHostess HaloJackson
12-15 Arl 1 1/8 ft 6000clm	:31^{3} 1:04^{3} 1:38^{3} 2:10^{3}	5 6 4o 2o 3^{3}	6^{4}	(2:11^{2})	6.20	(E.Was)	RcewayThndor RustyForbes CraigsWorthy

ORANGE $4000 — **9** – 3

FLEETWOOD KNOX

B g 1973, by Knox Hanover—Aggi Dale—Ross Hanover. Breeder: J. A. Konen
Owner: Joseph A. Konen, Croswell, Mich.

Lifetime—$8,219—3, 2:07.3

Driver—TOM WANTZ, White-Brown-Gold — Tr.—M. Goldschmidt, Jr.

1978 5 0 1 2 $ 935
1977 14 2 2 2 $ 3180 (2:09^{2} Nor)

1-31 PPk5/8 ft 65° 4500clm	:30^{3} 1:02^{2} 1:33^{1} 2:05^{2}	1 2 3 3o 2½	3^{ns}	(2:05^{2})	3.30	(T.Wan)	TeeniTime TennesseeSinger FleetwdKnox
1-24 PPk5/8 ft 72° 4500clm	:29^{4} 1:00^{4} 1:32^{1} 2:02^{4}	8 2o 2o 2o 3^{2}½	3^{9}¾	(2:04^{4})	11.40	(T.Wan)	ScottFashion FiftyGs FleetwoodKnox
1-18 PPk5/8 ft 70° 5000clm	:32 1:02^{3} 1:33^{4} 2:05	8 8 8 7 7^{6}	7^{5}¼	(2:06)	10.70	(T.Wan)	MrTrapp SkygoBoy MyBonnieLad
1-11 PPk5/8 ft 65° 5000clm	:30^{2} 1:01^{3} 1:32^{2} 2:03^{2}	3 3 3 3 4^{4}¼	4^{7}¼	(2:04^{4})	4.50	(T.Wan)	MrTrapp MynaMitzvah KmmysDreamHigh
1- 4 PPk5/8 ft 68° 6250clm	:29^{4} 1:03 1:33^{4} 2:05^{2}	4 2 2 3 3^{1}¾	2¾	(2:05^{3})	5.10	(T.Wan)	UnclesGirl FleetwoodKnox SantasGirl
12-28 PPk5/8 ft 55° 6250clm	:29^{4} 1:01^{2} 1:33^{2} 2:05	5 3 4 4o 4^{2}	2^{1}¾	(2:05^{2})	6.00	(T.Wan)	BarbaraBButler FleetwoodKnox LadyBillie

Trackman's Selections: 3—9—5—2

Pari-mutuel Race No. "A"

TENTH RACE
WARMUP SADDLE CLOTH—PURPLE
ONE MILE

QUINIELA & TRIFECTA RACE

CLAIMING PACE

Purse $1250

Claiming price $2500. With allowances.

Morning Line, PP Hd. No.	Date Trk	Cond. & Temp	Class	Dist 1/4	Leader's Time 1/2 3/4	Winner's Time	PP 1/4 1/2 3/4 Str	Fin	Ind. Time	Odds	Driver	First	Second	Third

RED $2500 / 1 — WHITE / 10

‡SURPRISE DANDY — Purple-White-Green
Driver—GARY LEWIS, Purple-White-Green
Lifetime—$18,640—6, 2:05 (⅝)

B g 1969, by Harrys Delight—Cascade—The Abbot.
Owner: Warren Woodcock, Boca Raton, Fla. Breeder: Mrs. W. E. Montgomery

						Tr.—Marthalou Cavalliere St.—G. Lewis								
1-28 PP⅝‡	:32	††60° qua	:32	1:03²	1:35¹	2:07³	3	5o 6o 4½	5³½	(2:08¹)	NB	(G.Lew)		
1-24 PP⅝‡	:31¹	††71¹¹ qua	:31¹	1:01⁴	1:34	2:06	3	4 6	6¹³½	(2:10)	NB	(G.Lew)		
1-17 PP⅝‡	:30¹	††72° 2500clm	:30¹	1:03¹	1:35²	2:07³	7	5o 5 7o	5²⁰½	(2:10)	10.20	(W.Woo)		
1-7 PP⅝‡	:31	††78° qua	:31	1:03¹	1:34³	2:06	5	2o 3	4³	3³½	(2:06³)	NB	(G.Lew)	
12-31 PP⅝‡	:30³	††qua	:30³	1:01	1:33¹	2:06¹	6	6 6	7¹¹½	7¹⁵½	(2:09¹)	NB	(G.Lew)	
9-9 VD¾	:29	††71¹¹ qua H-D	:29	1:02¹	1:35	2:07	1	2 3	4	3⁴	(2:07⁴)	NB	(I.Jew)	

BLUE $2500 / 2 — 5-2

DONS ANN RAIDER — White-Orange-Green
Driver—BERNARD GERVAIS, White-Orange-Green
Lifetime—$7,790—5, 2:04.3 (⅝)

B m 1972, by Florimec—Sue Adde—Easy Adios.
Owner: Robert R. Miller, Jr. (lessee), Pompano Beach, Fla. Breeder: D. G. Finlayson

						Tr.—R. Miller, Jr.								
1-28 PP⅝	:29¹	††55° 3000clm	:29¹	1:02²	1:34	2:06¹	4	1¹½	1¹	(2:06¹)	NB	(G.LaB)		
1-21 PP⅝	:29¹	††59° 3600clm	:29¹	1:01³	1:33	2:043	5	6°¾	6⁵¾	(2:06)	*2.70	(B.Ger)		
1-14 PP⅝	:29¹	††59° 3600clm	:29¹	1:02	1:33²	2:05²	5	2½	4²¾	(2:05⁴)	3.50	(B.Ger)		
1-7 PP⅝	:29¹	††72° 3600clm	:29¹	1:01³	1:33	2:04¹	3	3¾	3¾	(2:04²)	*1.10	(B.Ger)		
12-31 PP⅝	:30¹	††80° 3600clm	:30¹	1:01³	1:33¹	2:06	9	1²	1²	(2:06)	9.20	(B.Ger)		
12-27 PP⅝	:30³	††60° qua	:30³	1:02	1:33⁴	2:05¹	1	2⁷	4⁶¾	(2:05²)	NB	(B.Ger)		

3 / 8

G B GEE — Red-Green-Yellow
Driver—GUY LaBELLE, Red-Green-Yellow
Lifetime—$5,538—4, 2:07.3

B h 1973, by Success Saint—Freight Maid—Torpid.
Owner: Guy LaBelle, Montreal, Que., Can. Breeder: Greco Brothers Stable Inc.

						Tr.—G. LaBelle								
1-23 PP⅝	:29¹	††72° 2500clm	:29¹	1:01¹	1:33	2:05¹	6¹	8 7 7¹⁰	6¹²¾	(2:07⁴)	NB	(G.LaB)		
1-14 PP⅝	:29¹	††59° 3000clm	:29¹	1:03¹	1:35³	2:07¹	1	3 4	8⁴	8⁵³¾	(2:09)	*2.70	(G.LaB)	
12-31 PP⅝	:29¹	††80° 3125clm	:29¹	1:02	1:33³	2:05⁴	5	5o 5 5³½	2½¾	(2:06¹)	8.70	(G.LaB)		
12-26 PP⅝	:30³	††58° 3125clm	:30³	1:03	1:34³	2:07¹	5	5o 5 6⁷¾	4⁸½	(2:08⁴)	6.60	(G.LaB)		
12-8 PP⅝	:30²	††70° 3125clm	:30²	1:02¹	1:35	2:08¹	7	7 6	1ʰᵈ	(2:08¹)	4.30	(G.LaB)		
11-2 Stga s‖ 2500clm	:31²	1:04²	1:35⁴	2:09¹	1	2⁷	6⁶¾	(2:10¹)	4.80	(G.Ber)		

GREEN $3000 / 4 — 3

SOURDOUGH — Red-White
Driver—DON BRAINARD, Red-White
Lifetime—$32,715—10, 2:05.1 (¾)

Blk m 1967, by Isolator—Watchims Ollie—Watchim.
Owner: Donald E. Brainard, DeLeon Springs, Fla. Breeder: H. Haman Jr.

						Tr.—D. Brainard								
1-28 PP⅝	:29¹	††55° 3000clm	:29¹	1:02²	1:34	2:06¹	9	7o 7o 4⁴	4²½	(2:06³)	NB	(D.Bra)		
1-24 PP⅝	:30	††72° 3000clm	:30	1:02	1:33¹	2:043	9	8 7o 6o	2²½	(2:05)	4.50	(D.Bra)		
1-17 PP⅝	:30¹	††72° 3000clm	:30¹	1:03³	1:34¹	2:07	3	4 5 4⁵¼	3⁵	(2:08)	6.30	(D.Bra)		
1-10 PP⅝	:31²	††55° 2500clm	:31²	1:04	1:35¹	2:07²	4	5o 5 5o	4⁸½	(2:07⁴)	4.30	(D.Bra)		
1-3 PP⅝	:31²	††70° 2500clm	:31²	1:04¹	1:35²	2:07²	3	5 5 3¹¾	2¹¾	(2:07)	5.50	(D.Bra)		
12-28 PP⅝	:31¹	††55° 3000clm	:31¹	1:04¹	1:36	2:07⁴	3	5o 5 6⁹¼	6⁹¼	(2:09³)	4.20	(D.Bra)		

			QUINIELA & TRIFECTA		First	Second	Third
	1978	1	0 0 0 $	00			
	1977	1	0 0 5 $ 50				
	1978	2	0 0 0 $ 00				
	1977	4	1 0 $ 824	(2:06¹ PP⅝)			
	1978	4	3 0 $ 3501	(2:04³ PP⅝)			
	1977	18	4 3 1 $				
	1978	2	0 0 0 $ 00				
	1977	27	2 6 4 $ 3920	(2:07³ Stga)			
	1978	35	0 2 2 $ 904				
	1977	44	3 3 $ 6424	(2:05¹ VD¾)			

Breeder: Mrs. W. E. Montgomery
1977 — SimonesSkipper RosiesBaby Safapadi / Racso MyCompare WilliamF / HiVesta Edstime KeeneExpress / DrAlanHeritage Reindeer SurpriseDandy / CrestwoodBirdie ByrdK Tovim / StarConory StarletJ SurpriseDandy

Breeder: D. G. Finlayson
DnsAnnRaider LuddenhamBay MsuredFlo / AmexbroGinny FlanaryHan DoctorsReef / MiniPower VeraBest BlossomBelle / AlwaysNeato Esplanade DonsAnnRaider / DonsAnnRaider DougsDandy AlwysNeato / ScottKeyStar Aboline DougsDandy

Breeder: Greco Brothers Stable Inc.
PaperMoney Roywyn CrainMan / RntreesCharity ScrletTartan MissRoyalVic / Esplanade GBGee Boyduplicate / Edstime SiloWendi JerseySilk / GBGee Esplanade VanwayAndy / LeeOregon LittleDillie ScottiesExpress

Breeder: H. Haman Jr.
DnsAnnRaider LuddenhamBay MsuredFlo / Tuckabuck Sourdough AprilTryax / ByeByeChris FlanaryHan Sourdough / TomMagoo Sourdough CashBox / Esplanade ChoiceLeehy Sourdough / ArmbroRascal ToRiEdie BayStarBoy

5 YELLOW $2500 =

TARLO
B g 1971, by Adios Cleo—Upland Liz—Tar Heel.   Breeder: C. E. Voorhies
Owner: George Slavin & Scott Holman, Denver, Colorado

Driver—JOE SEIDERS, Green-Gold-White
Lifetime—$22,628—5, 2:03.3 (⅝)

Tr.—J. Seiders

1-28 PP⅝ ft 55⁰ 2500c.lm	:29⁴	1:02²	1:34	2:06¹	3	2	2	3³½	5²¾	[2:06¹]	NB	1978	4	1	0	0	$ 60	(J.Sei) DnsAnnRaider LuddenhamBay MsuredFlo
1-23 PP⅝ ft 72⁰ 2500c.lm	:29⁴	1:01¹	1:33²	2:05¹	9	9	9o	8¹0½	7¹5	[2:08¹]	23.90	1977	14	1	3	2	$1,987	(J.Sei) PaperMoney Roywyn CrainMan
1-17 PP⅝ ft 76⁰ qua	:30			2:06	1	2	2	4¹0¾	3⁹½	[2:08]	NB						(J.Sei) QuakerHallmark ByeByeDawn Tarlo
12-23 PP⅝ ft 68⁰ qua	:31	1:03	1:34¹	2:06²	8	7o6	8	8dis	8dis		NB						(J.Sei) VMarJ BudByrd StraightOak
6-15 Sem3⅛ ft 1500c.lmhcp	:31	1:03	1:37	2:08²	8		8	7²½	7²¹½	[2:12⁺]	*1.0						(J.Sei) SpudKSun DaytonasTerri SmallPins
6-3 Sem⅝ ft 3000c.lmhcp	:30¹	1:02½		2:06	4	1	2	2	3²½	[2:06²]	1.80						(J.Sei) DoctorsReef PartlysJunny Tarlo

6 BLACK $2500 =

OCMULGEE KID
B g 1971, by Melody Kid—Gentles Byrd—Poplar Byrd.   Breeder: S. Pettey Jr.
Owner: Norm Cohen, W. Bloomfield, Mich.

Driver—NORM COHEN, Black-White
Lifetime—$16,270—6, 2:03.2 (1)

Tr.—N. Cohen

1-26 PP⅝ ft 62⁰ 3500c.lm	:29³	1:02²	1:31³	2:03⁴	3	3	2	4³¼	5²¾	[2:05³]	6.70	1978	4	1	0	0	$ 757	(N.Coh) WilLorDoc ColonelRock DrexelDaryl
1-18 PP⅝ ft 70⁰ 3000c.lm	:30⁴	1:02⁴	1:34	2:05¹	5	5	5¹⁴½	5⁴	4⁹½	[2:06]	10.80	1977	25	4	3	3	$7,705	(N.Coh) DugoCleverWon BillyMahone SassyDevil
1-18 PP⅝ ft 67⁰ 2500c.lm	:31	1:04²	1:34¹	2:06¹	6	6	6o	3o1	1¾	*1.60							(N.Coh) OcmulgeeKid JustLeah LulleBelle
1-7 PP⅝ ft 78⁰ qua	:30³	1:03	1:34⁴	2:06¹	3	3	3	3²¼	2¹	[2:06²]	NB						(N.Coh) Surety OcmulgeeKid LulleBelle
12-9 PP⅝ sy 68⁰ 2500c.lm	:30⁴	1:03²	1:34	2:06²	8	9	8°8	8⁸¾	5⁸¾	[2:08¹]	19.60						(N.Coh) SandMonarch SterlingsCape JeansBabe
12-27 PP⅝ ft 49⁰ 4500c.lm	:30²	1:03		2:06	7	1	6	7o8.8⁸¾	7¹0	[2:08¹]	7.80						(N.Coh) MoneyMaker Madman Threat LushLife

7 GREY $2500   **9-2**

LE THON
Ch g 1970, by Adios Prince—Old Gold—Alpha Hal.   Breeder: P. Cyrenne
Owner: William J. Dufresne, Amsterdam, N.Y.

Driver—GARY GIBSON, Black-Gold-Green
Lifetime—$13,695—7, 2:06.1

Tr.—Y. Breton

1-28 PP⅝ ft 55⁰ 3000c.lm	:29³	1:02¹	1:33	2:05⁴	9	9	7o 9⁰7	6⁵¼	6⁹½	[2:07³]	NB	1978	4	0	0	2	$ 258	(G.Gib) BismBelle ChoiceLeeHy JollyGeneGiant
1-21 PP⅝ ft 59⁰ 2500c.lm	:30³	1:01³	1:31¹	2:04¹	8	5	5 5²²	3²	3²	[2:04⁴]	9.10	1977	32	3	3	5	$7,071	(G.Gib) TroutLine YankeeBeeBee LeThon
1-14 PP⅝ ft 59⁰ 2500c.lm	:31	1:02	1:34²	2:06¹	6	6	6o 3o2ⁿᵏ	2⁰	[2:06³]	*1.60							(G.Gib) MeasuredFlo YankeeBeeBee LeThon
1-7 PP⅝ ft 70⁰ 2500c.lm	:30³	1:02	1:33	2:06³	8	7	8 8⁸¼	6⁴	[2:07²]	4.40							(G.Gib) OBrien HenryAllanN HartKway
12-9 PP⅝ sy 68⁰ 2500c.lm	:30⁴	1:03²	1:36	2:09⁴	4	7o 4o3	3 x5³¾x	[2:11]	*1.40							(T.Tay) GoodyShoes MistyYates PopularDiamond
12-28 PP⅝ ft 55⁰ 2500c.lm	:37³	1:16¹	1:54³	2:32³	4	x4 x8x 8 pulled up	dnf	2.00							(J.Mor) CalebsFirst ScottiesExprs OneShotDirect

8 PINK $2500   **11-6** =

BAY STAR BOY
B g 1968, by Painter—Alema Jay—Alemite.   Breeder: E. E. Eads
Owner: Paul Hebert, Pompano Beach, Fla.

Driver—BRUCE KENNEDY, Maroon-Grey
Lifetime—$76,079—2, 1:59.3 (1)

Tr.—P. Herbert

1-28 PP⅝ ft 55⁰ 3000c.lm	:30¹	1:02²	1:33	2:05⁴	8	2	2 2³½	3¹½	8⁵¾	[2:07⁴]	NB	1978	5	0	3	1	$3,225	(B.Ken) JimMorrill CapeFineNibsen TyrinaPride
1-21 PP⅝ ft 59⁰ 3000c.lm	:29⁴	1:01²	1:33	2:04³	4	2	2 2¹	5³½	7⁷	[2:06]	4.80	1977	28	3	4	5	$4,418	(B.Ken) AmexbroGinny FlanaryHan DoctorsReef
1-16 PP⅝ ft 65⁰ 3000c.lm	:30²	1:01³	1:33²	2:05³	9	1	4 4⁴	6²⅜	5³½	[2:06¹]	17.70						(B.Ken) MaysTarBaby Brigadoon KootneyBrown
1-11 PP⅝ ft 65⁰ 3000c.lm	:30²	1:04	1:35¹	2:08²	1	4	4 4¹¾	4²	[2:08⁴]	4.20						(B.Ken) TarportBryn ThirtyKnots DoctorsReef
1-4 PP⅝ ft 68⁰ 3000c.lm	:30²	1:04²	1:34³	2:06	7	1	1 1³½	2ⁿᵏ	[2:06]	25.00						(B.Ken) PartlysChoice JimMorrill BayStarBoy
12-28 PP⅝ ft 55⁰ 2500c.lm	:31¹	1:04¹	1:34³	2:07⁴	7	1	2 2²	3²¾	3³½	[2:08²]	*1.00						(A.Sau) ArmbroRascal ToRIEdie BayStarBoy

9 ORANGE $2500 —

HERBARS DREAM
B h 1969, by Buxton Hanover—Royal Sara—Royal Blackstone.   Breeder: Capital Hill Farms
Owner: Sandra J. Pilote, Wakefield, Mass.

Driver—SAM LUSSIER, Green-Red-White
Lifetime—$53,392—4, 2:04.1

Tr.—S. Lussier

1-28 PP⅝ ft 55⁰ 2500c.lm	:30¹	1:02²	1:33	2:05⁴	6	3o3	3 3¹½	7¹6½	7¹6¼	[2:09]	NB	1978	4	0	1	0	$ 367	(S.Lus) BismBelle ChoiceLeeHy JollyGeneGiant
1-21 PP⅝ ft 59⁰ 2500c.lm	:30³	1:01	1:34²	2:07¹	7	1o1	2 5³½	1¹½	5²¾	[2:07⁴]	9.90	1977	30	4	0	4	$4,415	(S.Lus) TroutLine YankeeBeeBee LeThon
1-13 PP⅝ gd 65⁰ 2500c.lm	:31	1:03	1:35	2:07¹	4	3	3 3¹¼	1¹¼	5²¾	[2:08]	22.20						(S.Lus) JimmieCollins HerbarsDream DarlingMiss
1-4 PP⅝ ft 68⁰ 2500c.lm	:32¹	1:02	1:33¹	2:06³	7	7	7o 6²½	6⁸¼	5¹¾	[2:08¹]	39.50						(S.Lus) TomMaqoo OcalaStarRae Tuckabuck
12-9 PP⅝ sy 68⁰ 2500c.lm	:30³	1:04¹	1:37¹	2:11	8	8	8¹¼½	8¹1¼	8¹1¼	[2:13²]	3.60						(R.Eng) DrSpeedabit MyCompare YLMini
11-17 Rock sy 2500c.lm	:31¹	1:03⁴	1:35⁴	2:08²	6	6	6o 6¹0	5¹¼½	5¹¼½	[2:10³]	24.40						(Ra.Tre) LebanonJJ RstyBritten TomorrowsDarling

Result.

```
6th RACE — CLAIMING PACE — I MILE
Quarter Times—:30² 1:03⁴ 1:34² 2:05¹
5 MeigsMarauder      5  2  2  I   I¹¹₂  I²¹₂  (2:05¹)   2.80   (A.Jas)
7 Esther Herbert     7  8  8  7o 4²³₄  2²¹₂  (2:05³)   7.90   (A.LaL)
4 Little Etta        4  6  6  5o 6³¹₂  3⁵    (2:06¹)  19.00   (R.Bar)
2 Wildwood Earl      2  3  3  3  5³¹₄  4⁵¹₂  (2:06¹)   4.20   (W.Lam)
3 Threat             3  5  5  4o 2¹¹₂  5⁶    (2:06²)  *2.00   (B.Ken)
9 Fleetwood Knox     9  I  I  2  3¹³₄  6⁶³₄  (2:06³)   9.70   (T.Wan)
6 Time Way           6  7  7  8  9⁵¹₂  7⁷    (2:06³)  42.10   (T.Tay)
8 Pleasant Rhythm    8  9  9  9o 8⁵    8⁷³₄  (2:06¹)  31.70   (E.Was)
I Katu Star          I  4  4  6  7¹¹₂  9⁻³₄  (2:07 )   6.80   (M.Har)
Mutuels:    (5)—7.60  4.20  3.80    (7)—6.00  6.80    (4)—7.80
TRIFECTA—5-7-4—$402.20                 QUINIELA—5 and 7—$33.60
```

Pompano Park   Tenth Race   February 6, 1978

Although this is a cheaper claimer than the races we have handicapped up to now, it is nonetheless instructive.

Start by eliminating 1 Surprise Dandy, 3 G B Gee, 5 Tarlo, 7 Le Thon, 8 Bay Star Boy, 9 Herbars Dream. None have been contenders in any of their recent starts.

This leaves:

2 Dons Ann Raider

Current form	2
Class	0
Post position	3
Driver	3
Total	8

6 Ocmulgee Kid

Current form	2
Class	2
Post position	1
Driver	1
Total	6

4 Sourdough

Current form	2
Class	0
Post position	2
Driver	3
Total	7

Analysis. This looks like a close decision between Dons Ann Raider and Sourdough, but that is not the case. Both horses are front-runners, but Dons Ann Raider has the rail and can park Sourdough for part or all of the mile, as she did on January 28. For this reason, Dons Ann Raider is the better bet, even though Sourdough would

have more bonus points in a close decision. Ocmulgee Kid has not been in his two last ı

Result.

```
10th RACE — CLAIMING PACE — ı MILE
Quarter Times—:30 1:02¹ 1:34¹ 2:07¹
2 Dons Ann Raider    2  1  1  1  1¹      1²¹⁴   (2:07¹)  *1.70   (B.Ger)
7 Le Thon            7  8  8o 2o 2¹      2²¹⁴   (2:07³)  14.30   (G.Gib)
9 Herbars Dream      9  9  9  7  5⁶¹⁴    3⁶¹²   (2:08²)  39.50   (S.Lus)
6 Ocmulgee Kid       6  7  6o 4  4⁵      4⁶¹²   (2:08²)   2.80   (N.Coh)
5 Tarlo              5  6  7  6o 6˄¹⁴    5⁸¹⁴   (2:08¹)  15.50   (J.Sei)
4 Sourdough          4  3o 2  3  3¹      6˄³⁴   (2:09 )   2.40   (D.Bra)
3 G B Gee            3  5  5  9  7ˢ¹₂     7⁹¹⁴   (2:09 )  28.70   (G.LaB)
8 Bay Star Boy       8  2  3  5  8⁹      8¹⁹³⁄₄ (2:11¹)  12.00   (B.Ken)
ı Surprise Dandy     1  4  4  8ix9ᵈⁱˢ    9ᵈⁱˢ   (2:12¹)  22.00   (G.Lew)
Mutuels:   (2)—5.40 3.60 3.60    (7)—9.40 7.20    ( 9)—9.00
TRIFECTA—2-7-9—$1,277.40                QUINIELA—2 and 7—$53.80
```

Pompano Park   Seventh Race   February 7, 1978

Eliminate 2 Bay B. Echo, 3 Gobelet, 7 D W P, and 8 T C B for poor current form. 4 Rockville Chris has not shown enough in his last three starts to be an attractive bet; ditto for 9 Lynnwoods Major.

The remainder of the field:

1 Mays Tar Baby		6 Partys Choice	
Current form	4	Current form	2
Class	−1	Class	−2
Post position	3	Post position	1
Driver	3	Driver	2
Total	9	Total	3

5 Teeni Time	
Current form	3
Class	0
Post position	2
Driver	2
Total	7

Analysis. From the rail, Mays Tar Baby should have no difficulty staying in front from wire to wire; this horse is unquestionably the choice. Teeni Time can be given no better than an outside shot at taking this one. Partys Choice is clearly outclassed.

SEVENTH RACE

WARMUP SADDLE CLOTH GREY

ONE MILE

QUINIELA & TRIFECTA RACE

CLAIMING PACE

Claiming price $4500. With allowances

Purse $2000

		QUINIELA & TRIFECTA		
		First	Second	Third

Morning Line, PP Hd No.	Date Trk	Cond & Temp Class	Dist ¼	Leader's Time ½ ¾	Winner's Time	PP ¼ ½ ¾ Str	Fin	Ind Time	Odds		Driver

RED $4500

1

5-2 +

MAYS TAR BABY

Lifetime—$1,940—6, 2:04.3 (⅝)

Driver—BERNARD GERVAIS, White-Orange-Green

Br q 1971, by Tar Boy—Mayola—Thomas B Scott. Breeder: H. F. Harp

Owner: Howard W. Lawrence, West Farmington, Ohio

Tr.—R. Miller, Jr.

1-25 PP⅝ ft 76° 4000clm	:29¹	1:01	1:02¹	1:33¹	2:05¹	5	1	—	1¹	1½	(2:05¹)	*2.60	1978	2	2	0	0	$ 1425	(2:05 PP⅝)
1-16 PP⅝ ft 65° 3500clm	:30¹	1:01	1:02¹	1:33	2:05¹	1	1	1¹	1¹	1¹	(2:05¹)	3.90	1977	11	2	3	2	$ 1940	(2:04¹ PP⅝)
12-31 PP⅝ ft 80° 3000clm	:30¹	1:01	1:02¹	1:33	2:04¹	7	6	7 7o	1¹	1¹	(2:04¹)	7.90	(B.Ger) MaysTarBaby QuickNCrafty Goldock						
12-26 PP⅝ ft 58° 3500clm	:30	1:01	1:02	1:32	2:04¹	9	9x°	9	1²½	1¹½	(2:05)	5.70	(B.Ger) MaysTarBaby Esplanade Kootney Brown						
12-10 PP⅝ ft 70° 3000clm	:32	1:04¹	1:36	2:09¹	9	1o¹	1¹	8¹½	8¹½	(2:13¹)	30.00	(B.Ger) MaysTarBaby FlashinKash BlossomBelle						
10-27 Nfld ft 54° 3000clm	:30	1:02¹	1:34¹	2:07	9	7	4o 3o	4o 7²½	7²½	(2:07)	14.50	(M.Tur) DarbyL Janidawn FourOaksTia						

WHITE $4500

2

≡

BAY B. ECHO

Lifetime—$8,009—5, 2:04.4

Driver—R. W. DeSANTIS, Gold-Blue

B h 1972, by Smith Cress—Hopeful Elise—Adios Harry.

Owner: Sandra & David Shein, Schenectady, N.Y.

Tr.—R. W. DeSantis

1-31 PP⅝ ft 65° 4500clm	:30	1:02¹	1:33¹	2:05¹	7	3	6 9	8¹¼	8¹¼	(2:06¹)	74.50	1978	2	0	0	0	$ 4012	
1-21 PP⅝ ft 59° 5000clmhcp	:30²	1:00¹	1:31	2:02	7	8	8 8o²	8o³¼	8o³¼	(2:07¹)	62.20	1977	27	2	2	3	$ 7234	(2:04¹ PP⅝)
1-21 PP⅝ ft 55° 5000clm	:30	1:02	1:33	2:05	7	7o 7o	5o³¼	6¹	6¹	(2:07¹)	62.20	(R.W.DeS) TeeniTime TennesseeSinger FleetwdKnox						
12-10 PP⅝ ft 70° 6500clm	:36	1:01	1:32	2:04¹	8	6	6o 5o	6¹	6¹	(2:07)	21.60	(R.W.DeS) RecordClip TempermentalSinger						
11-16 PP⅝ ft 70° 6500clm	:36	1:14	1:50	2:25	3	9	9 9	9dis	9dis		30.00	(R.W.DeS) Tempermental MrTrapp KammysDrmHigh						
11-3 Siga by 5000clm	:38	1:01	1:32	2:04¹	3	8	7o 2	4	4	(2:27)	5.70	(K.Cra) SnapJudgement SaratogaStan BaysEcho						
11-3 Siga gd cdnw1000L5	:31	1:04¹	1:35	2:06	2	7	8o 4	3¹	3¹	(2:08)	9.40	(R.W.DeS) Namahana SpdyChrisTime SugarYally.Blle						

BLUE $4500

3

–

GOBELET

Lifetime—$46,622—5, 2:01.2 (⅝)

Driver—HOWARD LEVINE, Red-Blue-Gold

B h 1968, by Adios Mir—Fair Yankee—Sampson Hanover.

Owner: Laurent Belhumeur, Sherbrooke, Que., Can.

Tr.—L. Belhumeur

1-26 PP⅝ ft 62° 5000clm	:30¹	1:01	1:32¹	2:04¹	4	7	7 9	9⁰	9⁰	(2:06¹)	36.00	1978	4	0	0	0	$ 165	
1-19 PP⅝ ft 62° 5000clm	:29¹	1:01¹	1:32¹	2:04¹	4	8	6o 9	8⁷½	8⁷½	(2:06¹)	13.80	1977	20	4	2	4	$ 7234	(2:03 BB⅝)
1-13 PP⅝ gd 65° 6000clmhcp	:29	1:01¹	1:32	2:04	8	6	6 8¹½	7¹¹¼	7¹¹¼	(2:06¹)	23.30	(L.Bel) SkygoBoy KammysDreamHigh SantasGirl						
1-6 PP⅝ ft 70° 6000clmhcp	:29³	1:01	1:32	2:04	6	5	5¹ 5¹³⁴	5¹	5¹	(2:07)	62.20	(L.Bel) HighChance SantasGirl HappyCreed						
12-30 PP⅝ ft 72° 6500clmhcp	:29	1:01	1:31	2:03¹	9x	9	9 7	9dis	9dis		48.40	(M.Fil) SteadyHostess AdahsDream HaloJackson						
11-5 BB⅝ ft 7000clm	:31	1:03	1:33¹	2:04¹	3	3	3 3	3⁻	3⁻	(2:05)	36.50	(M.Fil) RompinRisa SteadyHostess HaloJackson						
						2	7	8o 2 4	3⁻	3⁻	(2:05)	10.65	(G.Gen) SomethingBetter ArmbroeNavajo Shout						

GREEN $4500

4

+

ROCKVILLE CHRIS

Lifetime—$1,984—4, 2:03.3 (⅝)

Driver—LEONARD ABBRUZZIO, Red-Gold

B h 1971, by Mighty Tide—Lourdeslan—Solicitor.

Owner: Raymond Abbruzzese, Fort Lauderdale, Fla.

Tr.—L. Abbruzzio

2-1 PP⅝ ft 66° 4000clm	:30¹	1:01¹	1:32¹	2:04¹¹	9	9	7o 6o 5³⁴	3¹	3¹	(2:04¹)	11.90	1978	3	0	1	2	$ 772	
1-27 PP⅝ ft 56° 4000clm	:30	1:01¹	1:32¹	2:04¹	2	1	1¹ 2¹	2¹	2¹	(2:05)	8.00	1977	7	0	0	0	$ 284	
1-21 PP⅝ ft 59° 4000clm	:30	1:01	1:33¹	2:05	4	5	5 7¹³⁴	3²³⁴	3²³⁴	(2:06¹)	40.80	(L.Abb) EstherHerbert RockvilleChris MeadowBet						
1-4 PP⅝/8 gd 60° qua	:31¹	1:03¹	1:34¹	2:06¹	6	5	5o 5 5¹	5¹	5¹	(2:08)	NB	(L.Abb) BoGator TeeniTime RockvilleChris						
12-31 PP⅝ ft 75° qua	:31¹	1:03¹	1:34¹	2:07	6	5	5o 3¹½	4¹½	4¹½	(2:08)	NB	(L.Abb) TemplarLobell GalaTag BugsyButch						
9-1 MR ft 72° 5000clm	:30¹	1:02¹	1:33¹	2:04	1x7	7	7 7dis	7dis		(2:05)	5.20	(L.Abb) OzarkChief GeneralMac Neebo						
												(L.Abb) BuckeyeRun FaithFarvel GenesBoy						

Trackman's Selections: 1—4—5—7

---

5 TEENI TIME
YELLOW $4500

Lifetime—$73,838—5, 2:00.2 (1)

Driver—GAETAN BRUNET, Green-Red-White

1-31 PPL⅝	ft 65"	4500clm	:30¹	1:02	1:33¹ 2:05
1-21 PPL⅝	ft 59"	4000clm	:30¹	1:01¹	1:31¹ 2:05
1-14 PPL⅝	ft 59"	5500clmhcp	:30¹	1:00	1:31¹ 2:04¹
1- 7 PPL⅝	ft 72"	5000clmhcp	:29¹	1:02¹	1:32¹ 2:03¹
12-30 PPL⅝	ft 72"	6000clmhcp	:29¹	1:01¹	1:32¹ 2:02¹
12-22 PPL⅝	ft 55"	5000clm	:31	1:04	1:34¹ 2:07

b g 1966, by Race Time—Reens Farr—Tar Heel.
Owner: Joe D'Amato, Fort Lauderdale, Fla.
Tr.—G. Brunet
Breeder: P. B. Dennis

| 1978 | 36 | 4 | 1 | 4 | $ 1,543 | (2:05 PPL⅝) |
| 1977 | 36 | 4 | 5 | 4 | $ 7,617 | (2:02¹ VD¾) |

---

4 PARTYS CHOICE
BLACK $5400

Lifetime—$4,026—4, 2:36

Driver—ALFRED LaLONDE, Red-White

1-30 PPL⅝	ft 55"	4200clm	:30	1:02¹	1:33¹ 2:05
1-20 PPL⅝	ft 66"	4200clm	:30	1:02	1:33¹ 2:05
1-13 PPL⅝	gd 65"	4800clm	:31³	1:05	1:36 2:07
1- 9 PPL⅝	ft 49"	4200clm	:30	1:04¹	1:33 2:04
1- 4 PPL⅝	ft 72"	3900clm	:30³	1:03³	1:34³ 2:03³
12-29 PPL⅝	ft 65"	6500clm	:31¹	1:03¹	1:33 2:03¹

B m 1973, by True Duane—Handy Girl—Victory Boy.
Owner: Alfred LaLonde, Huntingdon, Que., Can.
Tr.—A. LaLonde
Breeder: Teri Van Buren

| 1978 | 5 | 2 | 0 | 0 | $ 1250 | (2:05 PPL⅝) |
| 1977 | 23 | 1 | 4 | 3 | $ 2901 | (2:36 Stga my) |

---

6 D W P
GREY $4500

Lifetime—$17,897—4, 2:04.2

Driver—A. "TONY" MANNINO, White-Green-Orange

1-30 PPL⅝	ft 65"	4500clm	:30	1:02	1:33¹ 2:05
1-18 PPL⅝	ft 70"	5000clm	:30¹	1:02	1:33¹ 2:05
1-10 PPL⅝	ft 55"	4500clm	:31¹	1:03	1:36 2:05
1- 3 PPL⅝	ft 59"	cdmw1550L8	:30¹	1:04¹	1:34 2:06
12-16 PPL⅝	ft 72"	cdmw350L5	:30¹	1:03¹	1:34³ 2:06
11-26 DD⅝	ft 30"	5000clm	:31¹	1:03¹	1:34¹ 2:03¹

B g 1972, by Greentrees Pride—Miss McGuinea—McGuinea.
Owner: Ann Nunziata, Douglaston, N.Y.
Tr.—A. Mannino
Breeder: D. W. Parr

| 1978 | 23 | 4 | 0 | 1 | $ 375 | |
| 1977 | 23 | 1 | 6 | 1 | $ 2795 | (2:06¹ MR) |

---

7 T C B
PINK $4500

Lifetime—$27,099—6, 2:02.1 (⅝)

Driver—ROBERT CAMPBELL, Silver-Grey-Blue

1-30 PPL⅝	ft 55"	5000clm	:29¹	1:02¹	1:31¹ 2:04³
1-23 PPL⅝	ft 72"	5000clm	:30	1:02¹	1:34 2:05
1-16 PPL⅝	ft 65"	5000clm	:31¹	1:03¹	1:34¹ 2:04
12-17 PPL⅝	qd 72"	5000clmhcp	:30¹	1:04¹	1:34 2:08¹
9-28 MR	ft 55"	5000clm	:30	1:03¹	1:34 2:06
9-23 MR	sy 54"	5000clm	:30¹	1:02¹	1:35³ 2:07

B h 1970, by Vickis Jet—Dons Pride—Prince Richard.
Owner: Richard & Mary Gleeson, Fort Lauderdale, Fla.
Tr.—R. Schenck
Breeder: H. & E. L. Budin

| 1978 | 36 | 3 | 3 | 7 | $ 6734 | |
| 1977 | 22 | 1 | 4 | 5 | $ 2348 | |

---

9 LYNNWOODS MAJOR
ORANGE $5625

Lifetime—$7,930—2, 2:14.2

Driver—W. "BILL" LAMBERTUS, Gold-White-Black

1-24 PPL⅝	ft 72"	5625clm	:30	1:02	1:32¹ 2:04¹
1-17 PPL⅝	ft 72"	5625clm	:30	1:02	1:32¹ 2:05
1- 7 PPL⅝	ft 72"	6250clmhcp	:29¹	1:02¹	1:32¹ 2:03¹
12-31 PPL⅝	ft 80"	7500clmhcp	:29¹	1:01¹	1:32¹ 2:03¹
12-12 Nor	gd 6000clm		:31¹	1:04¹	1:36¹ 2:09¹
11-26 Nor	ft 7500clm		:31²	1:04²	1:36² 2:09¹

Br g 1974, by Major Goose—Jorinda—American Flag.
Owner: Terrigeo Stables, Loxahatchee, Fla.
Tr.—W. Lambertus
Breeder: B. & B. Downing

| 1978 | 3 | 0 | 0 | 1 | $ 591 |
| 1977 | | | | | $ 00 |

Overlay Betting.

Horse	Chances of winning	Acceptable odds	Actual odds	Overlay
1 Mays Tar Baby	50%	1 to 1	2.10	yes
4 Rockville Chris	20	4 to 1	3.20	no
5 Teeni Time	20	4 to 1	2.70	no
9 Lynnwoods Major	10	9 to 1	5.00	no

Result.

```
7th RACE — CLAIMING PACE — I MILE
Quarter Times—:30¹ 1:03³ 1:34³ 2:04²
  1 Mays Tar Baby      1   1   1   1   2ⁿᵏ    1½      (2:04²)  *2.10   (B.Ger)
  4 Rockville Chris    4   3   3   2o  1ⁿᵏ    2½      (2:04²)   3.20   (L.Abb)
  3 Gobelet            3   4   4   4o  4⁵½    3⁶¾     (2:05¹)  18.90   (H.Lev)
  5 Teeni Time         5   5   6o  6o  5⁵¾    4⁶¾     (2:05¹)   2.70   (G.Bru)
  2 Bay B Echo         2   7   8   8o  8¹⁰    5ˢ³¾    (2:06¹)  63.20   (R.W.DeS)
  9 Lynwoods Major     9   9   7   7o  7⁸     6ˢ³¾    (2:06¹)   5.00   (W.Lam)
  8 T C B              8   6   5   5   6⁷³⁴   7⁹¾     (2:06²)  52.10   (R.Cam)
  7 DWP                7   2o  2   3   3⁵¼    8¹⁰¹½   (2:06²)   9.60   (A.Man)
  6 Partys Choice      6   8   9x  9   9ᵈⁱˢ   9ᵈⁱˢ             21.10   (A.LaL)
Mutuels:   (1)—6.20 3.60 3.20   (4)—4.20 3.60   (3)—6.40
TRIFECTA—1-4-3—$376.80                    QUINIELA—1 and 4—$11.40
```

Pompano Park   Ninth Race   February 7, 1978

Throw out 2 Douro Lobell, 4 Bluegum, 6 Steady Brookdale, and 9 Mark William for poor recent efforts. 7 Windy David and 8 Steady Denny are back too far and in too tough here.

The contenders:

1 Fifty G's			**5 Kerry**	
Current form	4		Current form	2
Class	−2		Class	−2
Post position	3		Post position	2
Driver	3		Driver	3
Total	8		Total	5

3 Rompin Risa	
Current form	2
Class	0
Post position	2
Driver	2
Total	6

Analysis. Fifty G's, moving up in class, is nevertheless a genuine contender. The change of barn won't hurt this horse at all. (Note McNichol's record as a trainer.) Rompin Risa is in for a much tougher race than her last start, when we bet her on January 31. Kerry, a front-runner that came to life in his last effort, could take this one, especially if he can get to the rail easily. We will go with Fifty G's here.

Result.

```
9th RACE  —  CLAIMING PACE  —  I MILE
Quarter Times—:30 1:00⁴ 1:31 2:02³
```

5 Kerry	5	1	1	1	1^2	1^{nn}	$(2:02^3)$	*1.60	(A.Man)
I Fifty Gs	I	2	2	2	2^2	2^{nn}	$(2:02^3)$	1.90	(M.McN)
2 Douro Lobell	2	4	4	3	$3^{3\frac12}$	$3^{1\frac14}$	$(2:02^4)$	41.20	(C.DelG)
3 Rompin Risa	3	5	5	4	$4^{4\frac34}$	$4^{2\frac14}$	$(2:03)$	3.10	(G.Fol)
7 Windy David	7	6	6	5	5^5	$5^{6\frac12}$	$(2:03^4)$	10.40	(S.Buc)
6 Steady Brookdale	6	8	8	7	6^7	$6^{8\frac12}$	$(2:04^1)$	26.10	(S.Lus)
8 Steady Denny	8	9	9	8o	$8^{7\frac34}$	7^9	$(2:04^2)$	12.50	(D.Hal)
4 Bluegum	4	7	7o	6o	$7^{7\frac14}$	$8^{10\frac12}$	$(2:04^3)$	87.70	(C.Cus)
9 Mark William	9	3o	3o	9	9dis	9dis		65.00	(J.Smi)

```
Mutuels:    (5)—5.20 3.40 3.60    (I)—2.80 2.40    ( 2)—7.80
TRIFECTA—5-1-2—$379.00                    QUINIELA—I and 5—$9.20
```

The Meadowlands

The Meadowlands, in East Rutherford, New Jersey, is the leading 1-mile track in the United States. Not only are the purses high, ranging from a low of $7,000 to more than $20,000, but some claimers go for as high as $75,000. One result of these high purses is that the 2 percent fee for entering races is high enough to prohibit many stables from entering their horses merely as tighteners or to get them ready for future races.

Because Meadowlands is an elliptical 1-mile track, the horses circle the race course once from the start to the finish. This means that there are only two turns to negotiate, and since these turns are wide rather than sharp, horses parked on the outside are not at a great disadvantage. An inside post position is not as important on mile tracks as it is on smaller tracks As a result, horses generally run truer to form.

On the other hand, the track at the Meadowlands is very wide and accommodates a field of ten horses across the starting line. There is thus a chance of greater congestion during a race, and horses in the last two post positions have a greater distance to run to circle the entire field.

WARMUP SADDLE CLOTH ORANGE

ONE MILE

QUINIELA & TRIFECTA RACE

CLAIMING PACE

Purse $2500

Claiming price $6000. With allowances.

Date Trk	Cond & Temp	Class	Dist 1/4	Leader's Time 1/2 3/4	Winner's Time	PP 1/4 1/2 3/4 Str Fin	Ind Time	Odds	Driver

RED $6000

1 FIFTY G'S

Driver—MICKEY McNICHOL, Blue-White-Black

Lifetime—$8,874—4, 2:04.3 (⅝)

B g 1971, by 52nd Street—Everyone's G—Proud Scot.
Tr.—M. McNichol   Owner: Debra McNichol & Joseph Cirasuola, New Fairfield, Conn. & Margate, Fla.   Breeder: D. W. Snyder

2- 1 PP¼⅝ ft 66° c5000clm	:30¹ 1:03¹ 1:34	2:05⁴	5 6 6 5o 2¹	(2:05¹)	*1.20	(G.Lew)	1978 5 1 2 2 $ 2023	2:05 PP⅝
1-24 PP¼⅝ ft 72° 4500clm	:29¹ 1:01 1:32² 2:02	7 2 2 2¹ 2²	(2:02¹)	*2.20	(G.Lew)	1977 24 5 4 6 4889	2:04 VD⅞
1-17 PP¼⅝ ft 72° 4500clm	:30¹ 1:02 1:34² 2:05	6 1 2 3 1½	(2:06)	*1.70	(T.Eic)	HopefulOne FiftyGs SingleSmith
1-10 PP¼⅝ ft 55° 4500clm	:30¹ 1:03¹ 1:34² 2:05²	5 5¹ 1½	(2:05¹)	*1.40	(T.Eic)	ScottFashion FiftyGs FleetwoodKnox
1- 3 PP¼⅝ ft 59° 4500clm	:30¹ 1:02² 1:34 2:05	9 9 9 7o 5³	(2:05¹)	14.30	(T.Eic)	TennesseeSinger LynnwoodsMajor FiftyGs
12-22 PP¼⅝ ft 55° 5000clm	:31 1:04 1:34¹ 2:07	6 2o 1 2 3³¼	(2:08⁻)	2.40	(T.Eic)	Threat HopefulOne FiftyGs

WHITE $6000

2 DOURO LOBELL

Driver—CHARLES DEL GATTO, Orange-White

Lifetime—$88,241—4, 2:02.4

B h 1969, by Torpid—High Rock—Tar Heel.
Tr.—C. Del Gatto   Owner: Arthur G. Grodner & Harvey R. Goldberg, Forest Hills & Yonkers, N.Y.   Breeder: Lana Lobell Farms

1-31 PP¼⅝ ft 65° 6000clm	:30¹ 1:01² 1:33¹ 2:04²	2 2 3 3 3¹¼	(2:06)	21.30	(C.DelG)	1978 4 0 0 0 $ 150
1-24 PP¼⅝ ft 65° 6000clm	:29¹ :59¹ 1:31 2:04	1 1o 1 2² 5²¹²	(2:05¹)	34.40	(C.DelG)	1977 18 0 0 2 1214 (Q 2:08¹ PP⅝)
1-18 PP¼⅝ ft 70° cdmw800L9	:30¹ 1:02 1:33 2:05	9 9 8o 7o 6¹¼⁴	(2:09)	34.60	(C.DelG)	RompinRisa WindyDavid SteadyBrookdale
1-11 PP¼⅝ ft 65° cdmw800L10	:30¹ 1:01 1:32¹ 2:05⁴	4 5 8 8 9⁹	(2:05¹)	117.70	(C.DelG)	SteadyWnnah BnniesBetty SteadyMrLady
1- 5 PP¼⅝ ft 71° 7500clm	:29¹ :59¹ 1:31 2:02¹	7 6 6 5 8 8¹²⁴	(2:06³)	9.80	(C.DelG)	OcalaStarPrince JrbesJack KystneArdmre
12-29 PP¼⅝ ft 70° cdwL150hcp	:29⁴ 1:01 1:32 2:03³	7 2 4 5 4¹²⁴	(2:05¹)	33.00	(C.DelG)	LongTime GrunkosBoy ByrdBobby
12-22 PP¼⅝ ft 55° 7500clm	:31¹ 1:01² 1:32 2:05	8 8¹ 7o 6 6¹⁴	(2:08⁻)		(C.DelG)	GreenwdMuffey SteadyDenny PeterRobin

BLUE $7200

3 ROMPIN RISA

Driver—GEORGE FOLDI, Green-Red-White

Lifetime—$25,217—2, TT 2:02.4 (1)

Br m 1970, by Sampson Direct—Pizzeria—Knight Star.
Tr.—H. Purdy   Owner: J.A.A.W. Stable, So. Fallsburg, N.Y.   Breeder: M. G. Westfall

1-31 PP¼⅝ ft 65° 7200clm	:30¹ 1:01 1:32 2:04³	6 6o 4o 4¹¹²	1¹¹²	(2:04)	4.60	(G.Fol)	1978 5 0 0 1 $ 2249 (2:04 PP⅝)
1-24 PP¼⅝ ft 72° 7200clm	:30¹ 1:03 1:32² 2:02¹	5 5 5 5¹² 4²¹²	(2:06⁻)	9.30	(G.Fol)	1977 38 6 5 6 10344 (2:04 MR)
1-17 PP¼⅝ ft 72° 7200clm	:29¹ 1:00 1:31 2:04¹	6 7 6o 6o 5³⁴	(2:05)	9.30	(G.Fol)	RompinRisa WindyDavid Brookdale
1-10 PP¼⅝ ft 55° 7200clm	:31 1:04 1:34 2:05¹	7 6 6 5 4o 5⁴	(2:05)	*1.40	(G.Fol)	RCQuestor CreditableVon CoolupWay
1- 6 PP¼⅝ ft 70° 7200clm	:30 1:01 1:31 2:02	1 2 1 1o 1¹⁷³	(2:06¹)	7.60	(G.Fol)	UnclesGirl CoolupWay CreditableVon
12-30 PP¼⅝ ft 72° 7200clmhcp	:29¹ 1:01¹ 1:32 2:03¹	1 3 6 8²¹² 5¹²²	(2:05)	15.00	(G.Fol)	AndysCoho HatfieldChuck RompinRisa

GREEN $6000

4 BLUEGUM

Driver—CHRIS CUSIMANO, Green-White-Gold

Lifetime—$28,255—8, 2:03.4

B g 1968, by Van Hanover—Van Kitty—Van Dieman.
Tr.—C. Cusimano   Owner: Christopher Cusimano, Lake Ronkonkoma, N.Y.   Breeder: C. C. Devine

1-31 PP¼⅝ ft 65° 6000clm	:30° 1:02¹ 1:33¹ 2:04¹	1 4 4 5 6³¹⁴	7⁹	(2:06¹)	35.90	(C.Cus)	1978 3 0 0 0 $ 2430 (2:05 Fhld)
1-24 PP¼⅝ ft 72° 7500clmhcp	:30¹ 1:02² 1:32² 2:02¹	5 5 5 5¹² 4²¹²	(2:06⁻)	49.70	(C.Cus)	1977 23 1 0 1 70
1- 4 Fhld ft 35° cdmw150ps	:31 1:02 1:34 2:05	4 5 4o 5¹⁴ 5¹⁷	(2:06¹)	11.10	(O.Pis)	ShiawayDale RebelGrittan PeterHoprtn
12-27 Fhld ft 30° 10000clm	:30 1:01 1:34 2:05¹	6 2 2o 2o 8⁻	(2:08¹)	133.80	(C.Cus)	DesotaGB TheJokerA DoubleCopy
12-19 Fhld gd 45° 10000clm	:31¹ 1:01 1:35 2:07¹	3 4 4 7 8¹	(2:08²)	6.90	(C.Cus)	Deakon NeverKnowA Fullapoleon
12-12 Fhld ft 25° 10000clm	:31¹ 1:02 1:34⁻ 2:07⁻	7⁻	7¹³⁴	(2:08⁻)	12.70	(C.Cus)	RawlingsStreet RomansAugustus Deakon

(G.Fol) BarRTar MeadowMechanic Fahrenheit

(C.Cus) MikeMarvel FortWaikato OneAndAll

QUINIELA & TRIFECTA			
Driver	First	Second	Third

Trackman's Selections: 5—3—1—7

---

5 $6000

Lifetime—$47,609—8, 2:03.1

Driver—A. "TONY" MANNINO, White-Green-Orange

Owner: Dominick Satornino & Robert Fuoco, Miami, Fla. & Bellport, N.Y.

Tr.—A. Mannino   Breeder: J. R. Colvin

1-30 PP⅝ ft 55° 5000clm
1-21 PP⅝ ft 59° 5000clm
1-14 PP⅝ ft 72° 5000clm
1- 5 PP⅝ ft 71° 5000clmhcp
12-29 PP⅝ ft 65° 5000clm
12-15 PP⅝ ft 78° 5000clm

---

6 $6000

Lifetime—$20,894—4, 2:04

Driver—SAM LUSSIER, Green-Red-White

Owner: M. E. & S. J. Lussier, R. D. Jones, No. Amherst & Sunderland, Mass.

Tr.—S. Lussier   Breeder: B. R. & P. W. Mathewson

1-31 PP⅝ ft 65° 6000clm
1-23 PP⅝ ft 72° 6500clm
1-14 PP⅝ ft 72° 6000clm
1- 7 PP⅝ ft 72° 7000clmhcp
12-18 NE⅝ sl 7000clm
11-27 Rock ft 7000clm

---

7 GREY $6000

Lifetime—$10,931—4, 2:05.3 (⅝)

Driver—STERLING BUCH., Red-White-Black

Owner: Virginia Shell, Pompano Beach, Fla.

Tr.—R. Shell

1-31 PP⅝ ft 65° 6000clm
1-24 PP⅝ ft 72° 6000clm
1-17 PP⅝ ft 72° 6000clm
1- 9 PP⅝ ft 49° c5000clm
1- 2 PP⅝ ft 65° 6250clm
12-26 PP⅝ ft 58° 6250clm

---

8 PINK $6000

Lifetime—$15,907—5, 2:03.4 (1)

Driver—DON HALL, Grey-Red

Owner: Charles Federman & Marvin Schiffman, Southfield & Detroit, Mich.

Tr.—C. Federman   Breeder: J. R. Colvin

1-27 PP⅝ ft 54° 6000clmhcp
1-19 PP⅝ gd 72° 7500clm
12-29 PP⅝ ft 72° 7500clm
11-16 Nor gd 8000clm
11- 3 Nor ft 9000clmhcp
10-20 HP⅝ ft 10000clm

---

9 ORANGE $6000

Lifetime—$34,515—7, 2:02.2 (⅝)

Driver—J. (CARL) SMITH, Maroon-Tan

Owner: Arthur Brewer II, Haverhill, Mass.

Tr.—J. Carl Smith   Breeder: Hill Distributing Co.

1-31 PP⅝ ft 65° 6000clm
1-24 PP⅝ ft 72° 6000clm
12-26 PP⅝ ft 58° 6500clm
12-15 PP⅝ ft 78° 7500clm
11-23 Rock ft 8000clm
11-17 Rock sy 8000clm

5-2 + Lifetime—$47,609—8, 2:03.1 (with entries listed as STEADY BROOKDALE, B g 1971 by Steady Beau)

6 = STEADY BROOKDALE

9-2 = WINDY DAVID   B g 1973, by Major Goose—Amber Grey—Grey Demon.

8 = STEADY DENNY   B g 1972, by Steady Beau—Amy Quick—Amortizor.

10 MARK WILLIAM   B h 1970, by Knight Time—Margo Hill—Hoot Mon.

One more fact to note is that the Meadowlands must be characterized as a fast track. For example, in the chart of comparative track ratings, it is rated 4 seconds faster than Batavia Downs and 2 seconds faster than Pompano Park.

Reading the Meadowlands Program

Listed below are a number of symbols in the Meadowlands program that differ from those used in the Batavia and Pompano programs:

The modified sulky, permitted at the Meadowlands, is marked by a Ⓧ and the conventional sulky by (c).

A *z* notes that the horse has been claimed.

After the driver's name, his birth date and weight are given.

At the end of a horse's performance line for each of its races, the temperature is shown, together with a time allowance based on weather factors. Example: (23-2) means that a mile race is about 2 seconds slower than normal because of the chill factor.

The following changes in point assignments should be made:

Driver Standings

Because the Meadowlands furnishes the racing fan with a comprehensive list of driver standings, it will be convenient to base point assignments for the caliber of driver on UDR percentages. Virtually every driver at the Meadowlands with a percentage of .250 and higher has won about 15 percent his starts. This is a clear mark of excellence at a 1-mile track where there are ten starters in most races, but it is particularly impressive at the Meadowlands, where the best drivers in America compete.

To find a driver's level of performance, simply check his UDR rating in the program and make the following point assignments:

UDR .250 and up	3 points
UDR .225 to .250	2 points
UDR .200 to .225	1 point
UDR .000 to .200	0 points

Unfortunately, no list of leading trainers is given in the Meadowlands program.

Post Positions

Since there are ten starters in most races at the Meadowlands,

assigning points for post position can be done this way:

1 or 2   3 points
3 to 6   2 points
7 to 9   1 point
10   0 points

This scheme for awarding post-position points is in close accord with the results of more than fourteen hundred races at the spring and summer meeting. Post positions 1 and 2 produce more than 30 percent of all winners at the Meadowlands; 3 through 6, more than 45 percent; and 7 through 9, slightly more than 20 percent.

We do not go back further than one month from the date of the present race in assigning points for current form. Let's turn to a number of illustrative races at the Meadowlands on the evenings of June 7, 8, and 18, 1977, using the point system we outlined in chapter 5.

Examples of Races at Meadowlands

The Meadowlands   4th Race   June 7, 1977

Eliminate the following: 1 First Me, 2 Gaum Caton, 3 First Echo, 4 Special Byrd, 6 Neda Abbegale, 7 Lucky Miracle, and 8 Mitey Tonyjoe. None have finished in the money during the last month in regular starts at a distance of 1 mile.

This leaves:

5 Sandu

Current form	1
Class	0
Consistency	2
Post position	2
Driver	3
Total	8

10 Resume Fire

Current form	2
Class	0
Consistency	3
Post position	0
Driver	3
Total	8

9 Bobcat Sue

Current form	2
Class	0
Consistency	3
Post position	1
Driver	3
Total	9

Driver	Starts	1st	2nd	3rd	UDR
ABBATIELLO, C.	203	23	31	30	.229
ARONE, R.	14	2	2	1	.190
BALDACHINO, G.	92	6	8	7	.138
BATTAGLIA, L.	15	2	2	0	.198
BAYLESS, S.	22	3	1	2	.190
BERKNER, G.	89	7	14	11	.180
BERNSTEIN, J.	27	5	5	0	.285
BERTOLDO, B.	30	0	1	1	.040
BONACORSA, D.	32	1	1	2	.111
BOYD, C.	25	0	1	9	.198
CAMERON, W.	149	10	20	18	.175
CARAWAY, T.	17	0	4	2	.222
COBB, E.	205	16	13	20	.151
CONSOL, P.	36	0	1	1	.098
CONTE, J.	22	2	0	2	.033
COPELAND, L.	21	0	3	2	.285
COTE, D.	29	2	2	1	.144
CRANK, V.	16	4	4	5	.451
CRUISE, J., JR.	39	2	2	5	.195
DAIGNEAULT, R.	134	22	20	16	.295
DANCER, H., JR.	37	8	4	9	.390
DANCER, S.	42	5	6	8	.349
DANCER, V.	32	10	7	8	.277
DANDEO, A.	20	0	0	2	.068
DANOSKY, J.	21	0	2	0	.030
DAUPLAISE, N.	73	17	10	9	.313
DAVIS, E.	35	3	7	4	.197
DeMARCO, R.	19	2	1	3	.205
DEMERS, Y.	54	5	1	6	.216
DETERS, W.	179	21	22	22	.219
DOHERTY, JA.	587	75	78	63	.234
EVILSIZOR, J.	33	3	0	0	.130
FAGLIARONE, M.	35	1	1	4	.070
FILION, DEN.	150	14	19	16	.213
FITZPATRICK, C.	48	5	5	2	.232
FONTAINE, L.	27	2	1	6	.175
FREIDMAN, M.	30	1	2	4	.189
GAGLIARDI, M.	611	67	75	70	.222
GALBRAITH, C.	61	4	3	7	.150
GIAMBRONE, A.	45	0	4	6	.200
GIGANTE, L.	27	3	5	1	.027
GILLIS, D.	25	2	0	1	.219
GILMOUR, W.	509	61	70	62	.216
GILMOUR, L.	480	45	56	64	.196
GIORGIANNI, J.	65	5	5	9	.229
GOWER, JR., W.	18	2	2	8	.182
LeCAUSE, C.	150	13	19	20	.225
LIPARI, J.	78	6	6	6	.204
LOHMEYER, E.	145	18	22	24	.255
LUCHENTO, T.	72	6	4	10	.105
MACEDONIO, D.	20	1	1	4	.144
MALADY, C.	24	4	2	2	.204
MANZI, R.	159	16	18	12	.260
MANZI, JR., R.	11	2	2	0	.138
MARKS, W.	98	13	11	8	.203
MARSH, W.	10	0	0	0	.300
MARUSCO, D.	19	4	0	3	.327
McNUTT, K.	176	23	18	18	.269
MEGENS, W.	11	2	3	0	.259
MORGAN, T.	140	20	20	14	.208
MORONE, J.	18	0	0	2	.274
MYERS, R.	21	1	0	3	.203
NASH, J.	12	2	1	2	.141
McNUTT, J.	149	23	17	18	.269
OAKES, G.	18	12	4	4	.231
OKE, W.	110	10	10	13	.200
PAROLARI, P.	26	2	2	3	.160
PIERCE, D.	112	12	10	5	.076
POLISENO, D.	61	3	4	2	.222
PULLEN, L.	24	1	4	2	.262
QUARTAROLO, A.	28	4	3	2	.229
RATHBONE, J.	28	3	1	5	.174
RATHBONE, L.	444	46	57	53	.229
REMMEN, R.	60	5	6	2	.200
RIZZO, J.	18	3	3	3	.373
RODGERS, R., JR.	62	4	1	5	.195
ROLLA, L.	17	0	5	1	.255
ROSINO, J.	17	2	8	21	.182
SCARPA, L.	115	8	12	1	.244
SCHMIGEL, J. E.	10	1	2	2	.182
SCHWARTZ, M.	85	1	9	2	.211
SCORSONE, J.	17	1	1	2	.214
SEAMAN, J.	15	2	2	2	.292
SIMPSON, D.	27	7	5	6	.420
SPARACINO, S.	59	4	2	3	.148
STOLTZFUS, A.	154	24	17	23	.263
TALLMAN, J.	210	20	23	18	.089
TELYNONDE, L.	38	2	0	0	.055
THOMAS, R.	21	1	2	3	.092
TORRE, S.	12	0	1	0	.055
TURCOTTE, R.	51	6	6	4	.184
WARRINGTON, W.	70	9	7	8	.216
WEBSTER, B.	11	1	6	6	.276
WILLIAMS, L.	136	7	9	4	.222
WING, T.	674	121	90	59	.282
WRIGHT, G.	565	78	63	79	.244

LEADING DASH WINNERS
(15 Top Dash Winners As Of Thursday, June 16, 1977)

Name	Starts	1st	2nd	3rd
WEBSTER, B.	854	136	113	113
WING, T.	674	121	90	59
WRIGHT, G.	565	78	63	79
DOHERTY, JA.	587	75	78	63
GAGLIARDI, M.	611	67	75	70
GILMOUR, W.	509	61	70	62
REMMEN, R.	444	46	57	53
GILMOUR, L.	480	45	56	64
HAUGHTON, P.	194	29	45	21
McNUTT, K.	176	27	26	23
GRAHAM, J.	199	27	22	18
STOLTZFUS, A.	154	24	17	23
DAIGNEAULT, R.	134	22	22	16
MORGAN, T.	140	20	20	14
TALLMAN, J.	210	18	23	18

Name	Starts	1st	2nd	3rd	Pct
GRAHAM, J.	199	27	22	25	.224
GRAHAM, T.	15	3	-	1	.259
GREENE, J.	35	3	4	2	.181
HAMMER, R.	32	3	3	-	.198
HAUGHTON, P.	194	29	23	21	.328
HAYTER, R.	15	5	5	3	.511
HOCH, G.	18	4	2	3	.373
HOGAN, D.	29	3	5	4	.195
HOLLINGSWORTH, G.	12	1	1	5	.194
HOWARD, R.	32	1	0	2	.160
HUDSON, W.	76	6	11	6	.168
INGRASSIA, P., JR.	25	3	4	6	.280
INOKAI, S.	20	1	2	3	.269
INSKO, D.	69	4	2	2	.289
JOHNSON, D.	84	8	8	6	.220
KELLY, H.	70	8	8	8	.207
KING, J., JR.	207	17	20	26	.195
KLEINMAN, K.	21	1	0	5	.111
LARENTE, J.	53	13	4	8	.492

WINNING POST POSITIONS
THROUGH THURSDAY, JUNE 16, 1977

POST	1	2	3	4	5	6	7	8	9	10	11	12	13	14
WIN	238	208	178	150	184	151	118	87	83	27	0	0	0	1
PLACE	200	201	177	183	160	156	127	108	50	46	2	0	0	1
SHOW	175	157	192	187	164	174	142	116	76	47	0	2	1	0

Percentage Of Winning Favorites 33% (467 of 1420)
Percentage Of In The Money Favorites 64% (911 of 1420)
(Includes All Dead Heats)

TEMPERATURE AND RACING CONDITIONS:

Your official program now provides helpful weather conditions at the end of each horse's performance line. Temperature and, if necessary, time allowance due to cold weather, are shown

EXAMPLE: 23 minus 2 i.e. (23-2)

This means that actual temperature was 23, but with wind chill factor the mile may be approximately 2 seconds slower than normal performance. Racing officials determine the time allowance based on weather factors.

RECALL RULE

The starter may sound a recall only for the following reasons.

1. A horse scores ahead of the gate.
2. There is interference.
3. A horse has broken equipment.
4. A horse falls before the word "go" is given.
5. Where a horse refuses to come to the gate before the gate reaches the pole ⅜ of a Mile before the start, the field may be turned.

PACE–1 MILE
Warming-Up Saddle Cloth
GREEN

Exacta Wagering This Race

THE MONCLAIR K. OF C. PACE

PURSE $7,500

CLAIMING PRICE $10,000
(Four-Year-Old & Older Mares Granted 40% Allowance)
(Five-Year-Old & Older Mares Granted 20% Allowance)

ASK FOR HORSE BY PROGRAM NUMBER

8-1
1
10000
Red

FIRST ME
ch g, 5, by Nevele Bigshot—First Surprise by Tar Heel
S. K. Zimmerman, Glenn Prezocki & Sarah Jerome, Louisville, Ky.
Driver—MICHAEL GAGLIARDI, 8-25-48(175)WHITE-BLACK-MAROON

$20,904 — 4, 1:59¹ (1)
Trainer—B. Bertoldo
M((⅛)2:03 1977 13 1 1 1 7,685
Lat(1)1:59¹ 1976 36 7 7 2 20,077

6-1
2
10000
Blue

GAUM CATON (J)
b g, 9, by Caton Hanover—Jeannine Hanover by Axomite
Spiro L. Serbes & James S. Serbes, Brooklyn, N.Y.
Driver—SPIRO SERBES, 9-30-21 (170) WHITE-ORANGE-BLACK

$22,229 — 8, 2:02 (⅞)
Trainer—S. Serbes
Ppk(⅞)2:01¹ 1977 17 4 2 3 6,387
Ppk(⅞)2:02 1976 34 6 5 7 11,795

15-1
3
12000
White

FIRST ECHO
b m, 5, by Maynard Hanover—Echo Hills Seniah by Bay State Tom
T. Kiernan, F. Zentgraf, M. Mammes & J. Kelley, Jr., Westbury, N.Y
Driver—GREG WRIGHT, 1-26-46 (165) BLUE-WHITE

$16,740 — 4, 2:02¹ (1)
Trainer—J. Kelley, Jr.
Q-M((⅛)2:04³ 1977 15 0 2 1 5,045
M((1)2:02¹ 1976 41 6 6 7 16,740

12-1
4
10000
Green

SPECIAL BYRD
b g, 11, by Bye Bye Byrd—Nance Abbe by Gene Abbe
Jerry Glantz & Harry Chaiken, Tamarac, Fla.
Driver—CHARLES GIAMANCO, 2-14-54 (146) RED-WHITE-BLACK

$63,327 — 6, 2:02 (⅞)
Trainer—C. Giamanco—Tr.-A. Giamanco, Jr.
Ppk(⅞)2:02 1977 12 3 2 0 3,865
VD(⅝)2:03 1976 50 11 11 4 12,021

3-1
5
10000

SANDU
b g, 9, by Sunny O'Brien—Doc's Miss by Doctor's Adios
Patrick Tarsio, Newburgh, N.Y.
Driver—BEN WEBSTER, 11-8-39 (130) RED-WHITE-BLACK

$8,434 — 4, 2:05 (⅜)
Trainer—G. Baratta—Tr.-H. Kamm
M((⅛)2:02¹ 1977 16 4 2 0 17,485
BB(⅜)2:05 1976 27 6 3 5 8,434

Black														

6 20-1 | $11,668 — 4, 2:03
Black | 4-19 M1⊗ | 7000 ft 10000 clm cd mi 3111:0121:3232:033 | 4 | 5 | 5 | 4 | 42¼ 41¼ | 2:034 | 3.40 | (R.Remmen) | SprAlmah,PeppyJack,JayBBlz 61-0
| 4-11 M1⊗ | 7500 ft 12500 clm cd mi 2911:0011:3122:012 | 4 | 7 | 9 | 9° | 9⁵ 9⁶¼ | 2:024 | 5.50 | (R.Remmen) | Wckd.Mike,HalfNui,Mrion.Gun 52-0

NEDA ABBEGALE ro m, 5, by Gene Abbe—Annie Hardy by Hardy Hanover
Albert Racing Stable, Inc., Pompano Beach, Fla. (182)   Trainer—S. Demas

BLUE-WHITE
Driver—EDDIE COBB, 3-1-20

6 12000 Yellow | 5-24 M1⊗ | 7000 ft Qua mi 2941:014¹:321²:021 | 5 | 6 | 3° | 4 | 42¼ 43¼ | 2:024 | N.B. | (E.Cobb) | Stga2:03 1977 8 0 0 1 600
| 4-6 M1†⊗ | 7000 ft 10000 clm mi 30 1:021:352²:052 | 6 | 8 | 6°10⁶ 10¹8¼ | | | 2:091 | 14.90 | (E.Cobb) | Lynslee,RobRkt,BretScotchc. 80-0
| 3-26 M1⊗ | ft Qua mi 30 1:021:021:343:204 | 6 | 3 | 3° 2° 34¼ 39¼ | | | 2:054 | N.B. | (E.Cobb) | OneA.All,LkyMrcl,AftElectra 39-2
| 3-11 M1⊗ | 6500 ft 12500 clm cd mi 3021:011:33 2:021 | 4 | 4 | 3° 6¼ 87¼ | | | 2:054 | 51.40 | (E.Cobb) | Shanda,Raphael,NedaABlgyi 40-1
| 3-5 M1⊗ | 6500 ft 12500 clm cd mi 3031:001:121:22:023 | 7 | 7 | 74¼ 76¼ | | | 2:034 | 39.40 | (E.Cobb) | WckdMike,GinPtch,Chuck,lim 53-0
| 2-15 M1⊗ | 7000 ft 15000 clm cd mi 2911:014¹:333:2:033 | 5 | 6 | 5° 88¼ 81¼ | | | 2:06 | 23.10 | (C.Abbatiello) | BonExprs,RoyRights,WckdMk 56-0
| | | | | | | | | | | SkpBrba,SnwllExpr,MajCrm 20-3

7 5-1 Pink | $124,427 — 6, 2:02¹
LUCKY MIRACLE br g, 8, by Miracle Knight—Beau Time by Good Time
Milton & Sandra Keslow, Scarsdale, N.Y. (160)   Trainer—D. Sider

WHITE-BLUE
Driver—LLOYD GILMOUR, 10-3-45

7 10000 Pink | 5-17 M1⊗ | 7500 ft 10000 clm cd mi 2941:292²:004 | 4 | 1 | 1 | 1 | 2nk 7⁵¼ | 2:02¹ | 4.40 | (L.Gilmour) | RR2:03¹ 1976 30 4 5 6 31,615
| 5-3 M1⊗ | 7500 ft 10000 clm cd mi 292¹:012¹:33 2:021 | 9 | 9 | 9 | 31¼ 98¼ | 2:034 | 8.50 | (W.Gilmour) | ResumeFire,RsClns,PrdMmnt 89-0
| 4-21 M1⊗ | 7500 ft 10000 clm cd mi 29 :591:292²:011 | 2 | 4 | 6¼ 610 | 2:03¹ | 3.50 | (L.Gilmour) | FrllwyRed,Dkfeels,SirOmaha 69-0
| 4-13 M1⊗ | 7000 ft Qua mi 3041:002¹:322:02 | 6 | 6 | 6¼ 62¼ | 2:052 | N.B. | (W.Gilmour) | StubMite,PaulaLdr,ArmLofty 60-0
| 4-6 M1⊗ | 7000 ft 10000 clm cd mi 30 1:021:352²:052 | 9 | 9 | 2° 1nk 222 | *3.10 | (W.Gilmour) | MtBridge,BrndyMan,Overhaul 83-0
| 3-29 M1⊗ | 7000 ft 12500 clm cd mi 292 :591:29 1:594 | 7 | 3 | 3 4 4° 25 37 | *1.20 | (W.Gilmour) | OneA.All,LkyMrcl,AftElectra 39-2
| | | | | | | | | *1.10 | (L.Gilmour) | QuickSam,RomanLdr,LkyMrcl 75-0

8 12-1 Gray | $12,595 — 4, 2:03 (⑤)
MITEY TONYJOE br m, 4, by Worthy Jimmy—Derringer by Sharpshooter
Catello R. Manzi, Liberty, N.Y. (170)   St.-G. Regan—Tr.-A. Arone

WHITE-BLUE
Driver—CATELLO MANZI, 6-27-50

8 10000 Gray | 5-18 M1⊗ | 7500 gd 10000 clm cd ⑧ :283 :583 | 1:14 | 1 | 8 | - | 87¼ 89¼ | 2:02¹ | 9.60 | (C.Manzi) | Q-MR(112:024 1977 7 1 2 0 3,490
| 5-6 M1⊗ | 7500 gd 10000 clm cd mi 3011:004¹:322²:03 | 4 | 3 | 8° 8⁶ x9⁰¼ | 2:044 | 3.50 | (C.Manzi) | MR2:081 1976 23 2 4 2 3,424
| 4-30 M1⊗ | 7500 ft 10000 clm cd mi 3141:04 1:352:063 | 1 | 2 | 2½ 610 | 2:024 | N.B. | (C.Manzi) | LclSpark,SnkyChms,FirstMe 71-0
| 4-26 M1⊗ | 7000 ft Qua mi 3041:013¹:33 2:033 | 1 | 1 | 1 1 2nk | 2:052 | N.B. | (C.Manzi) | Sandu,HaliTFulla,ArmPigeon 69-0
| 4-23 M1⊗ | 7000 ft Qua mi 30 1:021:322:032 | 9 | 9 | 2½ 27 | 2:041 | N.B. | (C.Manzi) | Mty.Tnyj.,Bon.Expr.,Ryl.Gabe 60-0
| 4-20 M1⊗ | 7000 ft 12500 clm cd mi 293 :592¹:29 2:003 | 3 | 3 | 65¼ 64¼ | 2:044 | 10.30 | (C.Manzi) | BillyBrt.,MtyTnyjoe,StdyChckl 48-1
| | | | | | | | 9 9 923²82¹ | | | (C.Manzi) | RomanovH,MdMirN,JSMindg 76-0
| | | | | | | | | | | DuaneShow,BlueBrk,FrstMrk 61-0

9 4-1 Purple | $72,259 — 5, 2:02³ (1)
BOBCAT SUE br h, 5, by Bullet Hanover—Rosana by Star's Pride
Sanford Resnick, Springfield, N.J. (136)   St.-C. Manzi—Tr.-R. Arone

GREEN-WHITE-RED
Driver—TED WING, 7-30-48

9 14000 Purple | 5-19 M1⊗ | 7500 ft 10000 clm cd mi 31 1:022¹:33 2:032 | 10 | 7 | 5° 5° 23 13¼ | 2:032 | 6.40 | (G.Wright) | MR(112:004 1977 14 4 2 0 12,540
| 5-4 M1⊗ | 6000 ft C3 cd mi 31 1:022¹:331²:043 | 5 | 7 | 7x¹457¼ | 2:062 | 5.10 | (J.Chapman) | BbctSue,ArmLofty,RoyRights 65-0
| 4-28 RR⊗ | 6000 sy C3 cd mi 3141:04 1:352²:034 | 4 | 5 | 7o⁰53 1ns | 2:034 | 19.70 | (Den.Filion) | ResumeFire,RsClns,PrdMmnt 81-0
| 4-9 M1⊗ | 7000 ft 10000 clm cd mi 2931:002¹:313²:022 | 9 | 2 | 2½ 1 1 | 2:034 | 20.10 | (J.Chapman) | Pud,Almih.,Trp.Str.,Slwy.B. 62-0
| 3-23 M1⊗ | 7000 ft 10000 clm cd mi 3041:023¹:342²:04 | 3 | 2° 6²¼ 97³ | | | 2:043 | 6.90 | (B.Webster) | Hstllr.Bst.,Bbct.Sue.,Frm.Shan 47-0
| | | | | | | | | 3 1 1¹ 2nk | 2:04 | 13.10 | (A.Niles) | OfHrmBndg,BbctSue,RoseClns 61-0
| | | | | | | | | | *1.30 | (C.Manzi) | SprAlmah,PeppyJack,JayBBlz 61-0

10 5-1 Blue-Red | $10,926 — 4, 2:03²
RESUME FIRE b m, 5, by Bullet Hanover—Rosana by Star's Pride
Capital Hill Farms Inc., Montreal, Quebec, Can. (185)   St.-Her. Filion—Tr.-Den. Filion

RED-DK. BLUE-WHITE
Driver—DENIS FILION, 6-3-42

10 10000 Blue-Red | 5-17 M1⊗ | 7500 ft 10000 clm cd mi 292 :593¹:294²:004 | 5 | 7 | 9° 1nk 1³ | 2:04 | 14.70 | (Den.Filion) | FHld2:032 1976 24 2 4 2 6,651
| 5-4 M1⊗ | 10000 clm cd mi 3031:013¹:332²:05 | 3 | 5 | 5x 7x4¹57¼ | 2:062 | 5.20 | (Den.Filion) | ResumeFire,RsClns,PrdMmnt 81-0
| 4-26 M1⊗ | 7000 ft 10000 clm cd mi 3031:01:332²:034 | 2 | 5 | 6 7 o⁰53 1ns | 2:034 | 20.10 | (J.Chapman) | RsmeFire,HpfiNews,GeneTrip 48-1
| 4-19 M1⊗ | 7000 ft 10000 clm cd mi 3111:012¹:322²:023 | 6 | 6 | 7 53x5x1¼ | 2:034 | 11.40 | (Den.Filion) | SprAlmah,PeppyJack,JayBBlz 61-0
| 3-30 M1⊗ | 7000 ft 10000 clm cd mi 301:011:322²:022 | 5 | 7 | 8 9 66 610¼ | 2:042 | 13.00 | (Her.Filion) | Dainty,Countway,SidneyClns 63-0
| 3-16 LB⊗ | 3000 ft 10000 clm cd mi 291 :594¹:312²:024 | 3 | 3 | 2 2° 62¼ 97¼ | 2:071 | 23.10 | (RheoFilion) | ByeZoe,Superlative,Scott.Isle 50-0
| | | | | | | | | *1.30 | (RheoFilion) | |

C—Denotes Conventional Sulky
All Others To Use Modified Sulky

PACE—1 MILE
Warming-Up Saddle Cloth
BLUE-RED

PURSE $10,500

CLAIMING PRICE $20,000
(Four-Year-Olds Allowed 25% Allowance)
(Five-Year-Old & Older Mares Granted 20% Allowance)

ASK FOR HORSE BY PROGRAM NUMBER

5-1
1
20000
Red
CANADIAN RED ch g, 7, by Canadian Dares—Wing Ding by Mighty Storm
House Of Pagano, Woodbridge, N.J.
Driver—ABE STOLTZFUS, 4-9-42 (165) RED-WHITE-BLACK St.—W. Stoltzfus—Tr.—C. Boyd
Hol(1)1:59 1977 17 0 5 2 12,636
1976 24 3 2 5 11,163

6-1
2
25000
Blue
OVER T. b h, 4, by Overcall—Charming Gail by Bullet Hanover
Gerald Popper, Englishtown, N.J.
Driver—WALTER MARKS, 1-19-31 (137) BROWN-WHITE Trainer—G. Villemure
1977 16 2 3 0 19,040
1976 32 6 2 2 14,492

15-1
3
Blue
INFORMAL b g, 6, by Tempest Hanover—Jilaire by Stormway
Joseph Spero, Brooklyn, N.Y.
Driver—LLOYD GILMOUR, 10-3-45 (160) RED-GREY Trainer—G. Villemure
RR2:012 1976 7 1 1 1 3,676

8-1
4
20000
White
DODO LINER b h, 8, by Randolph Liner—Debby J. by Harold J.
Gary Boyle, Lowell, Mass.
Driver—GARY BOYLE, 2-9-39 (180) BLUE-WHITE Trainer—G. Boyle
M(1)2:00 1977 17 2 2 2 20,560
1976 22 4 7 2 10,921

7-2
5
25000
Green
ROYAL RAIDER N. b h, 8, by Ricochet (F)—Bonnie Princess by U. Scott
Kathy Horvath, Hamilton, Ont., Can.
Driver—TED WING, 7-30-48 (136) GREEN-WHITE-RED Trainer—K. Primmer
Brd(1)1:592 1976 24 1 3 6 15,684

4-1
Black
20000

6
4-1
20000

HAVE FAITH
b g, 11, by Greentree Adios—Amosson's Faith by Prince Richard

Driver—EDWARD LOHMEYER, 10-1-591 (⅝)

$150,686 — 10, 1:591 (⅝)

4-15 M①⊗	10000 ft 22500 clm cd mi 281 :591 3:022:00	3	6	5	6	5	4⁰⁰2¹¼	12¹	3.20	(T. Wing)	RylRdrN,HarMcElln,LitScmp
4- 9 M①⊗	9500 ft 20000 clm cd mi 301 3:031:312:02	3	6	5	4⁰⁰2¹¼	13	2:02	*2.40	(T. Wing)	RylRderN,ArmOctane,ShrBlk

St.—E. Lohmeyer—Tr.—L. Battaglia
Spk(⅝)1:591 1976 41 8 11 11 67,687
M(1)2:00¹ 1977 17 1 2 3 18,415

15-1
Yellow
20000

7

LOUISTON A.
b g, 6, by Raider Frost—Kirsty by Allegiance (F)

Kingsley Stable, Brooklyn, N.Y.

Driver—GEORGE BERKNER, 6-19-42

$17,689 — 5, 2:04 (1) Qua

5-24 M①⊗	10⁰00 ft 20000 clm cd mi 291 1:00 1:302:00¹	2	1	1	2¹	76¹	2:012	9.40	(G. Berkner)	HaveFaith,TrckyRhythm,Prcst
5-16 M①⊗	11000 ft 22500 clm cd mi 291 :59 1:292:593	3	6	2	2	4H³891	2:012	12.50	(G. Berkner)	BnbryBlcnt,Quartette,AddTch
5- 4 M①⊗	11000 sy 22500 clm cd mi 304 1:01 1:322:023	4	3	4	3	45½	2:03	12.30	(G. Berkner)	JmbDllr,ClvrTruax,MetaroHan
4-27 M①⊗	7000 ft 22000 clm mi 30 1:003 1:314 2:021	3	1	1	1nk	53	2:024	3.60	(C. Abbatiello)	Gd.Ritns,BillyB,Byrd.K.Sctt
4- 8 RR①⊗	7000 ft 22000 clm mi 31 1:033 1:35 2:063	1	4	5	76	77	2:08	8.80	(C. Abbatiello)	EchoB,Joe,Nvl,Prz,LouistnA
4- 2 RR①⊗	8000 sy 27000 clm cd mi 32 1:04 1:354 2:07	8	8	8	8	811	2:09¹	18.20	(C. Abbatiello)	PhilCllns,Key,Trmph,BroPer

St.—B. Norris—Tr.—Da. Russell
YR2:023 1976 45 11 7 4 45,799
1977 12 0 1 2 7,300

8-1
Pink
20000

8
24000

MISS MIKE'S LADY
b m, 7, by Lang Hanover—Mike's Lady by Rip MacArthur

Branislau Kulka & Anthony M. Cogianese, Queens, N.Y.

Driver—JAMES DOHERTY, 9-27-40   (155)

$82,630 — 4, 1:593 (1)

5-24 M①⊗	10⁵00 ft 20000 clm cd mi 291 1:00 1:302:001	1	1	1	1	76¹	2:012	6.40	(Ja. Doherty)	HaveFaith,TrckyRhythm,Prcst
5-16 M①⊗	11000 ft 22500 clm cd mi 291 :59 1:292:593	6	8	851	661	2:003	*3.20	(J.Tallman)	BnbryBlcnt,Quartette,AddTch
5- 7 M①⊗	10500 ft 20000 clm cd mi 293 1:01¹1:312:04	4	4⁰	6	6	78	2:04	28.20	(E.Lohmeyer)	FrstyZip,NchkoTar,CdrwdSam
5- 3 M①⊗	10500 ft 20000 clm cd mi 293 1:01 1:312:04	4	6	3	31	1nk P⁹	2:031	N.B.	(E.Lohmeyer)	TaroHn,FrstyZip,LyssGreen
1-31 YR①⊗	5500 ft 18000 clm cd mi 31 1:033¹:35 2:063	1	4	5	76	77	2:08	3.70	(N.Dauplaise)	ShiawyGale,Ambiguous,Trent
1-26 YR①⊗	5500 ft 18000 clm cd mi 32 1:04 1:354 2:07	8	8	8	8	811	2:09¹	4.00	(N.Dauplaise)	CarefreeKevin,Jckts,Trck,Barr,Geo.

St.—G. Wright—Tr.—W. Ecker
YR2:023 1976 3⅝ 5 2 11 34,100

20-1
Purple
20000

9

TRENT
br g, 8, by Smokey Hanover—Lucks Againstus by Lawn Raider (F)

Larry Pollock Stable. Montreal, Que., Can.

Driver—RONALD TURCOTTE, 12-12-33   (191)

$55,526 — 7, 1:592 (⅝)

5-27 M①⊗	10500 ft 20000 clm cd mi 2921:00³1:2941:584	7	7	5x	3	431	2:012	27.70	(R. Turcotte)	GldShdk,ShrBlck,LckySahbra
5-18 M①⊗	12000 gd 25000 clm cd mi 3041:041¹:3042:004	2	3	3	881	914	2:03	17.60	(R. Turcotte)	Shwy.Gale.OrkalyN..ThorLbll.
5-11 M①⊗	12000 ft 25000 clm cd mi 291 :592¹:30 1:593	1	2	32¼	54	422iP3	2:002	8.80	(R. Webster)	FrstyZip,NchkoTar,CdrwdSam
5- 4 M①⊗	10000 ft 22500 clm cd mi 291 :592¹:301 1:593	5	4	431	633	577	2:002	11.80	(R.Turcotte)	TaroHn,FrstyZip,LyssGreen
4-28 M①⊗	10000ft22500z clm cd mi 301 :5941:2931:584	4	343	33	2:034	3.70	(J.Graham)	HighHl.Yss,SnrsTime.FunMan
4-23 M①⊗	12000 ft 20000 clm cd mi 284 :5931:2931:592	5	4	453	33¼	2:011	3.10	(J.Graham)	Prmnthn,CsN,Blly,CdrwdSam

St.—G. Wright—Tr.—D. Johnson
Spk(⅝)1:592 1976 3⅝ 5 2 11 34,100
M(1)2:01 1977 24 4 5 5 33,685

5-1
Blue-
Red
20000

10

SHORE BLACK
br g, 8, by Eastern Shore—Lou Worthy by Worthy Boy

William Breyer & Gerald Krause, Leonia, N.J.

Driver—GREG WRIGHT, 1-26-46   (165)

$55,841 — 7, 2:01¹ (1)

5-27 M①⊗	10500 ft 20000 clm cd mi 2921:00³1:2941:584	1	3	4	431	233	1:593	4.80	(G. Wright)	GldShdk,ShrBlck,LckySahbra
5-17 M①⊗	10500 ft 20000 clm cd mi 284 :5821:29 1:583	6	6⁰	64	431	233	1:593	7.60	(G. Wright)	GldShdk,ShrBlck,LckySahbra
5- 7 M①⊗	10500 ft 20000 clm cd mi 293 1:01¹1:312:04	7	5⁰	52	42½iP3	2:011	3.40	(G. Wright)	FrstyZip,NchkoTar,CdrwdSam
4-30 M①⊗	9500 ft 22500 clm cd mi 3031:011:3112:004	4	6	643	543	2:002	6.10	(G. Wright)	HighHl.Yss,SnrsTime.FunMan
4-23 M①⊗	9500 ft 20000 clm cd mi 3031:0031:31 2:003	3	5	5	843	33	2:011	3.10	(G. Wright)	E.V.Pet,ShrBlack,RylTwinkle
4-16 M①⊗	9500 ft 20000 clm cd mi 284 :591:2931:592	2	5	5	9	453	33¼	2:00	*1.80	(G. Wright)	Mj-Duke,BeauChance,ShrBlck

St.—G. Wright—Tr.—D. Johnson
M(1)2:01 1977 24 4 5 5 33,685
M(1)2:01¹ 1976 42 4 4 5 26,483

C—Denotes Conventional Sulky
All Others To Use Modified Sulky

Close Decision

Sandu: No bonus points.

Bobcat Sue: 3 points for roughing it over the mile and 1 point for stretch gain on May 17. Total: 4.

Bobcat Sue is the clear choice and a reasonable bet at 1.30 to 1.

Result.

4th Race—1 Mile Pace—Claiming Allowance   Purse $7,500

Fractional Times: 294 1:001 1:314 2:031 FAST Off 9:01

H.N.	HORSE	P.P.	¼	½	¾	Str.	Fin.	Time	Drivers	Win	Place	Show	Eq.Odds
9.	BOBCAT SUE (14000)	2°	1	1	1	1½	1²	(2:03.1)	T. WING	$4.60	3.20	3.00	*1.30
4.	SPECIAL BYRD (10000)	1	3	2	2½	2½	2¼	(2:03.3)	C. GIAMANCO		13.40	12.00	29.20
2.	GAUM CATON (10000)	2	3	3	3²½	3¼	3¼	(2:03.4)	S. SERBES			5.20	7.40
7.	LUCKY MIRACLE (10000)	3	9	5	5¼	4¼	4½	(2:04.1)	L. GILMOUR				20.00
3.	FIRST ECHO (12000)	4	6	6°	6ʰᵈ	5½	5	(2:04.1)	G. WRIGHT				30.00
5.	SANDU (10000)	5	10	4	4ⁿᵏ	6⁵	6⁵	(2:05.1)	B. WEBSTER				2.50
10.	RESUME FIRE (10000)	8	18°	8	8	7¹	7¹	(2:05.2)	DEN. FILION				6.10
6.	NEDA ABBEGALE (12000)	6	9	7¹	9¹⁵	8¹³		(2:08)	E. COBB				73.10
1.	FIRST ME (10000)	5°	5°	10°	10	9¹⁹			M. GAGLIARDI				9.30
8.	MITEY TONYJOE (10000)	5°	2°x10°	10	10	10			C. MANZI				51.30

EXACTA — Nos. 9 & 4 PAID: $51.00

The Meadowlands   10th Race   June 7, 1977

Eliminate from contention 1 Canadian Red, 3 Informal, 4 Dodo Liner, 7 Louiston A, 8 Miss Mike's Lady, 9 Trent, and 10 Shore Black for poor recent form.

The contenders shape up as follows:

2 Over T.		**6 Have Faith**	
Current form	2	Current form	2
Class	0	Class	0
Consistency	2	Consistency	1
Post position	3	Post position	2
Driver	1	Driver	3
Total	8	Total	8

Close Decision

Over T.: Assign 1 point for roughing it and 1 for stretch gain in May 18 race. Total: 2 points.

Have Faith: 2 points for roughing it on May 21.

Analysis. Too close to call between Over T. and Have Faith. In addition, I have not counted 5 Royal Raider N. out of this race. Going down in class from $25,000 claimers, Royal Raider N. is a threat here. At odds of 4.80 to 1, though, Over T. is a good bet.

Result, 10th Race

10th Race–1 Mile Pace—Claiming Allowance   **Purse $10,500**

Fractional Times: 302 1:002 1:304 2:01 FAST Off 11:08

#	Horse						Time	Driver			
2.	OVER T. (25000)	5	5°	2°	23	11	(2:01)	W. MARKS	$11.40	5.00	$4.80
5.	ROYAL RAIDER N. (20010)	6°	3°	1	11	24	(2:01.1)	T. WING		5.20	3.20
6.	HAVE FAITH (20000)	1°	4°	4	32	3ns	(2:02)	E. LOHMEYER			3.20
10.	SHORE BLACK (20000)	7°	8°	6nk	4ns	(2:02)	G. WRIGHT			7.80
3.	INFORMAL (20000)	8°	7°	5nk	5nk	(2:02)	L. GILMOUR			3.90
1.	CANADIAN RED (20000)	3	6	6	4nd	6nd	(2:02)	G. STOLTZFUS			17.10
4.	DODO LINER (25000)	9	10	10	75	710	(2:02)	G. BOYLE			9.30
9.	MISS MIKE'S LADY (24000)	10	9	8½	81½	(2:04)	JA. DOHERTY			15.80
8.	TRENT (20000)	4°	1°	8nd	95	9°	(2:04.2)	R. TURCOTTE			35.00
7.	LEWISTON A. (20000)	2°	2	101	10	(2:06.2)	G. BERKNER			87.50

TRIFECTA — Nos. 2-5-6 PAID: $393.00

Result. 7th Race

7th Race–1 Mile Pace—Claiming Allowance   **Purse $11,400**

Fractional Times: 284 :594 1:30 2:00 FAST Off 10:18

#	Horse						Time	Driver			
3.	MAJOR SPEED (17500)	5	5	7°	12	12	(2:00)	V. DANCER	$10.00	5.00	$4.00
6.	E. B. TIME (17500)	7°	1	2nd	2nd	(2:00.2)	T. WING		7.00	4.40
8.	PETER PARKER (17500)	1	6	6nk	313	(2:00.2)	M. GAGLIARDI		5.80	9.00
2.	BERKSHIRE SKIPPER (21875)	6	4°	2nk	4nd	(2:00.4)	E. LOHMEYER			24.90
5.	FIRST MARK (21875)	2	3	3nk	51	(2:00.4)	M. FRIEDMAN			*2.00
1.	PINEHILL BELL (21000)	3	2°	71½	63	(2:00.4)	W. WARRINGTON			95.30
10.	MISS BILLIE VIC (21000)	9°	9	93	72	(2:01.2)	W. GEORGE			90.10
9.	RACING NEWS (21875)	10	8	83	8nd	(2:01.4)	W. MARKS			89.30
7.	ROYAL TWINKLE (21000)	8	10°	5°10	98	(2:01.4)	B. WEBSTER			7.60
4.	ADIOS RUN E. (26250)	4	7	81	10	(2:03.2)	M. PHILLIPS			9.70

EXACTA — Nos. 3 & 6 PAID: $49.60

The Meadowlands   7th Race   June 8, 1977

Throw out 1 Pinehill Bell, 2 Berkshire Skipper, 5 First Mark, 7 Royal Twinkle, 8 Peter Parker, 9 Racing News, and 10 Miss Billie Vic because of poor current form.

We are left with:

3 Major Speed		**6 E. B. Time**	
Current form	4	Current form	2
Class	0	Class	−2
Consistency	2	Consistency	1
Post position	2	Post position	2
Driver	3	Driver	3
Total	11	Total	6

4 Adios Run E.

Current form	2
Class	0
Consistency	1
Post position	2
Driver (unlisted)	
Total	5

Analysis. Major Speed, at odds of 4.00 to 1, is a clear choice in this race.

Exacta Wagering This Race

THE BERGEN COUNTY DENTAL ASSOCIATION PACE

CLAIMING PRICE $17,500

(Three-Year-Olds Granted 50% Allowance)
(Four-Year-Olds Granted 25% Allowance)
(Five-Year-Old & Older Mares Granted 20% Allowance)
(New Jersey Owned Or Bred)

ASK FOR HORSE BY PROGRAM NUMBER

5-1 **1** 21000 Red	**PINEHILL BELL**	b m, 6, by Pine Hill Star—Atomic Belle by Atomic Hanover

Driver-WALT WARRINGTON, 5-7-25 (155)   RED-GRAY-WHITE

Evelyn & Arthur Glasser, Fort Lee, N.J.

Trainer-W. Warrington

$18,652 — 5, 2:02¹ (⅝)
6– 1 M1⊗   11400 ft 17500 clm cd mi 30⁴1:00 1:29³2:00⁴   7   1°¹   1²   2¹   2:00¹ *3.60 (W.Warrington) HaveFaith,TrckyRhythm,Prcst 80–0
6–24 M1⊗   10500 ft 20000 clm cd mi 29¹1:00 1:30¹2:00¹   7   7   7°63   43   2:01   4.60 (W.Warrington) AdsRunE,PnhilBell,RylTwnkl 67–0
...

| **3-1** **2** 21875 Blue | **BERKSHIRE SKIPPER** | b h, 4, by Most Happy Fella—Meadow Bloom by Thorpe Hanover |

Driver-EDWARD LOHMEYER, 10-29-43 (140)   RED-GREEN-WHITE

Edward Lohmeyer Racing Stable, Mt. Holly, N.J.

Trainer-E. Lohmeyer

| **8-1** **3** 17500 White | **MAJOR SPEED** | b h, 7, by Speedster—Lynn Frost by Victory Song |

Driver-VERNON DANCER, 8-3-23 (141)   BLUE-GOLD

Niccolai, Dancer & Brummel, New Egypt, N.J.

Trainer-V. Dancer

| **12-1** **4** 26250 Green | **ADIOS RUN E.** | b g, 3, by Adios Ronnie—Star Mir by Burton Hanover |

Driver-MITCHELL PHILLIPS, 6-26-43 (145)   BLUE-GREEN-WHITE

Thomas Lail & Ella Borrelli, Swedesboro, N.J.

Trainer-T. Lail

| **10-1** **5** | **FIRST MARK** | b g, 9, by Mark Lobell—Hanover Chimes by Smokey Hanover |

Driver-MARK FRIEDMAN, 4-24-47 (162)   BLUE-GREEN-WHITE

Rosemary Friedman, Toms River, N.J.

Trainer-M. Friedman

21875		5-2	
Black			

E. B. TIME
$179,327 — 6, 2:003 (½)

Driver—TED WING, 7-30-48   (145)   GREEN-WHITE-RED   Trainer—T. Coyne

Jason, Inc., Secaucus, N.J.

b h, 8, by Race Time—Little Bee by Dale Frost

6-2	M1 Ⓒ	clm cd mi 292 :591¼ 2931:593 3 1 2 2 2nk 33¼	(T. Wing)

17500	6-1
Yellow	

ROYAL TWINKLE
$91,278 — 6, 2:03

Driver—BEN WEBSTER, 11-8-39   (130)   RED-WHITE-BLACK   Trainer—W. Marks

David Rosen & Tom Coyne, Flemington, N.J.

br m, 9, by Canny Scot—Twinkle Light by Light Brigade

21000	7
Pink	

PETER PARKER
$87,886 — 6, 2:022

Driver—LARRY RATHBONE, 1-5-47   (190)   WHITE-GREEN-BLACK   Trainer—L. Rathbone

Sark Stable, Freehold, N.J.

b g, 7, by Don Parker—Bonnie Fingo by Tar Heel

17500	8
Gray	

RACING NEWS
$16,174 — 3, 1:59 (⅝)

Driver—WALTER MARKS, 1-19-31   (107)   BROWN-WHITE   Trainer—W. Marks

Dead Heat Stables, Robbinsville, N.J.

b h, 4, by Race Time—Kiara Hanover by Tar Heel

21875	9
Purple	

MISS BILLIE VIC
$39,304 — 4, 2:003 (½)

Driver—CHARLES GEORGE, 5-31-27   (190)   RED-WHITE   Trainer—C. George

Stephen Sperone & Charles George, Dover, N.J.

ro m, 5, by Adios Vic—Miss Billie Rice by Meadow Rice

21000	20-1
Blue-Red	**10**

C—Denotes Conventional Sulky
All Others To Use Modified Sulky

PACE—1 MILE

Warming-Up Saddle Cloth
GRAY

PURSE $9,000

Exacta Wagering This Race

CLAIMING PRICE $15,000
(Four-Year-Old Mares Granted 40% Allowance)
(Four-Year-Olds Granted 25% Allowance)
(Five-Year-Old & Older Mares Granted 20% Allowance)

ASK FOR HORSE BY PROGRAM NUMBER

10-1 | CONTENTION
b m, 4, by Overall—Aunt Bess by Victory Song
Driver—PETER HAUGHTON, 9-22-54, (130) GREEN-WHITE-GOLD
Stephen M. Heller, Highland Park, Ill.
Trainer—J. DeSpain

$29,977 — 3, 2:013 (½)

21000 Red							
5–30 M1⊗	9000 ft 15000 clm cd mi 30:3021:01:1:3242:022	7	6	5°	5°	2½	21	2:023	4.10	(R.Remmen)	Crly,l.Nap,Mdw.Roy,E.B.Time	67-0
5–33 M1⊗	9000 ft 15000 clm cd mi 292 :5911:3022:004	4	8	7	3½	2½	2:012	4.00	(R.Remmen)	NrrmBrwn,Cntentn,DerryWall	73-0
5–11 M1⊗	9500 ft 17500 clm cd mi 2931:3031:593	2	4	4	3°	42½	66¾	2:01	7.50	(T.Merriman)	Crly,l.Nap,Mdw.Roy,E.B.Time	52-0
5– 4 M1⊗	8000 gd 12500 clm cd mi 29 :583:1:292:004	4	6	6	4°	32½	1ns	2:004	5.80	(T.Merriman)	Conten,OfHrmeBrdg,BluSue	47-0
4–28 RR⊗	6000 sy C3 cd mi 314:1:04 1:3522:063	8	8	5x 8	8⅕	6½	13.50	(T.Merriman)	Hslt.Bst,Bbct,Sue,Frm.Shn	55-0
4–21 RR⊗	6000 ft C3 cd mi 30 1:01:3122:034	5	3	1°	2½	6½	2:041	2.20	(T.Merriman)	Pud,Almh.,Hstlr.Bst,M.Edna

---

20-1 | FINE NOTE
b g, 9, by Fine Time—Riverview Hi Note by Mark Anthony
Driver—JAMES McGOVERN, 10-25-32, (167) GOLD-WHITE-BLACK
James McGovern, Cream Ridge, N.J.
Trainer—J. McGovern

$157,580 — 8, 2:024

15000 Blue							
5–26 M1⊗	10800 ft 15000 clm cd mi 30 :591:01:3042:004	6	7	7	6°	87	7103	2:03	57.40	(J.McGovern)	WtkiNrth,PlutusN,FrllwyRed	72-0
5– 4 LB½⊗	5000 sy 15000 clm cd mi 2911:0141:3312:042	8	8	85	8123	8123	2:044	43.80	(J.McGovern)	LothariohN,Mireille,VityNellie	53-0
4–28 M1⊗	9600 ft 15000 clm cd mi 2941:03 1:3442:031	1	4	4	3°	42½	66¾	2:044	14.30	(J.McGovern)	Tchr.Pet,StarKyle,BelleCntss	54-1
4– 2 M1⊗	8000 sy 15000 clm cd mi 322:1:03 1:3312:063	2	4	5°	78⅓	718¼	2:09	12.90	(J.McGovern)	KingOfIng.,Stdy.Sam.,Mr.Rod	44-1
3–28 M1⊗	8500 gd 17500 clm cd mi 30 :594:1:291:594	4	3°	9	101⅞	19⁹ⁱˢ	2:05	12.70	(J.McGovern)	SnrsTime,GdKgtStr,LrzzHan	48-0
3–23 M1⊗	8500 ft 17500 clm cd mi 2911:012:1:3332:023	2	1	2	2	84	781	2:041	6.80	(J.McGovern)	PcngDonut.Kill,Pat.Dr.Nrthrp	37-2

8-1 | ROYAL HORSE POWER
blk h, 5, by Blazing Comet—Miss Cleo Abbey by Spanish Abbey
Driver—GREG WRIGHT, 1-26-46 BLUE-WHITE
Roy Merlo, Windsor, Ontario, Canada
St.-G. Wright—Tr.-D. Johnson

$34,280 — 3, 2:002 (1)

15000 White							
5–30 M1⊗	9000 ft 15000 clm cd mi 282 :581:2821:594	7	1	2	2	32½	341	2:003	14.20	(D.Johnson)	GlenPatch,WPAdios,RylHPwr	72-0
5–18 M1⊗	9000 ft 15000 clm cd mi 2921:01	7	2	6°	87	751	98⅓	2:042	24.10	(G.Wright)	FbldYnk.,MoveAhd.,LegalHill	71-0
5– 4 M1⊗	9500 sy 17500 clm cd mi 3041:021:3222:024	2	1	3	6	7°	64¼	65¼	2:034	13.80	(G.Wright)	S.R.Bill, PinehillBell, Fab	52-0
4–25 M1⊗	8500 ft 17500 clm cd mi 2931:002:1:3121:2:003	2	4	2	2	2	2	2:012	16.60	(G.Wright)	ScottyGrtN.Fab.RylHrsPower	56-0
4–19 M1⊗	9500 ft 20000 clm cd mi 30 1:00:1:30 1:59	8	4	32½	84	871	2:02	17.00	(D.Johnson)	OrkalyN.PinehillBell,EBTime	61-0
4–12 M1⊗	ft Qua mi 2931:012:1:31 2:011	6	1	2	1	23	2:014	N.B.	(D.Johnson)	Owl,Ryl.H.Pwr.,Paula.Leader	82-0

12-1 | HOLLY RAINBOW
b m, 6, by Adios Vic—Honick Rainbow by Tar Heel
Driver—CHARLES GIAMANCO, 2-14-54, (146) RED-WHITE-BLACK
Stanley J. Sanders & John H. Larsen, East Meadow, N.Y.
St.-C. Giamanco—Tr.-A. Giamanco, Jr.

$35,504 — 5, 2:024

15000 Green							
5–25 M1⊗	9000 ft 15000 clm cd mi 282 :59 1:3042:011	4	7°	8	63¼	44¼	2:02	22.00	(C.Giamanco)	MjrSpeed,DuanShow,LgHill	79-0
5–13 M1⊗	9000 ft 15000 clm cd mi 2941:00 1:3132:004	6	8	87¼	611¼	2:02	11.40	(C.Giamanco)	BrvChris.DdlAlmh.DuanShow	68-0
5– 3 M1⊗	10500ft20000 clm cd mi 2931:00 1:30 1:59	2	4	4	4	64¼	79¼	2:004	22.80	(C.Giamanco)	FutureTm,SetGrtoN.,OrklyN.	69-0
4–18 Ppk⊗	1900 ft nw550 cd mi 2941:011:1:3042:012	5	7	7	711	67	2:024	11.50	(C.Giamanco)	EdieTwo.,EnsignG.,KellytuckJerry
4–23 Ppk⊗	2100 ft nw550 cd mi 3031:023:1:3242:024	2	5	5	651	56	2:04	4.90	(C.Giamanco)	Batabbe.KellytuckJerry.Sprkl.Lch.
3–12 Ppk⊗	2250 cd mi 2911:012:1:31 2:013	6	6	54¼	63¼	2:013	6.30	(C.Giamanco)	OwlRocket.,Mgc.Heels,L.Silvertime

---

6-1 | GOLD TRAIL N.
b g, 10, by Hundred Proof—Nithdale by Dillon Hall
Driver—HAROLD KELLY, 5-3-35 BLUE-GOLD-WHITE
Thelma & Marvin Collin & Helene & Roger Tinney, Old Bridge, N.J.
Trainer—P. Woitowicz

$11,785 — 9, 2:031

5–24 M1⊗	9000ft15000 clm cd 1¼:10232:0512:38 3:074	1°1	33	21	21	3:08	8.90	(H.Kelly)	FrtHest,GldTrlN.,JustlyFlirt	80-0
5–18 M1⊗	9000 gd 15000 clm cd mi :284 :59 1:3132:023	9	9	1° 2	1	44¼	712	2:05	13.10	(H.Kelly)	SplitDcsn,SmkyAfr,PatRich	71-0
5– 7 M1⊗	9000 ft 15000 clm cd mi 2841:0021:3042:001	7	2	2	33	36	2:012	11.60	(H.Kelly)	MrRdlf,DctrNrthrp,GoldTrlN.	70-0

6   15000   Black   15-1

$48,357 — 5, 2:02¹ (⅝)

MILLER KILLEAN   b h, 7, by Zip Tar—Mary Byrd by Poplar Byrd

Driver—BART SCARPA, 5-11-54 (145)

G.A.L.Young, J.Maratea & E.Napolitano, Brooklyn, N.Y.

Trainer-B. Scarpa

---

7   18000   Pink   3-1

$51,976 — 5, 2:00¹ (1)

†SNOWBALL EXPRESS   ro m, 6, by Bengazi Hanover—Miss Holly Dee by Kim Castle

Driver—CATELLO MANZI, 6-27-50 (170)

College Point Stables & Double C. Stable, New York, N.Y.

Trainer-D. Sider

---

8   18750   Gray   5-2

$11,256 — 2, T-2:00¹ (1)

IVALOT'S BOY   br h, 4, by Race Time—Ivalot by Thorpe Hanover

Driver—LLOYD GILMOUR

Milt Keslow, Scarsdale, N.Y.

Trainer-E. Soven

---

9   15000   Purple   12-1

$46,124 — 6, 2:01¹ (⅝)

CHUCKIE JIM   b g, 7, by Meadow Chuck—Henley's Dream by Harry's Dream

Driver—BEN WEBSTER, 11-8-39 (130)

Harry & Ruth Williams, Glen Rock, N.J.

Trainer-R. Remmen

---

10   15000   Blue-Red   5-1

$115,222 — 8, 2:00 (1)

SMOKY AFFAIR   blk g, 11, by Smoky Cloud—June Pick by Lord Pick

Driver—RAY REMMEN, 5-28-47 (180)

E. Larson, E. Thomas, H. Fleming & R. Remmen, Sask. Can.

Trainer-R. Remmen

C—Denotes Conventional Sulky

No. 4—FULLA BARON—Scratched

The Meadowlands   8th Race   June 8, 1977

The following horses can be eliminated because of poor current form: 2 Fine Note, 4 Holly Rainbow, 5 Gold Trail N., 6 Miller Killean, 8 Ivalot's Boy, 9 Chuckie Jim, and 10 Smoky Affair. Scratched: 3 Royal Horse Power.

The contenders:

1 Contention			7 Snowball Express		
Current form	2		Current Form	2	
Class	0		Class	0	
Consistency	1		Consistency	3	
Post position	3		Post position	2	(moves to
Driver	3		Driver	3	6 hole)
Total	9		Total	10	

Close Decision

Contention: 1 point for May 30 race.
Snowball Express: No bonus points.

Analysis. Snowball Express will be tough if he gets the lead easily or falls in early. At odds of 3.80 to 1, Snowball Express is a good bet. At 8 to 5, Contention is not.

8th Race-1 Mile Pace—Claiming Allowance Purse $9,000 Fractional Times: 291 :593 1:30 2:002 FAST Off 10:39

7.	SNOWBALL EXPRESS (18000)	6 1 1	12	12½	12½	(2:00.2)	C. MANZI	$9.60 4.80 3.80
5.	GOLD TRAIL N (15000)	4 2 2	2½	23	23	(2:00.4)	JA. DOHERTY	6.60 5.00
9.	CHUCKIE JIM (15000)	8 4 4	4½	32½	32½	(2:01.2)	B. WEBSTER	5.80
1.	CONTENTION (21000)	1 3 3	3½	41	41	(2:02)	P. HAUGHTON	16.10
8.	IVALOT'S BOY (18750)	7 8 8	63	5½	51½	(2:02.1)	L. GILMOUR	*1.60
10.	SMOKY AFFAIR (15000)	9 9 9	9	61	61	(2:02.2)	R. REMMEN	2.70
2.	FINE NOTE (15000)	2 6 6	5nd	7ns	7ns	(2:02.2)	J. McGOVERN	14.20
6.	MILLER KILLEAN (15000)	5 7 7	7	8¼	82	(2:02.3)	B. SCARPA	29.70
4.	HOLLY RAINBOW (18000)	3 5 5	8½	7½	9	(2:03)	C. GIAMANCO	61.20
3.	ROYAL HORSE POWER (15000)	Scratched						29.80

EXACTA — Nos. 7 & 5 PAID: $59.40

The Meadowlands   10th Race   June 8, 1977

Only E. V's Pet earns two points for current form. But for the sake of completeness, let's consider horses that have placed in a race during the past month.

2 Cedarwood Sam

Current form	1
Class	0
Consistency	2
Post position	3
Driver	1
Total	7

5 E. V's Pet

Current form	2
Class	-2
Consistency	1
Post position	2
Driver	3
Total	6

3 Metaro Hanover

Current form	1
Class	-2
Consistency	2
Post position	2
Driver	3
Total	6

7 Nechako Tar

Current form	1
Class	0
Consistency	0
Post position	1
Driver	not listed
Total	2

Analysis. Too difficult to call. Several horses seem evenly matched, or almost so, and none has the eight points required for a play.

Result.

10th Race—1 Mile Pace—Claiming Allowance   Purse $12,000   Fractional Times: 29 :58² 1:28¹ 1:59⁴ FAST Off 11:21

								Time	Driver				
7.	NECHAKO TAR (25000)	1	9	8	8	5½	1³	(1:59.4)	L. SPERENDI	$65.40	21.20	8.40	$31.70
1.	EAGLE ALMAHURST (37500)	9	2	4	4	2¾	2³½	(2:00.2)	J. LARENTE		15.00	11.80	20.10
9.	LEANIDES (31250)	9	7	6	5	6¹¼	3²	(2:00.4)	E. LOHMEYER			6.00	4.20
5.	E.V.'S PET (31250)	4	6	7	6°	6¹⁰	4ⁿˢ	(2:01)	T. MORGAN				3.30
4.	BOEHM'S DA PRIMA (25000)	3	6	5	2°	3ⁿᵏ	5ⁿᵏ	(2:01)	W. CAMERON				16.40
3.	METARO HANOVER (25000)	8	10	3	3°	4½	6ⁿᵈ	(2:01)	R. DAIGNEAULT				4.40
8.	P.K. (31250)	10	5	1°	7°	7ⁿᵏ	7ⁿᵏ	(2:01)	P. HAUGHTON				4.70
2.	‡CEDARWOOD SAM (25000)	2	1°	10	1	1ⁿᵏ	8¹¹	(2:03.1)	W. WARRINGTON				•3.10
10.	ARGYEL HARRY (25000)	10	3°	3°	10	9¹⁰	9¹³	(2:05.4)	J. ROSINO				70.10
6.	GAME BARON (25000)	6	8	9°	10	10	10		R. REMMEN				22.40

TRIFECTA — Nos. 7-1-9 PAID: $6,151.80

Trifecta Wagering This Race

PACE—1 MILE

Warming-Up Saddle Cloth
BLUE-RED

PURSE $12,000

CLAIMING PRICE $25,000
(Three-Year-Olds Granted 50% Allowance)
(Four-Year-Olds Granted 25% Allowance)
(Five-Year-Old & Older Mares Granted 20% Allowance)

ASK FOR HORSE BY PROGRAM NUMBER

8-1 Red 1 EAGLE ALMAHURST
$9,105 — 2, 2:03⅘
b g, 3, by High Ideal—Elegant Wick by Gene Abbe
Charter Oak Stable & Marie F. Boyle, Philadelphia, Pa.
Driver—JAMES LARENTE, 5-21-31 (160) BLUE-GOLD Trainer-J. Larente
M(1):59⅕ 1977 6 0 2 0 2,500
Fhld2:03⅘ 1976 9 2 2 1 9,105

5-30 M1⊗ 10000 ft nw4 cd mi 28⅘ :59⅕:2931:59⅕ 1 2¹ 76 2:02² 10.10 (J.Larente) SlapHappy,PureGeo,Sid A.Rqr. 72-0
5-21 M1⊗ 12000 ft 2c0000 clm cd mi 29⅘ :59 1:28⅕:1⅗33 10 8 4¹ 76 2:02² 48.40 (J.Larente) SilentCash,PureBret,J.C.Heel 74-0
5-13 M1⊗ 3000 ft nw10000 cd mi 29⅘ :294 1:01³:1:324²:024 4 6 6 4²⅘ 54 2:03³ *2.20 (J.Larente) MonarchHan,BuckDean,Newell
5-6 LB½⊗ 4500 ft nw12000 cd mi 291 :59⁴1:30²²:012 4 6 6 4²² 54 2:03³ *2.20 (J.Larente) BonitaVic,RiphHarry,DickChmp 68-0
4-29 LB½⊗ 4500 ft nw12000 cd mi 291 :59⁴1:31⁴:1:33 2:032 2 1 2 2²³ 54 2:04 *.80 (J.Larente) BonitaVic,EagleAlm,BudTrnto 54-0
4-22 LB½⊗ 4000 ft nw12000 cd mi 294 :59⁴1:02²:1:3172:022 2 2 2 2¹³ 2¹³ 2:02³ 1.90 (J.Larente) LavezzoHn,EagleAlm,GandLob 74-0

4-1 Blue 2 †CEDARWOOD SAM
$56,632 — 5, 2:00³ (⅝)
br h, 6, by Sampson Direct—Moonraker by Painter
Evelyn & Arthur Glasser, Fort Lee, N.J.
Driver—WALT WARRINGTON, 5-7-25 (150) RED-GRAY-WHITE Trainer-W. Warrington
M(1):59⅘ 1977 19 2 5 7 31,080
Gdn C(⅝)2:00³ 1976 36 5 7 4 22,179

5-28 M1⊗ 12000 ft25000 clm cd mi 283 :57³1:28 1:58⁴ 1 1 1 1¹³ 2¹ 1:59 12.40 (W.Warrington) ThorLob,Cdrwd.Sam,Leanides 83-0
5-21 M1⊗ 11000 ft25000 clm cd mi 304¹ :304¹1:01⁴:3042:004 7x 7 3x10 10 10¹⁰¹⁵:10¹⁵ 7.50 (W.Warrington) FrstyZip,NchkoTar,CdrwdSam 67-0
5-11 M1⊗ 12000 ft25000 clm cd mi 291 :59²1:30 1:593 9 4 4 53 41 1:591 4.70 (W.Warrington) CvlloRegale,Prsdbl,SunriseAll 52-0
5-4 M1⊗ 12000 gd nw8750 cd mi 303¹ :594 1:31³:1:584 1 1 2 1 74² 9¹1 2:043 10.00 (W.Warrington) PrmntHn,CsN.Blly,CdrwdSam 50-1
4-23 M1⊗ 12000 ft20000 clm cd mi 301 :59⁴1:2931:584 2 1 1 2¹ 33 2:00¹ 10.00 (W.Warrington) MetaroHn,MsE.Drct,MmiBch,ManCmro 62-0
4-16 M1⊗ 12000 ft30000 clm cd mi 2921:001:31:31 2:001 4 x4x10 10 10¹⁵10¹⁵ 6.70 (W.Warrington) ChrlSprks,MtroHan,RylSpctr 79-0

5-1 White 3 METARO HANOVER
$56,265 — 5, 1:594 (⅝)
b g, 5, by Best Of All—Miss Step N. by False Step
Andrew Palermo & P. & M. Corapi, Massapequa, N.Y.
Driver—REJEAN DAIGNEAULT, 2-19-48 (135) RED-BLUE St.-R. Daigneault—Tr.-S. Villante
M(1):594 1978 40 5 4 5 30,884
LB(⅛):594 1977 19 2 1 1 11,825

5-28 M1⊗ 11000 ft22500 clm cd mi 293 :59 1:28⁴1:591 2 3 3 2¹³ 2¹³ 1:592 5.90 (R.Daigneault) Shwy,Gale,OrkalyN,ThorLbll. 71-0
5-21 M1⊗ 11000 ft22500 clm cd mi 283 :57²1:27⁴1:59 9 4 4 41 41 2:032 20.60 (B.Webster) Har.McElln,PrB.Hope,Sun.Tm 74-0
5-11 M1⊗ 11000 ft22500 clm cd mi 294 :593¹1:302:001 1 2 1 74² 9¹1² 2:032 5.70 (R.Daigneault) MajorOk,OrkalyN,ClvrTruax 67-0
5-4 M1⊗ 11000 sy22500 clm cd mi 303¹1:01¹:3032:023 4 5 3 35 35 2:032 4.40 (R.Daigneault) JmbDllr,ClvrTruax,MetaroHan 52-0
4-29 M1⊗ 9500 ft20000 clm cd mi 284¹1:001¹:3232:022 5 5 2⁰¹ 1¹³ 2²² 2:022 3.30 (R.Daigneault) MetaroHn,CsN.Blly,CdrwdSam 50-1
4-22 M1⊗ 8500 ft 17500 clm cd mi 29 :59³1:2932:00 4 1 1 33 23 2:001 23.30 (R.Daigneault) ChrlSprks,MtroHan,BigBNck 79-0

10-1 Green 4 BOEHM'S DA PRIMA
$43,575 — 4, 2:02³
b g, 9, 4, by Airliner—Greentree Marie by Tar Heel
Bernard Isaacs, Shaker Heights, Ohio
Driver—WARREN CAMERON, 5-29-40 (154) RED-WHITE St.-W. Cameron—Tr.-M. Purcell
M(1)2:021 1977 16 1 3 0 10,605
YR2:023 1976 35 4 5 4 26,351

5-28 M1⊗ ft Qua mi 292¹1:003¹:3132:014 3 7⁵ 7⁰ 2⁰ 24 2:014 N.B. (G.Berkner) BhmDPrm,BrnBrat,TrueBrnss 81-0
5-25 M1⊗ 9⁰⁰ ft nw5500 cd mi 283 :57⁴1:28¹1:58 10 7 7 10¹²10¹¹10¹⁵ 24.60 (P.Haughton) BnbryBlcnt,AnmoHn,Qrtette 79-0
5-11 M1⊗ 9000 ft nw5000 cd mi 29 :593¹1:00⁴¹:3032:014 4 2⁰ 33 74⁴ 2:014 2.90 (W.Cameron) GtdM.Boy,DrmMaJR.,DrmDigt 67-0
4-25 M1⊗ 8000 ft nw5000 cd mi 293 :583¹:282¹1:593 4 4 4 2¹³ 2nk 1:593 22.70 (W.Cameron) DonLpz,BhmDaPrma,BigBNck 69-0
4-18 M1⊗ 8000 ft nw5250 cd mi 294 :59³1:31⁴2:012 5 3⁰ 1 1 3³ 10⁸³ 2:031 3.40 (W.Cameron) Fellowship,TopTrick,PlEHrtg 56-0

7-2 Blue 5 E. V.'S PET (J)
$47,803 — 3, 2:002 (†)
br g, 4, by
Driver—TERRY MORGAN, 8-15-43 (165) BLUE-BLACK-GOLD Trainer-T. Morgan
M(1):591 1977 17 3 1 1 17,610
M(1)2:002 1976 29 11 4 1 47,803

5-28 M1⊗ 11000 ft22500 clm cd mi 293 :59 1:28⁴1:591 2 3 3 2¹³ 1¹³ 1:591 6.20 (T.Morgan) E.V.Pet,MetaroHn,HarMcElln 83-0
5-20 M1⊗ 10⁰⁰ft+20000± clm cd mi 30 :59²1:30 2:001 2 3 3x 3x 9 9¹4 8¹3 2:031 7.80 (S.Sparacino) Sugarlane,Lky.Baron,EllLang 71-0
5-7 M1⊗ 11000 ft 22500 clm cd mi 301 :59²1:31¹:3032:00 8 7 7 78¹ 65¹ 2:01 7.80 (S.Sparacino) RumWave,BlRobB,BrkshrSkip 61-0
4-30 M1⊗ 10000 ft 22500 clm cd mi 301 :59²1:29³1:592 5 3⁰ 1 1 33 10⁸³ 2:002 8.80 (S.Sparacino) HiaHLyss,SnrsTime,FunMan 62-0

6 12-1 Black

GAME BARON $88,603 — 3, 1:59² (1)
br h, 6, by Baron Hanover—Miracle Bess by Miracle Knight
Eric & Harry Whebby, Dartmouth, N.S., Canada
Driver—RAY REMMEN, 5-28-47 (180) WHITE-GREEN-GOLD
Trainer—R. Remmen

4-23 M¹⊗	9500 ft 20000 clm cd mi 30³:30³:30³:2:03	4	4	6	4	1°	11¹	13	2:03	12.60	(S.Sparacino)
4-19 M¹⊗	ft Qua mi 29²⋅:58³:30²:2:021	4	3	1	1	11¼	22		2:023	N.B.	(S.Sparacino)

7 12-1 Yellow 25000

NECHAKO TAR $91,492 — 6, 1:58² (1)
blk g, 7, by Tar Duke—Glen Lady by Genghis Khan
Al Ochsner & Louis Sperendi, Freehold, N.J.
Driver—LOUIS SPERENDI, 6-21-41 (145) GREEN-WHITE-GOLD
Trainer—L. Sperendi

8 5-1 Pink 31250

P. K. $11,994 — 3, 2:05
b g, 4, by Adios—Pretty Peggy by Miracle Knight
Forecast Stable, Inc., Great Neck, N.Y.
Driver—PETER HAUGHTON, 9-22-54 (130) GREEN-WHITE-GOLD
Trainer—Tr. B. Peck

9 6-1 Gray 31250

LEANIDES $19,949 — 3, 2:01³
b g, 5, by Newport Duke—Amy by Tar Heel
Kal Leibowitz & Mark Goldman, Watchung, N.J.
Driver—EDWARD LOHMEYER RED-GREEN-WHITE
Trainer—E. Lohmeyer

10 15-1 Purple 25000
Blue-Red

ARGYEL HARRY $56,599 — 5, 2:00¹ (1)
b h, 6, by Lehigh Hanover—Argyel Florence by Steinway Grattan
G. & F. Moradante, S. Blackman & R. Rohde Ridgefield, N.J.
Driver—JULIAN ROSINO, 3-22-23 (155) ORANGE-GRAY
Trainer—J. Koth

C—Denotes Conventional Sulky
No. 10—FLYING TUFTS—Scratched

PACE—1 MILE

Warming-Up Saddle Cloth
RED

PURSE $11,000

CLAIMING PRICE $22,500
(Four-Year-Olds Granted 25% Allowance)
(Five-Year-Old & Older Mares Granted 20% Allowance)

ASK FOR HORSE BY PROGRAM NUMBER

1 · 4-1 · 22500 · Red
HURRICANE TODD ch g, 7, by Watchful—Handy Way by Handy Dillon
$28,870 — 5, 2:02¹ (½) Driver—NORMAN DAUPLAISE, 1-29-40 BROWN-GOLD-WHITE Evelyn Glasser, Fort Lee, N.J. (139) Trainer—N. Dauplaise

2 · 5-1 · 28125 · Blue
RUM WAVE b h, 4, by Rum Customer—Dixie's Shadow by Shadow Wave
$17,527 — 3, 2:03 (½) Driver—GREG WRIGHT, 1-26-46 BLUE-WHITE Carlini Bros. Stable, Windsor, Ontario, Canada (165) Trainer—G. Wright

3 · 12-1 · 22500 · White
JONATHAN HANOVER b h, 8, by Lehigh Hanover—Joanna Hanover by Tar Heel
$179,968 — 5, 1:59² (½) Driver—JIM MARCUS, 12-17-34 CREAM-MAROON Jim R. Marcus & Count Ricci Farms, Inc., N.Y., N.Y. (190) Trainer—J. Marcus

4 · 8-1 · 22500 · Green
BREV HANOVER br g, 7, by Star's Pride—Brief Romance by Victory Song
$32,321 — 6, 1:58³ (1) Driver—JAMES DOHERTY, 9-27-40 RED-WHITE-GREEN Alan Parker, St. Catharines, Ontario, Can. (155) Trainer—W. Wellwood

5 · 7-2 · 22500 · Green
FUTURE TIME b m, 5, by Race Time—Helen Jane by Dancer Hanover
$24,404 — 4, 2:02³ Driver—LLOYD GILMOUR, 10-3-45 RED-GREY Joseph Martorano & Meadowlark Stables, Poughkeepsie, N.Y. (160) Trainer—R. Bencal

6-1 Black 27,000
5-12 M(1)⊗ 13800 ft 27500 clm cd mi 28¹ :56⁴1²/¹1:5⁴ 8 2⁹ 2⁹ 5⁹ 9¹0⅞9³⅜ 2:02³ 4.60 (L.Gilmour) BrdStr,HighH,Lyss,V.H.Drm 73-0
5-3 M(1)⊗ 10500ft20000 clm cd mi 29²1:00 1:30 1:59 9 3 3 4 2¹3 12¹ 1:59 6.90 (L.Gilmour) FutureTm,SctGrtnN,OrklyN, 69-0

6 Yellow 22500
PRIMA IRISH
$34,246 — 5, 1:59⁴ (1)
b g, 6, by Irish Grattan—Ortance Adios by Champ Adios
J. Morrissey, M. Gawza & M. & R. Feagan, Dundas, Ont., Can. (140)
Driver—W. (Buddy) GILMOUR, 7-23-32. RED-GRAY Trainer—D. Sider
6-9 M(1)⊗ 13000 sy27500 clm cd mi 31⁴1:03 1:33³2:03⁴ 7 7 7 6⁶¹ 7⁹¹ 2:05³ 9.40 (L.Gilmour) M(1)1:2-0⅓ 1977 /13 1 2 1 11,730
6-2 M(1)⊗ 13000 ft 27500 clm cd mi 29² :59 1:29¹1:58³ 5 5 6 7⁷ 7⁴⅓ 5²¹ 1:59 12.10 (L.Gilmour) M(1)1:59⁴ 1976 18 5 1 0 12,320
5-28 M(1)⊗ 14000 ft 30000 clm cd mi 29³ :59³1:29¹1:59 6 6 5⁵ 5⁴⅜ 3²¹ 1:59² 7.10 (L.Gilmour) ThorLbil,BnbryBlcount,Bossill 55-0
5-23 M(1)⊗ 14000 ft nw11000 cd mi 28³ :57⁴1:28 1:57⁴ 8 8 8 6⁸ 5⁸ 1:59² 21.60 (L.Gilmour) ManCnmro,PrvtLabel,FrstyZip 75-0
5-13 M(1)⊗ 14000 ft nw11000 cd mi 28³ :59 1:29¹1:59⁴ 6 8 8⁸ 7⁹³ 6¹ 2:00¹ 19.40 (L.Gilmour) PnsvBrt,ShrpShtrA,RightOvr 83-0
5-4 M(1)⊗ 12500 gd nw8750 cd mi 30³1:00¹3122:02² 4 5 5 5⁵ 6⁴ 2:03 15.00 (L.Gilmour) TarpLouise,Lt.CoLJoe,KpCool 73-0
CvllorRegale,Prsdbl,SunriseAll 52-0

10-1 Pink 28125
OVER T.
$14,492 — 3, 2:02³ (1)
b h, 4, by Overcall—Charming Gail by Bullet Hanover
Gerald Popper, Englishtown, N.J. (137)
Driver—WALTER MARKS, 1-19-31. WHITE-BLACK-MAROON Trainer—W. Marks
6-7 M(1)⊗ 10500 ft 20000 clm cd mi 30²1:00²3042:01 2 2 2¹ 1¹ 1¹ 2:01 4.70 (W.Marks) M(1)2:02³ 1976 32 6 2 2 14,492
5-27 M(1)⊗ 10500 ft 20000 clm cd mi 29²1:00³3¹2941:58⁴ 1 5 3⁰ 2³⅜ 5⁶⅜ 2:00 6.00 (W.Marks) OverT.,RovalRaidaN,HaveFaith 60-0
5-18 M(1)⊗ 11400gd17500 clm cd mi 29⁴ :59 1:29¹1:59 6 6 4³ 3⁴³ 1⁵ 1:59 14.90 (W.Marks) GldShdk,ShrBlck,LckySahbra 84-0
5-7 M(1)⊗ 10500 ft 20000 clm cd mi 29³1:01³3¹22:004 1 2 1⁰ 2² 3³⅜ 2:01 10.20 (T.Wing) OverT.,Hurr.Todd,Tenn.John 71-0
4-23 M(1)⊗ 9500 ft 20000 clm cd mi 30³1:00¹3¹31:31 2:03 4 2¹ 4²¹ 7⁶³ 2:01⁴ 31.30 (W.Marks) +PmHllBill,+LckyShbr,+ShrBlck 61-0
4-14 M(1)⊗ 9500 ft 20000 clm cd mi 29²1:01 1:3142:02⁴ 9 9 8⁸ 9⁷³ 4³¹ 2:03 8.20 (G.Klein) RngrAndy,Ambiguous,Precast 59-0

12-1 Gray 22500
LUCKY SAHBRA
$11,920 — 4, 2:02¹
b h, 5, by Fashion Tip—Bianca by Torpid
Marvin J. Gross, Cleveland, Ohio
Driver—MICHAEL GAGLIARDI, 8-25-48 (175) Trainer—M. Gagliardi—Tr.—A. Modiano
6-10 M(1)⊗ 10500 ft 20000 clm cd mi 29 :59⁴1:3042:00 5 2 1 3¹¹ 2² 2:00 5.70 (M.Gagliardi) M(1)d2:02¹ 1976 16 4 6 4 7,620
5-27 M(1)⊗ 10500 ft 20000 clm cd mi 29²1:00³3¹2941:58⁴ 5 4 5³³ 6⁴ 6⁴¹ 2:004 3.70 (M.Gagliardi) Sugarlane, OrkalyN, Fab 66-0
5-17 M(1)⊗ 10500 ft 20000 clm cd mi 28⁴ :58²1:29 1:58³ 7 8 7⁸ 5³³ 3³⅜ 1:59³ 5.50 (M.Gagliardi) GldShdk,ShrBlck,LckySahbra 84-0
5-11 M(1)⊗ 10500 ft 20000 clm cd mi 29⁴ :59⁴3¹31:5941:58⁴ 6 6 5³ 4²¹ 2¹⅞ 1:59¹ 10.80 (M.Gagliardi) GldShdk,SctGrtnN,LkyShbra 81-0
5-2 M(1)⊗ 9000 ft nw5000 cd mi 29¹ :59³1:3¹31:3122:004 5 7 7⁷ 1⁰² 2nk 2:00² 5.50 (M.Gagliardi) +PmHllBill,+LckyShbr,+ShrBlck 61-0
4-25 M(1)⊗ 8000 ft nw5000 cd mi 30 1:00²1:3032:003 5 5 6⁶ 2²³ 1⅞ 2:00² *2.20 (M.Gagliardi) LckyShbr,ArrvJohn,BrgtTygr 67-0
ChrDplmt,FrthEst,TrtwdBud 56-0

5-1 Purple 27000
GOLDEN WALTZ
$64,622 — 4, 2:02¹ (‡)
b m, 5, by Golden Money Maker—Terpsichore by Dancer Hanover
Woodstock Stud, Monticello, N.Y. (160)
Driver—JAMES LARENTE, 5-21-31 BLUE-GOLD Trainer—J. Larente
5000 Lc mi 30³1:01¹31:32 2:003 2 1 3 3¹⅜ 2³ 2:004 11.35 (G.Gendron) BB(⅞)2:013 1977 14 3 4 3 13,269
6-6 BB⊗ 5000 Lc mi 30³1:01¹3¹31:312:003 2 1 3 4 3¹⅜ 2⅜ 2:004 31.10 (J.Bruyere) BB(⅞)2:021 1976 15 16 4 6 4 6,491
5-25 BB⊗ 600 ft Pref mi 30¹1:01¹3¹3¹3312:02 6 4⁰ 1⁰ 5⁵ 2⁰⁴ 5.70 (J.Bruyere) EdgarSen,Gldn,Waltz,ParsonLbil.
5-18 BB⊗ 600 ft Pref mi 31 :59 1:29¹1:58³ 5 5 5⁵¹ 3³³ 3⁴¹ 2:01¹ 8.75 (J.Bruyere) Mar.Best,Dtch,Almh.,Smn.O.Mrt.
5-11 BB⊗ 600 ft Pref mi 31¹1:03¹13¹3232:021 1 3 3⁰ 2² 2⁰¹ 2.40 (J.Bruyere) Daleirish,CavalierAngus,Mar.Best
5-2 BB⊗ 5000 ft w4000 Lc mi 30⁴1:00⁴13¹22:021 4 4⁰ 4² 2²¹ *1.40 (J.KingJr) Gldn,Blaze,Gldn.Waltz,KpCool
4-20 BB⊗ 6000 ft nw6250 cd mi 28²1:00²1:30 2:01 8 8 8⁴⁴ 6²¹ 2:01 16.80 (J.Bruyere) Gldn.Waltz,MoodMoney,Tarp.Ace
GigoloAngus,TwoT.Geo.,Bnkr.Lbil.

15-1 Blue-Red 22500
EIGHTY FOUR ACE
$31,314 — 4, 1:59⁴ (1)
br h, 5, by Tar Heel—Arlene Dares by Meadow Gene
Milton & Miriam Prince, Livingston, N.J.
Driver—JIM KING, JR., 2-16-52 (140) GREEN-RED-WHITE Trainer—E. Looney
6-11 M(1)⊗ 11000 ft nw22000 clm mi 28³ :59¹13:021:592 7 7 8⁷ :74¹ 7⁷³ 2:01 24.80 (J.KingJr) M(1)2:012 1977 20 3 0 1 15,095
6-6 BB⊗ 13000 ft 22500 clm cd mi 30¹ :59 1:29¹1:583 8 8 9 9⁵ 9⁵³ 2:004 63.90 (J.KingJr) M(1)1:594 1976 39 5 3 5 23,773
5-26 M(1)⊗ 14000 ft nw10500 cd mi 29⁴ :58²1:2831:582 6 6 4⁶ 85¹ 97 1:594 35.30 (J.KingJr) SnrsTm,HrrcnTodd,JnthnHan 72-0
5-13 M(1)⊗ 14000 ft nw11000 cd mi 29⁴1:00⁴13:022:002 5 4⁰ 104¹ 2:012 37.40 (J.KingJr) ManCnmro,PrvtLabel,FrstyZip 75-0
5-2 BB⊗ 14000 gd nw11000 cd mi 29² :59¹12:9¹1:59 5 8 9⁸ 10⁷ 104⅜ 2:002 19.90 (J.KingJr) Key.Atlas,DrmsBrm,KiwiBrmm 72-0
4-27 M(1)⊗ 9500 ft nw6250 cd mi 30²1:00¹31:31 2:021 8 8 8⁶³ 6²¹ 2:021 10.80 (J.KingJr) TarpLouise,Lt.CoLJoe,KpCool 68-0
PepLeeDir,WavEddie,V.Time 68-0
Egtly.F.Ace,Crg.Rom.,Mk.Mrv. 56-0

C—Denotes Conventional Sulky
No. 1—SUGARLANE—Scratched

Comment. An upset, but not unpredictable in this field.

The Meadowlands   1st Race   June 18, 1977

Eliminate 2 Rum Wave, 3 Jonathan Hanover, 4 Brev Hanover, 5 Future Time, 6 Prima Irish, 8 Lucky Sahbra, 9 Golden Waltz, and 10 Eighty Four ace for lack of success over the past month.

The contenders:

1 Hurricane Todd		7 Over T.	
Current form	4	Current form	4
Class	0	Class	−2
Consistency	3	Consistency	2
Post position	3	Post position	1
Driver	3	Driver	1
Total	13	Total	6

Analysis. Hurricane Todd is a real overlay at odds of 2.60 to 1.

1st Race—1 Mile Pace—Claiming Allowance   *Purse $11,000*   Fractional Times: 284 :59 1:283 1:582 FAST   Off 8:00

Horse							Time	Driver				
1. HURRICANE TODD (22500)	1	2	1	1	1²	1ns	(1:58.2)	N. DAUPLAISE	$7.20	4.40	2.80	*32.60
9. GOLDEN WALTZ (27000)	3	3	4	4	2³	2²	(1:58.2)	J. LARENTE		8.00	6.20	7.40
2. RUM WAVE (28125)	4	4	5	7	4⁴	3³	(1:58.4)	G. WRIGHT			3.40	4.70
8. LUCKY SAHBRA (22500)	9	9	7	6°	7¹	4¹	(1:59.2)	M. GAGLIARDI				23.80
10. EIGHTY FOUR ACE (22500)	10	10	10	10	8ⁿᵈ	5³	(1:59.3)	J. KING, JR.				56.80
7. OVER T. (28125)	8	2	3	2	2¹	6¹	(1:59.4)	W. MARKS				8.50
6. PRIMA IRISH (22500)	7	7	9	9	9¹	7¹³	(2:00)	W. GILMOUR				4.80
4. BREV HANOVER (22500)	6	6	8	3	6³	8⁴	(2:00.1)	JA. DOHERTY				10.20
3. JONATHAN HANOVER (22500)	5	5	6	5°	2°	9¹	(2:01)	J. MARCUS				22.30
5. FUTURE TIME (27000)	5	7	8	8	5ⁿᵏ	10	(2:01.1)	L. GILMOUR				4.80

PACE–1 MILE

Warming-Up Saddle Cloth
BLACK

PURSE $14,000

ASK FOR HORSE BY PROGRAM NUMBER

Exacta Wagering This Race

CLAIMING PRICE $30,000
(Four-Year-Olds Granted 25% Allowance)

5-1 — 1 — 30000 Red
MANERO'S CANONERO ch g, 6, by Bullet Hanover—Calico Hanover by Hickory Smoke
Driver—JAMES GIORGIANNI, Gary Safier, Milt Joseph & James Giorgianni, Dover, N.J.
Trainer—J. Giorgianni

12-1 — 2 — 37500 Blue
G. C. CHILDS br g, 4, by Egyptian Dancer—Cita Song by Gay Song
Driver—TED WING, O. M. R. Company, Inc., Beverly Hills, Calif.
Trainer—A. Craig

5-1 — 3 — 30000 White
GOYO ro h, 7, by Canadian Dares—Betty's Folly by Callie G.
Driver—WALT WARRINGTON, Evelyn & Arthur Glasser, Fort Lee, N.J.
Trainer—W. Warrington

4-1 — 4 — 37500 Green
BANBURY BELCOUNT ch g, 4, by Tarport Count—Rona Belle by Direct Rhythm
Driver—JAMES DOHERTY, Milton S. Wahl, Wilmington, Del.
Trainer—D. Marusco

8-1 — 5 — 37500
SUNRISE G. B. b h, 4, by Scotch Luck—Saunders Speed by Laguerre Hanover
Driver—EDDIE COBB, Nevacal Stable, Inc., & H. Thompson, Passaic, N.J.
Trainer—E. Cobb

CAMERAS ARE NOT PERMITTED ON THE PREMISES

C—Denotes Conventional Sulky
All Others To Use Modified Sulky

---

6   Black   6-1
TUTTI FRUITI   b h, 7, by Tar Heel—Lumber Bonnie by Adios
East Shire Stable, Inc., Massapequa, N.Y.
Driver-REJEAN DAIGNEAULT, 2-19-48   (135)   RED-BLUE   St.-R. Daigneault—Tr.-S. Villante

$113,245 — 6, 2:01³

4-30 M1⊗	9500 ft nw9500 cd mi 29¹ :59⁴1:29¹:59¹	4	6	6	4	3⁴	1:59³	13.30	(E. Cobb)
3-31 M1⊗	9500 ft nw4 cd mi 30 1:01¹1:32²2:02	6	6	4	2°	3¹¹	2:03	2.50	(E. Cobb)

---

7   Yellow   3-1
STORY BOOK CHIP   b h, 6, by Gene Abbe—Select Time by Race Time
Albert G., Jerry & Melvin P. Segal, Matthews, N.C.
Driver-PETER HAUGHTON, 9-22-54   (130)   GREEN-WHITE-GOLD

$84,199 — 5, 2:00² (1)

---

8   Pink   8-1
THOR LOBELL   b g, 5, by Noble Victory—Title Freight by Titan Hanover
Glenn Stables, Penn Valley, Pa.
Driver-ABE STOLTZFUS, 4-9-42   (165)   RED-WHITE-BLACK   St.-A. Stoltzfus—Tr.-C. Boyd

$51,452 — 4, 1:59⁴ (1)

---

9   Gray   12-1
GOOD YANKEE   b h, 4, by Good Time—Virginia Yankee by Yankee Hanover
Milton Keslow, Scarsdale, N.Y.
Driver-W. (Buddy) GILMOUR, 7-23-32   (140)   RED-GRAY   Trainer-D. Sider

$19,281 — 2, T-2:02 (1)

Purple   37500

The Meadowlands   5th Race   June 18, 1977

None of the following score enough points for current form to be considered contenders: 2 G. C. Childs, 3 Goyo, 5 Sunrise G. B., 6 Tutti Fruiti, 7 Story Book Chip, and 9 Good Yankee.

This leaves:

1 Manero's Canonero

Current form	2
Class	0
Consistency	2
Post position	3
Driver	2
Total	9

8 Thor Lobell

Current form	4
Class	−2
Consistency	1
Post position	1
Driver	3
Total	7

4 Banbury Belcount

Current form	3
Class	−2
Consistency	1
Post position	2
Driver	2
Total	6

Analysis. Manero's Canonero has enough of an edge over the remaining contenders to be the play here, particularly at the attractive odds of 4.20 to 1.

Result.

5th Race—1 Mile Pace—Claiming Allowance   Purse $14,000   Fractional Times: 29² :59¹ 1:29 1:58² FAST Off 9:44

1.	MANERO'S CANONERO (30000)	1	3	3	2	1¹¹	1ʰᵈ	(1:58.2)	J. GIORGIANNI	$10.40 6.60 5.00	$4.20
9.	GOOD YANKEE (37500)	2	2	2	3	2¹¹	2²¹	(1:58.2)	W. GILMOUR	13.80 9.20	15.20
5.	SUNRISE G. B. (37500)	5	5	5	4°	3²¹	3²¹	(1:58.4)	E. COBB	13.60	29.50
3.	GOYO (30000)	9	4	4°	6	4¹¹	4ⁿᵈ	(1:59.2)	W. WARRINGTON		*2.20
6.	TUTTI FRUTTI (30000)	6	7	6	7°	5¹³	5²³	(1:59.2)	R. DAIGNEAULT		8.30
8.	THOR LOBELL (30000)	8	9°	7°	7°	6¹³	6ⁿᵏ	(2:00)	A. STOLTZFUS		9.20
2.	G. C. CHILDS (37500)	2	6	8	8	7¹²	7²¹	(2:00)	T. WING		15.00
4.	BAINBURY BELCOUNT (37500)	4	1	1	1	8¹³	8²¹	(2:00.3)	JA. DOHERTY		5.90
7.	STORYBOOK CHIP (30000)	7	8	8	9	9	9	(2:01)	P. HAUGHTON		3.90

EXACTA—Nos. 1 & 9 PAID: $189.60

8
Conclusion: Beating the Races

We can best summarize the results of previous chapters by discussing the recommendations John Scarne, an expert on gambling, gives to the horse-racing bettor. Scarne first advises us to stay within a pre-planned total budget, including the price of transportation, etc., when we go to the races. He then advises us to bet the favorite to show. "I don't say that this advice will win you any money, but it will cut down your losses."

We have already discussed the advantages of win, place, and show betting and will not repeat the arguments in favor of "one way" betting, whether to win, to place, or to show.

Scarne then adds the following "rules":

1. Bet cash only, never on credit; the temptation to bet beyond your means in trying to recoup your losses is too difficult for most people to resist. Credit betting ruins more gamblers than anything else. Remember that "money you don't have on you, you can't lose."
2. Bet on a horse running at a track where the state and track percentage cut is the smallest, because if you win, the mutuel payoff price will be more.
3. Make as few bets as possible so that the money wagered, if lost, won't disturb you mentally.
4. Bet your horse to show if you can.
5. Stay away from parlays, "if" money and back-to-back bets.
6. Always remember that when you pick a winner, you were lucky; it wasn't good handicapping. And don't forget that "you can beat a race, but not the races."*

For the most part Scarne's rules are well thought out and constitute good advice for the majority of horse players. However, I would like to comment a bit more fully on each rule.

*John Scarne, *Scarne's New Complete Guide to Gambling* (New York: Simon & Schuster, 1974), p. 85.

195

1. The advice to bet only cash is excellent. The temptation to make up losses as soon as possible is almost always counterproductive. If you hit a losing streak, the only reasonable thing to do is to cool off for a while before you resume wagering. Don't insist to yourself that you *must* recoup your losses immediately. Instead, write off what you have lost, insisting to yourself that you will begin fresh. This will relieve you of the pressures and anxieties of having to win back money you have lost. Scarne rightly stresses that it is essential for you to keep within your means. Never play with the rent money.

2. The advice to bet at a track where the state and track percentage is the lowest is obviously sound. But if you live in New York and raceways in California take the smallest cut of your racing dollar, it will not be worthwhile for you to fly back and forth from New York to California, to take advantage of the better break in the pari-mutuel system on the West Coast.

3. The advice to make as few bets as possible is obviously good. One of the central contentions of this book is that spot betting is the only route to success. To win at the races, you must pick and choose your spots, never wagering on every race on the card.

4. Show betting is one route to success, but it is not the only route, and it is not paved with gold. However, if you are willing to settle for smaller profits, you can unquestionably make money at the races by confining your wagering to show bets.

5. According to the 5-percent rule, your wagers should not exceed 5 percent of your kitty at any one time. If you follow this advice, you will avoid parlays and other "do or die" kinds of wagering.

6. Only with Scarne's last recommendation do I find myself in complete disagreement. For the able handicapper, selecting winners is not a matter of luck. If it were, it would be difficult to understand why some persons win over the long haul while others are constant losers. It would also be difficult to understand how, if the outcome of a race cannot be handicapped, more than 35 percent of all winning horses in harness racing are favorites and 70 percent or more of all favorites finish in the money. If the outcome of a race were due to chance or luck, it would be very unlikely that the public's choices could enjoy such a high degree of success.

The advice that "you can beat a race, but not the races" is also open to question. The reason for taking this adage seriously is that each dollar wagered successfully returns only 80 cents to the bettor. In racing, unlike many other forms of gambling, you are pitting your

handicapping skills against the public (more accurately, that percentage of the public which is backing other choices).

Here is where you can realize your margin of profit. The public often makes a horse that cannot possibly win, or even finish in the money, the favorite or the second choice in a race. By wagering on horses chosen by sound methods of handicapping, you will overcome the initial 20 percent taken by the state and realize a profit.

So it is not true that Old Man Percentage will wipe you out eventually. You will not "beat the races" if that means betting on every race and winding up ahead, but you will beat enough races to finish ahead of the game.

Most books on racing conclude by wishing the reader good luck at the races. The assumption, no doubt, is that the reader will need all the luck he can get. However, with a sound approach to handicapping and an intelligent betting plan, racing *luck* will not be significant at the races. Your success will be the result of your own handicapping skills.

GLOSSARY

This list will help the reader understand and use the vocabulary of harness racing. No effort has been made to be exhaustive, but most of the important technical and everyday expressions of the sport have been included. For some definitions, the "Rules and Regulations of the United States Trotting Association" were consulted.

Across-the-board wagering   Covering your bet by placing an equal amount of money on the horse to win, to place, and to show. This is also called buying a combination ticket.

Age   No matter what time of year a horse is born, every horse in Standardbred racing is given an arbitrary birthday of January 1 of the year it is born. It is thus an advantage to a horse to be born late in the year. Two horses, one born in March and one in December, will both be considered the same age. The horse born in December thus has an advantage over the older horse.

Aged horse   A horse of either sex that is four years of age or older.

Appeal   A request for a review of any official decision. An appeal can deal with penalties, order of finish, or the rules by which races are conducted.

Backstretch   The area of the race track between the clubhouse turn and the far turn.

Barn   A stable under a single management or ownership.

Beaten favorite   A horse that, as a favorite, lost its last race.

Bike   A sulky.

Blowing out   A fairly fast training mile, generally two days before a horse is scheduled to race.

Box a bet   Betting every combination of three or more horses in a race or races. For example, boxing three different horses in

an exacta or trifecta wager.

Boxed in   A situation in which a horse is trapped on the rail behind the horse in front and another on the outside. The driver has nowhere to go and cannot get out. Unfortunately, past-performance lines do not show when a horse was boxed.

Break   A break occurs when a horse goes off stride, failing to maintain its proper gait. A Standardbred may break stride because of interference, accident, faulty equipment, inexperience, tiredness, or inadequate training. Trotters break far more often than pacers. When a horse goes on a break, the driver is required to take it to the outside, losing ground, until the horse is able to resume its proper gait.

Breakage   Money the state and track take from the pari-mutuel payoff to the bettors. Breakage is computed by first deducting the state's takeout (15 percent or more) from the "natural payoff" and then rounding this figure to the next lower dime ("dime breakage").

Example: $50,000 is the total win pool in a specific race; $10,000 of this was wagered on horse A, which wins. The natural odds on A are therefore 4 to 1. Now deduct, say, 17 percent from the *total* win pool, for a takeout of $8,500. The winning bettors will divide the remaining $41,500, which figures to a ratio of $3.15 to $1.00. So a $2.00 bet should return $8.30, of which $6.30 is profit. But breakage is always computed to the next lower dime, so that the payoff is only 3.10 to 1, and a $2.00 wager nets the winning bettor only $8.20. By this means the state and track rip off the public for millions of dollars each year.

Breaking the maiden   A horse breaks its maiden upon winning its first pari-mutuel race.

Breeding   The science of mating horses to produce the most desirable set of qualities possible for a race horse. These qualities, for the Standardbred, are speed, stamina, durability, and affinity for the pacer's or trotter's gait.

Bridge jumper   Someone who restricts his play to favorites.

Brush   A horse's ability to put on a burst of speed at some point in the race.

Career earnings   A horse's lifetime earnings or its earnings up to the present.

Catch driver   A driver who races a horse he does not train or own. Some drivers, because of their skill, are in great demand as catch drivers. In this age of specialization, it's not unusual for a horseman to devote himself entirely to catch driving for different stables.

Chalk player   A bettor who consistently wagers on favorites (a bridge jumper).

Champion   Technically, a horse that travels the fastest mile of the year for its age, gait, and sex. A world champion is one that sets an all-time speed record.

Choked down   When a driver tries to restrain or rate a horse and the animal's breathing is accidentally cut off. The horse may black out and fall.

Claiming-allowance race   A claiming race in which allowances are made for certain types of horses. For example, a mare may be claimed for 20 percent more than the specified claiming price and a horse under five years old for 30 percent more.

Claiming race   A race in which every horse can be purchased for a specified sum. There may be a range of prices in a claimer, for example, from $5,000 to $7,500. It is more common to find aged horses in claiming races than two- and three-year-olds.

Class   The level on which a horse is able to compete successfully. A horse's class at a given time is determined solely by the level of competition it is capable of fitting in with, not by its lifetime or previous year's earnings.

Classified race   A race in which the entries are selected solely on the basis of ability or performance.

Clocker   Someone who records a horse's fractional and final times in its workouts and warmups. Clocking times, often used as an index of a horse's actual performance, are unreliable.

Closer   A horse with a strong move in the stretch. A closer is able to make up ground in the final stages of a race.

Colt   A horse of male sex up to the age of four.

Comparison handicapping   A method of handicapping in which one horse is chosen over another because the first finished ahead of the second when the two were in direct competition. Again, if horse A beat B, and B beat C, the comparison handicapper will conclude that A will beat C. This method is

obviously faulty because it does not take into account specific conditions since the previous race, such as improvement in horse C and decline in A, which can make the outcome of the present race very different.

Conditioned race   A race in which the racing secretary specifies certain conditions of eligibility, such as nonwinners of three races lifetime or winners of $3,000 in 1978–79. The racing secretary's aim is to ensure as even a level of competition as possible among the entries.

Consistency   The capacity of an animal to perform on an even or near even performance level from race to race.

Cooling out   Walking a horse after a race or training mile until its body signs return to normal.

Corking   Sending out a horse at the beginning of the year as if it were in midseason form. Corking is destructive to a horse's future level of performance.

Covered up   A horse in a race is covered up when other horses are in front of it.

Current form   A horse's performance in its last race or two, providing these races are recent (within the last two weeks or so).

Daily double   A form of pari-mutuel wagering that requires the bettor to select the winner of the first and second races on a ticket.

Dam   A horse's mother.

Darkened form   A stable's attempt to conceal the real capabilities of a horse. Example: For a number of races at the beginning of the season a horse is raced lightly. As the odds continue to rise, the stable primes the animal for a winning effort. Darkening a horse's true form also occurs for several races after a lengthy layoff before coming back strong to win.

Dash   A race decided in a single trial. Every race is a dash unless it's decided in more than one heat.

Dead heat   A tie between two or more horses. In a dead heat for the win, there will be a separate payoff for each co-winner. There can be a dead heat for place and show as well, with a resulting increase in the number of payoffs. However, with the advent of the photo-finish camera, dead heats are few and far between.

Dime breakage   Breakage to the next lower dime, as illustrated in

the account of breakage, above.

Distanced   A horse that finishes so far (at least twenty-five lengths) behind the winner that the number of lengths is not recorded.

Dollar odds   The natural odds on a horse before takeout and breakage have reduced them. If the win pool is $60,000, $20,000 of which has been bet on A, the dollar odds on A are 2 to 1.

Driver   The individual who reins a Standardbred. A driver must be licensed in a state before he can drive in a pari-mutuel race. The driver ordinarily receives 10 percent of the purse money won by the horse he reins. More importantly, the driver's skill often makes a crucial difference to the outcome of a race.

Due-column betting   A system of betting in which the bettor requires a certain profit from the races and increases the size of his wagers until he realizes that profit. Example: I require a profit of $50, so I bet $25 on a 2 to 1 shot in the first race. I lose my initial investment, so I increase my wager to $75 in the second race, now betting on a horse that goes off at even money. Should I lose this bet, I will be out $100 and must recoup by making a wager that will return $150 in winnings. A suicidal approach to wagering.

Early closer   A race with a specified closing date for entries. A stable with a promising young horse may enter it in an early closer, paying out the entry fee in a number of installments.

Early pace   The pace set in the early stages of a race.

Early speed   A horse may be trained to move out quickly at the start of a race, thereby showing early speed.

Elimination heat   The division of a race into separate heats, in which only some of a large number of contestants can qualify for a final heat. Each part of an elimination is called a division.

Entry   Two or more horses in the same race belonging to the same stable or under the same management (the same trainer or owner).

Even money   A horse that goes off at odds of 1 to 1. Usually the favorite in a race, unless there is a small field.

Exacta   A form of pari-mutuel wagering in which the exact order of the horses finishing first and second in a race must be selected. It's sometimes a good strategy to reverse the order

of the horses you select, particularly if the race figures to be close.

Far turn   The turn on a race track leading to the homestretch.

Favorite   The most heavily bet horse in a race. A favorite can go off at odds of anything from a low of 1 to 20, to odds of 4 to 1 and even higher in an evenly matched contest of eight or more animals.

Field   For wagering purposes, the field consists of one or more horses above the usual number (eight on a ½-mile track) that can be wagered on as a group. If *any* horse in the field finishes in the money, the bettor can win by wagering on the field to win, place, or show as the case may be. In a more general way, the field refers to all the horses starting in a particular race.

Filly   A female horse less than four years old.

Final time   The winning time of a race.

Fixed-percentage betting   A system of watering in which one bets a fixed percentage of one's bankroll, say 5 percent, on every wager. As one's bankroll increases, so does the size of one's bets; as it decreases, the size of a bet decreases correspondingly.

Fixed race   A race in which some or all of the drivers, owners, etc., conspire to predetermine its outcome.

Flushed out   A driver is flushed out when he is forced to make his move too early in a race.

Form   A horse's ability to perform on a specific level; its racing fitness.

Fractional times   The times of each quarter of a race, as set by the horse pacing in front. On past-performance charts, fractional times are recorded for each race a horse has been in.

Front-runner   A horse trained to take the lead at the start of a race and hold it to the finish.

Futurity   A stake race in which the competing animal is nominated at least a year in advance and possibly as early as when its dam is in foal.

Gait   A horse's gait or leg movement can be either natural or artificial. In harness racing there are two different gaits—pacing and trotting—and both are artificial. Standardbreds are therefore trained to pace or trot, although as a breed improves its

gait becomes more native to each succeeding generation of Standardbred.

Garden spot The position directly behind the leader during a race. It's considered ideal by drivers for striking position throughout the race.

Gelding A desexed male horse. A horse is gelded to make it more tractable and stable in its performance habits. Geldings are among the most consistent and steady of Standardbred performers.

Grand Circuit The Grand Circuit is a continuous schedule of topflight racing events in which the leading stables of the day compete for large purses. It is held for several months each year, and the nation's major raceways host the Grand Circuit for a week or more each. Virtually every big name in the business is on hand to compete, often commuting from one raceway to another to drive separate divisions of their stable that are competing on different racing circuits.

Green horse A horse that has never trotted or paced in a race.

Groom An attendant who assists the trainer in the care and management of his stable.

½-mile track Most of the harness tracks in the United States and Canada are ½-mile ovals, in which the horses make two complete trips around the track in a standard 1-mile race.

Handicapper's notebook The notebook kept by many careful handicappers on the performances of many Standardbreds at the track. By keeping these records, one will have a stronger basis for predicting, for example, whether a horse will perform well in the mud or whether a horse seems to be tiring or getting stronger from race to race.

Handicapping The art of selecting winners in races. It depends upon an acquired skill in reading and interpreting pastperformance charts.

Handle The total amount of money wagered on a race, a nightly program, or an entire season.

Heat One competitive mile in a race that requires two or more dashes to decide.

Hedging Hedging a bet is a means of recouping one's losses if the horse one bets finishes in the money but doesn't win. So betting a horse across the board is one way to hedge a bet,

betting it to win and place, or to win and show, is another. But hedging a bet is profitable only if the place or show price more than compensates for money lost when the horse doesn't win.

Hobbles   Leather or plastic hoops, one encircling each leg of a pacer and connected to one another by a strap on each side. As the animal's right front leg moves forward, its right hind leg is also forced forward, and so with its left legs. Only pacers wear hobbles; it is impossible to trot with them. A free-legged pacer is one that races without hobbles, either because it does not need them or because they cause injury.

Horseman   A word used loosely to refer to a driver, trainer, or owner of horses or to whoever cares for or maintains horses.

Hot streak   A succession of in-the-money finishes by a driver, usually extending over a substantial number of races. A cold streak, by contrast, is a lengthy succession of races in which a driver seldom or never finishes in the money.

Hung   Parked out; obliged to race on the outside.

Inside information   Information from someone directly connected with a stable (owner, trainer, groom, etc.) about a horse's condition or its chances in a race.

Interference   When a horse's progress in a race is impeded, for example, by a horse that breaks stride in front of it, the first horse is the victim of interference. A horse can be interfered with in a variety of ways, by being bumped, having another horse cut in front of it, etc.

Invitational   A race in which the fastest pacers or trotters on the grounds are invited to participate. These are the feature events with the largest weekly purses and are generally held at the major tracks.

Iron men   Pari-mutuel machines.

Jogging   Slow, steady workouts on a race track or training track.

Judges' stand   The place occupied by the officials who have final authority for the outcome of every race. The judges are responsible for imposing fines and penalties, hearing appeals, and determining all questions of fact relating to a race.

Jump   To break or go off stride.

Key race   The race used in certain handicapping systems to deter-

mine a horse's chances in a given race. The key race is usually one in which the horse apparently performed up to the limit of its capabilities.

Lapped on break at the wire   When a horse breaks while crossing the finishing line and at the same time overlaps one or more of the other horses in the race, the breaking horse is set back by the judges and finishes behind the horse or horses lapped on at the wire.

Late closer   A race for a fixed purse to which entries close less than six weeks and more than three days before the race.

Lay over   To beat easily. A horse is said to lay over a field when it can trounce that field easily.

Leading driver   A driver among the top ten or fifteen at a meet in terms of the Universal Driver-rating system (q.v.).

Length   The distance used to measure the relative position of a horse with respect to the leader in a race. There is no settled definition of a length in harness racing. Measured by the average size of a horse, a length would be about 8 feet. However, if the sulky is included as well, a length is at least 10 feet. In New York State, a length is measured by the horse and sulky together.

Long shot   A horse that goes off at high odds in a race. There is no precise definition of long shot, but a horse at odds of 5 to 1 is not a long shot, whereas one at 10 to 1 is.

Maiden   A horse that has never won a pari-mutuel race.

Mare   A female horse at least four years old.

Match race   A race arranged according to a set of conditions agreed upon by the contestants.

Meeting   A sustained period of pari-mutuel racing at a raceway.

Mile track   A track 1 mile in length, upon which the contestants circle the track just once in a mile race.

Mobile starting gate   A moving gate or barrier used to get a harness race underway. An automobile is equipped with a barrier behind which horses move quickly to the starting line. The automobile then speeds away, leaving the animals on their own. The procedure is controlled by an official called a starter, who is responsible for seeing that the race starts fairly. The mobile starting gate is unique to harness racing and is in large measure responsible for harness racing's success.

Modified sulky   After being officially sanctioned a few years ago, the modified sulky has proved its value by adding precious seconds to the performance times of many—though not all—horses. The modified sulky places the driver's weight behind, instead of directly above, the sulky's wheels. As a result, horses are spared an extra burden. The modified sulky was not allowed at Canadian tracks until recently.

Morning line   The opinion of the track handicapper of the probable odds on each horse entered in each race on the card. The morning line is printed in the official program and flashed on the tote board before actual wagering gets underway.

Move theory   A theory of handicapping based on the estimate of a horse's ability to brush, or show a burst of speed at one or more points in a race. Most Standardbreds, it is said, are capable of no more than one brush in a race, some of two, and outstanding competitors of three. On the move theory, one combines an analysis of each horse's brush potential with the aim of predicting the pacing in a specific race ("how the race will be run").

For example, in a race made up largely of front-runners, an advocate of the move theory will conclude that a horse that can put on a good brush in the stretch is the best bet, for the front runners are apt to use themselves up in a fast pace while contesting for the lead. This will provide the stretch horse with ample opportunity to make up ground in the last half of the race.

Although this theory has clear limitations—many races don't unfold as expected—it can be used to advantage in a handicapping system.

Mudder   A horse that competes especially well on an off track, particularly on a muddy or heavy track.

Multiple betting   A multiple bet is one in which the bettor is required to select two or more horses in the same race (e.g., exacta, trifecta) or in different races (e.g., daily double, twin double).

Mutuel handle   The total amount of money wagered on a given racing program.

Odd-distance race   A harness race at a distance of more or less than 1 mile.

Odds   The potential payoff on a horse in a pari-mutuel race. A horse that goes off at odds of 3 to 1 to win will pay $8 for a $2 win ticket *if it wins*. The payoff is determined by multiplying the amount bet by the odds reduced to a function of one and then adding the amount bet to this sum. So $2 bet on a 3-to-1 shot to win will return (3 × $2 = $6 + $2) to the winning bettor.

Odds-on choice   A favorite that goes off at less than even money.

Off track   A track whose condition is not fast, but good or more often sloppy, slow, muddy, or heavy.

Off-track betting   A legalized off-track betting operation run by the state of New York that permits wagering on horse races in and occasionally out of the state.

Open Race   A race in which several horses are evenly matched and can be given an equally good chance of winning.

Overlay   A horse that goes off at lower odds than it should in a race. As a result, the horse may be a good to an exceptional bet in that race.

Pacer   A Standardbred that races by moving its right front and hind legs simultaneously, followed by the same movement by its left front and hind legs. From in front the pacer gives the impression that it is waddling forward.

Pacing   How a race is run. Pacing depends on the fractional times of the quarters of a race in relation to the final time. Consider the different pacings of two races, each of which is run in a final time of 2:05. In the first, there is a battle for the lead, with the result that the half goes in 1:01, offering horses that sit back an excellent chance to win. In the second, a slow first half of 1:04 will favor those horses in front. In each case pacing is crucial to the outcome of the race.

Paddock   The area at the race track containing the horses' stalls.

Paint a horse   To substitute a counterfeit horse for the horse really entered in a given race.

Parked out   A horse which is parked out during one or more quarters of a race is on the outside of those horses which keep to the rail. A horse can be parked two or three wide, especially at the beginning of the race when its driver tries to take the lead. During a race a driver may take his horse to the outside to make up ground, rather than waiting until the stretch, when it may be too late to overtake the leaders.

Parlay   A series of wagers in which the entire payoff on one winning bet is used to make a second bet, etc. A two-horse parlay, such as the daily double, is restricted to two successive winning bets, a three-horse parlay to three, etc.

Past-performance charts   The charts in a racing program that show past performances of horses in a race.

Perfecta   Another name for exacta wagering.

Perfect trip   A race in which a driver sits second or third behind the leader, pulls out in the stretch, and wins easily. This is a perfect trip for the winner because the pace-setting horse acts as a wind screen until the precise moment at which the driver makes his move, winning easily while taking an absolute minimum out of his horse.

Place bet   A bet that pays off if the horse wagered upon either wins or places (finishes second).

Playable race   A race in which a definite betting choice at attractive odds is present. If a race is to be playable, the bettor must believe that his selection has the best chance in the race and is going off at more than acceptable odds.

Pole horse   The horse that leaves from the rail, which is the most favorable post position.

Post parade   The procession of horses before the judges' stand about 10 to 15 minutes before the start of their race. The parade to the post gives the spectators a chance to size up the animals before the race.

Post position   In a harness race the horses approach the starting gate side by side. The horse on the rail has post position 1, and so on through 8 or 9. In some races there is a second tier of horses that line up behind the first. As a general rule, the better a horse's post position, the better its chances in a given race, although this applies more clearly to ½-mile tracks than to larger ones. As track size increases, the post-position advantage decreases.

Preferred race   A race limited to the fast horses on the grounds. Such horses are not allowed to compete in regular conditioned races.

Price   The payoff on a bet.

Program   (1) The schedule of races held on a specific occasion. (2) The official raceway program, which contains, among other things, the past-performance charts of the horse entered

for each race on the card.

Progressive betting   Any of a variety of wagering systems that require the bettor to increase the size of his bet after a loss. The assumption behind progressive-betting systems is that at some point the player is bound to win and that his increased wagers will make up for previous losses. Example: doubling your bet after each successive lost wager.

Protest   A charge lodged with the judges that could disqualify a horse from winning or competing in a race.

Provisional driver   A driver who has not yet completed a year's driving experience at extended pari-mutuel meetings, as required to be fully licensed.

Public selector   A handicapper whose choices are communicated to the public via newspapers, television, etc.

Puller   A horse that requires a tight hold on the reins. Pullers are usually bad bets because, being hard to restrain, they are prone to build up a big lead, only to fade later in the race.

Punter   A horse player, particularly one who bets every race.

Purse   The total amount of money distributed to the horses in a race according to their order of finish. The winner usually gets 50 percent of the purse and the second-place finisher 25 percent. The next three finishers receive a varying percentage of the remainder.

Qualifying race   A nonbetting race in which all horses must run before they can enter competitive pari-mutuel races. It sets minimum standards for competition. Horses that break stride too often, misbehave behind the starting gate, have been running too slowly, etc., are put back to qualify again before they can reenter pari-mutuel races.

Quick leaver   A horse able to get to the front quickly.

Quinella   A form of betting in which the first two horses in a race are selected in any order. Example: A quinella ticket on 1 and 2 pays off whether the win-place combination is 1 and 2 or 2 and 1.

Quitter   A horse that fades in the stretch.

Racing life   Standardbreds are permitted to compete in pari-mutuel races at two, although many trotters are erratic at this age. The most dramatic improvement in speed occurs between the ages of two and three. A Standardbred reaches its top racing

form between four and six, at least in the case of pacers. Most go into decline at seven, especially if they are trained and raced very hard. An aged horse is allowed to compete through the age of fourteen, and it's not unusual for a senior citizen with class to whip its younger colleagues week after week in cheap claiming races.

Racing secretary   The official responsible for making up the races on each card.

Rating a horse   A driver's skill in moving a horse at precisely the right moment in a race to maximize the animal's performance potential and chances of winning.

Recall   The starter of a race can sound a recall for any of the following reasons: a horse scores ahead of the gate; a horse has broken equipment; there is interference; a horse falls before the word *go* is given; a horse refuses to come to the gate before the ⅛-mile pole prior to the start of the race.

Record   A horse's fastest winning time. This is a lifetime mark for the animal and may have been made in a qualifying race or at a distance less than 1 mile.

Reinsman   A driver.

Results charts   The charts that record the running and outcome of a previous day's races. These may be useful to the handicapper.

Reversing a bet   Betting an exacta both ways—for example, 3–6 and 6–3.

Reversal of form   A horse's turnabout from winning to losing form, or vice versa.

Roughing it   A horse's racing on the outside or being parked out for a quarter or more of a race.

Score   The two final warmup dashes, about ¼ mile each, that a horse takes after the post parade and just before the race. These are taken "the right way of the track," or counterclockwise.

Scratch   Withdrawal of a horse from a race, usually due to illness, lameness, etc.

Scrug   A cheap horse.

Short price   A horse that goes off at low odds, such as even money, is said to be at a short price because the potential profit to be had by betting on it is comparatively low. But the return on an even-money bet is 100 percent, and a bettor who avoids

short prices can be criticized for sometimes being penny wise and pound foolish.

Short shot   A horse that goes off at low odds.

Show bet   A bet that pays off when the horse wagered on finishes first, second, or third (win, place, or show) in a race.

Shut out   Arriving at a betting window after the wagering has closed.

Sidewheeler   A name for a pacer.

Sire   The father of a horse.

Spot betting   Betting only on selected races, rather than on every race in the program.

Stable   A number of horses under a single owner or management.

Stake race   A race that requires nominations and entry fees to be made while the horse is still a foal. Stake races are held primarily for two- and three-year-olds and often feature large purses.

Stallion   A male horse that has not been desexed.

Standardbred   A horse bred to either pace or trot, the two artificial gaits of horses in harness racing.

Starter   The official responsible for overseeing the start of a race.

Stiffing a horse   Causing a horse to lose a race by holding it back. If detected, a driver can be suspended indefinitely from a track for this action.

Straight betting   Wagering on a horse to win only.

Stretch   The area of the race track from the far turn to the finish line, in front of the grandstand and clubhouse.

Stretch drive   The capacity of a horse to make up ground on the leaders by its rush in the stretch.

Stretch gain   The amount of ground, recorded in lengths, a horse picks up from the head of the stretch to the finish line.

Sucked along   A horse may run a faster time than usual because it is "sucked along" by the pace of the other horses in the race. A reversion to a slower time in its next start is likely.

Sulky   A two-wheeled seat, pulled by the horse, on which the driver sits.

Superfecta   A form of wagering in which the bettor must select the winners of four successive races. Often called the twin double because it is equivalent to a parlay bet on successive doubles.

System betting   Wagering according to a set scheme or plan. Fixed-

percentage betting, due-column betting, and progressive betting are types of system betting.

Take and breakage   The combined percentage of takeout and breakage the "house"—the state treasury and raceway management—deduct as their share of each dollar wagered. Take and breakage together reduce the margin of profit on the "natural odds" by at least 20 percent.

Takeout   The percentage of each dollar wagered, apart from breakage, deducted by the state and the raceway as their joint profit. The takeout percentage varies from state to state, from a low of 14 percent in California to a high of 17½ percent in Ohio.

Tip sheet   The sheets sold at raceway entrances that contain a handicapper's selections for the races on that day. Anyone who blindly follows the advice of a tip sheet from day to day is headed for financial ruin at the track.

Tightener   A race that sharpens and prepares a horse for future races.

Tote board   The tote board (totalizator board) flashes the odds on each horse in a race, including the betting pools for win, place, and show, up to the start of the race. It also communicates such information as the condition of the track, driver changes, and late scratches and the time at which the next race is expected to go off. In addition, the tote board flashes the fractional and final times of each race as it progresses.

Tout   Someone who sells a tip or expects to be compensated later if his information turns out to be correct.

Track handicapper   A handicapper hired by the raceway to put out a morning line of probable odds on each horse in each race on the card. These appear in the raceway's program.

Track size   Although the great majority of harness *races* are run at a distance of 1 mile, the actual size of harness tracks differs from one major raceway to another. Roosevelt and Yonkers Raceways, both in New York, are ½-milers; Liberty Bell (Philadelphia), Sportsman's Park (Chicago), and Brandywine (Wilmington) are ⅝-mile tracks; Hollywood Park (Los Angeles) and Washington Park (Chicago) are 1-mile tracks.

Trainer   The individual responsible for keeping a horse in fit condition and priming it for races. A good trainer is able to

maximize a horse's effectiveness, as is shown by the difference a change in barn can make to an animal's level of performance.

Trotter   A Standardbred that races by the artificial gait of moving right front and left hind leg simultaneously, then the left front and right hind leg. Only about 20 percent of all Standardbreds are trotters, the rest being pacers.

Twin double   A name for the superfecta, in which one must select the winners of four straight races to win. The twin double is bet as a parlay of two doubles.

Twin exacta   A parlay bet that one wins by selecting the one-two horses in their exact order of finish in successive races

UDR   Universal Driver-rating system.

Underlay   A horse that goes off at higher odds than would make it a worthwhile bet.

Universal Driver-rating system   A system used for computing the success of drivers at a meet in terms of the frequency of their in-the-money finishes. According to the system, a driver is awarded 9 points for each win, 5 for each place, and 3 for each show finish.

The driver is charged 9 points for each start. The system assumes that a victory is 80 percent better than a place finish and three times as good as a show finish. The rating is computed by adding the combined points earned for first-, second-, and third-place finishes and dividing the sum by the points for all his starts. Consider the following two drivers:

	Starts	Wins	Places	Shows
A	10	1	3	4
B	10	3	0	0

Driver A's UDR is .400, although he has won only .100 of his starts. Driver B has a UDR of just .300, even though he has won three times more often than A.

Assuming that these figures are representative for A and B, a show bettor will undoubtedly fare better with A in the long run, whereas a straight bettor will ignore the UDR ratings and play drivers with a high winning percentage like B.

Unplayable race   A race that, for any of a variety of reasons, cannot be handicapped adequately. Examples: The horses are too

closely matched in ability; the horses are all breakers or are all inconsistent performers; a contestant's advantage in one department (post position), which might otherwise be decisive, is offset by a second or third contestant's having an equivalent advantage (driver). As a result, no wager is solid enough to be a worthwhile risk.

Warmups   The exercise a horse is given before the race. This may take place not only before the first race, but between races as well, usually for 1 mile or more. It's sometimes possible to find a winner by catching an animal in peak form during its warmups.

Weanling   A horse is a weanling from the time it is taken from its mother until it reaches its first birthday on January 1.

Wheeling a bet   Combining a bet on one horse with a bet on every other horse that can be coupled with it to win. Example: Wheeling a daily-double bet on number 1 in the first race with every horse in the second.

Wire   The finish line, defined as an imaginary line from the center of the judges' stand to a point directly across the track.

Working a horse   Exercising or training a horse.

Yearling   A horse is a yearling from the time it reaches age one until it reaches age two.

MW01601540